MW01440759

The Word On Wheels

Highway to Heaven

Bob Dennis

Copyright © 2023 by Robert (Bob) Dennis

All rights reserved. (Revision 1)

No portion of this book may be reproduced in any form without written permission from the author, except as permitted by U.S. copyright law. All scripture reference are from the inerrant King James Bible.

Introduction to Praise

I started thinking about what I would do my dissertation on back in my freshman year of Shepherd School of Ministry. I did not really nail it down until the summer before my senior year. I had several ideas running through my mind of what I thought I would do, but never had a peace of mind about any of them. During my third year of Shepherd School, one of the instructors led a class on praise. Ultimately praise, service, and worship became tied together. One of the assignments was to do a fifteen-page paper on praise. My first thought was how in the world could I do that? I would have other homework, I had my secular job, and I would need to prepare for tests at the end of each trimester. I found out since then that fifteen pages on praise, service, and worship is nothing. I made a commitment to spend the summer and the first part of my senior year doing a word study on praise and I included service, and worship. I initially wondered if I could come up with a devotion for every day of the year. Praise God that He did indeed help me through it, and I believe I benefited from it. With all that said, let us get into the world of praise, service, and worship and see what we can apply personally. My goal will be to compile 366 devotions that we can apply and grow closer to God the Father, Son, and Holy Spirit. My goal upon completion of this book is that it will not only stimulate me in the area of Praise, Service, and Worship, but would motivate others to a better understanding of how to Praise, Serve, and Worship God in the way it was intended. God has given us many examples in His word concerning these three topics. As individuals, are we setting an example in the way we praise, serve, and worship or are we setting an example of how we do not praise, serve, and worship? I pray you will be blessed as you go through one simple devotion per day and apply what you read. I pray that you will be drawn closer to the Lord Jesus Christ. **Before we head on into praise, I must thank my wife Beverly as she is such an encourager for me in many walks of life. It was seeing how she lived for Jesus that turned me to Jesus**. We all must promote the name of Jesus and encourage one another in how we praise, serve, and worship. If necessary use words, but please note that our actions are very loud and powerful as well.

January 1

Genesis 29:35
And she conceived again, and bare a son:
and she said, Now will I praise the LORD:
therefore she called his name Judah; and left bearing.

We have here an account of the fruitfulness of Leah's womb. When Leah realized the fruitfulness that God had allowed her, she praised Him. When I consider what God has allowed me to do for Him, such as souls I could lead to Christ, preaching His word, serving in some capacity, or producing fruit because of what He has done, I should be more than the song; "I am satisfied". Praise should be pouring from my tongue because of the understanding that God does not need me to do anything. How fortunate any of us are that God would even consider for a moment using us. Praise God that He can use any of us to bear fruit for Him. As a man I cannot bring forth children from a womb, but I can spread forth the gospel and bring new babes to Christ and to the Kingdom of God. The word of God is likened unto a seed that can bring forth fruit. I must sow the seed, (Word of God), and pray that God will bring forth fruit. You and I can only sow the seed, but God is the one responsible for giving the increase. Praise God that He would use any of us to handle the seed, (the Word of God). Praise God for the fruit He wants us to acquire through praise, service, and worship. What were we like before Jesus Christ became our Saviour? Many bad tempers and unhealthy habits had to be laid aside. We laid them aside with the help of the Holy Spirit guiding us. We were able to exchange the bad fruit we had for the fruit of the spirit. Praise God we can bear the fruit of love, joy, peace, longsuffering, gentleness, goodness, faith, meekness, and temperance, as recorded in

Galatians 5:22-23. May the fruit of our life coincide with the list in *Galatians 5:22-23* as we tell others about Jesus. The sweetest nectar in the world is Jesus' love for all of mankind. Let others know today just what you think about God's love for you and His love for them. You never know, you just might get some fruit handed to you as you share this good news that Jesus came, died, was buried, and arose from the grave triumphantly. All believers can bring people to a saving knowledge of Jesus Christ and produce new babes in Jesus!

January 2

Genesis 49:8
Judah, thou art he whom thy brethren shall praise:
thy hand shall be in the neck of thine enemies; thy
father's children shall bow down before thee.

Judah, out of all the brethren, is the one who will be praised, and the scepter will not be taken out of his hand. Judah, (type of Christ), will be the protection from our enemies. Why would we not praise God when we consider how He has His hand of protection on us? The worst possible thing to happen to us physically is death. Even then we can say *O death, where is thy sting? O grave where is thy victory*? according to *I Corinthians 15:55.* We will praise an employer for a raise, but how much sweeter to praise God for an eternal life with Him. Recently we had an election year that covered filling everything from State level positions to the President of the United States. No one knew until the ballots were counted who had really won the high office of President of the United States. All anyone could do was speculate who they thought had won. For the president position, if he wins twice, the best he can do is serve 8 years. There is going to be a time in the future when another office, (throne), will be filled in a New Jerusalem. Jesus is the only one on the ticket, so there is no uncertainty of who will win. When Jesus establishes His kingdom in a New Heaven and a New Earth for those who have trusted Him as their Saviour, the scepter He will have will never be removed. There will not be such a thing as a dishonest or corrupt government. Christ will not allow it and believers will not even think of it. Praise God even now that there is coming a day when Jesus Christ will take the throne, and He allows us to reign with Him in a perfect world for all of eternity. As far as the end of the verse and bowing down to Jesus, the time to bow down and worship the Creator is not in the future. It is today.

January 3

Leviticus 19:24
But in the fourth year all the fruit thereof
shall be holy to praise the LORD withal.

Israel has been told not to eat of the trees the first three years, but to wait upon the fourth year. It did not matter if some trees happened to bear fruit early, do not eat from the trees until the fourth year. Sometimes when raising fruit trees, it is good to simply pick the fruit off young trees early and discard the fruit. Fruit trees will produce better fruit if they are given time to mature in their own time. As born-again believers we need to develop that same patience. God's word says in *I Timothy 3:6 we are not to use a novice*. Give a new believer time to grow and mature. When that new saint is ready God will decide when they will become a useful fruit tree. God wants what is best for His children. God knew it would take some time for fruit trees to produce the best fruit. Fruit trees that are allowed to mature will bear an abundance of fruit. As a lesson to us, God is always on time. He is neither early nor is He late. The best thing you and I can do for Him is to wait upon Him and what His word says for our life. There will be a day when we reach the maturity God wants us to have, and then how the praise will pour out. When we realize it is God who matures us, we must praise, worship, and serve Him. We do this because of who He is and for what He has done in our lives. A discipleship program at a Bible believing Church follows the same process. We take a young fruit tree, take them through some Bible lessons, develop a special relationship with them, and then turn them loose. We then pray for them that they will in turn produce the best fruit possible. Praise God we are like fruit trees, and He does not burden us with things we should not be burdened with. This is the reason for plucking the fruit off the tree early. It keeps the tree from having to nourish the fruit and allows it to concentrate on what's important for the tree. For a fruit tree, what is most important is not necessarily the fruit, but how deep its roots run. Concentrate on your personal walk with Jesus Christ, (your roots), and let God bring forth the fruit when it is time. Maintain your own walk first and then nourish the fruit that God brings your way. It will be a lot easier for you to praise, serve, and worship God if you wait on God. Pray for your walk with Jesus and then sing praises about what are "His" results in your life.

January 4

Deuteronomy 10:21
He is thy praise, and he is thy God, that hath done for thee these great and terrible things, which thine eyes have seen.

It is apparent that there is praise or worship in everything God does. We are not to look for ways to praise God, but to simply praise God because He is our praise. The verse in essence says, *"He is our praise, and we need no other"*. God is our praise because of the relationship we can have with Him. What an honor to be able to proclaim to the world that we know God personally and God knows us. No matter what our social status or position in church, God is our praise. Unbelievers and believers alike cannot wait to brag when they meet a celebrity or some superstar. How much better to let the world and the brethren know through our praises that we praise God because we know Him. When you know Him, you will praise Him. We sing the following song. *"Praise ye the Lord, Hallelujah, praise ye the Lord"*. Do we mean it or are we just paying Him and those around us lip service? Another thought in this verse about praising God is that He is a personal God. This is not just somebody's god to praise but He is "thy" God. Being saved is a personal matter between a person and the Lord. Satan knows about God, but he certainly will not praise Him, serve Him, or worship Him. Knowing about God is not good enough as the devils know all about God. Knowing Him through salvation by way of Jesus makes it personal. When you know Him, you will love and praise Him. Do not worry about whose God He is. Make certain that He is your God and then praise Him for it! If necessary, look back at your life before you met Jesus and compare it with where you are at today. Most people I know never want to go back to their old life when it was not filled with their Savior Jesus Christ. Be encouraged, God can and will do some mighty things in your life if you will just obey the word of God and submit every area of your life to Him.

January 5

Deuteronomy 26:19
And to make thee high above all nations which he hath made, in praise, and in name, and in honour; and that thou mayest be an holy people unto the LORD thy God, as he hath spoken.

Moses reminds Israel of what God has done for them. God has exalted His people above all others. Here we discuss praising God and yet many times God allows praise to rain down upon us. God will make His people high above all nations. The Hebrew word is elyown, (el-yone'), meaning a name above all names. It is used in a sense of the utmost highest, which is where God has put His children. We will be above the nations in praise, name, and in honor. In staying within the boundaries of the theme of praise, service, or worship, none will praise God like we will. Those who have a different doctrine for salvation beyond Christ and Christ alone should not have the ability to out praise God's children. There are lost people in churches who do not know Jesus Christ as their Lord, but they are singing about Him. Those lost or spiritually dead are simply that, spiritually dead. Somebody spiritually dead should not be able to out-praise someone who has been made alive or a quickening spirit, *I Corinthians 15:45,* by the blood of Jesus Christ. Because of what God has done for us how can any nation or any branch of people out praise those who are a Christian? The brethren are those who are born-again, those who boldly claim Jesus as their Saviour. There are times when at home or just maybe in the car when you just sing out because you know God loves you. In return you love Him, and it can be an awesome time of worship and praise. We cannot out give God and there are times when we cannot even out praise God. God's praise of His people cannot be surpassed. Because of God's love for us, how can we not praise Him, and it should be a natural response? Praise is who we are and what we do. Praise should not be manufactured, but consistent. Our praise should be something that does not need a lot of preparation. There is nothing wrong with being spontaneous. It should be as natural for a believer to worship the Lord as it is for us to talk about a favorite sport's team or hobby. We consider God's love by reading *John 3:16* and that in and of itself should be sufficient for us to want to praise "OUR" Almighty God. *1 John 4:19 We love Him because He first loved us.*

January 6

Judges 5:2-3
2) Praise ye the LORD for the avenging of Israel, when the people willingly offered themselves. 3) Hear, O ye kings; give ear, O ye princes; I, even I, will sing unto the LORD; I will sing praise to the LORD God of Israel.

Deborah and Barak both sing out and praise God because He has avenged Israel. In *Judges Chapter 4* God avenged Israel and the first thing to take place is praise to God. They do not wait several chapters to begin the praise of God. In the last verse of *Judges Chapter 4* the enemy is dealt with and in the first verse of chapter 5 the praise begins. We are not to hesitate in our praise. Just as God defeated the enemy of

Israel, God has defeated our nemesis and his name is Satan. Jesus defeated him when He went willingly to the cross. God who would not even spare the anguish and torture of His only begotten Son should not have to wait one verse for our praise. God deserves the praise, service, and worship of all humanity because of what He did through Jesus Christ. We should not become guilty thinking we are to only praise God when we receive something materially. God earned our praise long before *Genesis 1:1* and He will be worthy long after *Revelation 22:21*. Praise came in verse 2 of our text when the people willingly offered themselves. Do we readily offer ourselves up completely to God? There was a day when God wanted rams and bullocks for an offering. Today we are to be those rams and bullocks, but not as a sacrifice to die, as we are to "LIVE" for Him. We sacrifice everything to serve the risen Saviour. There must be a <u>willingness</u> to offer up ourselves with thanksgiving and then our praise will fill the air. I also want to look at verse 3 of Judges 5. The leaders were proclaiming that they would praise God. Praise from you just might solicit praise from others as they join you. If leadership cannot praise God, then will the followers praise Him? They may, but many times we learn, follow, and do by example. Just maybe you are not to be the follower of worship, but the leader?

January 7

I Chronicles 16:4
And he appointed certain of the Levites to
minister before the ark of the LORD, and to record,
and to thank and praise the LORD God of Israel:

The ark had been restored to its rightful place. That place being right in the heart of His people. The ark had been in a place of obscurity, but now it was visible to all that would come to it. David was so excited about the return of the ark that he personally appointed the Levites to praise God. What an honorable position in being the one who could stand before a congregation and lead worship to God. The Levites were the ones David, (a type of Christ), thought was worthy of that position. When Jesus Christ died, the veil that covered the "Holy of Holies" was rent in twain from the top to the bottom, *Matthew 27:51 and Mark 15:38.* Those who accept His atoning death would become worthy to lead or participate in the praises to God just as the Levites. The veil was rent from the top to the bottom and the "Holy of Holies" became visible and available to any who wanted to enter God's presence. Most churches have a praise team, and they are appointed to praise God. Do they stand before the congregation and perform for our enjoyment and pleasure? I would think not. I do believe that their praise and worship of an Almighty God solicits praise from the congregation. What a very important position to be in as part of the praise team. I wonder if the people watched the Levites to see how they performed FOR THE LORD. Did the people see praise on the faces of the Levites? Does praise show forth in the countenance of our own praise team. I wonder if the praise team sees praise on the faces of the different members of the congregation. Is the praise team the only ones appointed for praise? Have we ever pondered whether we were being called into the ministry of a praise team or choir? Do not let Satan steal your joy through fear of singing in front of others. Allow the Lord to use the gift of song as a tool to bless others and in doing so you will bless God as well. God knew us even before we were born. He was worthy of our praise before we drew our first breath, and He will be worthy when we draw our last breath. As you feel led, rejoice in the name of the Lord because God is not just the God of Israel. He is the God of the universe and you!

January 8

I Chronicles 16:35
And say ye, Save us, O God of our salvation, and gather us together, and deliver us from the heathen, that we say give thanks to thy holy name, and glory in thy praise.

The cry here to "save us" is not in a sense of God we are lost and need to be saved. It is an intercessory request to God to assist the brethren who may be experiencing some hardships because of their stand for Him. The cry is to gather us together. Together and united is where the brethren belong. The request continues by acknowledging to God that when we come together let us rejoice and glory in his praise. When we gather together for worship and a message through preaching it is often preceded with songs of praise. As a unified body of believers are we praising God for what He has done, is doing, and will do in the lives of believers? Do we give thanks to God that we are saved? Have we thanked Him today because He has not appointed us to wrath, *I Thessalonians 5:9 For God has not appointed us to wrath, but to obtain salvation by our Lord Jesus Christ.* There will be a day when we will gather together and will forever live and reign with Jesus. Have you praised Him today for what He has appointed for you for all eternity? The day is coming when we will be in the presence of nothing except believers. No sin, no sickness, and no death, *I Corinthians 15:55 O death, where is thy sting? O grave, where is thy victory?* Finally look two verses farther and read in *I Corinthians 15:57, But thanks be to God, which giveth us the victory through our Lord Jesus Christ.* Look at

1 Chronicles 16:35 one last time and you will see that we have asked God to save us, gather us, and to deliver us. God has honored His part, but have we honored ours? God deserves our praise and are we praising Him? By the way, a heathen can come in many sizes, shapes, and colors. Ask God to give you discernment as to who you are to attach yourself to or are running with. We are to witness to everyone, but we are not to be attached spiritually to anything except God. Not everyone we know is spiritually healthy for us to be consistently hanging with. Not only would God separate Israel from the heathen, but God will help you lay aside who is not healthy for you.

January 9

I Chronicles 23:5
Moreover four thousand were porters; and four thousand praised the LORD with the instruments which I made, said David, to praise therewith.

In the four verses before our text today, there are a total of thirty-eight thousand Levites on hand to render a given service. To break it down, twenty-four thousand attended to the work of the house of the Lord. Six thousand were officers and judges and four thousand were porters. The remaining four thousand would be responsible for taking the instruments that King David had prepared before his death and using them to praise God. I am still amazed at how some churches believe you cannot use instruments in your worship time. David felt the need to appoint four thousand to lift up instruments to praise God. He not only believed in it, but instead of letting Solomon his heir take care of it, David addressed the matter and made sure praise was in place. Everybody should have a place of ministry where God wants us and where we should be. *Romans 12:1* reminds us to render reasonable service. No matter what we may have believed, one of our reasonable services that we should offer is in the praise service. Isn't it amazing that four thousand men were chosen to lead the praise? Our various choirs should reflect what King David would do. We surely would not get so busy in our different ministries that we would forget to take the time to praise God. Men should be leaders in our churches and in their homes in the area of praise. Do those we are closest to us see us praising, serving, and worshipping God? Because of our attitude, do those around want to join in and participate with us? Are we making a joyful noise or an awful racket? My last comment is not directed to those who may not be able to carry a note in a basket. The awful racket is produced from a heart filled with sin and no repentance. The quality of our voice is not what produces praise. It is the quality of our heart. Jesus cleaned us up when He saved us, and we are to live a life that shows praise regardless of what we sound like. Our song to the Lord Jesus when done with a right attitude is a beautiful sound to the ears of God. It is never too late to mimic the four thousand who would praise God.

January 10

I Chronicles 23:30
And to stand every morning to thank and
praise the LORD, and likewise at even;

We are given a time when we should praise God. This particular verse tells us to stand and praise Him in the morning and in the even. *Proverbs 8:17 I love them that love me; and those that seek me early shall find me. Proverbs 8:17* indicates when God wants our attention. It is not at the end of our day when there may not be much left in us. God wants us first thing, which is when we are or should be at our freshest. Our offering of time should be of our first fruits and not the leftovers. As in the tithing of money, God does not want what is left, but what is right. Offer your praise early in the morning. Be sure and praise your "Lord" before your feet ever hit the floor or you leave your bed. The verse not only teaches that we should start our day with praise, but to end it in the same manner. If we start and end our day with praise to God, we have only the time in the middle to concern ourselves with. If we can intermingle praise within our day, what a day it would be. It would appear that as long as we are a living breathing soul, we should be praising God. We can praise God anytime we choose. Praise and worship can be done quietly just like prayer if need be. Our job or our attitude should not inhibit our praise to Him. Praise can be just like prayer where you can do it, and no one has a clue. Praise is not just singing, but it is what we do to let others see Jesus in us. The only way they could know would be from the countenance on your face. There are worse things that could happen besides having a silly grin on your face because you are praising God on the inside. The verse does not mention when we sleep. If we will start our day with praise, and our last thoughts are praising God, we may praise Him in our sleep. Praise Him in the Morning! Praise Him in the Noontime! Praise Him in the Evening! Before I forget; "Please be sure and fill in the gap between getting up and lying down with your praise". You just might be amazed at how your day starts, goes, and then finishes. Look forward to someone asking why you are so happy so you can point them to your one true joy and that being the Lord Jesus Christ. Always end your day reading scripture, take what you just read to your pillow, and sweet dreams.

January 11

I Chronicles 25:3
Of Jeduthun: the sons of Jeduthun; Gedaliah, and Zeri, and Jeshaiah, Hashabiah, and Mattithiah, six, under the hands of their father Jeduthun, who prophesied with a harp, to **give thanks** and **to praise** the LORD.

We have two words used in the same breath and they are thanks and praise. Read the account of the last 24 hours of Jesus before He went to the cross and consider just how thankful we should be. When we count our many blessings and name them one by one we should become thankful. When thankfulness to the Lord arrives so does praise. Thankfulness is an attitude or awareness that should run 24 hours a day and 7 days a week. We should not count our blessings only on Sunday morning, but include the other six days of the week. Praise and thankfulness should not be restricted to one day a week. I want to address the men once again. What a sweet picture we have here of a father and his children. Can you think of a greater blessing for a father than for his children to join him in praise to God? I have had the opportunity to preach the word of God outside of my regular church home. My own son has gone along with me and was a part of that experience. What a joy to be able to lead a song of praise to a group of strangers knowing my son was singing along. When we sing songs of praise is it genuine? Do our children see us singing because that is what we are expected to do, or do they see us sing because it is what we desire to do? *Proverbs 22:6 Train up a child in the way he should go: and when he is old, he will not depart from it.* What kind of training are we providing in the area of praise? There is more to life in the training of a child than making sure they make a good living. Do not misunderstand, making a good living and providing for one's family is very important, but do not put praise as a second-rate gesture. I have a friend who shared one time just how awful her dad could sing and that he would be the loudest in the church. She was never embarrassed, but she was very proud of her dad. She knew her dad was not trying to be the loudest but was worshipping his God and Savior Jesus Christ. May we all pattern that example daily.

January 12

I Chronicles 29:13
Now therefore, our God,
we thank thee, and praise thy glorious name.

If we were to back up to the verse preceding this one and then read down to verse 13, we would see that a lot of people gave willingly for the building of God's house. I believe King David in all his splendor realized that everything he had belonged to God. He gave willingly and with great joy because his affection was on pleasing his God. *Colossians 3:2 Set your affection on things above, not on things on the earth.* Here is a leader who could not contain the joy he had in giving back to God what was God's already. Whether it was silver, gold, or brass is not relevant. The important thing to remember is the attitude reflected when the giving took place. Verse 9 of this chapter says the people gave willingly and with a perfect heart. We read verse 9 and then we can understand why we are looking at verse 13 of *I Chronicles 29*. The right attitude in recognizing God and what He deserves from us will result in praise, service, and worship. Look again at just where the leader is. He is setting the example of giving back in verse 1 of this same chapter. In verse 13 David is setting the example again in praise. I see over and over in scripture where praise produces praise. The bottom line in praise is that it is a giving of a gift that we cannot hold in our hand. It is a gift manifested in our heart and given to God as a token of the love we say we have for Him. What each of us must decide is what kind of token are we offering Him? A token that is genuine and pleasing to the Lord or a token that is simply conjured up in our mind so that we would feel good about ourselves? Praise cannot be done while one is in sin. Oh, we might sound pretty to others, but God knows our heart. We must offer beautiful praise because we are living a beautiful life for Him. Many of us change the pipes on our motorcycles to make it sound special. Does our giving of praise sound special to God or is it simply a lot of noise? As you walk or ride your highway to heaven with Jesus, may it be a joyful walk and a joyful noise. Remember, there is only one highway to God and that is through Jesus Christ who is the same yesterday, today, and forever and may you shout out Hallelujah!

January 13

II Chronicles 7:6
And the priests waited on their offices: the Levites also with instruments of music of the LORD, which David the king had made to praise the LORD, because his mercy endureth forever, when David praised by their ministry; and the priests sounded trumpets before them, and all Israel stood.

All the instruments David had prepared before his death would be put into use. King David knew just how merciful God was. In this verse David says, *"his mercy endureth forever"*. Both David and Solomon knew what Israel deserved. They knew the nation had turned their back on God more than one time. The kings knew what could happen if God unleashed his wrath upon them. In this particular text a consuming fire comes down and takes up the sacrifice. The people had two options, one would be to run, and the other would be to stay reverent and praise God. They stayed because God had accepted their sacrifices and their offerings. Had they offered God anything with impure motives I would suppose fire would have come down, but I am not too sure what it would have consumed. Would it have consumed the people or the sacrifice? Israel offered sacrifices willingly so they could praise God obediently. It is interesting the order of events if we backed up to verse 1 of this same chapter. There is prayer first, sacrifices second, and praise third. *I John 1:9* covers the prayer part, *If we confess our sins, he is faithful and just to forgive us our sins, and to cleanse us from all unrighteousness.* We need to be prayed up before attempting to enter into His presence by prayer. *Romans 12:1* covers the kind of sacrifice God wants from us, *I beseech you therefore, brethren, by the mercies of God, that ye present your bodies a living sacrifice, holy, acceptable unto God, which is your reasonable service.* Third, praise is offered up so let us apply *Psalm 34:1 I will bless the LORD at all times: his praise shall continually be in my mouth.* Psalm 34:1 offers up a specific time frame for our personal praise. It is not part of the time but at all times. I do not believe I need to give a definition for the word ALL in conjunction with praise. They go hand-in-hand so hang on to the Lord with all of your praise.

January 14

II Chronicles 8:14
And he appointed, according to the order of David his father, the courses of the priests to their service, and the Levites to their charges, to praise and minister before the priests, as the duty of every day required: the porters also by their courses at every gate: for so had David the man of God commanded.

King Solomon puts into place where the Levites would be serving. Here is the important part of the whole plan. The verse ends with the words, *(for so had David the man of God commanded)*. We make sure we teach our kids manners, respect, obedience, and on and on and on. Do we make sure they understand the significance of praising, serving, and worshipping God? Have we prioritized things in order of importance? In other words, do we emphasize the importance of tithing, and everything involved with tithing and forget praise? My concern for any church is do we understand the importance of praising God? I would hope that a song service is not used by any fellowship or worship leader as an alarm clock or a call to order. In plain terms, do we sing a song or two to indicate that class or worship time is supposed to start now? I try and picture in my own mind how God would feel if leadership offered up a song of praise as a means of a call to order. I know God would appreciate the brethren singing praises with the right motive. Just how would God respond if the motive for the song service was just an alarm clock and time to go? We teach to give of our first fruits. We teach to not regard iniquity in our heart as the Lord will not hear us, *Psalm 66:18*. Do we teach to sing with purity, honesty, and integrity to the One who died for us? Hey dad and mom, what legacy are you passing on to your children? Will your children and grandchildren praise God because their father and grandfather did the same? One, we are to be an example of praise. Two, our children, grandchildren, and possibly even great grandchildren just might follow our example in singing praises to God.

January 15

II Chronicles 20:19
And the Levites, of the children of the Kohathites, and of the children of the Korhites, stood up to praise the LORD God of Israel with a loud voice on high.

In this text the children of Ammon and of Moab are swarming Israel. It appears evil is getting worse and worse. The world today is calling good evil and evil good. There is a great multitude on the way with the intentions of destroying and pilfering the Israelites. Next, the Spirit of the Lord comes upon Jahaziel, and he proclaims, "Do not worry, this battle will be fought by the Lord". Many people feel that if the Lord cannot handle a situation, then we are all in big trouble. I am one of those who feels the same way. Jahaziel prophesies to Israel that they need to simply go to the battle and stand still. Try and picture what is going to happen in your mind. Multitudes of fighting men are coming to destroy you and God says, "Go and meet them, **but** stand still and see the salvation of the Lord". This is what most would consider testing your faith. Jehoshaphat and Israel have only two choices, to trust God's deliverance from the enemy or to not trust God's deliverance from their enemy. Here is the order of events. They fell down and worshipped God and I believe we are looking forward to *I John 1:9* in the New Testament. Israel got right with God and what happens next? They are no longer prostrate on the ground, but they are standing and praising God. I was not there, but I have a feeling these people were not standing there looking pious, but they were doing some serious praying and praises to God. Picture in your mind what the countenance on each face must have been like when they came together in one accord to praise the One who would deliver them from their enemy. We have an enemy and his name is Satan and consider how often God must intervene for us each and every day. Do we even begin to understand what Satan would do to us if God removed His hand from us? When we understand God has his hand upon every area of our life, we will do some praising. What a time we could have if we laid down feeling embarrassed because others may think we are singing too loud, or we do not sound quite right. When we sing, we are not trying to make a soundtrack of our voice or make a record deal. We are not here to start selling records because of our singing talent. We are simply lifting our voice to a God who will deliver us today from our enemies in the same way He delivered Israel. God will continue delivering, so let us continue praising. As we go through life witnessing about Jesus, people are watching to see what we are really made of. It will not be what car you drive, the motorcycle you sit on, or the size of your house that may impress them. It will be in how you live your life for Jesus daily. Do not worry about how big your enemy is. You need to concentrate on just how big your God is!

January 16

II Chronicles 20:21
And when he had consulted with the people, he appointed singers unto the LORD, and that should praise the beauty of holiness, as they went out before the army, and to say, Praise the LORD; for his mercy endureth forever.

We have only moved forward two verses from the last thought. Did the people praise God for what He would do or had done and call it good? As they went out before their enemies, they continued to praise God. I mentioned earlier how King David proclaimed that the Lord's mercy endureth forever. Israel was now singing the same song. Is your desire to be a good leader at home, work, or at church? Start with being an example in the area of service and then feel free to pass on things that have eternal significance, *Matthew 6:19 Lay not up for yourselves treasures upon earth, where moth and rust doth corrupt, and where thieves break through and steal.* Israel and their king had gotten right with God so there was no reason not to continue in praising and serving the One who would deliver them. One thing must happen before we praise and serve God. We must go to Him with pure motives. We must enter His presence prayed up and repentant before Him. We must be as clean in our praise with regards to sin in our life as when we approach the Lord's Table for the Lord's Supper. We have a time of quietness before we partake of the bread and the juice. It is a time to reflect on Him and address any unconfessed sin we may be clinging to. Would we want to do any less when we come to Him offering up our praise? Would I even want to be in God's presence knowing I am dirty with sin? If we approach Him dirty with sin, then it is shame on us. I understand that when God looks at us, He sees the mark of His Son Jesus and our sins were forgiven. However, when we come to Him, we need to be clean spiritually and maintain a repentant heart. Then and only then can we rejoice for Him. The thing to remember about approaching His throne with purity, is that when we get there with purity, we will leave with purity. Keep in mind that our purity is His purity and without it we are nothing. Praise God that we can Praise and serve God and seek to apply *Psalm 66:18 If I regard iniquity in my heart, the Lord will not hear me:*

January 17

II Chronicles 20:22
And when they began to sing and to praise,
the LORD set ambushments against the children of
Ammon, Moab, and mount Seir, which were come
against Judah; and they were smitten.

Once again, we have only moved forward one verse from yesterday and look what happens when the people **BEGIN** to praise God. God puts His plan into action. It appears that the enemy was defeated when the singing started. You would have to read the next three verses and see what the Lord does to the enemy. He utterly destroyed everything in the path of Israel. When God does something for His people it is not half done. God is a perfect God, with a perfect plan, and with perfect timing. Here is the deal; sometimes the victory is not won on the front line. Sometimes the battle is won in the trenches where the preaching, praying, and praising are taking place. Keep in mind that Israel could see their enemy. Their enemy happened to be someone they could see, touch, and with God's help defeat. There are times when our battle is not against something we can see. There is a constant spiritual battle going on all the time around us. It would probably scare us to death if we knew spiritually what was going on around us all the time. Some battles can be seen and maybe it is with drugs, alcohol, lying, or stealing. Maybe it is refusing to be obedient in serving God. If you are dealing with any of those things, God can deliver you the same way He delivered Israel. I wonder if we spent more time in praise if it would make a difference in other areas of our life. Most believers want the ability to harness their thoughts and keep them pure and holy. Our thoughts are sometimes the last stronghold we let Satan have control of. If we were to keep an attitude of praise **in the front of our mind** we would spend less time thinking foolish thoughts **in the back of our mind**. *Psalm 34:1 I will bless the Lord at all times: His praise shall continually be in my mouth.* One thing I do not want to do is come across as if the only kind of praise is through song. Praise is given when we make the decision that is based on *Joshua 24:15 "as for me and my house we will serve the Lord"*. That is for sure a great sign of praise to decide every single day to serve Jesus with your family. Praise comes in many forms and in many wrappers, but praise must be a daily commitment to an Almighty God.

January 18

II Chronicles 23:13
And she looked, and, behold, the king stood at his pillar at the entering in, and the princes and the trumpets by the king: and all the people of the land rejoiced, and sounded with trumpets, also the singers with instruments of music, and such as taught to sing praise. Then Athaliah rent her clothes, and said, Treason, Treason.

Athaliah heard something she probably was not accustomed to hearing. She heard sounds of praise for the new King. Historically, it is obvious the people were excited about a new King named King Joash. Skip the historical implications and get to the inspirational side of things. Some of the people under Athaliah's authority were not as excited about her running the show as she was. Athaliah's pride brought her to proclaim treason assuming the people would side with her. The pride from her heart brought her to the point of the sword and she was executed. There is going to be a day when some will not be happy about Jesus sitting on the throne in a New Jerusalem. The lost will have to deal with it for eternity. Why was all this joy exuberating from the people? Israel was excited because they knew they did not have just any old king. They now had a king that was a son of David. We have a King, and His name is Jesus Christ. Jesus just happens to come from the line of King David, but Jesus never knew any sin. Now if a secular king of the lineage of David brought on this much stir, how much more for a King of the lineage of David who is the Son of God. Here is my subtlest contrast concerning praise. We get all excited over a new car, new motorcycle, new home, or a new anything. Where is the excitement for our King Jesus? When we got saved, did we get excited about our decision? Have we stayed excited because we now have a new King or in a short amount of time did the excitement subside? Are you still rejoicing today because of the King you met when you got saved? Surely, we would not miss praising our King because we were too busy with more important ministries or other activities. We whoop and holler for our favorite sports team, but how about whooping and hollering for the one who is "the chief and captain" of our salvation! Athaliah was a very evil ruler, and I am sure most of the people knew that. Joash would be a very honorable king and the people knew that as well. You and I must be careful who we look up to as not everyone is honorable. The Bible is clear about separating ourselves from those who are unclean or better put, in sin. Do not yoke yourself to an unbeliever through dating, marriage, or friendships. Trust God to lead you in discernment before you haphazardly follow or look up to someone you should not.

January 19

II Chronicles 29:30
Moreover Hezekiah the king and the princes commanded the Levites to sing praise unto the LORD with the words of David, and of Asaph the seer. And they sang praises with gladness, and they bowed their heads and worshipped.

We would have to back up in this chapter 29 to verse 18. The Levites go to King Hezekiah to let him know that the house of the Lord had been cleansed and restored. Hezekiah does not tarry, but he goes early to the temple. There are sacrifices and burnt offerings offered up. Significantly, in verse 23 of this same text there is a sin offering and the entire congregation laid their hands upon it. They all acknowledged the sins they had committed. I am not sure exactly how to picture a revival breaking out, but I believe right here, that this is what is happening. Forgiveness of sin takes place, and the very next activity is the people break out in songs of praise to God. The verse says they sang with gladness. There is a difference between singing with gladness and singing because we feel obligated. When there are people singing all around me, I must freely want to join in and participate in the praise. Keep in mind that Israel used a goat for their sin offering. Our sin offering is Jesus Christ. We simply need to go to him for forgiveness and we are made holy by His blood. By the way, a goat was only used once for a sin offering. We use the same Jesus 24 hours a day and 7 days a week. We do however need to stay prayed up. In laymen's terms, be prayed up and confessed up that we might look up and praise up. The result will be the same as this verse and we will sing with gladness. We have a Saviour that died for us and that should result in gladness not sadness. It requires fewer muscles to smile for Jesus Christ than to frown with the world! May you keep your hands, heart, and mind fixed towards our sin offering in the person of Jesus. Goats had to be offered for sin continually, but on the cross Jesus said, "It is finished". When the Lord says something is finished then it is finished. Amen!

January 20

II Chronicles 31:2
And Hezekiah appointed the courses of the priests And the Levites after their courses, every man according to his service, the priests and Levites for burnt offerings and for peace offerings, to minister, and to give thanks, and to praise in the gates of the tents of the LORD.

It is interesting here that the people went out and utterly destroyed all the images and idols. When a person makes up their mind to address sin, the result should be that they will address ALL sin. The result of addressing ALL sin is a cleanness or an inner cleansing that brings about praise to God. God desires that we should come to Him with a childlike faith. Addressing sin can bring upon all of us a sweetness that you can only see in a newborn baby. Not only do we see a newborn baby as sweet in appearance, but for most of the time a newborn baby even smells sweet. Jesus took upon himself all our sin. We simply need to make a conscientious effort to keep sin in check. We are to monitor and avoid sin instead of letting sin monitor or control us. I believe the word I am looking for is repentance. Hezekiah realized the importance of order within the house of the Lord, so the Levites were appointed for certain tasks. If everyone knew what their responsibility was there would be no chaos. God is a God of order, *I Corinthians 14:33 For God is not the author of confusion, but of peace, as in all churches of the saints.* We can all have a place of service, but we do not need to use scorecards and grade the ministry we do. If you are where God wants you to be, and we used a scale of one to ten with ten the best, you will score a ten. If this is a time when you are not sure where God wants you then look around where you see God active and go there. Your praise can become where you are serving Him. You will never know what gifts God has given you until you let Him stretch you in your ministry. Allowing God to stretch you to new things is your praise. For those who would sing or lead praise in the gates of the tent, they had a tremendous responsibility. Do not miss that they sang praises in the doorways. Are we restricted to praising only in the sanctuary? You praise God anytime it is on your heart to do so. It will be extremely difficult to have praise in your heart when you have sin on your mind! God cannot be in your house if Satan is paying your rent.

January 21

Ezra 3:10
And when the builders laid the foundation of the temple of the LORD, they set the priests in their apparel with trumpets, and the Levites the sons of Asaph with cymbals, to praise the LORD, after the ordinance of David king of Israel.

In Ezra chapter 3 we have some industrious people trying to get some things accomplished. The laws Moses had passed on were being carried out. An altar to God was erected and offerings for sin were being carried out. We have Israelites working in unity to bring about the work of God. The Levites do not wait until the temple is completely erected. Just as soon as the foundation is laid, here come the trumpets and the cymbals. After the ordinance of King David the instruments come out. King David had left behind a legacy in music and praise to God. When God allows us to do anything for Him, we do not need to hold it in. If we were to build a new worship center, would we wait until the last brick or board was hung in place? No, we would rejoice before the first shovel of dirt was dug. That is exactly what Israel is doing here. Giving thanks to the One who deserved it, God, their deliverer. Apply this same verse to us today. How about if we all worked together in unity to accomplish what God wants accomplished? What God wants accomplished is that we would lead lost and dying souls to Him. God calls, we witness, and He brings forth the increase. What would the result be if we all worked, prayed, and praised together as one? We would all be blessed as we watched God work for the good of one lost soul. When we start sharing the goodness of God in unity, we will praise Him in unity. It will be no more of what I did, but what WE did. Then we will praise God for what He did in and through all of us collectively. Individually we might be bronze but working collectively together for the souls of men we are gold. Hallelujah!

January 22

Nehemiah 9:5
Then the Levites, Jeshua, and Kadmiel, Bani, Hashabniah, Sherebiah, Hodijah, Shebaniah, and Pethahiah, said, Stand up and bless the LORD your God for ever and ever: and blessed be thy glorious name, which is exalted above all blessing and praise.

In this verse Israel is going through spiritual healing. They will be praising God when they complete the process, they have laid out for themselves. That process begins in *Nehemiah 5:1.* Fasting is being carried out and they have separated themselves from strangers, *II Corinthians 6:16-17 16)And what agreement hath the temple of God with idols? for ye are the temple of the living God; as God hath said, I will dwell in them, and walk in them; and I will be their God, and they shall be my people. 17) Wherefore come out from among them, and be ye separate, saith the Lord, and touch not the unclean thing; and I will receive you.* It can be a sad time for any believer to come to the place where they must lay aside old friendships. Not all friendships are healthy for spiritual growth. Not only does a decision need to be made of who we attach ourselves to, but confession of sin must take place. Israel gets into the word and starts making wise decisions for the welfare of themselves as well as for the entire nation. For six hours they read the book of the law, six more hours there is more confession and worship made. Israel had made confession in verses 2 and 3 of this chapter 9. Why would they feel they needed to do so twice? There is no better way of knowing what you need to confess than by applying the word of God. Once you read what you should not do, there should be no doubt as to what needs to be confessed. We now arrive at today's devotional verse. There is one more thing Israel needed to be reminded of and that is what an awesome God they had. Israel had fasted, confessed, worshipped, and now it was time to praise. I understand the time frame for Israel is different than for us in the year two thousand and twenty-two, but the plan for spiritual healing is exactly the same. There needs to be some fasting, confessing, and worshipping that we might get to the praising. Let me paint a mental picture for you. Picture God sitting on His throne receiving praises from His children who have come to Him with a clean heart. We are living in a busy world and there needs to be a preparation process taking place for every believer with regards to praise. It must be our goal to leave the cares of this world and to concentrate on our praise to Him. We must concentrate on what we are trying to accomplish for Him and praise God for who He is. Picture this one more time. An entire body of believers has prayed, confessed, and worshipped together and are now ready to praise God. Imagine when an entire body of believers come into His presence with praise. I mentioned an entire body of believers as an example. To have an entire body of believers singing praises together to God starts with one thing. You and I must serve in unity praising the Lord. Is our heart prepared to praise God in the way He deserves? If not, repentance to God is just a prayer call away and His line has no busy signals.

January 23

Nehemiah 12:24
And the chief of the Levites: Hashabiah, Sherebiah, and Jeshua the son of Kadmiel, with their brethren over against them, to praise and to give thanks, according to the commandment of David the man of God, ward over against ward.

We have in this verse an attachment of giving thanks through the giving of praise. In many songbooks there is a song titled, "Give Thanks". The jest of the song is giving thanks to the Holy One because He has given us Jesus Christ. That should be more than enough reason to celebrate with praise. We need to give thanks to God for His son Jesus Christ. Amen? There still needs to be a time when we are singing those praises because of the continual blessings God rains down upon us. If it was required of all of us to write a song expressing our thanks for what has been done in our lives, I would suggest that it would be very lengthy. This verse repeats the following, "*according to the commandment of David*". There has been a legacy passed down to Israel and at this point they are carrying it out. What legacy are we passing on to those around us in the area of praise with consideration given to thankfulness? Do those around us know who we are thankful to by our thoughts, words, or actions? If people around us do not recognize our thankfulness to God, I wonder if He does? One thing I hear parents say sometimes to their kids is, "you need to say thank you" and normally the child does just that. If we really want our kids or grandkids to say such a thing to another person, then why would we not as an individual set aside some time to do the same? To say thank you God does not cost us anything, but to God it just might be priceless.

January 24

Nehemiah 12:46
For in the days of David and Asaph of old there were chief of the singers, and songs of praise and thanksgiving unto God.

There have been a few sunsets since the days of David and Asaph. Asaph was the chief musician appointed by David to serve in the tabernacle until the temple was completed. Here is my case in point. There have been songs of praise and thanksgiving for several hundred years. I would suggest that Asaph more than likely passed on a few thoughts to generations that would follow behind him. I hate to ride a good horse to death, but what are we passing on in the area of praise to those around us? I will remind you of a friend who shared how she could remember her dad singing so loud in church. She recognized his lack of talent, but she also recognized his gratefulness, gentleness, and genuineness when he sang. There is a difference between singing loud to be heard and singing out because of the sheer necessity to worship. God is not interested in someone you must pry a microphone out of their hand. God is interested in praise from you and I and no sound system is needed. You cannot let praise out if there is none on the inside to let out. Do you have praise to offer? The Lord is looking for a few good praisers. Just like my friend's dad, he probably was considered chief of all the singers. This verse also mentions *in days of old*. With that said, will others look back at my life or yours and remember how we praised Jesus? May we be found singing and not sinning.

January 25

Psalm 7:17
I will praise the LORD according to his righteousness: and will sing praise to the name of the LORD most high.

This verse says we are going to praise the Lord according to "His" righteousness. Let us check out in the word of God His righteousness. First, let us compare his righteousness to ours. Our first example must be *Isaiah 64:6 But we are all as an unclean thing, and all our righteousnesses are as filthy rags; and we all do fade as a leaf; and our iniquities, like the wind, have taken us away.* These filthy rags that are talked about are in reference to the old cloths women would sit on during their menstruation period. Yes, a filthy menstruation cloth is the best our righteousness can be in comparison to God. We are as those filthy rags, but praise Jesus, that when we made Him our Savior, we were made clean. Our righteousness is not based on who we are, but on what Jesus did. On our own merit we will never compare with God and His holiness and righteousness. The only righteousness we can portray is through the shed blood of Jesus Christ. To throw in another reference check out *Romans 3:10 As it is written, There is none righteous, no, not one.* Compare these verses with what Daniel had to say in *Daniel 9:14 Therefore hath the LORD watched upon the evil, and brought it upon us: for the LORD our God is righteous in all his works which he doeth: for we obeyed not his voice.* If we consider the text we are in and are to sing praises because of His righteousness, we should not have any problem. *Daniel 9:14 God is righteous in all His works.* It is not a matter of trying to drum up what righteous things God has done. Everything God has done will fall under the category of righteousness. This verse mentions the word praise twice. The second use is to sing praise unto the name of the Lord most high. What does the word of God say about the name of the Lord? We only must travel to one verse to see what the Psalmist says in chapter 8 and verse 1 and then again in verse 9, *Psalm 8:1 To the chief Musician upon Gittith, A Psalm of David. O LORD our Lord, how excellent is thy name in all the earth! who hast set thy glory above the heavens. Psalm 8:9 O LORD our Lord, how excellent is thy name in all the earth!* According to *Acts 4:12 there is only one name under heaven given among men, whereby we might be saved.* Why would we not want to praise the name of the One who could give eternal life? Are we praising the holy name of Jesus?

January 26

Psalm 9:1
To the chief Musician upon Muthlabben, A Psalm of David. I will praise thee, O LORD, with my whole heart; I will show forth all thy marvellous works.

Thus far we have seen many cases of congregational praising. Another key to proper praise is seen in this verse. It is the word "I". David says, "I" will praise the Lord". Do not wait for those around you to start the praise or jump start you to praise. You have the same Lord who died for you and the need of prompting should not be necessary. For those married, does our spouse or children ever hear us praising God around the house? It is now time for the first couple of stupid questions in this book. One, do we need a song leader in our living room leading us in praise? Two, do you feel it is of the utmost importance that any time you feel the need to praise God, you look for the remote control so you can lower your projector screen that contains the words to the hymn you want to sing? I admit both are easy questions to answer, but are you praising God in your home? By the way, praise also involves what is running through the radio and TV. Trust me, even as I ride my motorcycle down the highway, I do not need to have Christian radio on. I choose to, but I do not need a song to inspire me to praise Jesus. I will admit that I will probably not raise my hands towards heaven and remove them from the handlebars. I remember like it was yesterday riding my Harley Davidson to Maine for the sole purpose of getting a lobster tail and taking that off my bucket list. I found myself on my motorcycle motoring down the highway and thinking about God all day long. What a huge blessing that was for me, and I will bet it was a blessing to God. It was sobering and honoring for me to lift my heart to Jesus as I rode. As far as no praise in the home, there obviously is no joy in the heart. Does God want half-hearted praise from any of us? According to this verse the Psalmist says he will praise God with his **whole** heart. If we were to use the whole heart for praise it will show us that all the other affairs of this life need to be laid aside to concentrate on praise. I am not talking about needing a song service before a devotion is given. Praise rolling off our tongue is a good indicator of where we are spiritually. God created us, lived with us, died for us, and arose again for us. Praise Jesus for His sacrifice for ALL.

January 27

Psalm 9:2
I will be glad and rejoice in thee:
I will sing praise to thy name, O thou most High.

We only traveled one verse from yesterday, but there are a couple of different things I want to point out. The Psalmist is glad and rejoicing in his heavenly Father. Because of that attitude the Psalmist will sing praises. I mentioned this earlier, but it is time for the same reminder. Have you ever sung the hymn Count Your Blessings? Not just sang it, but realized what Johnson Oatman, Jr. meant when he penned the words of that song? Let me recap a few of the stanzas of that song for you. One, are you burdened down with the cares of the world? Then check out what the Lord has done. Two, do you realize the wealth coming to us from Jesus Christ and it is just down the road? Three, are you discouraged at times and need a little encouragement? Christ will be there when your journey ends. Of course, I paraphrased the entire song, but my point is we sing these songs, but do we sing these songs with the same heartfelt emotions that the writer must have had? He felt blessed or he probably would not have written it. We ought to feel blessed or probably should not be singing them! Keep in mind this life is only a coffee break and we are only passing through. Guess what will happen when we face that reality. We will do what the Psalmist just wrote and we will be glad and rejoice. The Psalmist is rejoicing and praising the Most High God. There is none higher, greater, and more worthy than our heavenly Dad. You are not singing about just anyone in particular. You will be praising the name above all names, Jesus Christ our Lord. His name alone is worthy of our attention in not just our prayers or preaching, but in our praise. *Psalm 148:13 Let them praise the name of the LORD: for his name alone is excellent; his glory is above the earth and heaven.*

January 28

Psalm 9:14
That I may show forth all thy praise in the gates
of the daughter of Zion: I will rejoice in thy salvation.

Do you not just love this verse? The Psalmist is not only going to praise God, but he is going to show-it off. If we go to God and confess every sin He brings to mind, it is not going to be a problem showing forth praise. It is going to be written all over our face. The Bible calls it *"of a good countenance"*. Why wouldn't the Psalmist rejoice, he is giving thanks for his salvation. I would assume that anyone who is saved would naturally praise God because their soul has been rescued from a burning and eternal lake of fire. The Bible teaches more about hell than heaven and if that alone isn't cause for rejoicing then I do not know what is. If you are not happy about being saved, then you may need a refresher course about what salvation really is. Make a request from someone who can teach you of the state of eternal damnation, the place we refer to as hell, and ultimately a lake of fire. If that does not inspire you to praise Jesus, then I do not know what will. You need to have the gospel explained again because you are not saved. I can assure you that God gives and gives and gives and that in itself should merit our praise to Him. Do you feel blessed yet? Well then let God hear you praising Him. Keep in mind every day that we serve a Saviour that loved you so much he said, *"Father, forgive them for they know not what they do"*. And then Jesus died. Rejoice in your salvation as there was a huge price to pay for it. For those who will trust Jesus for salvation it cost nothing. For Jesus to give us an offer of salvation it cost Him everything. That thought should give you a spirit of rejoicing. Jesus died so you and I could live!

January 29

Psalm 21:13
Be thou exalted, LORD, in thine own
strength: so will we sing and praise thy power.

Many things take place in our life that we cannot take care of on our own. There is a spiritual battle going on every day and every second of our life. We need God to come to our rescue and He monitors everything that goes on. Some things require the Lord's strength, as we just cannot handle some situations. We have an adversary, and he walks around seeking who he may devour, and you will find that in *I Peter 5:8 Be sober, be vigilant; because your adversary the devil, as a roaring lion, walketh about, seeking whom he may devour*: The greatest strength a believer in Christ has is to recognize our weaknesses. We needed strength right out of the womb, *Psalm 8:2 Out of the mouth of babes and sucklings hast thou ordained strength because of thine enemies, that thou mightest still the enemy and the avenger*. God knows when we are in trouble, and He will intervene by His strength and deliver us. *Psalm 37:39 But the salvation of the righteous is of the LORD: he is their strength in the time of trouble*. We really need to have a steady diet of prayer in the areas where we know we need help. We just as well recognize our weaknesses because our adversary the devil figures them out. One more thing about prayer is that sometimes we do not recognize our weaknesses and we can pray God will point those out as well. We need to sing and praise as it says in this verse, because of the strength of the

Lord. Think of the mess we would be in if God were not intervening? Go back to the start of the verse and the first words are *"be thou exalted"*. When we exalt God, we will praise God. There are occasions in just about every church where banners may be used during special events. We attempt to create an atmosphere of what praise will be like in eternity. People are waving banners, God's name is exalted, the choir is singing, and we are sitting back drinking it in. It can be a wonderful experience in being there and participating, but we can and should exalt God as an individual in the same way. All those experiences with the brethren are good and we must wave our banner of praise that is contained within us and exalt our King, Let the banner of praise that we contain on the inside wave proudly on the outside.

January 30

Psalm 22:22
I will declare thy name unto my brethren:
in the midst of the congregation will I praise thee.

I want to look at the definition of declare since it is mentioned in this verse. Here the word declare means to emphatically make something known. It would almost seem like the same setting for the Psalmist is to what we would do in a song service on any given Sunday morning. The Psalmist is in the midst of a congregation and the brethren are there. The Psalmist had, **(past tense),** already decided that he would do his part among the brethren. In the midst of the congregation, he will render praise to God. I wonder when he made his decision to praise God? Do you think he decided to praise God after he had shown up in the middle of the congregation or did he start preparing before he got there? I guess a more fitting question would be, when do I start preparing to praise God? Is it right after we have had an argument with our spouse or yelled at the kids? Here is food for thought; if I spent more time concentrating on praising God as an individual then it is highly possible that I would not have had an argument with the wife or yelled at the kids. This verse makes it a personal choice as the verse starts with the word "**I**". Do not worry right now about what your neighbor is doing in the area of praise, but instead concentrate on what you are doing. Back to about all the fighting and yelling before church. Do not think for a second that the neighbors are not in on the yelling as well, as they have ears. The Psalmist says he will be emphatic in declaring the name of the Lord to his brethren. The bottom line is all of us have people we really love and enjoy talking to. Through our conversation to people closest to us, can they tell we love Jesus as much as we say we do based on our conduct? Talking about Jesus Christ to the brethren should be a natural and an everyday occurrence for us. We praise the Lord when we share the Lord with others. How much praise are we declaring to our brethren about Jesus? It is one thing to talk about fast cars, motorcycles, or horses with someone, but it is a whole new level of conversation when we lift up the name of Jesus. Do not leave the Lord out of your conversation with anyone because it just might be that what you have to say about Jesus is exactly what they needed to hear at that moment. It may even be the last thing they will ever hear.

January 31

Psalm 22:23
Ye that fear the LORD, praise him; all ye the seed of Jacob, glorify him; and fear him, all ye the seed of Israel.

We are told here that if we fear the Lord, we will praise Him. If the fear of the Lord is the beginning of wisdom according to *Psalm 111:10 The fear of the LORD is the beginning of wisdom: a good understanding have all they that do his commandments: his praise endureth forever. Proverbs 9:10 The fear of the LORD is the beginning of wisdom: and the knowledge of the holy is understanding*, Would it not be safe to say that praising the Lord is wise? It does say here if ye fear the Lord, praise Him. I guess if we refused to praise the Lord could we read into this verse that we do not fear Him? Being as though this verse is located in the latter half of *Psalm twenty-two* I want to point out one thing. We have here in this *Psalm 22* a picture of Christ as a suffering servant. If Christ as a suffering servant can proclaim, *"ye that fear the Lord, praise Him,"* I would think that would be sufficient counsel and would be carried out. *Psalm 22:25 My praise shall be of thee in the great congregation: I will pay my vows before them that fear him.* I need to remind you that we are still in the twenty-second Psalm. Jesus Christ back in verse 6 even calls himself a worm. Ever heard the expression you cannot keep a good man down. Christ was belittled, scorned, despised, and literally poured out like water. He went through all that and what does He do? He reminds us here in verse 25 of the need for praise in the great congregation. I can give you two schools of thought here. One, when you gather with the brethren, we are to be praising God. Two, when all the brethren are gathered together in His kingdom, (**great congregation**), we will praise Him. Think of the praise that will take place when Jesus is physically reigning as our King. If there is no joy in praising Christ now, how will we feel when He is on the throne as our King? How much remorse will we feel when we look back and recall we never praised Him? Can you think of a better time to start practicing for that day than right now? I could not either!

February 1

Psalm 22:26
The meek shall eat and be satisfied: they shall praise
the LORD that seek him: your heart shall live forever.

We have another bit of advice from Jesus Christ who will reign one day. Those that seek the Lord will praise the Lord. We preach and teach that through the word of God you can know Him. We have a greater source of information in our King James Bible about knowing God and the future than what Moses did. I know the relationship between God and Moses was special. I also know that everything I need to know about God is contained within the confines of 66 books of our King James Bible. I only need to take the time and seek Him out. If we diligently open one of 66 books and seek Him, then we should praise Him. That is exactly what this verse says. Let me repeat parts of this verse; *they shall praise the Lord that seek him.* Is it safe to say that those who are not seeking Him are not praising Him? Or would it be better if I said, "those who will not praise Him must not be seeking Him"? You decide which of the two questions you prefer. The first few words of *Psalm 46:10 be still and know that I am God.* Do we take the time to be still with God? When we get to know God, we should praise God. If our lives are so busy that we have no time to be still, it is time to evaluate what we are doing. I am not suggesting that what we do during the day is not important, but there must be some checks and balances. If there is no time for stillness, then there is no balance. We must establish biblical priorities. As followers of Jesus Christ, we must set priorities and boundaries. I love riding my Harley Davidson every single day in Florida, but there are times to leave the kickstand down and park it! Our priority is for us to be still and know God, *Psalm 46:10*. Our boundary is that we will not operate outside of our first priority. To Know Him, Love Him, Seek Him, Serve Him, and Praise Him. There is an order to the list I just gave you. Here is what I believe is significant to this order. When you Know Him, you will Love Him. When you Love Him, you will Seek Him. When you find Him, you will want to serve Him. When you serve Him, you will praise Him. Your praise is a joyful sound and the LORD will hear you.

February 2

Psalm 28:7
The LORD is my strength and my shield; my heart trusted in him, and I am helped: therefore my heart greatly rejoiceth; and with my song will I praise him.

Our Psalmist has decided to praise the Lord with his song. Do you have a special song that speaks to you? Do you ever just sing that song for the sole purpose of ministering to the Lord and to yourself? I mention singing to the Lord and ministering to yourself in the same breath. You praise God with a rejoicing heart and the praise will rain right back down on you. There are many reasons why we should sing to the Lord. The Psalmist mentions a few right here in this verse.

He says the Lord is my strength and my shield. You cannot find a better advocate to stand up for you than Jesus Christ. What good news that a born-again believer has the Lord's strength to depend on. Jesus is not just your strength. He is your shield. The enemy does not stand a chance against Jesus. Not only does Satan have to get past a shield of protection, but it is the Lord himself who is holding the shield. To be an armor bearer required faith on the part of the warrior you were in front of. Can you think of anyone you could put more faith in than Jesus Christ to be your armor bearer? The Psalmist says he has trusted the Lord with his heart. He trusted in the Lord's help and that is what he received. Do you have any personal examples of when you know the Lord bailed you out of a bad situation? If you trusted in the Lord for your strength, your shield, and for your protection then where is your song? When was the last time you sang for the Lord? If you do not have a song for Christ, then I recommend that you find one. If you find the right song that will minister to you then it will minister to Jesus as well.

February 3

Psalm 30:9
What profit is there in my blood, when I go down to the pit? Shall the dust praise thee? shall it declare thy truth?

David had been delivered several times from his enemies thanks to God. At the start of *Psalm 30* David gave thanks for the prosperity, answered prayer, his life, and so on. He also wondered if there was any profit in his death, (his blood). David asks a simple question, *"What profit is there when I go to the grave"*? If you could die and then do real service for God wouldn't that be awesome? It does not work that way. There are times at a funeral when people get saved. I guess that would depend on the epitaph we leave behind. Why would someone want to accept Jesus as their Savior if it made no difference in your life? The theme is praise so I will pose a familiar question. During the course of the day, does anyone ever see praise in how you live your life? Do we really try and carry ourselves as if we do have the joy of the Lord within us? The word dust is also used in this verse. We were started from the dust of the earth, and we will return to the dust of the earth. The Psalmist asks another question of us. *Shall the dust praise thee?* I believe there is a prescribed order of preference regarding praising God. I would suggest that during the course of this life, and before a casket is needed, that we might want to consider praising God. The time for praise is when we are alive not when we are a pile of dust. Not only will the dust not praise God, but it will not testify of God's truth. Are we a new creature in Christ? *II Corinthians 5:17 Therefore if any man be in Christ, he is a new creature: old things are passed away; behold, all things are become new.* Our praise is not only vital to our walk with God, but it testifies of the truth of God's word. The truth is that through Jesus Christ we are a new creature. The next time someone asks you to stand up and testify, you might try singing them a little song. There is power in the songs of praise so stand up and flex your muscles. I am talking about the muscles contained in your throat that should be used for praise. A dead body with a dead soul cannot praise the LORD, but an alive body with a saved soul certainly can. Which one are you?

February 4

Psalm 30:12
To the end that my glory may sing praise to thee, and not be silent. O LORD my God, I will give thanks unto thee forever.

We moved forward three whole verses from yesterday. King David had been doing a little lamenting of his own here. In two verses earlier all the lamenting is gone. All the mourning has now turned to dancing. The old sackcloth is gone, and David is girded up with gladness. The reason we praise the Lord is because He is able to reassure or calm us when our spirit is troubled. Here in this verse 12 David wants to praise God right up to the end. Recently a co-worker was called back to Alabama because his mother was dying. His mother had lived a good life of eighty-four years. I say a good life because of what her son had said about her when he returned to work. All of her children were in the hospital room, and she shared one particular thought with them. It is as follows: "kids, I have lived as a Christian most of my life. I have waited the biggest part of my life for the day that I would meet my Saviour Jesus." She was ready to meet her Saviour and she testified of it on her deathbed. She was praising God for her life and was now ready to give it up to be with Him. Her tombstone should read as follows; born March 12, 1916, and gone to her real home July 16, 2000. Above the dash between the dates should be the words, loved Christ, lived for Christ, and is presently with Christ. The date of her birth and death are not what is important. The important date is the day she accepted Christ as her Saviour. That date is referred to as her born-again date and is somewhere on the dash between the two dates. Does this story sound familiar with what David now thought? I agree with his statement at the start of the verse, *To the end that my glory may sing praise to thee.* We have no glory in ourselves. The only glory we have is what God will let shine forth through us. Do you want a little glory of God to shine forth? Sing praises, serve Him, and see what happens. When Moses came down from the mountain he had a glow about him because he had spent time with God. I believe we need to praise God and our purpose for doing so is to bring glory to Him. Who knows, we might just need that same veil that Moses wore.

February 5

Psalm 33:1
Rejoice in the LORD,
O ye righteous: For praise is comely for the upright.

I would like to include Webster's dictionary at this point. I want you to see Webster's definition of the word upright. One of Webster's definitions is that it means morally correct. So here is the first test question for you concerning this verse. Are you morally correct? Second question is, are you praising God anytime you get the opportunity? I can only assume you would be praising God because this verse says it is comely for the upright, (**morally correct**), to praise God. I hope that you are upright. I did not write this verse. I am only trying to help both of us understand it. Let us back up to the first word in the verse. Rejoice is the first word recorded. Who is to rejoice in the Lord? The verse says, "*O ye righteous.* I know it is confusing, but let me help straighten things out. The righteous are to rejoice, and if you are morally correct, (upright), praise is comely and should be natural for you and me. Another definition from the Webster's dictionary would be to consider the word comely. This verse says praise is comely. Comely is defined as good looking or handsome. Are you tired of your same old looks? You may not need a barber, beautician, makeover, or a facelift after all. Praise will make you comely and it will not cost you one red cent. Jesus **on a cross** paid the cost for you to look comely, beautiful, or handsome spiritually almost two thousand years ago. Want to look good, (comely), to those around you today? Then rejoice in the Lord and start Praising Him right now! Live a life that points to Jesus. Yes, you can praise your Saviour even while you work or play. Please do not tell me you have been too busy to praise Him? Jesus took the time to drag a cross to Golgotha for us. If He had the time for that, then you and I have all the time we need to thank and praise Him. If you believe that you have been too busy to praise the Lord, then you are too busy and Jesus knows that as well.

February 6

Psalms 33:2
Praise the LORD with harp: sing unto him
with the psaltery and an instrument of ten strings.

I must regretfully report some bad news and some good news. The good news is should you decide to use an instrument to praise God, good for you. The bad news is if you feel like the only thing allowed in the aid of praise is a hum-a-zoo then do not argue with me I did not write this verse. Just to be on the safe side, let me give you a few verses where other instruments were used to praise God. *I Chronicles 16:42 And with them Heman and Jeduthun with <u>trumpets</u> and <u>cymbals</u> for those that should make a sound, and with <u>musical</u> <u>instruments</u> of God. And the sons of Jeduthun were porters. Psalm 98:6 With <u>trumpets</u> and sound of <u>cornet</u> make a joyful noise before the LORD, the King.* Did you realize that above fifty five psalms the words **To the Chief Musician** appears in the superscription or heading? My point is to not get so anxious about how to praise God. The next thing you know there is no praise because you are scared you may do it wrong. The wrong way to praise is the refusal to praise. I went on about instruments, but the verse says to sing. Musical instruments can complement a song service, but you still need participation from the congregation. For the musicians out there, I do understand that you can praise God with your instrument alone and you should do just that. I recall a young piano player saying one time that he felt closest to God when he played for God. For the musically inclined please play for the Lord. For the not so musically inclined, make a joyful noise unto the Lord, *Psalm 95:1 O come, let us sing unto the LORD: let us make a joyful noise to the rock of our salvation.* The most important thing I can tell you is to keep in mind that you are performing for Jesus Christ and not for those around you.

February 7

Psalm 34:1
A Psalm of David, when
he changed his behaviour before Abimelech; who drove him away, and he departed. I will bless the LORD at all times: his praise shall continually be in my mouth.

If you need to be reminded of this incident in David's life simply turn to *I Samuel 21:12-15.* Before we belittle David for his behavior with King Abimelech, we need to consider the situation. Saul wanted to kill David, so David fled the scene. He was then taken before a king and I would trust he was more than a little nervous. Many of us would have done the same thing if we consider the circumstance and recall

David was probably a young man. We may have not acted like a mad man and allowed spit to run down our face like David did. However, when we were first saved, and before any type of spiritual maturity had developed, did we ever do anything foolish? David's behavior, however foolish, did result in him being released by the king. We can think that David was foolish for his act and should have trusted God for deliverance. That may be true, but when you were first saved did you ever act in a certain way and never consulted with God in how you should act? You may have never stood before a king, but did you ever act foolish or rude towards a checkout person or a salesclerk in a store? To move on in the verse David realizes ultimately who delivered him from King Abimelech and later on realized God could have rescued him. After it all came to pass David is content to praise God at all times. So if you were looking for a time frame to bless the Lord in, here it is. You are to praise the Lord at all times. We bless the Lord and bring honor upon Him by what we do or how we act. When we concentrate on blessing the Lord, the verse says praise will continually be in your mouth. Can we assume that when we focus on the Lord and what He would have us to do, praise will be present? David brings this to our attention in the context of deliverance. Imagine going through life and God kept His hands off of you in the area of deliverance or protection? We are delivered from Satan in some way every single day. Even for Job, God dictated what could and could not be done, *Job 1:12* and *Job 2:1-6*. I bring up Job because it is probably a safe bet that when he was going through his ordeal the only thing he really had to lean on was God. If there is a key verse in the area of praise in the whole Bible it has to be this *Psalms 34:1*. I will repeat the end of the verse one more time, *his praise shall continually be in my mouth*. By the way, the verse says His praise, (which translates God's praise), shall be in your mouth and not your praise. God is your praise and you are just returning it to its rightful owner.

February 8

Psalm 35:18
I will give thee thanks in the great
congregation: I will praise thee among much people.

I have mentioned more than once the need as an individual to praise and serve an Almighty and Sovereign God. I do not want to be remiss and forget that it is very important to praise God within the confines of the body of Christ. All churches should come together in one place for praise and worship. I cannot help but think that God would sit back and drink in the praise from all people at one time. Do not misunderstand the importance of your individual praise. The only way to praise God in a great congregation is to have a lot of individuals. Here is the deal, are you and I doing our part within the confines of the congregation in the area of praise? Even if five thousand people come together, but only two are praising God then that is what God will receive. He will receive the praises of two people. If five thousand people come together and all five thousand are in one accord, then God will receive the praise of five thousand. Have you ever received praise from someone for doing a good job? Have you ever received praises from more than one person on a given day for doing a good job? If that would make you feel good, then why wouldn't God feel good when several thousand or hundred come together to praise Him? Oh, and by the way, do not ever think that God does not desire and enjoy your individual praise and service every day. As a parent we want our children to be in love with us and we enjoy the affection we receive. Why would God want any less from us concerning praise and affection? More importantly, why would we want to do anything less for God than what we enjoy? If Christ is your Saviour, you are a child of God. God enjoys the affection from His children as much as you do from your kids. I would suggest you join in and praise God with others and that you would present that praise in a childlike manner. The pay you receive for your singing in terms of money may be low, but the eternal rewards of blessings are significant. There will be a day when all believers will be gathered together in one place, and we will sing praises to the One who saved us. That my friend is the Great Congregation. Are you looking forward and longing for that day? It is going to be awesome and unforgettable. Last thought is that you just as well start practicing your praise today, as you just might be standing in the middle of the great congregation tomorrow or possibly today?

February 9

Psalm 35:28
And my tongue shall speak of thy
righteousness and of thy praise all the day long.

I am guilty of tying praise to singing a lot, but here our Psalmist will be praising God through the words he uses. Let me share a verse with you from the book of James and then maybe we can both gain some understanding of the need for praise being spoken by us and through us. *James 3:5-6 5)Even so the tongue is a little member, and boasteth great things. Behold, how great a matter a little fire kindleth! 6) And the tongue is a fire, a world of iniquity: so is the tongue among our members, that it defileth the whole body, and setteth on fire the course of nature; and it is set on fire of hell.* If we took every opportunity we are given to speak praises to God or to others about God, then how much boasting could we do? It is amazing how the same tongue we use to praise God can be used for spewing out profanity. If you are tired of the cursing and swearing then let me give you a cure-all for it. Praise God with your mouth for a certain amount of time every day and do not put filth in your ears. I cannot set a certain amount of time for you to praise God, but the Psalmist obviously did in this verse. Go back and see how long he says to praise God. It says all day long. If I spent all day long praising God in some way, then how much time would be left for any foolishness to flow out of my mouth? The answer is zero. Are we taking a little time each day to speak praises about God and to God? It is amazing how natural it can be for us to make small talk with our friends, but how much sweeter for it to be a natural thing to brag on our heavenly Father. One thing I have noticed when I am talking with a brother in Christ is the conversation always turns toward God, Jesus, and the Holy Spirit. We can share praises about what God is doing in our life, our church, and in our family. I would think it fitting that even when we believe we may be talking with a lost person that we could still share that God is alive and well. The sobering news is somebody dies every few seconds and I wonder if one of them had ever heard us or another believer praise the name of Jesus. I am not talking about praise through a song. I am talking about the praise of our tongue and the testimony of our lifestyle. Have you praised God today through what you might have said? Have you praised God by your actions or conduct? Have we praised God by our unspoken words? Are we a living breathing testimony for Jesus Christ? Are we living a life that says we are a peculiar creature that is constantly being molded into His image?

February 10

Psalm 40:3
And he hath put a new song in my mouth, even praise unto our God: many shall see it, and fear, and shall trust in the LORD.

I absolutely love this verse and I hope you do as well. We must include the first two verses of this Psalm 40. Verse 1 says the Lord heard the cry and inclined unto me. Have you ever needed the Lord in the worst way and you cried out to Him? You are comforted because you know He heard your request and will answer that prayer perfectly. Even considering our salvation there was a time when we had to ask God for forgiveness of sin and recognize a need for a Saviour. Both the Psalmist and anyone saved have been delivered from a horrible pit, (hell). We are no longer sinking into the miry clay because we are standing on a Rock, (Jesus Christ). Because we are saved, verse 2 says He is even going to establish our goings. If we will be obedient, then He can even help us know how to walk and where to walk. This brings us to the third verse where we are going to sing a new song. You sing a new song to be heard on the outside because we have a new Saviour on the inside. Have you heard the expression, "they are singing a new song now"? Many times that expression is used in a negative sense. Here it is used in a positive sense. When we received Christ as our Saviour we should sound differently. I do not believe it is up to the lost to sing praises to God. The song we sing for Christ can be a real-life testimony. The verse ends by saying we will sing, so many will see it, fear it, and then be saved because of it. Many people go through a drastic change when they receive Jesus Christ as their Saviour. When God begins a work in you and others see that change, many will want what you have. Part of that change is letting God mold us into His image and singing a new song. Singing a new song is like saying one has put on a new and improved attitude. There are times when the only one who can change us for the better is the Lord. Has God changed you? Are you singing a new song and dancing a different dance? *Jeremiah 17:7 Blessed is the man that trusteth in the LORD, and whose hope the LORD is.* If we trust in the Lord, as our hope is in the Lord, can we not enjoy praising the Lord? We must come to the place when we simply drop our arms in humbleness and place everything we have in His hands. Praise God for the times when we feel so close to Him. When we feel as if God is distant, He is right at our fingertips. He never leaves or forsakes us, but we distance ourselves from Him if we are not careful. Praise him today and feel your Savior's nearness. Do not just sing a new song, but live like you are a new song. No one can sing your song to Jesus like you can.

February 11

Psalm 42:4
When I remember these things, I pour out my soul in me: for I had gone with the multitude, I went with them to the house of God, with the voice of joy and praise, with a multitude that kept holyday.

When is an important word in this verse and I will come back to it shortly. In the preceding three verses there are some pictures painted for us. A hart/deer that is very thirsty panteth after a drink. Have you ever been so thirsty you could hardly wait to get where you were going just to get that drink? As bad as you wanted to take that first drink of cool water it does not even begin to compare with how we should thirst for the "LIVING" God. The Psalmist even cries because of his search for God. He realizes the importance of seeking God and developing a relationship with Him. Let us both get back to the word when in this verse. <u>WHEN</u> he remembered all those things he went with the multitude into the house of the Lord for the purpose of praising God. <u>WHEN</u> was the last time we recalled just how much we needed God? <u>WHEN</u> was the last time we expressed our joy for what God has done for us? <u>WHEN</u> did we enter into the house of the Lord filled with joy and praise? I trust that if we set aside a little quiet time with God and recall His goodness daily, we will be filled with joy and praise. I believe it is necessary to do this with regularity and not sporadically. Once a year is not going to cut it when it comes to praise. Do your best to focus Monday through Saturday on just what God means to you, and guess what will happen come Sunday morning? You will enter with the multitude into your perspective church with joy and praise. For the record, more than likely praise will become a daily event if you continually meditate on the goodness of God. Start applying that you have a need for God daily. <u>WHEN</u> do we start applying just how much we need God every single day? That <u>WHEN</u> is this exact moment of time in your life.

February 12

Psalm 42:5
Why art thou cast down, O my soul?
and why art thou disquieted in me? hope thou in God:
for I shall yet praise him for the help of his countenance.

It would be safe to say that everyone, including myself, has felt at times a little downcast for whatever reason. Have you ever noticed that whenever you are feeling more than a little blah that you cross paths with someone, who at least physically, is a little worse off than you are? We do need to lay aside for now the physical side of things as we are trying to address spiritual matters. It appears that even the Psalmist had a little downtime in his spiritual walk, or he would not have mentioned it. God knows we needed to hear this or He would not have inspired it to be written. The key to laying aside feeling mundane is to, and I quote, *{hope thou in God"};* and then the praise will begin. Look at the definition of hope. Hope is to cherish or have a desire with the expectation of fulfillment. Hope is to long for and includes an expectation of obtaining something. When was the last time you met someone that no matter what they did or said had that kind of hope in all matters? We have a Saviour that died for us, was made our mediator, and gives us the hope of expecting God to answer our prayers perfectly. We have hope that what God does in our life will be perfect. In my own personal life I have had days where I had to go back to *Jeremiah 17:7 Blessed is the man that trusteth in the LORD, and whose hope the LORD is.* We must maintain an attitude of lowering our hands in complete humility and surrendering totally to Him. We must take up our cross daily and trust that what God is doing is what is best for us. When sin raises its ugly head and we succumb to it there are repercussions. Even then God can give us comfort, peace, and hope in order to endure and get through it. The Psalmist is going to praise God for the help of His countenance. What do you think God's countenance is like? Do you think it possible that it is such a glorious light that you cannot even look upon it? Is it possible that when we praise God for His assistance in our life that just maybe we can take on a little of that glow? Is it possible that if we were to daily praise God we could maintain or keep that countenance? Is it possible that we have no joy of the Lord upon our face because there is no praise upon our breath? Moses' face shined from spending time with God, but he reflected God's glory from the outside. You will develop a shine upon your face when you have spent time with God. Look at Stephen, the first Christian to be martyred. *Acts 6:15 And all that sat in the council, looking stedfastly on him, saw his face as it had been the face of an angel.* God is not only on the outside looking in. If you are saved, God the Holy Spirit is monitoring from the inside looking out. Would you prefer an external glow on your face due to your praise for God, or a frown on the inside because we do not praise Him at all? If God is your hope in all things, then praise God at all times.

February 13

Psalm 42:11
Why art thou cast down, O my soul? and why art thou disquieted within me? hope thou in God: for I shall yet praise him, who is the health of my countenance, and my God.

Did you think you were back reading verse 5 of this same chapter? It is identical until the very last few words. In *Psalm 42:5* the Psalmist needs God's assistance with whatever has him downcast. He is going to praise Him because of the help of His countenance. In essence, the writer needs a little of God's countenance, (**God's glory**), rubbed off on him. The major difference between verse 11 and verse 5 of Psalm 42 is in verse 5 the Psalmist needs help, and in verse 11 he recognizes God's help. The Psalmist recognized that it is God who helps him keep HIS countenance healthy. In verse 5 he needed to be lifted up spiritually, and in verse 11 he needed help staying up. In verse 5 God was the physician. In verse 11 God is the vitamins. If all we were to receive from the time of our birth was one measly meal and then we received nothing else, we would die. Since our thought today is based on our praise, the Psalmist is going to praise God first because God came to His aid. The Psalmist will continue to praise God because he knows it will be God that will stay as his aid. What a tragedy to call on God for some spiritual uplifting, receive His uplifting, and then demonstrate that thanks by saying, "thanks, I will get a hold of you when I need you again. Do not call me, I will call you". Praise is not carried out when it is convenient for us. It is to be carried out when it is convenient for God, which is all the time! When is it a suitable time for God to receive our praise? If you will take the time to praise and worship Him, then He will take the time and listen. What does God hear from us on a consistent basis? Does He hear our moaning and groaning and nothing else? Does He occasionally hear our praising and rejoicing? If I am trusting a God who would die for me, then I want him to trust me with praise for Him. In reality, any praise I could have is His praise anyway. God gives the praise, and I am only returning that praise to its rightful owner. After all, what good is praise if we keep it contained within us? God will lift you up, but it will be Satan who will try and drag you down. Try praising God right now and see if Satan flees the area.

February 14

Psalm 43:4
Then will I go unto the altar of God, unto God my exceeding joy: yea, upon the harp will I praise thee, O God my God.

In looking at the previous three verses of this Psalm 43 it would appear King David is a little beside himself. He is confronted by an ungodly nation and David would like some deliverance from a problem clear back in *Psalm 40:1*. Apparently, he is having a problem with some ungodly man. If you know your bible at all concerning David, then you understand how Saul could be that ungodly man. Saul chased David up one hill and down another for the sole purpose of killing him. If this is the case, it is understandable how you could get a little more than disturbed. David states he is oppressed by the enemy and obviously needs a little help. He does have the foresight to know where he needs to go for help. He needs to go to the throne of God. We are in the same boat as David. We have an enemy, (Satan), and there are times when we need to go to the throne of God. How would you suppose we ought to approach the throne of God? Look what it says in *Hebrews 4:16 Let us therefore come boldly unto the throne of grace, that we may obtain mercy, and find grace to help in time of need.* What kind of attitude should we take with us to the throne of God? David went with the attitude that it is God who was his exceeding joy. King David is so filled with that joy that he intends to praise God with the harp. The harp would be a very fitting instrument for David to use. It was the harp that David used to help soothe the spirit of Saul. If you have the talent to play for the Lord, then play for the Lord. Play in a manner that would show your exceeding great love for the Lord. Praise God in whatever manner you deem appropriate. A final though to ask, "is God our exceeding joy"? It appears throughout this Psalm that when God becomes our exceeding joy, praise will be following along right behind it. Hey, shout out some praise to God right now and you just might enjoy it yourself.

February 15

Psalm 43:5
Why art thou cast down, O my soul? and why art thou disquieted within me? hope in God: for I shall yet praise him, who is the health of my countenance, and my God.

Have you heard the old cliche, "if something is not broke then do not fix it." A previous verse we discussed is almost word for word with this one. That verse being none other than *Psalm 42:11*. That verse has only one word that is different. In the verse we are looking at today, it says hope in God, but back in *Psalm 42:11* it says hope thou in God. Let me give you some food for thought on this one. When the Psalmist wrote thou it is very personal. Help thou or help me. When something is repeated twice it necessitates our attention. If you look at *Psalm 42:11* and *Psalm 43:5* at the same time it really speaks to you. It is like the Psalmist is saying in the first recording, "hey it worked for me", and then here in this verse he repeats the thought and says, "Worked for me, it will work for you". When we recall what God has done, is doing, and will do in our life it will result in praising and serving Jesus. Why would we not praise and serve God who constantly comes to our rescue when we call? If God answered your call, were you grateful for His rescue and did you let Him know about it? Are you as grateful now for the rescue as you were when it occurred? Did you praise God for His assistance? It would be pretty sorry of us to praise God for His help at that time and then forget about it. We do not necessarily want to live or stay in the past, but some things are sacred and worth hanging on to. It was around two thousand years ago when Christ died for us. Christ's death, burial, and resurrection is as important now as it was when it first happened. Where the rubber meets the road are the words in this verse, *health of my countenance*. To maintain a healthy countenance will require a genuine attitude of gratitude for Jesus Christ and His commitment to us. To go another step, I need to add that it is very important for our health to have a genuine commitment to Him. Even medical workers through studies have indicated how much more improvement there is when a person, even with a terminal disease or impending death, has placed their trust in God. In many cases that person either recovers quicker, lives longer, or goes quieter. The Lord is our health, and we are not to take it for granted. Whether you are on top of a mountain or down in a valley is not what is important. What is important is that when you are on top of a mountain or down in a valley who or what do you have your faith in. Many times you show your praise for the Lord by how you live for the Lord. How are you living on the mountain and in those valleys? Can those around you see a healthy countenance upon your face? Praise flowing from your lips will produce a healthy countenance on your face. Make praise a daily commitment and you will be the better for it.

February 16

Psalm 44:8
In God we boast all the day long,
and praise thy name for ever Selah.

It is only fitting once again to go to Mr. Webster for a definition of a very important word in this verse. That word is **boast**. One of the definitions of boast is to mention or assert with excessive pride. I hear with frequency from some people a new name for God. Some would have us to believe through cursing that God has a last name, and it is thrown out flippantly. Fools will throw God's name out as a curse word, but in comparison how do we use His name? How do we conduct ourselves when we are not sitting in church with our ties and Easter bonnets on? How do we boast of God during the course of the day? Has anyone ever wondered why you work so hard? Has anyone ever taken notice that when you speak it is not filled with cursing? Do people see us as understanding, patient, and compassionate people? We were all taught that if you could not say something nice about someone then do not say anything at all. If that were true, would people have anything good to say about us? My point is this, *Romans 13:14* says *to put on the Lord Jesus Christ and make no provision for the flesh*. When we put on Jesus Christ we boast of God. It is the power of God that changes us. We boast of God and at the same time we bring praise to God by how we carry ourselves. We are to praise or boast of His name forever. When we trusted Jesus Christ as our Saviour, we became children of God by adoption. We took on His name. A child can do one of two things to his earthly name. He can either bring about the praise of men or he can utterly destroy it. We do the same thing for God if we claim to be born again believers in Jesus Christ. We will bring about the praise of men or we can destroy God's name through our witness. If we were to ask someone if we could explain how Jesus has changed our life would they be interested in what we had to say? Would they run us off because of what they had witnessed in our life for a long time? Whether we like it or not people are monitoring what we do. If what we do during the day were to be replayed for us at the end of each day would it receive a G., P.G., or an R. rated movie? G would be for a Godly day, P. G. for a Partly Godly day, or R as a Rejected-Godly day. By the way, do not worry about how the world is rating you. You best concentrate on how Jesus is rating you. Do not get nervous about it because Jesus loves you. God loved you unconditionally and not because of who you were or who you are. God knows better than we do of the potential we have in and through Jesus Christ. We will never reach our potential for Jesus Christ without being the person God wants us to be. Boast of God today because of how you conduct yourself for Him. Potential is what God can do through us. Reality is what we are letting Him do.

February 17

Psalm 45:17
I will make thy name to be remembered in all generations: therefore shall the people praise thee for ever and ever.

There are a lot of issues to be covered in this verse. Psalm 45 is a picture of a royal wedding. The royal wedding of Jesus Christ and His church. You can be certain that there is a lot of celebrating going on in anticipation of the bridegroom showing up. Celebrating the coming of Jesus Christ ought to bring on a celebration, (praise), for us. The Psalmist tells us he is going to make the Bridegroom's name to be remembered in all generations. When we participate in making known the name of Jesus Christ, we bring praise to Him forever and ever. As followers of Jesus, (who is the Groom), we are to participate in soul winning and give others the opportunity to become a part of the wedding celebration as well. We praise Jesus Christ when we speak of His name. Those who will accept Jesus receive the opportunity to share the gospel and pass on more praise. Praise will continue for all of eternity. Spreading the gospel is a continuing chain that should never be broken. By keeping the chain in tack, we keep a continual line of praise for the Bridegroom that is coming. From generation to generation the gospel must continue on with praise. Someone told each of us about Jesus Christ and that He died for us. That person brought praise to Jesus Christ. To whom are we telling the good news? Are we passing on to others the good news of Jesus Christ in hope that they would do the same and spread the good news to the next generation? We praise our coming Bridegroom when we testify of His love for us and of our love for Him. Do not count on someone else to spread the gospel to another generation. We praise God by our witness of how Jesus has changed our life. It is not the date of your birth or the date of your death on a tombstone that most will remember. It will be the dash that separates the dates. Within the confines of that little dash, are we doing our part to see that the praise of Jesus goes on forever in the lives of those around us? A man going to hell due to our lack of participation in God's mission does not or will not constitute him praising God forever. It is doubtful he will be singing praises to God from a fiery pit we refer to as a Lake of Fire. Not only that, but the older a man gets the harder it is to win him to Jesus. Try and win just one member of your generation today, so that he might just possibly win one from his generation tomorrow.

February 18

Psalm 48:10
According to thy name, O God, so is thy praise unto the ends of the earth: thy right hand is full of righteousness.

Backing up to verse 1 of this Psalm 48 we would see that Jerusalem is the city of God. Continuing to verse 3, we have a promise of God's eternal place of refuge. When God sets up His eternal physical kingdom in Jerusalem, *Revelation 21:1-4,* people are going to be filled with joy.

God, Psalm 48:8, will establish His kingdom forever and praise will continue throughout all of eternity. The reason we should praise God now is to get practiced up for eternity. Practice makes perfect and there is no better time than the present to work on that perfection. Here in this verse 10 of our chapter, it says the praises of God will continue according to His name. God's name being that of the Alpha and Omega, *Revelation 18:11, 21:6, 22:13*, and it is an eternal name. He has always **been** here, and He will always **be** here. So how long will God's children praise the Father? As long as His name says we will, for eternity. The verse also gives a geographic location of where that praise for God will be. It says unto the ends of the earth. Every nation you can go to will inhabit people who love God as much or more than we do. None of us have a monopoly on the praise of God. He desires praise from all of us and it is amazing just how many languages there are on this planet that praise God. We may not understand or speak seven different languages, but God speaks and understands them all. Anyone who lives outside of the written word of God is really missing out on joy. One single church today contains more hymns of praise for Jesus Christ than all the Muslims and Buddhists do about their so-called god combined. We sing of a living God, and they promote a dead god. At any given moment of the day there is someone praising God. Remember, we are all on different time zones and just because you may be in your bed does not mean someone else isn't singing to Jesus. Let me remind you of *Acts 4:12 Neither is there salvation in any other: for there is none other name under heaven given among men, whereby we must be saved*. Remember, it is His praise not your praise. It is our obligation to return the praise from our lips to its rightful owner. God is that rightful owner.

February 19

Psalm 49:18
Though while he lived he blessed his soul:
and men will praise thee when thou doest well to thyself.

The Psalmist gives us an unmistakable contrast of those rich in wealth and those rich in Jesus Christ. I guess it is possible, but I have yet to see a hearse with a U-Haul trailer behind it at a graveside service. If someone were to have all their earthly possessions buried with them, it all stays in the grave. There has been a popular question over the years and it is as follows; when so-and-so died how much did they leave behind? The answer is all of it. *Luke 12:16-21 16) And he spake a parable unto them, saying, The ground of a certain rich man brought forth plentifully: 17) And he thought within himself, saying, What shall I do, because I have no room where to bestow my fruits? 18) And he said, This will I do: I will pull down my barns, and build greater; and there will I bestow all my fruits and my goods. 19) And I will say to my soul, Soul, thou hast much goods laid up for many years; take thine ease, eat, drink, and be merry. 20) But God said unto him, Thou fool, this night thy soul shall be required of thee: then whose shall those things be, which thou hast provided? 21) So is he that layeth up treasure for himself, and is not rich toward God.* There is not anything wrong with being wealthy monetarily. There is something wrong when a Christian longs for the next buck more than He longs for the LORD. As far as receiving the praise of men there is absolutely nothing wrong with that. We should praise someone for a job well done, but do not solicit it for yourself. If we understand verse 7 of this Psalm we would understand the significance of praising God instead of others or ourself. We praise and serve God when we tell others of the saving power of Jesus. We share the gospel with others in hope that they will gain an understanding of eternal rewards, *Matthew 6:20 But lay up for yourselves treasures in heaven, where neither moth nor rust doth corrupt, and where thieves do not break through nor steal.* Let us be quick to give God the praise if and when we receive any. We are only what we are because of the grace of God. If perhaps today you are not feeling too blessed, then let me list a couple of things you should rejoice over. First off, if you are reading this then you are alive, and God wants to use you to the fullest. That is if you are willing to be used. Some of you have kids and have you told them today you loved them? I recently had a conversation with my younger brother Jimmie and neither one of us could ever remember a time growing up when our dad said, "I love you". Parents, do you want to feel rich? You are rich if you are certain, you and your children will spend eternity together with Jesus Christ on the throne. I trust the Holy Spirit is leading me to share this next thought with you. If you are feeling poor, is it because some sin such as drugs, drunkenness, lying, adultery, and so on is keeping you at the bottom of the barrel? Are you letting Satan's foolishness rob you of your joy? Now just think about sin for one minute. Is any sin such as drugs, drunkenness, lying, or adultery worth living a life of total degradation? We wonder why we have days of not feeling any joy or feeling rich in Jesus and it is all due to our own foolishness. I do not apologize for the statement I am about to share with you. Christ died for you and me that we might experience a deep understanding and love for Him. If you believe you or your kids do not need Jesus then you absolutely must be either stoned, drunk, or lost. If that is the case, then you my friend, deserve what you get. Some joke and call alcohol courage in a can. See how much courage you have while spending eternity in hell because you chose the joy of drugs and drunkenness over the joy of the Lord. Are you ready to feel rich yet? Then get off your duff and on your knees and ask the Lord to forgive you and set you free. Do not be guilty of blaming Satan for everything you may be into. It is not Satan buying your sin. It is you and Satan is nowhere in the area. Jesus is only a prayer away and you can receive Him, or you can reject Him. The decision to accept Jesus Christ today might just determine where you will spend eternity tomorrow or possibly even today?

February 20

Psalm 50:23
Whoso offereth praise glorifieth me: and to him that ordereth his conversation aright will I show the salvation of God.

This Psalm 50 is filled with warnings to the hypocrite. We all must make choices in how we are going to live. Some will choose to do their own thing over doing God's thing. Remember the last verse of the book of Judges, *Judges 21:25 In those days there was no king in Israel: every man did that which was right in his own eyes.* If anyone chooses the same path Israel did, there is a price to pay. If we backed up one verse in this Psalm 50 you would see the demise for those who exercise foolishness. God will tear them to pieces, and no one will be able to deliver them. Is it possible for someone to do whatever they deem appropriate and then praise God? I think it is possible to do whatever you want and then sing a hymn. I am not convinced it is praise that is being offered. When we approach God's throne through intercessory prayer or praise, we need to be a holy vessel. *Psalm 66:18 If I regard iniquity in my heart, the Lord will not hear me.* The first order of business is repentance to God for cleansing us and getting close to Him relationally. God will pardon, *I John 1:9*, but do not fail to ask for that forgiveness. We bring dishonor upon God if we claim to be a Christian and then live the life of a heathen. In this verse we are instructed that whosoever offers praise to God glorifies Him. Are we offering praise to God that He would be glorified? Keep in mind that just because you are singing does not mean you are praising. Be mindful that your actions, words, or deeds can either praise God or they can undermine God. The writer James said it best in *James 3:10 Out of the same mouth proceedeth blessing and cursing. My brethren, these things ought not so to be.* Your words and actions can make you appear hypocritical. In my own personal reading just yesterday, I was reminded of a couple of things in *John 9:38 And he said, Lord, I believe. And he worshipped him.* The story is that of the blind man who was healed by Jesus and then kicked out of the synagogue for testifying of Him. When the blind man believed he then worshipped. Worshipping goes hand in hand with believing. Think on this, if you are not worshipping the Lord, then are you absolutely certain that you really do believe in Him? If you respond, "Yes I believe", then what are you believing in right now that would hinder your worship? God asks so little of believers so please do not offer up less than the little He now asks.

February 21

Psalm 51:15
O Lord, open thou my lips;
and my mouth shall show forth thy praise.

What a beautiful picture in Psalm 51 of a man who wants God to dictate everything he does. King David acknowledges that he was born a sinner. He realizes his need for the forgiveness of sin. David records a list of things he desired. He had a desire for wisdom, forgiveness of sin, to be white as snow, a clean heart, a right spirit, and to walk in the Spirit. David desired to have the continual presence of the Spirit, joy in salvation, the ability to share the message of salvation, and the ability to sing aloud of God's righteousness. David desired all those things so he could get to our verse 15. David wanted God to lead him in his conversation. He says, *"Open my lips and my mouth shall show forth thy praise"*. We should desire the same things David did. David was just as human as we are. We should daily request from God that He would help us live blameless in a perverse and wicked world. The result of the request to live a holy life will end in praise. I do not understand how we could petition God for His help and then not praise Him as David mentions. The book of James states that it is difficult to steer the tongue, which is why we should place that task in God's hands. *James 3:5-6 5) Even so the tongue is a little member, and boasteth great things. Behold, how great a matter a little fire kindleth! 6) And the tongue is a fire, a world of iniquity: so is the tongue among our members, that it defileth the whole body, and setteth on fire the course of nature; and it is set on fire of hell.* Let God be the author of our words and see what happens. I believe we would have a chaste, (pure in thought), conversation. *Philippians 1:27 Only let your conversation be as it becometh the gospel of Christ: that whether I come and see you, or else be absent, I may hear of your affairs, that ye stand fast in one spirit, with one mind striving together for the faith of the gospel*; Can you imagine what the praise is going to be like when Christ sets up His kingdom? The list of things David desired will be put into place for all of eternity. Are you able to visualize the praise that will take place when all believers are gathered together in one place?

There will be a complete absence of sin, and everyone gathered together in one accord for the sole purpose of praising God. Can we come together at our perspective church in one accord for praise? How do we arrive at such a praise service? We do it one person at a time and as a favorite hymn states, "Will you be the One". It is an individual commitment to confess daily our iniquities and to enter His house <u>prayed up</u> in order to <u>praise right</u>.

February 22

Psalm 52:9
I will praise thee forever, because thou hast done it: and I will wait on thy name; for it is good before thy saints.

Here is another Psalm of King David where he introduces another character to us in verse 1 by the name of Doeg the Edomite. If you check out scripture you can see that Doeg was not a very nice person to anyone. He did have one good quality in that he was very obedient to his master. If he were told to kill, then he would kill. Apparently, Doeg had another age-old problem, which was the lack of ability to control his mouth. I would think it next to impossible to praise God in one breath and bring forth lies and deceit in the next breath. That would be a very unhealthy balanced life. Doeg had made a choice for himself. He chose the riches of the world over a relationship with God. He strove for strength in wickedness instead of relying on the strength of God. In verse 8 of Psalm 52 David says he is a green olive tree, and he will trust in the mercy of God forever. According to Romans 11:24 have we not also been grafted into an olive tree. God gave us His only begotten son, John 3:16, so we should give forth praise for the mercy of

God. If God gave us what we deserved, we would be in a heap of trouble. God did not give us what we deserve. He gave us His Son Jesus. David is going to praise God for His eternal mercy. That would indicate that it is important for us to praise God for His eternal mercy. Are we praising God with an attitude of thanksgiving? The same mercy that saved us is the same mercy that continually keeps us saved. If anything, we praise God because He sealed us with His Spirit, *Ephesians 4:30 And grieve not the holy Spirit of God, whereby ye are sealed unto the day of redemption.* Are we as grateful today for that seal of the Spirit as we were when we were first sealed? How about our gratefulness yesterday and the day before? Our gratefulness to an awesome and Almighty God will be reflected in our praise to God! To wrap things up, be sure and extend the same mercy to others that has been extended to you. The results will be eternal, and your praise will become more significant to yourself. We will either take on the appearance of an evil Doeg or the appearance of Jesus.

February 23

Psalm 54:6
I will freely sacrifice unto thee:
I will praise thy name, O LORD; for it is good.

In the previous 5 verses of this same Psalm, King David is not praying for vengeance. He is praying in faith that God would deliver him from his enemies. He knew better than to think he could take care of everything on his own. Vengeance is not ours to carry out, *Romans 12:19 Dearly beloved, avenge not yourselves, but rather give place unto wrath: for it is written, Vengeance is mine; I will repay, saith the Lord.* Our goal is to pray for those who despitefully use us, *Matthew 5:44 But I say unto you, Love your enemies, bless them that curse you, do good to them that hate you, and pray for them which despitefully use you, and persecute you;* We must recognize the need for God to come to our aid. God not only comes to our aid, but He is always watchful of what is going on in our life. God knows when to intervene and we ought to know when to call for His intervention. Due to David's knowledge of who the great Deliverer was brings us to our current verse. First, he would sacrifice freely to God. That is exactly how we are to take our tithes and offerings to Him. *II Corinthians 9:7 Every man according as he purposeth in his heart, so let him give; not grudgingly, or of necessity: for God loveth a cheerful giver.* The best sacrifice we can give is of our self. *Romans 12:1 says we are to present our bodies as a living sacrifice.* When we freely give and present our bodies a living sacrifice praise will follow close behind. When someone does something nice for us, we praise their name. We have our list of who we really want to be around, and I would assume that we would want to spend time with God. If we can praise the name of a friend, should we not praise the name of the Lord? David will praise God's name because it is good. I trust we would follow King David's example. I cannot emphasize enough the importance of fellowship with other believers. We relocated to Florida and currently I have made a lot of friends/acquaintances. I pray daily for godly men to show up where we can spend time together. I promise you one thing, going to church a couple of days a week may not be fellowship. Fellowship can occur outside the church building and can be profitable spiritually as well.

February 24

Psalm 56:4
In God I will praise his word, in God I have
put my trust; I will not fear what flesh can do unto me.

When we read God's word and apply it to our life, we should praise His word. Let me paraphrase a few verses of scripture of what would solicit praise from God's word. *John 3:16*, God loved us so much He let the world kill His son. *Romans 10:13*, anyone called of God to repentance can receive it, they need only to ask. In *I John 2:1*, Jesus is our advocate, (someone who will stand up for us). *I Corinthians 15:45*, instead of being dead, Christ has made us alive, a quickening spirit. *I Timothy 2:5*, we have a Christ who will go to the Father with our requests. I doubt I would have enough paper to list every good thing about God's word. This is why praise should be natural for us. We should praise His word for its goodness and how it applies to each one of us. I would dare say that every one of us has had a moment in time when we can do nothing, but trust in the Lord with all our heart, soul, and mind. I would say that every single one of us has had at least one occasion where we had no other option than to trust the Lord because anything aside from that would be futile. On my own screen saver on my computer I display a constant reminder of what I need to do. *Jeremiah 17:7 Blessed is the man that trusteth in the LORD, and whose hope the LORD is.* We have God's word that we can trust Him. It is refreshing how we serve a God that cannot lie or mislead us. To change gears, look at the last few words of this same verse. It reminds me of not being concerned with what my flesh can do or for that matter what someone else can do to my flesh. Let our fear be towards the one that after the flesh is dead can then cast the soul into hell. *Matthew 10:28 And fear not them which kill the body, but are not able to kill the soul: but rather fear him which is able to destroy both soul and body in hell.* Praise God His word says that if I am saved, I need not worry about it. The verse basically says, "Praise his Word, practice to trust in His Word, and perfect your walk by the Word." It all points back to Jesus Christ.

February 25

Psalm 56:10
In God will I praise his word:
in the LORD will I praise his word.

"Praise His word" appears twice in the same verse as you quickly noticed. There is however, one distinguishing difference. David uses two different titles: one being "God" and the other being the "LORD." He says first, "In God will I praise", and second, he says, "In the LORD will I praise". In the first case the Hebrew word for God is Elohim. Our Psalmist is addressing God himself and in the second case there is the Hebrew word for Lord. It is what we would pronounce as Jehovah. Isn't it amazing how some people cannot see Jesus in the Old Testament? David is going to praise Him, (the Lord). Throughout all scripture we cannot separate the Father from the Son. If it were not for God, we would not have received the Son and if it were not for the Son we could not get to the Father. We know from New Testament scripture that Jesus is "the eternal One". By comparing *John 1:1* and *John 1:14* we know that Christ is the Word, and He has always been here. How can you not praise Christ, (the Word), when He was so willing to praise us by dying for us? Are you in the Word, (Christ), on a consistent basis? If so, then praise should be a natural thing for you. What if you are not praising the Lord Jesus Christ? Then I would ask, "How much time are you spending in God's word"? How much time are you spending with Jesus Christ the Lord? You will never have a desire to praise Him unless you get to know Him. You will never know more about Him unless you spend time with Him. You will not find a better place to spend time with Him than studying the Word of God. You have at your fingertips the written word of God available. You have 66 books you can choose from and not one will lead you away from Jesus the Saviour. The key is not sitting around trying to pick the right book to read in your Bible, but to start somewhere and stay with it day after day after day. Give some thought to fasting every now and then. It will change you physically and spiritually. It will help you focus your mind on what is essential and important.

February 26

Psalm 57:7
My heart is fixed, O God,
my heart is fixed: I will sing and give praise.

What is your heart fixed on? David has his heart fixed on praising God. King David back in verse 1 of this same Psalm has gone to prayer. He has some things troubling him and he wisely chooses to take it to God. David starts out with a case of anxiety and distress and ends up comforted. How does he do that? He focuses on God instead of on his circumstances. What we must do is decide what we are going to focus on. David is not considering praise here. Praising God is not a matter of debate. He is fixed on singing and giving praise to God. He says his heart is fixed on it. Isn't it amazing how scripture says the heart is desperately wicked? *Jeremiah 17:9 The heart is deceitful above all things, and desperately wicked: who can know it?* If we corral our heart towards praise instead of our heart corralling us towards sin, we will experience the joy "<u>of</u>" the Lord. Then we can give way to praise "<u>for</u>" the Lord. We need to take on one of Christ's characteristics found in *Isaiah 50:7 For the Lord GOD will help me; therefore shall I not be confounded: therefore have I set my face like a flint, and I know that I shall not be ashamed.* Jesus Christ had something to do, so He set his face like a flint. Jesus had predetermined ahead of time the course of action He would take, and He would not be turned aside from it. What do we set our face like a flint for? We can set our face like a flint for anything. You and I can determine "IF" we will entertain sin and lose the ability to praise or we can predetermine as Joshua did in *Joshua 24:15 And if it seem evil unto you to serve the LORD, choose you this day whom ye will serve; whether the gods which your fathers served that were on the other side of the flood, or the gods of the Amorites, in whose land ye dwell: but as for me and my house, we will serve the LORD.* Our complete focus can be on the things of this world if we are not careful. When that happens, we become guilty of setting our thoughts and affections towards whatever comes our way and give way to the devil. Colossians 3:2 *Set your affection on things above, not on things on the earth.* If we consider the example of Jesus Christ and set our face like a flint with regards to praise and service, then we have predetermined that we will not let anything keep us from praising and serving God. Do not let situations or frustrations keep you from praising your Lord. If you do, it will be the blessing of praise you forfeit, and that is a place you do not want to be in.

February 27

Psalm 57:9
I will praise thee, O Lord, among the people:
I will sing unto thee among the nations.

If we backed up to verse 7 of this same Psalm, we would see that David has just gotten his heart right in the area of praise. He made a conscious decision that as an individual he would praise God. He had predetermined that he would praise God. Praising God in our own private time is wonderful, but there is a time to lift up our voice with the people as this *Psalm 57:9* says. King David had predetermined he would praise God among the people. I mentioned in an earlier scripture one particular thought and I will repeat it again. We need to do whatever is necessary when we come together as a body of believers to praise God as a congregation. We need to predetermine before we walk through the front doors of our perspective church that we will do our part during the praise service. You cannot have <u>congregational</u> praise without <u>individuals</u> committing themselves to praise. Are you one of the individuals participating in praise or are you sitting on the bench? Even on a professional sports team there are starters and there are backups. Here is the noticeable difference between the two. Usually, the starters are the best of the best and play nearly every minute of the game. Now the second team sitting on the bench is dying to get in the game. I realize some may have more talent, but those on the bench have a huge desire to participate in the victory. In the praise team or choir some members have the ability to get up and sing solos as they have the talent to do so. Some do not have the ability to grab a microphone and share a song. Here is what we need to remember. If we will predetermine to praise God as an individual in the midst of the people, there are no second-string participants. Those who can sing solos will receive no more recognition from God than from those who will make a joyful noise to Him. Here is an awesome thought to ponder. I may be a second-class singer, but I do not have to be a second-class worshipper. God's children are not second-class citizens. Do you want to participate and have victory in Praise? When you stand to sing, leave any attitude, sin, or whatever else you might be clinging to on the seat. Rise with repentance in your heart, have your attitude in check, and then let your voice ring out in adoration.

February 28

Psalm 61:8
So will I sing praise unto thy name for ever,
that I may daily perform my vows.

Let us get into the context of this verse. King David is petitioning God for the things that will help him be the kind of man God would have him to be. We have already discussed prior to this verse the implications alone of praising God's name forever. The emphasis being on the time of forever. Praise throughout all of eternity means plain and simple that praise for the name of the Lord will never cease. Look back to our verse to see that David recognizes some areas of his own life where he needed a little assistance. You would have to read the first 6 verses of this same Psalm, but it is there. In the first 6 verses he recognizes his need for help, and he does the wise thing. He seeks God for guidance. We just as well seek God to help us in the areas where we are weak. I can assure you that Satan will try and tear you down where you are the weakest. There is no doubt that God knows our strengths and our weaknesses. Do not think for a second that eventually Satan does not figure it out. Satan will be quick to jump on any opportunity, especially if it will drag us down and make us look like fools to the world. Many times it is not hard for Satan to know our weaknesses because they can be very obvious. Obvious, and because of a lack of eloquent words, we act foolish. What we should sing praise for is the fact that God alone will build us up, exalt us, and protect us. David ends this verse by saying he wants to perform his vows daily. He says he will praise God daily that he might perform his vows. The decision we must make is are we performing daily our vows? Have we made a vow to God that we will bless the Lord daily? Will we always praise God? *Psalm 34:1 I will bless the LORD at all times: his praise shall continually be in my mouth*. Here are your choices you can make with regards to making a vow to God. One, you can vow to be in sin or two, you can vow to ask God to help you with your walk with Jesus Christ and rely only on Him. The result of your dependence <u>toward</u> the Lord will be praise <u>to</u> the Lord. Do you think it is difficult living for the Lord and praising His name? Look around at those who think they do not need a Savior and listen to what kind of a tune they are whistling. There may be those occasions where they are whistling "Happy Trails", but they do not know at any given time during their walk what they might step in on that trail!

February 29

John 7:33
Then said Jesus unto them, Yet a little while am I with you, and then I go unto him that sent me.

Jesus told them He would return to Heaven. Basically, He is saying, "My dad sent me and to my dad I will return". The good news is what He told us seven chapters later and what we are to look forward to. *John 14:1-3 1) Let not your heart be troubled: ye believe in God, believe also in me. 2) In my Father's house are many mansions: if it were not so, I would have told you. I go to prepare a place for you. 3) And if I go and prepare a place for you, I will come again, and receive you unto myself; that where I am, there ye may be also.* Believers are only temporarily separated from Jesus Christ. I do not care where someone lives as it will not compare to what is coming. Not just a mansion is built for us, but we have other HUGE blessings on the horizon. *Mark 14:62 And Jesus said, I am: and ye shall see the Son of man sitting on the right hand of power, and coming in the clouds of heaven. 1 Thessalonians 4:17 Then we which are alive and remain shall be caught up together with them in the clouds, to meet the Lord in the air: and so shall we ever be with the Lord. Mark 14* is an account of the second coming of Jesus. *1 Thessalonians* is an account of the rapture of the church. The exact word used for rapture is harpazō. Harpad'-zo is the word for caught up in *1 Thessalonians*. It means to seize, catch, pull, or to take by force. There is nothing or nobody that will stop believers from heading to the clouds to meet Jesus Christ and experiencing God the Father, God the Son, and God the Holy Spirit to the fullest. Jesus did tell them that it would be a little while before it happened. Now I know that since Jesus made this statement it has been about two thousand years. In our finite minds that seems like a long time instead of a little while. Keep in mind that God does not operate in time because time will not be a reality in eternity. Also remember and ask, "How does two thousand years compare to eternity"? It will not even be a drop in the bucket.

March 1

Psalm 63:3
Because thy lovingkindness
is better than life, my lips shall praise thee.

If we back up to verse 1 of this Psalm 63, we will see at what time David says he sought God. David sought him early and that must be the best time of the day. Early in the morning means we have not been out and immersed ourselves in the world yet. David is longing for God in the way you would thirst for water in a dry and thirsty land. Keep in mind that water mentioned in scripture is also used in reference to Jesus Christ, the living water, or the Word. We should long for Jesus over and above how we would long for a glass of water. In verse 2 David says he has seen God's glory and power. Look around and see if you notice God's glory and power? Those who accept Jesus Christ as their Saviour are examples of God's glory and power. If you do not believe that statement, then you obviously have not heard a believers' testimonies of how God has supernaturally changed their life. David knew where his strength was and says in our verse for today, *"God, even your lovingkindness is better than life"*. Can you imagine what this world would be like if God was not a compassionate and forgiving God? David recognized it and chose to praise God for it, {*my lips shall praise thee*}. The reality is when we let "something" flow from our lips, will it be praise to God where we can lift up His name, or will we let something else fly out from those same lips and disgrace His name? *Matthew 12:35 A good man out of the good treasure of the heart bringeth forth good things: and an evil man out of the evil treasure bringeth forth evil things.* Do we desire to be an evil or a good person? Will we bring forth good things or evil things? What will come from our mouth? Will it be praise, disgrace, blessings, or cursing? David said he was in a wilderness, but he still chooses to praise God. We may be placed in the wilderness, but we are to still praise God. Praising God should not occur when you think you are on top of the mountain and everything is just peachy for you. The God on the mountain is still the God in the valley. Here is something for you to think about. When you sing in a valley the sound resonates for a long time. We would refer to that as an echo. It is as if God lets your praise linger or resonate so nature itself can enjoy it with him over and over and over.

March 2

Psalm 63:5
My soul shall be satisfied as with marrow and fatness; and my mouth shall praise thee with joyful lips:

In backing up one verse in this Psalm 63 David defines when he will praise God. He is going to praise God while he is still alive. Praise will not come from those in the grave, it will come from those still living. That would make me wonder that if you are not praising God while you are still living, then are you dead spiritually? David will not only sing, but he will lift holy hands when he does it. It sure does not sound like a man with any reservations about praising God does it? Now in this verse David's soul is blessed and content. He says his soul is satisfied. When we accepted Jesus Christ as our Saviour our soul was blessed, contented, and satisfied. David then records that he will praise God with joyful lips. Two verses earlier David would praise God with his lips. Now he will praise God with **joyful** lips. In two verses David has grown a little bit spiritually. I hate to repeat things, but he will not sing with lips, but with **JOYFUL** lips.

I am certain that David had experienced his own moments when things appeared that they could not get any worse. Praising the Lord can take your mind off your immediate predicament. Here is a test for you to try sometime if you would like. The next time you feel like things just cannot get any worse, try focusing on the Lord and praising him with your own song. You ask yourself, "What is my own song as I am not a song writer." Your song is the song that you choose to sing when it is just you and God alone. Praise in the congregation can be an awesome thing to participate in, but do not think for a minute that you cannot nor should not praise God by yourself. You can praise him for no other reason than the fact that He is God and that He loves YOU. Go back to the start of this verse. It basically says that the blessings of God are not just skin deep, but run clear to the bone. Now if the blessings of God run clear to the bones, then our praise should start at the bones and end up on the outside. Let our praise we exhibit externally reflect the blessings we possess internally. Praise is something we can continually work on. Practice will make perfect when it comes to praise. Only time will tell how you are doing with praise, service, and worship. If you are saved the greatest thing you have is time. You are looking at eternity with God and where I grew up eternity meant eternity.

March 3

Psalm 65:1
To the chief Musician,
A Psalm and Song of David. Praise waiteth for thee,
O God, in Sion: and unto thee shall the vow be performed.

David does not do a lot of petitioning in *Psalm 65*. He gets right to the heart of what he wants to sing about. David's song is one of anticipation as he knew the Lord was coming and he would be ready to praise Him. I would encourage you to look way down the road at what is coming for us as David did. Jesus will be sitting on a throne as the One and only King in a New Jerusalem. No one gathered around His throne will ever experience death and there will be no health problems to deal with. Those who gather around Jesus' throne are those who have trusted Jesus as their Saviour prior to His coming or prior to their death. Really meditate for a moment on what it will be like with absolutely no sin anywhere. We will not be worrying about wars and rumors of wars. We will not have to sit back and watch riots or any other type of chaos take place. If there were to be a news program, there will not be one segment devoted to the bad news for the day. There is not going to be any bad news and just think how blissful it will be. Think also of the loved ones you will never be separated from. Think of the "PERFECT" praise we will possess for the Lamb of God. Now look at what is going on in your life in the present. When we gather on Sunday God promised where two or more gather in His name, He will be in the midst, *Matthew 18:20*. I have to believe that on any given Sunday at our own church there ought to be at least two there who have gathered in His name. Make sure you are one of the two or more who are ready to praise Him. Do not count on someone else to praise the Lord. He is counting on you for that. If the Lord is in our midst I can assure you He will He hear the praise directed to Him? If Christ were to return today for His children, what will we be found doing? When we meet Him in the clouds, what were we right in the middle of? Will Christ find us in the middle of a debate, some good old-fashioned cursing, or did He hear praise from us? Please understand that you do not have to wait for Jesus to sit on

His throne in a New Jerusalem to praise Him. The time to start perfecting your praise for the Lord is NOW.

March 4

Psalm 66:2
Sing forth the honour of his name:
make his praise glorious.

In looking at verse 1 of this Psalm 66 the key word is joyful. Everybody has heard the phrase, *make a joyful noise unto the Lord*. There is a specific group addressed here in verse 1 and it says, *All ye lands*. The entire world is to lift up praise to God. Here is something to exercise your mind with. What would happen if the entire world at one time praised God? I would be willing to bet there would be one less murder, rape, abortion, or Lord knows whatever else should not take place? By considering verse 1 and 2 together it becomes obvious that God desires the praise of every country and nation. Everyone is to sing about the honour of His name and the praise should be glorious. *John 5:23 That all men should honour the Son, even as they honour the Father. He that honoureth not the Son honoureth not the Father which hath sent him.* Do you realize that those who possess only head knowledge of Jesus Christ cannot honor the Father? You cannot honor or praise the Father's name until you accept His Son's name for your Salvation. *Acts 4:12 Neither is there salvation in any other: for there is none other name under heaven given among men, whereby we must be saved.* You will only honor the Father when you personally accept Jesus Christ as your Lord and Saviour. Satan absolutely does not want people to believe that just trusting in Jesus is sufficient for your eternal soul. It really does not matter what Satan thinks. It is a matter of what the Bible says and how you respond to it. It says and I quote from *John 14:6 Jesus saith unto him, I am the way, the truth, and the life: no man cometh unto the Father, but by me.* The Father, Son, and the Holy Spirit are a package deal. You do not get one without the other. Where should you be when you praise God you ask? You praise Him right where you stand, and if you are too tired to stand, then it is wherever you happen to be sitting. The verse does not say that you are to praise God only on Sunday at your church. It does say to make His praise glorious. Now go back to the key word used in verse 1 and that being the word joyful. Are we presenting to Him a joyful noise? To joyfully praise Him is to honor Him. Before we can be honoring to Him, we need to be humble before Him. Do we seek humbleness that we would be prepared to make a joyful noise and to bring about honor due His name? Do unbelievers around us recognize our love for the Lord? If those who have made Jesus their Lord cannot praise His name then who will? Praise God consistently and if you are not doing that, you can let God know why not? However, God already knows our answer.

March 5

Psalm 66:8
O bless our God, ye people,
and make the voice of his praise to be heard:

Those who have trusted Christ as their personal Saviour are God's people. Where else should praise come from other than His children? I understand the examples given at the start of this Psalm 66 are examples of Israel's deliverance. God parted the Red Sea so they could flee from their enemy. If need be, go back to the start of this Psalm 66 and check it out. How many times has God had to part a Red Sea for us and then lead us to safety? How many Pharaohs has God protected us from and we did not know? Do you realize what our lives would be like if God completely took his hand of protection off of us? I do not know about you, but I am extremely glad that I serve a God who is concerned about every detail of my life. Look at *Luke 12:7 But even the very hairs of your head are all numbered.* Do you not think that if God knows every hair on your head that there could be anything He does not know about you? God is concerned about even the smallest of details concerning our life because He loves us. Is it too big a request from the Psalmist that we should let others hear our praise for Him or to be a blessing to Him? When we manage to get ourselves into a mess what does God do? Just like He rescued Israel from the Egyptians in the Red Sea, God made a way at Calvary upon a cross to rescue us. None of us need to give in to sin. God always makes a way for us to escape sin. Look at *I Corinthians 10:13 There hath no temptation taken you but such as is common to man: but God is faithful, who will not suffer you to be tempted above that ye are able; but will with the temptation also make a way to escape, that ye may be able to bear it.* So are you feeling good about yourself yet because the light just came on and you know God is watching your every move? Here is a bit of good news for you. If you are feeling good on the inside, you do not have to keep that feeling known as praise held captive any longer. Feel free to let it out. Our verse says to make known His praise or let it be heard. Whatever is on the inside wants to come out. There are times to ask what are we harboring on the inside? Is it praise or something else? Whatever we cling to internally will eventually be seen and heard externally. You can only keep something hid for so long and it will eventually be revealed. Do you love Him? Do not just tell others about it, tell God. Is it quite possible you do not know the words to speak to Him at this time? Sometimes we need to just be still and let God reveal what we ought to be saying to Him.

March 6

Psalm 67:3
Let the people praise thee, O God;
let all the people praise thee.

The Psalmist has a desire in *Psalm 67:1* to praise God because of God's mercy. He wants to praise God for he knows it is God who blesses. He wants to praise God because he knows it is God that gives us His glory that it might shine upon us. If you do anything today, think about God's mercy. We hear and know of God's grace, but consider grace with mercy. Grace is receiving something we do not deserve, (Jesus Christ). Mercy is not receiving what we do deserve, (hell). You might have to let that soak in for a while. If necessary, go back and read it again. If it helps, let me give you an acronym for G.R.A.C.E., {Gods Riches At Christ's Expense}. He continues in verse 2 expressing his desire to make known God's way. Something to think about is how we can make known God's way if we continually get in God's way. Are we a bold witness for Jesus or a big nuisance? In our verse you can almost sense the ending of a song where the cymbals come crashing together. The Psalmist would be the one with the cymbals in his hand and ready for the grand finale. Picture this thought in your mind. The musicians are playing with a fervor, *{let **the** people praise thee},* the last chord is played and everyone is praising God, and then boom the cymbals crash together, *{let **all** the people praise thee}.* For me in this verse we have one excited Psalm writer. Look back again at *Psalm 67:2*. God is going to be the one who can bring about a saving health to our nation. The thing that makes a sick nation is the rejection of God. A nation may be filled with people who are physically healthy, but that same nation who turns their back on God is spiritually sickly. You can be a nation of wealth and yet be spiritually poor. You could be a part of a nation that has the greatest of technology or sophistication and still be spiritually ignorant. The word to dwell on in our verse here is the word **all**. An individual must decide if they will be a part of the **all**. Just because your neighbor chooses not to praise God does not mean you join your neighbor. Maybe you should be heard or seen praising the Lord and maybe your neighbors will join you. Why would your friends, family, or even your enemies want what you possess if they do not know what you have? I am not referring to what you have in your home, but by what you have dwelling in your heart. Does your heart possess praise or is there something in your heart that is possessing you and keeping you from praise? *Matthew 15:8 This people draweth nigh unto me with their mouth, and honoureth me with their lips; but their heart is far from me.*

March 7

Psalm 67:5
Let the people praise thee,
O God; let all the people praise thee.

The Psalmist quotes word for word our devotional verse on praise from yesterday. *Psalm 67:3 Let the people praise thee, O God; let all the people praise thee.* Even the punctuation is the same. For the sake of recollection, it is obvious the writer is not only inspired to write this, but he is extremely excited about what he is writing. Back up one verse and we see what the Psalmist knows. He knows there will be a day when the whole world will be praising the Lord. Coming down the road for believers in Jesus, and for all of eternity, Jesus will govern the world and His judgment will be perfect. Things will be perfect as it was from the beginning with Adam and Eve. It will start with a King who is holy, perfect, and just. What a day it will be when Jesus Christ will sit on the throne for all of eternity. When is the last time you sat very still and tried to picture in your mind what it will be like with Jesus on the throne? *Hebrews 4:16 we can go boldly to the throne.* Think about that verse for a moment. If you wanted to go to another country and see the king or queen, you probably had best been invited. I am only speaking for me, but I have my doubts that I can go to another country and see the king. I probably will not even be allowed to see the throne. Jesus not only died for us, but when He returns for his children, He will spend time with us. All things will be in perfect harmony for "ALL" that have trusted Jesus Christ for salvation. For all of eternity we will praise him for what He did. Who do you know who would be willing to leave heaven, come to earth as a baby, die for us, and then lay 3 days in a grave? Here is the good news, the grave could not hold him, and we are back to why we should celebrate. He arose from the dead and is available to each one of us. We were given a throne that we can approach with boldness. At the Second Coming of Jesus, the world will finally be in one accord and in perfect unity. There will be no sin, sadness, or sickness, but there will be praying, playing, and praising. I will close again with the same key word I used in the last verse we discussed. That word is the word "ALL." An individual must decide if they will be a part of the "ALL"! Remember, the last three letters in the word fall is all. You can fall to the left or you can fall to the right. Jesus Christ must be your Saviour before you die or it will be hell for you.

The ramification for denying Jesus is eternal death and you absolutely do not want to experience that!

March 8

Psalm 69:30
I will praise the name of God with a song,
and will magnify him with thanksgiving.

Earlier in this Sixty-Ninth Psalm it would appear the writer was a little put out with his circumstances. He could have chosen to wallow in self-pity, but he did not. He came to the place where he obviously looked at the blessings he had and opted to praise God for them. Instead of comparing what we have with those around us, we need to be thankful for what God has provided to us. It is a hard thing to do, but even when things look their bleakest, we must thank God for those experiences and ask Him what we are to learn from it. It is rare to talk to another believer about trials or tribulation and not have them admit that even though it was a rough time in their life, they became closer to God relationally through the ordeal. We must keep in the front of our mind that the God who is with us on the mountaintop is the same God down in the valley. Look at the last half of *Hebrews 13:5 Let your conversation be without covetousness; and be content with such things as ye have: for he hath said, I will never leave thee, nor forsake thee*. This is exactly why we can sing songs of Praise and know they will be heard. You will not find a place where you can escape the watchful eye or listening ears of God. I think most have seen movies where someone is dancing through a field of daisies and singing their heart out. Trust me, life is not always filled with fields smothered with beautiful flowers. However, we can be in any circumstance, and still have a flower available to us right at our fingertips.

The flower is known in scripture as the "ROSE OF SHARON", or better known as Jesus Christ. In moving on, the Psalmist would not only talk about God's goodness, but he would also sing of it. Our writer says he will magnify God with thanksgiving. When you magnify something, it would normally mean to make something larger than it really is. I know of only one way to magnify God, and John the Baptist gave us the example, *John 3:30 He must increase, but I must decrease.* Life is not about us, it's about Jesus. Trust me when I say the sun does not rise nor set on our backside. When we take the focus off of self and put it on God, praise will follow. When we focus on Him it puts us into the position of counting our blessings and naming them one by one as the hymn says. There are many things we could focus on. The question here is what will we choose to focus on? I can only remind you of what God's word says in *Colossians 3:2 Set your affection on things above, not on things on the earth.*

March 9

Psalm 69:34
Let the heaven and earth praise him,
the seas, and everything that moveth therein.

Are we in agreement that anything that has breath should be praising God? Backing up to verse 31 of this Psalm 69, it makes mention of our praise in comparison to sacrifice. He writes that our praise is more pleasing than a sacrifice with horns or hoofs. There was a time when sacrifices were required, but I am quite sure that unless God tells me to do so, I would not want to wrestle with a bullock, sheep, or a goat. Even if I were to get the best of any of those three animals, I would still not be done. I would still have to take a knife, kill it, gut it, and then lay the parts in a particular order upon an altar. If God tells me to do that I would, but He hasn't. Therefore, yours truly is grateful that I have a sacrifice already and His name is Jesus Christ. There was a time when Jesus became our sacrifice as He willingly laid down his life for you and me. I would encourage you to stop reading this and go back and read this entire Sixty-Ninth Psalm. Keep in mind that in the first thirty verses you read that what the Psalmist wrote is what Jesus experienced. If it is, then Jesus still took the time and made sure that even during a time of great persecution He found it fitting to make sure we knew how important praise is. His death for us mandates our praise of thanksgiving for Him. Now back in verse 32 of this Psalm the humble will rejoice and the heart will be made alive. The opposite of our heart being alive would be to have a heart that is dead. Before any of us met Jesus Christ as our Saviour we were spiritually dead. The day we prayed and asked God for forgiveness for our sin, scripture says that through Jesus you were made a quickening spirit. *1 Corinthians 15:45 And so it is written, The first man Adam was made a living soul; the last Adam was made a quickening spirit.* Someone taking up space in a pew and singing an old hymn such as Amazing Grace does not mean they are saved. However, if you know you are saved you should not sit in your pew and look like someone just shot your favorite pet either. Not to be redundant, but if Jesus is your Saviour, and He made us a quickening spirit, we should act like we are alive instead of dead. If you have ever watched an old western movie, you may have noticed that on the tombstone the letters R.I.P.? That stood for Rest In Peace. If you act like you are spiritually dead you may have the same letters on your tombstone someday only it will stand for Really Insignificant Praiser! When we praise God, our heart is not made alive, but carries the appearance that we are alive and excited about being followers of Jesus. We should be joyful and grateful to our creator. This is exactly why we should want to sing and live for Him. Because you sing a hymn in church does not mean you have a heart that is alive. You become spiritually alive when you accept Jesus as your Saviour. The result of not having Jesus as your Saviour is a dead heart. You can sing till the cows come home, but if you do not know Jesus Christ you are SPIRITUALLY "DEAD"! Would it be safe to say that if we refuse to praise God, we either have a dead heart or a bad attitude? If you believe you have either a dead heart or a bad attitude you need to address that problem head on. No one I know has ever experienced what Job did and even he said in *Job 1:21 And said, Naked came I out of my mother's womb, and naked shall I return thither: the LORD gave, and the LORD hath taken away; blessed be the name of the LORD.* In comparison with Job, we have no excuse not to praise God! Satan's victory will be in keeping us from praising God on a consistent basis. I will simply throw out this thought. Who will win today with regards to your praise to the Lord? Will it be the Lord who died for you and wants to lift your spirits? Will it possibly be Satan, who wants to destroy you and keep you down in the muck and the mire? Seems like an easy decision, but how we fight that at times. Can you say a hearty Amen, or would it be more fitting to say, "Oh my"? The verse says Heaven and Earth will praise the Lord. That puts you among exceptionally good company.

March 10

Psalm 71:6
By thee have I been holden up from the womb:
thou art he that took me out of my mother's bowels:
my praise shall be continually of thee.

What a thing to recognize by the Psalmist. He records his gratefulness to God for letting him live. To put it another way the Psalmist knows who gave Him life. He knows who his help was, and as a youth, he knew who his hope was. We praise God because we have hope in Him. *Romans 5:5 And hope maketh not ashamed; because the love of God is shed abroad in our hearts by the Holy Ghost which is given unto us.* To stay within the confines of praise, can I assume that if we praise God, we have hope in God? He ultimately is the One who will deliver us from any circumstance should we desire His help. Is it also safe to assume that if we bring forth no praise then we are not hoping in God? This earth is not your permanent home. We are only renting until God takes us to His mansion He has prepared, *John 14:1-3 1) Let not your heart be troubled: ye believe in God, believe also in me. 2) In my Father's house are many mansions: if it were not so, I would have told you. I go to prepare a place for you. 3) And if I go and prepare a place for you, I will come again, and receive you unto myself; that where I am, there ye may be also.* I would remind you of when praise should be done according to this verse. Our praise to Him should be continual. The definition of continual with regards to praise is to be unbroken or steadily recurring. Is our praise just that? Does praise steadily occur outside of the worship time when we are in our church home? I would certainly hope so.

March 11

Psalm 71:8
Let my mouth be filled with thy praise
and with thy honour all the day.

We talked yesterday about having continual praise and look what happens. We move forward two verses in this Psalm 71 and that is exactly what the Psalmist says. We are not confined to praise God only on Sunday. Since I started this book of devotions on service, praise, and worship I find myself continually throughout the day singing praise to God. Praising God does not require a microphone and an amplifier. Praising God is in how we live our life and do our jobs. We praise God in ways other than singing. Maybe someone pulls out in front of you in your car or on your motorcycle. Do we respond Christ-like or do we throw a brick at them? We praise God because we are a new creature, *II Corinthians 5:17.* We are to reflect that by the way we witness to others. We praise the Lord by how we treat our spouse and children. Grab a pencil and record the reasons you should praise God. Number one on your list is the day that you received Jesus Christ as your Saviour. If we praise God all day something else will occur. The Psalmist writes that honor will come forth from our mouth. Is our conversation honoring to God? *I Timothy 4:12 Let no man despise thy youth; but be thou an example of the believers, in word, in conversation, in charity, in spirit, in faith, in purity. Matthew 12:36 But I say unto you, That every idle word that men shall speak, they shall give account thereof in the day of judgment.* If we were arrested for being a Christian on the merits of our conversation, lifestyle, or church attendance would we be found guilty?

March 12

Psalm 71:14
But I will hope continually,
and will yet praise thee more and more.

Once again, we need to read verses 12 and 13 of this Psalm 71. The Psalmist knows there is an enemy out to destroy him if possible. In verse 12 he cries out for God to hurry. I can understand being a little distraught from time to time, but I also understand that God is always on time. In verse 13, it reminds me of where I work on occasion. Every now and then someone will start some backbiting about another employee. It always gets back to the one being talked about and usually causes more than a little turmoil. Actually, it is usually the same two involved each time. My advice to the one taking the heat is to treat the backbiter extra special. His response is, "why"? I told him when you do, you heap coals of fire upon their head, *Romans 12:20 Therefore if thine enemy hunger, feed him; if he thirst, give him drink: for in so doing thou shalt heap coals of fire on his head.* I am not talking about a phony kind of nice. I am referring to a genuine kind of niceness. Not only does it heap coals on them, but it frees you up to praise God, which brings us to our verse we need to concentrate on. What an awesome thing to be able to hope continually in God. With God we will never be let down. His response to us is timely and perfect. We need to praise Him continually for His faithfulness. Not only is the Psalmist going to praise God at time of deliverance, but he is going to praise Him more and more. Can you think back to when you first started to learn how to tie your shoes? You did not do too whoopee of a job on your first attempt did you? No, you practiced until you got it right. That is how we are to praise God. It is to be in a manner that is natural for us. There is absolutely no thought or effort on our part. We simply thank God for what He has done, is doing, and will do. Praise will only become a <u>way of life</u> when we put it into action and it becomes a <u>part of our life</u>.

March 13

Psalm 71:22
I will also praise thee with the psaltery,
even thy truth, O my God: unto thee will I sing
with the harp, O thou Holy One of Israel.

In looking at the text we see gratefulness from the Psalmist for God lifting him up when he needed it. He mentions his appreciation for the comfort he has received from God. We should express the same thanks. I know both of us have had times when we needed to be lifted up spiritually by God. I know we have felt the need to be comforted by God. We must acknowledge God for the comfort He has given. If we will acknowledge that it is God who lifts our spirit when we are low, we will be praising God as the Psalmist has instructed. The Psalmist plans on praising God with the psaltery. Some believe you cannot use a musical instrument to aid in the worship of God. My thoughts about that is God delights in our praise whether using an instrument or not. Are you overjoyed that at church we can use every instrument in the area of praise? Most of you have never heard hymns played on a regular household saw. Trust me it can be done, and the music is something to behold. For me personally, I do not know how to play a Psaltery, and at this point in my life I am not looking to purchase one and learn how. The point is, if you are prompted to praise God by beating two bricks together then buy the bricks.

March 14

Psalm 74:21
O let not the oppressed return ashamed:
let the poor and needy praise thy name.

Asaph is the writer of this Psalm 74. The first word used and usually found recorded above many Psalms is Maschil, meaning understanding or instruction. Asaph is apparently sharing what he understands about God by way of prayer. There is nothing wrong with communicating to God what we believe we understand. I would trust that through the teaching of the Holy Spirit, and when our understanding is correct, our minds "WILL" be changed. What Asaph is sharing here is all the awful things being done. Synagogues are being burned, sanctuaries defiled, and everything tied to God is forsaken. I have not witnessed what Asaph had, but if I did, I am certain I would be a little bit on the oppressed side. I may have missed Asaph's cry for himself, but I do recognize his plea for other people who are experiencing the same thing. Asaph's desire is for the poor, afflicted, and oppressed to praise God even in the midst of a storm. I have never seen anyone martyred or beaten for Jesus. I have only read about it in books and heard of it on the news. I would hope that if I were in that exact same situation that I would stand strong for the Lord. What a compassionate prayer for his fellow Jews. Asaph was concerned for their spiritual welfare. As the body of Christ, we need to maintain unity, *I Corinthians 1:10 Now I beseech you, brethren, by the name of our Lord Jesus Christ, that ye all speak the same thing, and that there be no divisions among you; but that ye be perfectly joined together in the same mind and in the same judgment.* In the verse we are looking at today, Asaph's desire is that the poor and oppressed will have their spirits lifted and praise God. There will be things we will experience that may be a little unpleasant. My prayer for you and I is that God will lift us up and help us to continue on in the praise of God. I do understand that our adversary Satan wants us feeling oppressed. God warns us of not worrying about those who can destroy the body, but to be concerned with who can destroy the soul, *Matthew 10:28 And fear not them which kill the body, but are not able to kill the soul: but rather fear him which is able to destroy both soul and body in hell.* Praise God for His grace in helping us keep our chin up when the chips are down. The best place for us to be if we are feeling oppressed is down on our knees in prayer to God. Praise the Lord that we can all stand a little taller when we kneel a little longer.

March 15

Psalm 76:10
Surely the wrath of man shall praise thee:
the remainder of wrath shalt thou restrain.

In verse 1 of this Psalm 76 the word Neginoth, (smiting), is used. Asaph is referring to victory or deliverance from God. There was an occasion when Sennacherib came to destroy Jerusalem and God intervened supernaturally killing one hundred and eighty-five thousand soldiers. Be glad and rejoice if Jesus is your Savior because that one hundred and eighty-five thousand soldiers that were killed, will not hold a candle to what will happen during the tribulation period for the lost. There is coming a day when the wrath of God will be fully released and nothing or nobody can stop it. The reason we witness to others with our words and our actions is to bring reconciliation between them and God. Without Jesus in the equation there is no reconciliation to God and

His wrath is in their future. Watch the news in the evening and you can see the degradation of our society. The only thing that can change an individual and the world is Jesus the King. There is coming a day when even the vilest will bow the knee to the King, *Isaiah 45:23 I have sworn by myself, the word is gone out of my mouth in righteousness, and shall not return, That unto me every knee shall bow, every tongue shall swear.* The key thought here is praise. Who will be bowing the knee in praise willingly, and who will be forced? With that in mind, who is praising God in the flesh, and who is praising God in the spirit? God is a spirit and not flesh, *John 4:24 God is a Spirit: and they that worship him must worship him in spirit and in truth.* Our hope and promise is that God, in His time, will put everything into its proper place. Man's wrath would seem that it has no boundaries, but it does. God's forthcoming wrath has no boundaries, and every lost man and woman will experience what they have never experienced before. God is running this show and I am confident that everything is going to turn out right if you know Jesus as your personal Lord and Savior. Praise God for that! Need confirmation about how things are going to be all right? Read the beginning, middle, and back of your Bible. WE WIN!

March 16

Psalm 79:13
So we thy people and sheep of thy pasture will give thee thanks for ever: we will show forth thy praise to all generations.

Asaph is our writer again. We are compared to sheep, which is more than likely not any updated news to you reading this. Sheep become dependent on their Shepherd. If sheep stay within eyesight of their Shepherd, they are safe. No matter what predator comes slinking along in the brush, the Shepherd's ever watchful eye is on top of it. Naturally, when that sheep wanders a little too far, trouble is on the horizon. The Shepherd will do everything possible to keep his sheep within the confines of his sight. Even if it means breaking that sheep's leg, the shepherd will do it. It sounds bad, but if that sheep's leg is broken there is only one way he can follow. The Shepherd will have to carry him wherever he goes. Another example is when a sore develops on a sheep. The Shepherd will pour a type of medicated oil upon that sore. Oil is symbolic of the Holy Spirit in scripture. We know that when we are sick spiritually, God will give us a fresh out-pouring of His Spirit. The protection God can give us is limitless. God has no restraints with regards to His protection. With God's limitless protection for His children, we should be working to pass on praise from generation to generation as Asaph writes. One way we can participate in passing on praise is to first exhibit that we do indeed praise God. Second, who are we training to praise? Within the walls of our personal place of worship, where does praise fall in order of importance? Is it the most important things we do, or is it used as an alarm clock to start the service? In your Sunday School classes, is there praise among the sheep? Are the leaders of the various fellowships or Sunday School classes using songs for praise or are the songs used simply to let the people know class is starting now? Big question, are the leaders praising with the sheep or are the sheep praising the leaders? Only one leader is deserving of our praise, and it is God the Father, God the Son, and God the Holy Spirit!

March 17

Psalm 86:12
I will praise thee, O Lord my God, with all my heart:
and I will glorify thy name for evermore.

We have before us another Psalm of King David. Starting back in verse 1 of this Psalm 86, David lists a few things he wants to praise God for. The things David will praise God for are the same things we should praise God for. In verse 1 David petitions God to hear him. David, (a king), realized that without God he was poor and needy. This is a king saying this. He knew without God he had nothing and was nothing. In verse 3 David prays daily. To maintain communion with God there must be communication with God. Not only when we are in despair, but daily, *Philippians 4:6 Be careful for nothing; but in everything by prayer and supplication with thanksgiving let your requests be made known unto God.* Looking at verse 11, David wants God to teach him His truths. There is no doubt in my mind of the necessity to be in prayer when you open the word of God. David has been in prayer up to now. We know that because back in verse 1 it says, "a prayer of David". He now declares that he will praise God with all his heart. Let me repeat that, David will praise God with all his heart. David spent 11 verses in prayer and then in verse 12 he will praise God with his whole heart. When we recognize everything God does for us on a daily basis, how could we not praise God? My question is do we acknowledge God consistently for what He does? I believe if we would pray first thing every day and acknowledge God's provisions in our life, we would praise God on a daily basis. If we acknowledge God's provisions, we should be praising Him. So can I assume if there is a refusal to praise God that you are declaring God does not provide for you?

March 18

Psalm 88:10
Wilt thou show wonders to the dead?
shall the dead arise and praise thee? Selah.

In this Eighty-Eighth Psalm our writer appears to be in some sort of a deplorable condition. What all the Psalmist is experiencing physically we cannot be certain of. What I am sure of is the Psalmist knows that if he is going to praise God it must be when he is among the living. I would agree that dead souls in hell cry out as they now recognize it is too late! I would also agree that when the saved die physically and enter the presence of God spiritually, there will be a greater understanding of the lost opportunities we had. We will all feel more than just a little remorse, but God will dry all our tears. It is at this juncture that there is no going back to praise the LORD as that ship has sailed. The good news is that when we are standing in the presence of Jesus, praise will be nonstop. Let me share what one Psalm says about how we are to enter into God's presence, *Psalm 100:4 Enter into his gates with thanksgiving, and into his courts with praise: be thankful unto him, and bless his name.* How are we going to enter His courts? The answer is with thanksgiving and with praise. How in the world are we to enter into His presence today? The answer is with thanksgiving and with praise. The Psalmist was possibly in dire strait, but he recognized when praise would be carried out and when it would not. Our bodies are a tool to be used for something. We can use them to assist us in sin, or we can use them for praising God. Either path we choose to go down is an individual choice. I think it is only fitting to leave the theme verse of praise in scripture with you, *Psalm 34:1 I will bless the LORD at all times: his praise shall continually be in my mouth.*

March 19

Psalm 89:5
And the heavens shall praise thy wonders, O LORD:
thy faithfulness also in the congregation of the saints.

Ethan the Ezrahite is sharing his understanding in this Psalm. In this verse we have a certain place where men and women will praise God's wonders. That place is being declared as the heavens. The bible speaks of the three heavens. The first heaven that contains the birds and the air we breathe. Second, we have a heaven that contains all the planets. Finally, the third heaven which is the dwelling place of God. If we consider all the heavens will be praising God, then what area is not covered? The heavens will praise God's wonders. The word wonders is also translated as God's judgment and redemption. Could we possibly think of a better reason to praise God than for His perfect judgment or His plan of redemption? Ethan ends the verse speaking of his thankfulness to God in the context of praise. We have much to be thankful for. Imagine living in a place where there was NO God. We may be living in times where many people will reject God and His gospel, but imagine a place where there was not a trace of the presence of God. Ponder that thought and then consider if God is worthy of continual praise? Maybe we can thank God for His faithfulness towards us by our praise. With that being said, what are we saying about the faithfulness of God when we do not praise Him? Actually, what do we say of our own character if we do not praise God for His faithfulness? Grab a hymnal sometime and find the song "Great is Thy Faithfulness". Read it a few times and see if you change your mind. You and I reside under and within the first heaven and every single word we utter and every song we sing is under God's perfect hearing. What if everything God heard was played back for our friends or enemies after the fact. Would we be ashamed and disappointed in ourself? If so, turn it around and head in the direction of praise to the Lord.

March 20

Psalm 98:4
Make a joyful noise unto the LORD, all the earth:
make a loud noise, and rejoice, and sing praise.

Here is the infamous saying every good Bible-believing person has heard. *Make a joyful noise unto the Lord.* My bible does not say you need to be a professional singer, songwriter, or musician. Therefore, it should be safe to say that when we go to God with praise it is joyful UNTO the Lord. The key in this verse is to whom are we directing the praise? I mention singing as far as making a joyful noise unto the Lord. There are more ways than one to deliver the joyful noise of praise to God. How about our conversation, is it joyful unto the Lord? How about the way we perform our jobs? Is it a joyful noise unto the Lord? How do we treat our spouse and our children? Is it a joyful noise unto the Lord? How do we praise God during our worship time on Sundays? Is it a joyful noise unto the Lord? In our church attendance how are we doing in our praise? Is it a joyful noise unto the Lord? At the end of the verse there is an order of events taking place. One, make a loud noise, (be determined that you will praise God). Two, we are to rejoice, (in the fact we are praising God). Three, sing praises, (make a joyful noise). For those who believe it would be better if they did not open their mouth at all for fear of what they might sound like, I have good news for you. The verse says make a loud noise, not carry perfect pitch, or perfect harmony. It is not the quality of your voice; it is the quality of your HEART.

March 21

Psalm 99:3
Let them praise thy great and terrible name; for it is holy.

When I look at a Strong's Concordance there are different choices of words for terrible, name, and holy and it helps me to understand this verse. First glance and we think God's name is terrible. Our minds have been trained to interpret terrible as something that can only be negative. We need to look at the first 3 verses of this Psalm 99. We have the Lord on a throne in Zion. The Lord is none other than Jehovah, (the existing one). He is reigning on the earth and verse 1 says the people tremble. I like the use of the word tremble. We are to fear God and I understand that. Here tremble is also rendered as agitated or sometimes it is used as excited. If you know Christ and He establishes His kingdom and is on the throne in Zion you are going to tremble, (be excited). If you do not know Christ and you get through the tribulation you may tremble, (be agitated or perturbed). To make it clearer, the saved should be looking for the day of Jesus sitting physically on the throne reigning. The lost will be burning in hell, which is where they chose to be. I say chose because if they did not want hell then they would not have rejected Jesus. With all that said let us return to the name of God. We are going to praise that great and terrible name of God for it is holy. There must be positive meanings for the word terrible if God's name is holy. It can also be used in a sense of reverencing God's name. The verse says His name is holy meaning to be set apart. It must be set apart as there is no other name given unto men whereby they must be saved, *Acts 4:12 Neither is there salvation in any other: for there is none other name under heaven given among men, whereby we must be saved.* Let me put things in their simplest form. We will praise God like we have never praised God when He sets up His kingdom and we are there reigning with Him. Here is the deal; we are to praise God in that exact way right now. We have been commissioned to serve God like there is no tomorrow. We have been recruited to tell the world about Jesus. We have been sworn to duty by God to tell others about how awesome and holy He is and that they need Him. When we tell others how magnificent the Lord is we praise the Lord. By sharing the good news of Jesus, we praise the name of Jesus. So now it boils down to just how often are we sharing the good news? Lift up the name of Jesus Christ and then praise HIM, praise HIM, and then praise HIM some more.

March 22

Psalm 100:1
A Psalm of praise.
Make a joyful noise unto the LORD, all ye lands.

The opening of this Psalm mandates praise. This Psalm is not only to be read, but it is to be sung. We had just looked at making a joyful noise unto the Lord and the implications to do so. What I want to look at this time is where geographically this praise is to be carried out. The verse says "all" ye lands, so we can assume world-wide praise. By living in the United States most would probably think that in every nook and cranny of the world someone is praising God. I do not know if that is a true statement or not. What I am certain of is this, when all nations are discipled and the gospel is preached to every living soul, then the call for the lands to praise will be carried out. If we were to back up one verse to Psalm 99 and verse 99 we would see the people praising the Lord at His holy hill. There will be a day when Jesus will have everything in its place and His kingdom is filled with nothing except believers. Praise will then come from all lands. Can you picture the jubilation that will take place by everyone participating? That same jubilation probably ought to be written or seen on our face every day. Consider the quality of the sound of that praise. When we gather on Sunday to praise God, the number of those singing is not as relevant as to how many are really praising God. The only one we can be certain about who is praising God is self. We do not need to wonder about whether the person next to us is praising God or not. The question is, am I?

March 23

Psalm 100:4
Enter into his gates with thanksgiving, and into his courts with praise: be thankful unto him, and bless his name.

How else would you want to enter God's gates and courts? My choice would not to be standing in His presence with a bad attitude. Here is a thought: I wonder how many times we do not have our attitudes in check and still sing a hymn in Church? Is not the sanctuary HIS home or HIS court as well? I think that it is. Here is something for you to consider. There was a time when you could not enter the place established as the Holy of Holies. Only one person could do so, and he was the high priest assigned to that task. To perform those duties in the Holy of Holies would have been an extremely high honor. We have a different High Priest and His name is Jesus Christ. When Jesus died the veil was rent in twain, (torn from the top to the bottom). Jesus' death allowed us to enter the Holy of Holies. For us to enter God's gates and courts is still a high calling for us. Jesus has made those who trust Him as their Saviour worthy to enter. Jesus Christ is the gatekeeper, and He knows who belongs to God. With all that said, how will you approach the gate? You cannot get to the court without passing through a gate. The time to start praising God is not after we get to the gate, but before. The time for believers to start preparing for praise is before we walk through the front door of our church. The preparation process for praise should start before we leave our home and not in the parking lot of the church. It is definitely a shame at how many times there have been some ridiculous knock down argument between husband and wife on the way to church and then to smile all pretty and sing, "O Victory in Jesus". Where is that victory? Victory in praise does not just reside in the sanctuary, it is to be a way of life.

March 24

Psalm 102:18
This shall be written for the generation to come:
and the people which shall be **created** shall praise the LORD.

This psalm is written as a prayer of the afflicted and *Psalm 102:1* is your cross reference. We know some of the afflictions that past Christians endured. Many died promoting the gospel of Jesus Christ. Some died because they would not reject Jesus Christ as their King. How can we know of these things? We know because someone under the influence of the Holy Spirit recorded it for us in book form. If you desire to trace Christian roots, then read the book entitled The Trail of Blood. Do you wonder about the persecutions and afflictions of prior believers in Jesus Christ, then read Fox's Book of Martyrs. We know the history because it was written for generations to come. Back to our Psalm where the Psalmist records a prayer of affliction. He also records the Lord will be faithful. The Psalmist knows one day he will die, but he writes in verse 12 of this Psalm that God will live forever. The goal in this Psalm is to pass on praise to those who have not even been born yet. If every church deemed it was unbiblical to have a song service, what would future generations of believers probably be doing? You guessed it, probably no praise. What are we doing to preserve for the coming generation the teaching of the importance of praise? It is very important to pass on to future generations in every bible believing church that we not only believe praise is important, but we have the Word of God to prove that it is. It is a very vital and integral part of what we should be doing in every church where two or more are gathered. I get the importance of the preaching/sermon from the Pastor, but I also understand the importance of dedicating time singing about our Savior as well. The praise service is a great opportunity that can lead right into the message. If everyone is prayed up, I can assure you that the song service and the preaching will complement each other.

March 25

Psalm 102:21
To declare the name of the LORD
in Zion, and his praise in Jerusalem;

I would like to approach this devotion from two different directions. If we read the previous two verses of this same Psalm, we see there are groanings from those who are prisoners and crying out to God. We know that God heard His people's groanings and used Moses to bring the captive Jews out of Egypt into the promise land. Israel had been set free. Israel was taken into captivity later because they turned their back on God. God used key men to rebuild the walls of Jerusalem and they were set free from captivity. The great news for Gentiles is we need to praise God that the gospel came to us. God heard our groanings and we have the same Savior. Gentile and Jew apart from God have no hope. The good news is we have received a Deliverer and we have been set free. We are set free *To declare the name of the LORD in Zion, and his praise in Jerusalem;* and that is in a future sense. For now, we are to declare the name of the Lord wherever we happen to reside. At every opportunity that arises we are to declare the name of the Lord around the world. We are to praise Him in any city, county, state, and country that we live in or pass through. Why? Because God is worthy of all of us declaring His greatness.

March 26

Psalm 104:33
I will sing unto the LORD as long as I live:
I will sing praise to my God while I have my being.

Psalm 104 gives an account of the creative work of God. How sweet it is to investigate God's word and see the creative power of God. Every place is covered in this Psalm. This Psalm takes us from the place of God's glory and majesty to all the heavens, lands, and waters. Should you desire a better picture of God's handy work in creation read Genesis chapter one. When we recognize how God's hand has touched everything under the sun we should sit back in awe. Without God things would have stayed without form and void. There came a day when the things God created were no longer good enough for man and he succumbed to Satan and fell, Genesis chapter three. God had to enact another plan for humanity later. He sent His only begotten Son to earth to die for the whole world. To make a long story short, without Jesus Christ in a person's life as their personal Saviour, we are like the earth before God fixed it. We may have had form, but we were void. It is Jesus' redeeming work that can take away being spiritually void. We now come to the verse of our devotion for today and find out how long this Psalmist will sing praises to God. He records that he will praise God as long as he lives. Some things bear repeating so here it is. The Psalmist will praise God as long as he lives. Our Psalmist writes at the end of *verse 33* that he will praise God as long as he has his being. Let me paraphrase what the Psalmist just said about his being. As long as I can witness for God with praise, I will. Our being is our witness. Are we witnessing for Jesus Christ? Not only can we be soul winners using a bible, tracts, or a godly lifestyle, but we can witness for the LORD with praise. The only way to witness for Jesus Christ with a song requires genuineness on our part. Are we real in our praise and service or are we phony? We just as well answer honestly because God already knows where our heart is with regards to praise and service. Finally, a thought from a Matthew Henry's commentary about Psalm 104 and it is most fitting. *Man's glory is fading; God's glory is everlasting: creatures change, but with the Creator there is no variableness. And if meditating on the glories of creation were so sweet to the soul, what greater glory appears to the enlightened mind, when contemplating the great work of redemption! There alone can a sinner perceive ground of confidence and joy in God. While he with pleasure upholds all, governs all, and rejoices in all his works, let our souls, touched by his grace, meditate on and praise him.*

March 27

Psalm 104:35
Let the sinners be consumed out of the earth,
and let the wicked be no more. Bless thou the LORD,
O my soul. Praise ye the LORD.

We continue in Psalm 104 today. God's word is clear on what we should be thinking about. The best example I can think of is *Philippians 4:8 Finally, brethren, whatsoever things are true, whatsoever things are honest, whatsoever things are just, whatsoever things are pure, whatsoever things are lovely, whatsoever things are of good report; if there be any virtue, and if there be any praise, think on these things.* Let me name one good thing we can and should meditate on. We need to back up to verse 34 in this same Psalm to see what it is. The Psalmist says he is going to meditate on God, and it is going to be sweet, and he will be glad in the Lord. Why, because the verse we are in today says the wicked and the sinners will be no more. The Psalmist will be praising God with all he has. Do you find yourself praying with frequency for the safety of those you care about? Even if it is a simple trip to town to grab a gallon of milk or a newspaper. Here is another picture for you to ponder. Picture living in a place where there is no wickedness, evil, demons, or Satan. I have good news for you who have trusted Jesus Christ as your Saviour. There will be a day when everything unholy will be put in its proper place. Death and hell will be cast into a lake of fire and the wicked and the vile will be no more. When that day occurs and everything is perfect as God intended, what do you suppose is going to happen? Praise my friend, praise! Let us practice our praise that we may testify to the lost of how God has changed our life through Jesus Christ. Remember, it is quite possible that we were one of the mean ones before we met Jesus, which is a good reason to praise and brag about His holy name. No one I know wants to go back to their old life before meeting Jesus Christ as their personal Lord and Savior. I doubt you do either.

March 28

Psalm 105:45
That they might observe his statutes,
and keep his laws. Praise ye the LORD.

Psalm 105 takes us from Abraham to the present. The entire Psalm gives us an account of the faithfulness of God. He made a covenant with Abraham and God kept His word. Every time God's people needed a deliverer, He provided. God brought Israel over the course of forty years into the land He had promised. He gave them land others had worked so that they could reap the benefits of what others had sowed. God did many things for Israel over the course of forty years of wandering in the wilderness. Whether Israel desired water, meat, or manna God came through. Israel needed to do one simple thing. They were to observe His statutes so they could keep His laws. For twenty-four hours a day God monitored everything going on so He could bring His children to the land He had promised. His only request, "*observe my statutes so you can keep my law*". God is no different today for us than He was for Israel. God's desire for us is to keep His statutes and keep His law. I understand we live in an age of Grace. We are blessed in that alone. In order for us to live a life that is pleasing to God requires some things on our part. One, the accepting of Jesus Christ as our personal Saviour. Two, live a life that reflects that we do indeed have the indwelling of the Holy Spirit. How do we do the latter? We read God's word every day and apply it to our life. When we commit to live what God's word says, we will have a joy and peace that the world will never understand. When we recognize that joy and peace it will result in praise. It would be difficult to praise God and not live out what His word teaches. If there is an order of things recorded here it would be as follows. Obedience precedes praise and not praise before obedience. Final two questions: Are you praising God because of your obedience? Are you not praising God due to disobedience? Remember that disobedience is the same as rebellion and according to *1 Samuel 15:23 rebellion is as the sin of witchcraft*. Final thought: Nothing you do will earn you a spot in Heaven. Only accepting Jesus Christ by faith for salvation is sufficient and is required for everyone.

March 29

Psalm 106:1
Praise ye the LORD. O give thanks unto the LORD;
for he is good: for his mercy endureth forever.

Many times it becomes obvious how one Psalm leads right into another and there is no exception here. Psalm 105 gives us an account of God as a deliverer, and Psalm 106:1 begins with praise to the Lord because of His goodness and His mercy. Have you ever considered what would happen to us if God was not a merciful God? I cannot even begin to understand and appreciate the patience God shows to me. We have all heard the statement, "if we got what we deserved God would send us all to Hell". You can agree with that or not. Praise God that we now have an advocate. An advocate is someone who will stand up for us and plead our case. That advocate is none other than Jesus Christ. Think on *1 Timothy 2:5 For there is one God, and one mediator between God and men, the man Christ Jesus;* For those who are saved there will be a day when we will die and it will be Jesus Christ who tells the Father we are one of His. We can certainly praise God for that. Do those around us really know we are His? Do those we are around recognize that there is something peculiar about us? Not peculiar in a sense of acting like a nerd, but peculiar because we love Jesus. Not to get too far off track, but it is really important about who we hang out with all the time. If I have said it once I have said it a thousand times. Not everyone we attach ourselves to is good for us physically, mentally, or spiritually. God's word is clear on just how merciful He is, but do not let bad influences control you. We praise God for His infinite mercy, but do not act infinitely foolish. Mercy is the chance to receive from God a fresh start and what we do not deserve.

We deserved hell, but we received Grace. As far as praising the Lord, my hope for you is that praising HIM is a natural and daily routine and something none of us will take for granted.

March 30

Psalm 106:2
Who can utter the mighty acts of the LORD?
who can show forth all his praise?

If you were required to make an exhaustive list of every mighty act of God, you would need eternity to do it. Let us start out with a verse from the New Testament. *John 21:25 And there are also many other things which Jesus did, the which, if they should be written every one, I suppose that even the world itself could not contain the books that should be written. Amen.* Let me make the list shorter for us both. Make a mental note or write out your own list of what God has done for you specifically. Everything God does in the life of an unbeliever is for the sole purpose of bringing that person to Jesus Christ. Let us both look at past experiences prior to being saved and then sing praise about it. This verse has an interesting question attached to it. Who can praise God in a manner that would truly be a measure of what God has done for each of us? Our goal should be to praise God in a manner that would be pleasing to Him. God recognizes our weaknesses, and we recognize His strength. Remember the first few words of the hymn, "Just a Closer Walk with Thee". The first six words state, "I am weak but thou art strong". Find yourself a hymnbook sometime and sing this song for yourself and direct it to God. I believe you will see that Jesus Christ is our strength and our praise. We should all praise God because of our strength being in Jesus Christ alone. Can

I assume that if there is no praise in your life then maybe Jesus Christ is not your strength because He is not your Savior? Scary thought isn't it, but worth pondering. I want to end this with what the verse starts with. Who can utter the mighty acts of God? As a born-again believer it is my responsibility and a gift to praise and serve the Lord. It will not be a lost and dying world that will praise the Lord. No sir, it will be you and me that have claimed the name of Jesus for salvation. It is not about a denomination or our place of prominence in society. It is about God's children praising the Creator for taking something that was broken and fixing it. You ask, "What was broken that God fixed"?   You and me friend, You, and me.

March 31

Psalm 106:12
Then believed they his words; they sang his praise.

Read the first twelve verses of this *Psalm 106* and there is an attachment of praise to the believing of God's word. Miraculous examples are given of God leading the Jews to the Promised Land. Even today, if Israel needs a reason to celebrate, they only need to read the Old Testament. Everything God did to bring them where He promised is written down. I do not want to rail on Israel so I will pick on the Gentiles. We have an account also recorded within the word of God. Read Matthew chapters four, twenty-six and twenty-seven to see what Jesus Christ went through as our Deliverer. We have God's word on what God sacrificed in order to take us to the Promise Land. Read what God sacrificed enabling us to spend eternity with Him in heaven, which will be our Promised Land. *I John 3:16 Hereby perceive we the love of God, because he laid down his life for us. John 15: 13 Greater love hath no man than this, that a man lay down his life for his friends.* We praise God because we are trusting in His word. Can we reason then that if someone is not praising God it is because of a lack of trust in His word? We can prove our trust in His word by our praise for our Saviour. If you are trusting, then you should be praising. The other side of the coin would be that a lack of praise must be due to lack of trust! We drive down the highway probably about every single day and the only thing between us and the car coming towards us is a stripe. If we can trust a painted stripe for our safety, and assume that the car coming will not cross that stripe at 70 miles per hour, can we not trust God through His Son Jesus? God's word says HE sent his Son and I believe it. If I can trust the stripes on the road, I can trust the stripes that were put on Jesus' back when He was beaten for my sin. Those stripes on Jesus' back are why I will take praising the Lord to my last breath. Will you join me?

April 1

Psalm 106:47
Save us, O LORD our God, and gather
us from among the heathen, to give thanks unto
thy holy name, and to triumph in thy praise.

I can only encourage you to read this entire Psalm. Repeatedly Israel turned their back on God. Anything that pertained to being vile they were guilty of. Here is an account of their story. Israel sinned and God forgave, Israel sinned and God forgave, Israel sinned and God forgave. Are you getting the picture I am painting for you? We do the same thing. More than likely different sin, but sin just the same. We go to the cross asking for forgiveness for something we have done. So far so good up to this point, but when we turn and walk away, we stop and pick the sin back up instead of leaving it at the cross. We get ourselves in a jam and we do just as the Psalmist has written here. We cry, *"Save us oh Lord"!* The word save here has other meanings such as Saviour, deliver, help, preserve, avenge, defend, rescue, safe, and victory. Every one of these translations requires the hand of God to carry it out. We get ourselves in a bind and then God comes to our rescue. The Psalmist wants to be separated from the heathen and that is not such an unusual request. *II Corinthians 6:17 Wherefore come out from among them, and be ye separate, saith the Lord, and touch not the unclean thing; and I will receive you.* Eventually, we will be separated from the heathen. There will be no unclean thing to touch when Jesus returns for those who have trusted in Him for salvation. Okay, so we recognize God for His saving, delivering, redeeming, victorious, defending, and preserving grace. So what do we do with what we know? Read the end of the verse please. We are going to triumph in praise. Here is some good news for you. We already have victory in Jesus Christ. We have already conquered the grave because of Jesus Christ. We already have victory over Satan. We have already been saved, delivered, redeemed, and defended by Jesus Christ. The worst thing to happen to us is death. God tells us not to worry about those who can kill the body, but to concern ourselves with the One who can destroy the body and the soul, *Matthew 10:28 And fear not them which kill the body, but are not able to kill the soul: but rather fear him which is able to destroy both soul and body in hell.* Because of all the things Jesus Christ has conquered for us we can live a triumphant life. Here are a couple of last thoughts to consider. One, are you living a triumphant life filled with praise? Two, are you living a defeated life with no praise?

If you are feeling a little mundane or discouraged try reading *I Corinthians 15:57 But thanks be to God, which giveth us the victory through our Lord Jesus Christ.*

April 2

Psalm 106:48
Blessed be the LORD God of Israel
from everlasting to everlasting: And let all the
people say, Amen. Praise ye the LORD.

The last time the word praise appeared was in the verse right ahead of this one. In our devotion yesterday I mentioned that believers in Jesus Christ will be separated for eternity from unbelievers. It is only fitting that this verse follows. When Jesus Christ sets up His kingdom and puts everything into its proper place then the things of this verse will happen. We will praise the Lord God of Israel for eternity. I want to try and place another thought in your mind. Picture nothing except believers gathered to one place. Nothing except believers, and Jesus Christ is sitting on the throne. The entire crowd breaks out in unison in praise to the King. Can you see it and maybe feel it? Believers singing and crying for the complete surrendering of their love for Jesus Christ. A complete submissiveness to the praise of our Saviour. Humbleness will be abounding everywhere. Gives me goose bumps just thinking about how we will have no inhibitions in praising Jesus Christ to the fullest. We will be part of a perfect choir, perfect sound, and perfect praise forever. Amen! I am excited because we do not have to wait for Jesus to be sitting on a throne to praise HIS holy name. Brothers and Sisters, we can start perfecting our praise right now. We perfect our praise today by being frequent in our praise yesterday and tomorrow.

April 3

Psalm 107:8

Oh that men would praise the LORD for his goodness,
and for his wonderful works to the children of men!

If there is one thing I understand, it is this verse. There are times if you mention the name of Jesus Christ in the wrong place, some will look at you with disdain. When someone rejects Jesus Christ as their Saviour, we ask why? When someone attaches a last name to the name of God in cursing, we ask why? When the name of Jesus is thrown out as nothing more than profanity, we ask why? It should always cause anguish in our soul when the name of God is spewed out maliciously. Even at the point of this book I cannot make anyone understand how this research has changed me forever in the area of praise. There was a day when I abused the name of God just like most do. I still recall the day when Jesus became "my" Lord and all that was laid aside. I try to be understanding of those who do not know any better than to curse the name of God. I hate it, but I understand they need to be saved. They do not need me rebuking them for it, they need the word of God shared with them. It will be Jesus who will change their language and not me. *II Corinthians 5:17 Therefore if any man be in Christ, he is a new creature: old things are passed away; behold, all things are become new.* Finally, God is so good, and He is worthy of our praise. One of the greatest blessings we can miss is when we skip the opportunity to praise God. When we send praise to God, He always sends it back a hundred-fold. Try it and see for yourself. We praise God for He is good. Are you praising God because you know God is so good? Are you not praising God because you do not think God is good? I can only answer for me, and you must answer for you.

April 4

Psalm 107:21
Oh that men would praise the LORD for his goodness,
and for his wonderful works to the children of men!

The main idea in this Psalm 107 is the fact that God comes to the rescue when we are in distress. Distress is a condition of danger or a desperate need. I would say we have all experienced distress at least once in our life. I am not insinuating that the problem will disappear, but I am suggesting God can help us cope in any situation if we will allow Him to help. The greatest sedative we can ask for is the calming effect only the Holy Spirit of God can minister. *John 14:26 But the Comforter, which is the Holy Ghost, whom the Father will send in my name, he shall teach you all things, and bring all things to your remembrance, whatsoever I have said unto you.* It would probably behoove us all to make a list of everything good about God. I would suggest you wait until pencils and paper are on sale as you will need several of both. I repeated the same thing I did in our last devotional verse. Praise God because He is so good, and this verse ends by mentioning children. God loves the children of men, and we are to be an example to our children or other children in the area of praise. Look at what Jesus said in *Mark 9:42 And whosoever shall offend one of these little ones that believe in me, it is better for him that a millstone were hanged about his neck, and he were cast into the sea.* God loves the children, and they are so accepting of the teachings of Jesus. Adults could learn a thing or two about children and their faith about spiritual matters. The only way we should approach God is with a childlike attitude. *Matthew 18:3-4 3) And* Jesus *said, Verily I say unto you, Except ye be converted, and become as little children, ye shall not enter into the kingdom of heaven. 4) Whosoever therefore shall humble himself as this little child, the same is greatest in the kingdom of heaven.* Are we praising God for his goodness? You and I can maintain a <u>childlike faith</u> in God if we will stay in His word with a <u>childlike longing</u> for truth.

April 5

Psalm 107:31
Oh that men would praise the LORD for his goodness, and for his wonderful works to the children of men!

Are you starting to think maybe I have made a mistake and keep recording the same verse over and over again? The answer is no! The Psalmist, (inspired by God to write), thought it worthy to repeat the same verse three different times in this same Psalm. When you hear something more than once you probably ought to take notice of it. Many times, the best way we can learn is by repetition. Have you learned anything from this Psalm? The verse appears exactly in the same manner three times in *Psalm 107*. There is a sad note to the verse I must point out to you. What makes this verse sad is the use of the word would. How much sweeter if it said men will praise God for His goodness. The use of the word "would" makes praise a matter of choice. In other words, some will choose to praise God for His goodness, and some will not. God could force His children to praise Him, but what kind of praise would that be? I want to stimulate your thoughts through pictures and examples. Here is one more thing for you to picture in your mind. The sole reason for painting a picture is to help us both gain understanding in the area of praise. Sit back, close your eyes, and picture God sitting on the throne. He hears a pleasant and joyful noise. It is you praising God because you chose to, not because He forced you. Nothing can be sweeter than unsolicited praise. I would rather have God see me praising Him instead of what Peter received when he denied Jesus. What a feeling that must have been for Peter when he saw Jesus looking at him when he had just denied Him. What did Peter do next? He went out and wept bitterly. *Luke 22:61-62 61) And the Lord turned, and looked upon Peter. And Peter remembered the word of the Lord, how he had said unto him, Before the cock crow, thou shalt deny me thrice. 62) And Peter went out, and wept bitterly.* The best thing I can pass on here is the key verse for praise. *Psalm 34:1 his praise shall continually be in my mouth.*

April 6

Psalm 107:32
Let them exalt him also in the congregation of the people, and praise him in the assembly of the elders.

I will begin with a verse from *Hebrews 10:25 Not forsaking the assembling of ourselves together, as the manner of some is; but exhorting one another: and so much the more, as ye see the day approaching.* I mention this verse first so all understand that gathering together for worship should not be an option. Praise is to be done in the congregation of the people. Praise is to be done privately as well as corporately. What can edify the saints quicker than praising the Lord? I want to address the men here. The Psalmist writes let "them" exalt Him. In order to see who the them is, we only have to back up one verse. It is men that are being referred to. We have a job as men to be the example in the area of praise. I do not believe praise is an option for us. How else can we contribute to the continuance of praise from generation to generation if we do not participate? There is another group mentioned in this same verse. Praise is to be carried out among the elders. Elders being those who are possibly aged men, eldest, and those in authority. Authority, does that mean leadership among the men? Is their praise among the leadership? In considering praise, there are going to be two types of men. You are going to be either a spectator or a participator. Here is what the men will have to decide. Are we going to be nothing more than an onlooker when praise is going on? Will we be a participator of praise among the congregation? Seems like a simple question, but many men and women will choose to be an onlooker and refuse to praise God. In sports there are starters and there are those just waiting for the opportunity to play. In praise to God there are no benchwarmers as everyone is a starter. The only requirement is to get up off the bench and get into the game. Maybe you just do not like the songs they are singing. Here is a piece of relevant information for you. They are more than likely not singing to you and me. They are singing to Jesus Christ, and I am fairly sure He loves it.

April 7

Psalm 108:1
A Song or Psalm of David. O God, my heart is fixed;
I will sing and give praise, even with my glory.

King David himself has some instructions again for us. Let me give you a verse that indicates we ought to pay attention to what David would write. *I Kings 11:4 For it came to pass, when Solomon was old, that his wives turned away his heart after other gods: and his heart was not perfect with the LORD his God, as was the heart of David his father.* David's heart was perfect. That is an awesome thing to be recorded in the word of God for all of eternity. David says his heart is fixed. He is addressing God here in the same breath of singing and praising. David says He WILL sing and praise God. He does not wait for an occasion to make that decision. He had already predetermined it would be something he would do. He continues and says I will praise God even with my glory. Brethren, the only glory we have is through Jesus Christ. We show forth the glory of Jesus Christ by having our mind fixed on things holy or upright. The key here is having our heart fixed on the right things. *Colossians 3:2 Set your affection on things above, not on things on the earth. Philippians 4:8 Finally, brethren, whatsoever things are true, whatsoever things are honest, whatsoever things are just, whatsoever things are pure, whatsoever things are lovely, whatsoever things are of good report; if there be any virtue, and if there be any praise, think on these things.* What is robbing our focus off praising God? Many things can distract us. Identify problem distractions and deal with them. The important thing is making a diligent effort to turn our attention back toward God. However hard, we must struggle to maintain focus on the praising of God, and it will be worth it. Are we struggling with praise? What are we focusing on or what is stealing our time? What is consuming our thoughts? What is really driving our actions or conduct? Is there anything or anybody that is hampering your relationship with Jesus or your praise? I strongly suggest that if there is, you lay it at the foot of the cross. You will be so blessed with that decision to do the right thing at the right time for the right reason for the right Savior. For the record, not everyone that we have in our social circle is healthy for us spiritually. We will eventually identify with who we should run with. May your identity be in Jesus Christ and not with the world. Nothing or nobody should influence who you are in Jesus. You are a child of the most high God and He loves you dearly. He loved you so much He was even willing to die to show it.

April 8

Psalm 108:3
I will praise thee, O LORD, among the people:
and I will sing praises unto thee among the nations.

King David has pulled out all the stops with regards to praise. It is not relevant where he is at, he will praise God. Backing up one verse in this same Psalm we see a time when David will commence with the praise. He says I will wake up early. When could there be a better time to praise the LORD than first thing every day? We have not been immersed in the hustle and bustle of the day and we are fresh. Sing a song of praise to God before your feet hit the floor and God will hear you. A good habit to get into before stopping for the day or starting a day is letting the Lord know that you love him. I end every day by reading the Proverb for the day that coincides with the date. For example, if today is the eighth then I read Proverbs 8. Some months do not have thirty-one days and there are thirty-one Proverbs. If you read additional Proverbs the last day of the month you will read the book of Proverbs twelve times a year. That was free advice and now back to King David. David continues praise outside of the congregation as well. He praises God among the people and nations. Regardless of the nation or ethnic group, David praises God. He is a perfect example of a leader praising God. King David decided to praise God as a leader in front of and with all people. I would say many eyes were on the King and would follow his lead. What do people see us doing? In considering praise, are we leading, following, or getting in the way? You know the old saying, "Either lead, follow, or get out of the way." Not to be harsh, but I believe that would also mean we are to either lead the praise, follow along in the praise, or do not be a hindrance during the praise. It is amazing how someone with a bad attitude can quench the work of the Holy Spirit. I pointed out one page ago that praise is not about us, to us, or for us. It is for a King and a kingdom, and the Lord is coming back soon. Let Him find you in praise and in His word.

April 9

Psalm 109:1
To the chief Musician, A Psalm of David.
Hold not thy peace, O God of my praise;

God can be many things to many people. Right here King David refers to God as the God of his praise. In a country that seems to be abounding in riches it could be quite easy to be praising everything except God. *Matthew 6:20-21 20) But lay up for yourselves treasures in heaven, where neither moth nor rust doth corrupt, and where thieves do not break through nor steal: 21) For where your treasure is, there will your heart be also.* There is a time to praise our child, spouse, co-worker, or another believer in Jesus Christ who has done a good job. The only concern we need to have is that whatever we are praising does not become our god. Let God be the God of our praise. We do not want to be guilty of having a plastic, wood, or even gold god. In the order of things to do, God needs to be the first one we praise, and He needs to be the last one we praise. In order of importance in praise, God does not come second to anyone or anything. God does not want our leftovers. He wants our best and what is first. I love how the verse uses the phrase, *"hold not thy peace"*. God wants our internal praise. It is okay to release the praise we have on the inside so our praise will be revealed on the outside. How we praise the LORD externally is a direct revealing of our praise internally.

April 10

Psalm 109:30
I will greatly praise the LORD with my mouth;
yea, I will praise him among the multitude.

King David is again the author of this verse as inspired by God. There are several directions we could go, but there is one clear message all of us may be guilty of overlooking. Read this entire Psalm and watch for the times David prays for his enemies. Even for believers, our first instinct when someone does us wrong is to go on the offensive and go into the attack mode. If we live a holy life, we really have nothing to defend. What someone says can hurt, but we need to make sure their statements about us are not accurate. The bottom line about our adversaries is to use good common sense when addressing them and to let God have charge of the situation. I have learned that two wrong attitudes do not make a right attitude. There is a commonly used expression, "misery loves company". If your desire is not to be miserable then praise God and do good to those who want to cause you harm. *Romans 12:20 Therefore if thine enemy hunger, feed him; if he thirst, give him drink: for in so doing thou shalt heap coals of fire on his head.* Let me share the only choices we have in dealing with our enemies. One, treat your adversaries the way they are treating you. Two, treat your enemy the way you would want to be treated. I would suggest the latter of the two. Romans 12:20, (listed above), gives us a good look at a proper response to someone who is against us. Back to our verse on praise we read that David uses the word praise twice in the same verse. He is going to praise the Lord with his mouth and in the midst of multitudes. The multitudes David will praise the Lord in front of is not necessarily a bunch of born-again believers, which would make sense to me. We are not restricted to praising God in front of believers only. When we do good to our enemies, we are praising God. What an excellent way of bringing glory, honor, and praise to God. *Romans 13:14 says to put on the Lord Jesus Christ*, which means to act like Christ would act. Jesus was surrounded everywhere He went with enemies. The good news is Jesus Christ even died for His enemies and we must praise God for that as well. Remember, before you accepted Jesus as your Savior, you were not a child of God either.

April 11

Psalm 111:1
Praise ye the LORD. I will praise the LORD with my whole heart, in the assembly of the upright, and in the congregation.

Praise appears twice again within this same verse. Who can be surprised since the word praise appears in the book of Psalms 160 times? The Psalmist jumps right into verse 1 with praise. With his whole heart, in the assembly of the brethren, and in the midst of a congregation, he will praise God. Here is something you can study in scripture on your own sometime. Study to see how many times we are to praise God half-heartedly. Let me know if there is a place in scripture where the upright gathered to praise God and they did not do it with diligence. I am comfortable with the thought that if a believer knows they are in sin, and will not deal with sin, praise is not going to come. I understand it is Jesus and only

Jesus that makes us upright. I find it interesting that in our verse we are looking at today that there seems to be a division where the Psalmist is. He says, "I will praise with the upright, and in the congregation." It appears there may be some in the midst of the congregation who are not praising God. It obviously is not going to stop the Psalmist from praising God. Here is the only thing we must determine. Are we part of the upright praising God or are we just a part of the congregation singing? Singing a hymn does not necessarily mean someone is praising God. The upright will be praising God as the Psalmist testifies here. Final questions: Are you praising God because you are upright through Jesus Christ? Are you not praising God because you are not upright, as you have never accepted Jesus Christ as your personal LORD and Savior? I can assure you it is so much better to be upright than to be downcast!

April 12

Psalm 111:10
The fear of the LORD is the beginning of wisdom:
a good understanding have all they that do his
commandments: his praise endureth forever.

It would be fitting to read all of *Psalm 111* to gain a greater understanding of why we should praise God. The Psalmist records just a few of the reasons why he will praise God. He mentions how great the works of God are. Everything God does is done in truth and righteousness. Imagine what kind of place we would be living in if everything was done in truth and righteousness? The best thing he lists is how God sent redemption unto His people. If God chooses to do something there is nothing anyone can do to stop it. This is probably why today's verse is quoted with frequency, *The fear of the*

LORD is the beginning of wisdom. This verse ends by stating praise will endure forever. God's truth and uprightness are forever. The only way God can operate is through the works of truth and uprightness. When we mentally picture the truth and uprightness that God performs in our life praise should follow. Without God working through us we would be in serious trouble. One verse comes to mind if we consider what our righteousness is like in comparison to God's. *Isaiah 64:6 But we are all as an unclean thing, and all our righteousnesses are as filthy rags; and we all do fade as a leaf; and our iniquities, like the wind, have taken us away.* To move on let us ask ourselves the following questions. Are we praising God because of His truth and uprightness that He is doing through us? Are we not praising God because we are lacking truth and uprightness? The best place to start receiving God's truth is through Jesus. Uprightness only happened because of Jesus' sacrificial death and on to an empty tomb. If you have never received Jesus as your personal Saviour do so now. It will give you the reason you need to participate in the praising of God. Praising God will probably not make any sense to a lost man or woman. Praising God ought to make sense to every believer. God expects it and He sure deserves it. If you are not sure how to receive Jesus, simply ask Him for forgiveness, to save your soul for eternity, and it is a done deal.

April 13

Psalm 112:1
Praise ye the LORD. Blessed is the man that feareth the LORD, that delighteth greatly in his commandments.

Many times the word praise is used in a way to depict what the Psalmist is going to do. The word of God is personal and that is exactly what this verse is about. This verse makes praise personal by the simple word "*ye*". We want those around us to praise God with us. Guess what, those around us who are already praising God, want us to praise God with them. Praising God is a matter of choice. If we are doing what God wants done, then there is only one choice to make, and that is to praise God. God's word is clear on praise. Praise in our life is not what saves us, only Jesus Christ can save a soul. Praise is something every believer should want to do. When we come to the place where walking with God daily becomes important, then and only then, will praise start occurring with regularity. Praise will become a way of life. Are "*ye*" praising the Lord? If not, then why not? I do not want to leave this verse without pointing out the words, feareth the Lord. *Psalms 111:10* and *Proverbs 9:10* says *the fear of the Lord is the beginning of wisdom.* Do you fear or have reverence for the Lord, or is He just some BIG guy up in the sky that you kind of believe in, or who you have heard about? The Lord is so much more than a "Big" guy up in the sky somewhere. He is our Savior, Redeemer, and someone we can know very intimately and personally. Rejoice and praise God for that!

April 14

Psalm 113:1
Praise ye the LORD. Praise, O ye servants
of the LORD, praise the name of the LORD.

This is the first time that praise appears three times in the same verse. By the time we read the third use of praise in this verse you should be sensing the excitement the Psalmist is conveying. Stop right here and read this verse again with joy and excitement before reading any farther. Can you hear the

Psalmist addressing individuals by using the word once again *"ye"*? We have individuals mentioned who are to praise the Lord and then he moves on and addresses the servants of the Lord. The Psalmist writes, *"praise the Lord"*. The Psalmist addresses both groups and repeats his thought to both, *"praise the name of the Lord"*. To inspire you from all this, imagine the Psalmist filled with excitement while penning these words. You know that as soon as his pen places the period down at the end of this verse the cymbals come crashing together in a sense of finality of what he had just written. The enthusiasm the Psalmist has in this verse is the same kind of excitement I pray both of us will develop. We can develop that excitement by doing one simple thing. Choose to praise the name of the Lord! Praise Jesus out of habit instead of feeling obligated. Praise is a necessity, and it is profitable. Praise is not mandatory and demanded, but why would a believer decline from doing so? Praise is to be from those who love the Lord and are sold out to Him. Praise should be as natural of a thing to do as it is getting dressed before going to work. I assume you do dress for work.

April 15

Psalm 113:9
He maketh the barren woman to keep house,
and to be a joyful mother of children. Praise ye the LORD.

We have moved on to a different verse, but we have stayed in the same Psalm. Our Psalmist uses nine verses to name just a few wonderful things about the God we can serve. The bottom line of this entire Psalm is his ending, *"praise ye the Lord"*. Most people are in a rush all the time. It would behoove anyone reading this to stop right here for a couple of minutes and just reminisce on the goodness of God in your life. The older I get the more it appears everyone is in a rush to get somewhere or do something. I would suggest at this time you stop again and reread this entire Psalm. The Psalmist does not give us an exhaustive list of God's goodness. He does bring up things we sometimes take for granted. He covers things such as the deliverance of the poor, to thanking God for good moms who are a joy to their children. Are we thankful for God and His goodness? Are we praising the Lord for His goodness? If we would stop our fast-food lifestyle and do a little reflecting on God's goodness, praise will follow. Take the time to slow down and appreciate life. Do not use a day planner to fit God in to your schedule. Let God be the day planner and allow HIM to fit us into HIS plans. There is a time to run ninety miles per hour and there is a time to stop. *Psalm 46:10 Be still and know that I am God.*

April 16

Psalm 115:17
The dead praise not the LORD,
neither any that go down into silence.

Our Psalmist throughout this *Psalm 115* contrasts the unbeliever with the believer. It is interesting how the heathen trusts in things that are dead, and the believer puts his trust in God. One thing is certain, upon death the body is not going to praise the Lord. How many will regret their lack of praise or service while they were alive? I wonder how many spiritually dead people are singing on Sunday with no clue as to what they are doing. They may be singing hymns, but their gospel is based on something other than the atoning death of Jesus Christ. Our salvation is based upon a personal relationship with Jesus Christ. It is not a religion where the name of Jesus Christ is only casually mentioned in passing. It is Christ who changed us and made us alive, *I Corinthians 15:22 For as in Adam all die, even so in Christ shall all be made alive.* When our bodies hit the grave there will only be silence. A dead body will not jump up and down in the casket and praise God. The time to use this body for praise is while there is still breath in it. Let us consider our bodies as nothing more than a tool. We can use our body for praise, or we can choose not to use the body for praise. Seems like an easy decision to make, but let us take inventory at the end of the week and figure out just how much time was spent in praise. Instead of looking back and wishing we had praised God more, decide today to praise God daily, and build on the future.

April 17

Psalm 115:18
But we will bless the LORD from this time
forth and for evermore. Praise the LORD.

My last thought on our verse yesterday is exactly what this verse is telling us. The Psalmist tells us of how the heathen is trusting in idols that cannot speak even though it appears there is a mouth. Idols appearing to have hands, but hands that cannot hold. Idols having legs and feet but there is no movement. The Psalmist recognizes there is only one living God and praise should be reserved for Him only. A decision is made in this verse concerning praise. The decision is that from this day forward he will praise God forever. An incredibly wise decision that would dictate our doing the same if we have not already. A decision starting today that we will praise the Lord and never stop. We develop daily routines in what we must do. Make praising the Lord part of your daily routine. Praise has never been something we try and squeeze in if there is time. God wants of our firstfruits, not what is left at the end of the day. In wrapping up, we cannot let any idols of our own raise its nasty little head and distract us from praising Jesus. Our idols may not look like some Star Wars character or unholy creature that you will recognize right off. Idols come in many sizes, shapes, and colors. Sometimes an idol can be too much work. Maybe an idol will look like too much play time. It may look like anything under the "SUN" that will take our mind off praising the "SON". We do not want to be idle in our praise of God, but we might have to put away some idols in order to praise God. Do not be idle in destroying your idols.

April 18

Psalm 116:19
In the courts of the Lord's house,
in the midst of thee, O Jerusalem. Praise ye the LORD.

In reading this entire *Psalm 116* it becomes clear the writer recognizes his weaknesses and God's strength. The Psalmist renders a decision to pay his vows publicly, {*not to boast*}, but to show he is not ashamed of serving God. He has the credentials to be a good leader. He writes in this verse that the courts of the Lord's house is where all ought to praise the Lord. Some follow by example, so as a leader what example are we setting? We can either set a good example or a bad example in about everything we do. I can guarantee that no matter where we are working or ministering, people monitor us constantly. In the area of praise what kind of example are we setting? Praise may not be in our singing, but in how we work for our employer. In verse 12 of this same Psalm the writer recognizes that there is not a lot he can possibly give in trinkets and ornaments to God because all of it belongs to the Lord anyway. The best sacrifice is the sacrifice of self. I would not consider praise a sacrifice, but it is something we can return to God as He is worthy. The Psalmist will pay his vows now. He will not wait until his body hits the grave because then it is too late for the body to participate. The writer notes he is going to praise the Lord in the midst of Jerusalem. We do not need to fly to Jerusalem to praise Jesus. What we must do is find our own Jerusalem or our own quiet spot. Find a place of quietness where it is just Jesus and you together. Have no distractions so that you can praise HIS awesome and HOLY name.

April 19

Psalm 117:1
O Praise the LORD,
all ye nations: praise him, all ye people.

This Psalm does not give us a whole lot of information as it has only two verses. Please recognize whom the writer is addressing. His desire is for all nations and all people to praise the Lord. To stress the importance of praise across the lands let me give you something to think about. Imagine if the news reported that there was absolutely nothing bad happening around the globe. Imagine if the only news that could be televised were scenes of every group in the world praising the Lord. Imagine if no one lifted up hands of violence, but instead lifted up holy hands to heaven in praise to Jesus Christ. I have good news to report. This kind of day is rapidly approaching and are you prepared to participate? If Jesus Christ is your Saviour, you can trust He will return one day and establish a perfect kingdom. Then every believer will be in one accord, and I guarantee we will be singing at the top of our lungs. The issue of praise as far as congregationally or corporately, is we do not need to concern ourselves with whether the person on our left or right is praising God. The question we ask is one that is personal and can only be answered individually. Where am I at spiritually today as far as praise goes? Is my life a reflection of joy for the Lord Jesus Christ or not? It is never too late to start! Do you ever wonder if the person on your right or left is praising Jesus? They may be wondering the same thing about you.

April 20

Psalm 117:2
For his merciful kindness is great toward us: and the truth of the LORD endureth forever. Praise ye the LORD.

Are you interested in understanding more about God's mercy? If so, this would be a good stopping point for you. Before reading on with this devotion go to *Psalm 136* and read all 26 verses. You will quickly see that the phrase "*mercy endureth forever*" appears in every single verse. I pray you read *Psalm 136* in its entirety. The Psalmist takes the time to record a few things concerning God's mercy. I make mention of this Psalm as one of the reasons we praise God is because of His mercy and that is the topic at hand here in this verse. Where would all of us be if not for the mercy of God? Here is something for us both to chew on. Are you thankful for how God has provided in your life, or would you rather get what you deserve? For me personally, I will take what God gives and not what I deserve. *Psalm 136* tells us God's mercy endureth forever and right here in our devotional verse today it says *His truth endureth forever.* God's truth is His word, *John 17:17 Sanctify them through thy truth: thy word is truth.* We can look in scripture at just exactly WHAT the "WORD" is. We only need to go from *John 17:17* to *John 1:1* and on to *John 1:14* to discover that the truth is the word, which is Jesus Christ. *John 1:1 In the beginning was the Word, and the Word was with God, and the Word was God. John 1:14 And the Word was made flesh, and dwelt among us, and we beheld his glory, the glory as of the only begotten of the Father, full of grace and truth.* Now considering all that, here is good news for all. First, God was so merciful He sacrificed His son Jesus Christ for us. Second, Jesus will never leave us nor forsake us. He is eternal and will never change, *Hebrews 13:8 Jesus Christ the same yesterday, and today, and forever.* The only changing that needs to take place is in us. Praise cannot be an option in our Christian walk. Study out what Jesus experienced during His last twenty-four hours before He was put on the cross. As soon as you finish the study, wipe the tears from your eyes, count your blessings, and praise the Lord.

April 21

Psalm 118:19
Open to me the gates of righteousness:
I will go into them, and I will praise the LORD:

Our Psalmist recognizes where his strength lies. He acknowledges that he has enemies and is trusting in the Lord for victory. Back in verse 8 of this *Psalm 118* says it best, *It is better to trust in the LORD than to put confidence in man.* Most have heard the following expression used at one time or another; *"if it were not for the grace of God there go I"*. The Psalmist's choice is to enter the gates of righteousness. In order to get into the gates of righteousness we had better know firsthand the gatekeeper. The gatekeeper is Jesus Christ. It is Jesus Christ that makes us righteous in the eyes of God. Do you desire to enter the gates of righteousness? Be certain Jesus knows you are one who has trusted in Him for salvation. Upon entering through the gates of righteousness the Psalmist intends to praise the Lord. Is it just me or does it appear that those who accept Jesus Christ and enter through the gates of righteousness through Him will praise the Lord? Be certain that I did not say we were righteous by our own merits, *Isaiah 64:6 But we are all as an unclean thing, and all our righteousnesses are as filthy rags;* We must take up our cross daily, trust Christ for deliverance, and praise the Lord for it. Without Christ it is truly clear that we are nothing and can do nothing worthy of pleasing God, *John 15:5 I am the vine, ye are the branches: He that abideth in me, and I in him, the same bringeth forth much fruit: for without me ye can do nothing.* It is question and answer time once again. Are we praising God for the shed blood of Jesus Christ? Are we praising the Lord because we are righteous in God's eyes because of Jesus Christ? Are we not praising God because we have never claimed the righteousness Jesus Christ brought to us? If anyone tells you joy and praise is based on anything but the shed blood of Jesus Christ, you need to find another church to participate in or fellowship with. That is a huge Amen!

April 22

Psalm 118:21
I will praise thee:
for thou hast heard me, and art become my salvation.

Salvation is positively the issue here. Have you ever had someone speak to you and you were not paying attention? Finally, you hear that familiar, "Hello, is anybody home"? You come back down to earth because you are hearing them now. You engage your brain, your antenna is finally back up, and you are receiving a signal. God does not work that way. The idea being brought to us in this verse is salvation. There has never been a time when God was preoccupied and failed to hear a sinner asking for forgiveness and salvation. God's mind does not wander, it focuses on those who are his children and those who want to be His child. The Psalmist is praising God because he was heard, and he was saved. There is no doubt the Psalmist is overjoyed at what has occurred in his life. Remember your own salvation experience? The same joy or gratefulness we felt at the exact moment we were saved should be the same today. The salvation we received from God is more than reason enough to praise Him. It is fair to say that if we are saved we will praise God. Would it also be fair to say that if we will not praise God then we probably are not saved? I am not saying that you can lose your salvation if you refuse to praise the Lord. This is not a question of can you lose your salvation. The question is have you ever had salvation? There is no doubt the Bible teaches that once saved always saved. You would also think that once you have praised you will always praise? If thinking about Jesus' death, burial, and resurrection does not bring us to the point of praise then something spiritually is wrong. Never forget the day you met Jesus as your Savior. If you do not know of a day, then I would advise you to stop right now and pray to receive Jesus Christ to be your personal Lord and Savior. They are remarkably simple steps. By faith receive Jesus into your heart for eternal salvation. Nothing you can do or offer will take you to heaven. The only thing you can do to be saved is to ask Jesus to save your soul for eternity. If you just said that prayer or something similar, then let your rejoicing begin.

April 23

Psalm 118:28
Thou art my God, and I will
praise thee: thou art my God, I will exalt thee.

In this *Psalm 118* our writer has been expressing thanks to God. Here in verse 28 God becomes personal to him. He says, "Thou art **my** God". We just finished discussing the joy of the Psalmist's salvation. It is only fitting that now God becomes personal to him. We receive Jesus Christ as our "personal" Saviour not as just a Saviour. Think about this, God, who is all knowing and all powerful, can be our personal friend. Here is Webster's definition of a friend. A friend is a person attached to another by respect or affection. Isn't that good news? When we got saved, we become attached to God and nothing can break that attachment. Is that reason enough to praise God? Our Psalmist records here that he will praise his God. We praise God because He is a personal God. He is not just some god, but he is your God. A person must understand that just knowing of God is not sufficient in itself to be saved. Satan knows of God, *James 2:19 Thou believest that there is one God; thou doest well: the devils also believe, and tremble.* Satan knows some things, but he is not saved, and he certainly is not praising God. God is a personal God who desires our personal praise. Those who know Him intimately and personally will praise and exalt the name of God. Do you know Him personally for your salvation and are you praising Him daily for it? We only get one opportunity to live out our life and then we face physical death. Praise God that when believers draw their last breath they will be escorted by angels to their heavenly home where praise will last forever. The body may go to the grave, but the soul is headed to its heavenly home. The body will eventually be reunited with our soul and our body will be incorruptible and perfect. We look expectantly for the rapture of the body of Christ. When that event takes place, it will be quick. How fast you ask? It will be in the twinkling of an eye according to *1 Corinthians 15:52*. If there is one thing I know about heaven, there will be praise forever. If there is one thing about hell it is that it is eternal as well. No praise of God in hell, only an eternal horrendous torment.

April 24

Psalm 119:7
I will praise thee with uprightness of heart,
when I shall have learned thy righteous judgments.

Is getting into the word of God important? To the Psalmist here it is as he devotes the entire Psalm to it. *Psalm 119* has 176 verses filled with knowing God's commandments or instructions from Him and keeping them. In this verse we have a Psalmist whose desire is to praise with uprightness of heart. The thing to consider is how is he going to get that uprightness of heart? He tells us at the end of the verse. When the Psalmist learns of God's righteous judgment he will praise with uprightness of heart. Do you see the comparison of learning and keeping the precepts of God and praise will be following? It is learning God's word and applying it in a personal way that we are changed for the better. The way we are molded into Jesus Christ's image is through a daily walk with God through His word. It is pretty safe to say that the more we take in the word of God and apply it to our life, the greater our understanding and the greater our praise. Where would most of us be if it were not for the word of God in our life? The Psalmist is going to praise God for the perfect judgment He renders in scripture.

We gain better judgment of things when we judge like God would judge. We are to render a righteous judgment the Bible points out in *John 7:24 Judge not according to the appearance, but judge righteous judgment.* We can only do that by applying the word of God in our decision-making process and then praising God for it. If you are like me, you have the ability to make an occasional stupid mistake. We praise God that when we do goof up, He helps us to grow up spiritually. There is only one set of standards that we should use in rendering good and sound judgment and that is the word of God. By the way, judging righteously begins with judging self and not simply judging others. We cannot judge nor can we praise in the flesh. Are we praising in the flesh or praising in the spirit? Righteous judgment will never be found outside of the word of God. What you will find outside of the word of God is rebellion and rebellion is as witchcraft according to *1 Samuel 15:23 For rebellion is as the sin of witchcraft, and stubbornness is as iniquity and idolatry. Because thou hast rejected the word of the LORD, he hath also rejected thee from being king.* Judge righteously according to God's standards and we must not start with others. Judging outside of God's standards is just an opinion of what someone thinks is right.

April 25

Psalm 119:164
Seven times a day do I praise thee
because of thy righteous judgments.

The key here is understanding praise is to be done daily. It is not just an event to take place on a Sunday morning or Wednesday night or whenever you go to church. David would not only praise God once, but seven times. Praise is to be done with frequency. Daniel knelt and prayed to God three times a day in order to maintain fellowship with God. It is good to stay in constant communion with God through prayer. It is also essential to maintain communion through praise. David would praise because of God's righteous judgment. Let us all thank God that we do not get what we deserve and His mercy endureth forever. Let me share a few thoughts again from Matthew Henry's commentary: *<u>Those whose hearts stand in awe of God's word, will rather endure the wrath of man, than break the law of God. By the word of God we are unspeakable gainers. Every man hates to have a lie told him, but we should hate more telling a lie; by the latter we give an affront to God. The more we see the beauty of truth, the more we shall see the hateful deformity of a lie. We are to praise God even for afflictions; through grace we get good from them. Those that love the world have great vexation, for it does not answer what they expect; those that love God's word have great peace, for it outdoes what they expect. Those in whom this holy love reigns, will not perplex themselves with needless scruples, or take offence at their brethren. A good hope of salvation will engage the heart in doing the commandments. And our love to the word of God must subdue our lusts, and root out carnal/worldly affections: we must make heart work of it, or we make nothing of it. We must keep the commandments of God by obedience to them, and his promises by reliance on them. God's eye is on us at all times; this should make us very careful to keep his commandments</u>*. Many will accuse us of judging them and they will always say, "You are not God so you should not judge me". I get what they are saying, but if we do not judge then we are in essence agreeing that everything is okay. That is a lie right out of the pit of hell. *John 7:24* is written in red to indicate it is Jesus talking, and he addresses the subject of our judgment. Here is what Jesus said, "*Judge not according to the appearance, but judge righteous judgment*". We do not judge on the merits of what the media or our neighbors say, but we judge according to what the word of God says. It is a lot easier when we police ourselves and do the right thing. We are not Christian cops, but there are times you and I may have to separate ourselves from things or people that are not healthy for us spiritually or physically. I guess what I am wanting all of us to see is that we cannot let anything such as people, friends, or enemies deter us from praising the Lord.

April 26

Psalm 119:171
My lips shall utter praise,
when thou hast taught me thy statutes.

Praise is still personal in this verse. The first words are *my lips*, we want to praise God with the brethren, but the issue here is **our** praise. Instead of worrying about what our neighbor is doing in the next pew, what are we doing in the area of praise? It is imperative that we allow the Holy Spirit to teach us the statutes of God. God inspired what He wanted written for our admonition not His. God was not in seminary doing a final research paper and then submitted the Bible for a grade. He inspired the word of God for our benefit that we could learn from it and then praise Him for it. It was interesting how the word utter in this verse can be defined. The word utter is defined as the example of putting money into circulation. How much better to utter praise, to put forth praise, or to put into circulation our praise. How else can we learn what God expects from us if our Bible is collecting dust on the shelves? Learn His statutes from the word of God not a man. Apply it to your life and then praise Him more for the statutes the Holy Spirit is teaching you. It would be awesome if while we are out circulating in the world that we hummed a bar or two of our favorite Christian song. Since it is your mouth, you can use it anyway you see fit.

April 27

Psalm 119:175
Let my soul live, and it shall praise thee;
and let thy judgments help me.

King David continues with a real desire to praise God. David's request is for more time on earth so he could praise the Lord. In this life, what should be our number one priority? We must provide for our family, but our first responsibility is in how we can serve God. We are to praise Him and to find ways to honor Him. In this verse, David knows he needs God's judgments to help Him. For us, we have a complete inerrant Bible available, and we need to use it. We need to study and read the word of God with the hopes that we would continue to understand more and more of God's precepts. *II Timothy 2:15 Study to shew thyself approved unto God, a workman that needeth not to be ashamed, rightly dividing the word of truth.* The more we understand His word and apply it to our life, the more we are equipped to praise Him and to bring honor to Him. I do not necessarily believe we need to rate everything we do on a scale of one to ten, but in this case, it is only fitting. With ten being the most important and one the least, where would we fall right now in our praise? Would others judge us as a ten, a one, or God forbid a zero? More importantly, where would we place ourselves on that same scale? None of us are sitting on a ten, but we do not want to fall short and not strive to get off number one either. I just realized that what others see that we are closest to may give us an accurate account of where we are spiritually. Most people will probably rate themselves at a ten when in reality they are a five. Why is that you ask? More than likely it is because we live with ourselves twenty-four hours a day and seven days a week. What does that have to do with anything? When you or I are around something long enough, some bad habits will soon become acceptable to us. Through bad habits we can become a real stumbling block to someone else. I think it would behoove us all to have an accountability partner that is around us a lot to help keep our mind right and our attitude correct. Just how would we accept any criticism from an accountability partner? *Ecclesiastes 7:5 It is better to hear the rebuke of the wise, than for a man to hear the song of fools.* After reading *Ecclesiastes 7:5* I would hope we would receive rebuke graciously and praise the Lord for the friend with the courage to help us do the right thing. Every Friday, I and a friend share with each other where we are at in God's word. You might find an accountability partner and see how that works for you as well.

April 28

Psalm 135:1
Praise ye the LORD. Praise ye the name
of the LORD; praise him, O ye servants of the LORD.

Here is another time when praise appears three times in the same verse. You must sense the excitement of the Psalmist. He is applying this verse to us to help inspire us to praise. He says, "Praise "ye" the Lord". You cannot get ten people to praise the Lord until you have ten "Ye's" praising. It is an individual choice to praise or not to praise. The Psalmist continues and says, praise the name of the Lord. I wanted to use the same verse I had used earlier about the name of our Saviour, *Acts 4:12 Neither is there salvation in any other: for there is none other name under heaven given among men, whereby we must be saved.* Our writer makes mention that the servants of the Lord are to praise the Lord. Are you a servant of the Lord? This verse follows the same order of salvation. Let me give you an example of what I mean. We are to make a choice to praise. We are to praise His name, be a servant of the Lord, and we are to praise. What is the order of salvation? First, it is a personal issue, do I want to be saved? Second, there is only one way to be saved and that is by the name of Jesus. Third, I become a servant of the Lord. The awesome thing is that the Psalmist is making praise a priority in His life. We need to work on making praise the same priority in our own life. We are to serve the Lord by the best of His ability and praise is a big part of how we will serve Him. After all, how can you serve someone you will not praise? I honestly do not believe we can pull that off and I doubt you believe it either. Do not concern yourself with what others are doing as you can only control you. Be the best you can be, and everything will fall into place. Some servants loved their master, and some hated their master. I pray you have a huge amount of love as a servant for your master, which is Jesus Christ.

April 29

Psalm 135:3
Praise the LORD; for the LORD is good:
sing praises unto his name; for it is pleasant.

We are to praise the Lord for He is good. Let me give you a rather lengthy list of what good can mean from a dictionary perspective. Good: of a favorable character, bountiful, comely, suitable, fit, sound, whole, agreeable, pleasant, salutary, wholesome, considerable, ample, full, well-founded, true, real, recognized, valid, adequate, satisfactory, competent, and loyal. There are twenty-three reasons from Webster's dictionary concerning the word good that would mandate our praise to the Lord. Pick one and then praise Him for it. I have mentioned in the past the necessity to make a list of reasons to praise the Lord. We really do not need a lengthy list made up. All we need to do is to simply praise the Lord for He is good. "God is good all the time, and all the time God is good"! The list of reasons for praising God is a reminder for each of us of what the Lord has done for us. We can praise Him for the list we compile or simply praise Him for He is good! On any given day we have no idea of what God has done for us and what He has protected us from. Did He keep a speeding car or drunk driver from hitting us? Did you have a meal today and did you thank God for that? I know a lot of bad things happen, but I assure you it would be a lot worse if God was absent. I also know that if I was killed in an accident that my soul is in the hands of God for safekeeping. People are quick to blame God for bad things and He had nothing to do with it. God may have allowed it, but He does not orchestrate it. Terrible things happen to good people and good things happen to bad people. We are a sinful race, and thanks to Adam, we sink lower and lower with each passing generation. No matter how the generations before me praised God for His goodness has nothing to do with me. My praise and service for Him is personal and at times it is private. Whether out in the open or privately, God is in fact good all the time.

April 30

Psalm 135:21
Blessed be the LORD out of Zion,
which dwelleth at Jerusalem. Praise ye the LORD.

In this *Psalm 135* there are distinct groups of people mentioned. The Psalmist mentions the house of Aaron, house of Israel, or the house of Levi. Every house mentioned played their own special part in scripture. Whether we play a big part or a small part in God's big plan is up to God and us. I mention both of us as it is God's will we serve Him in some way, and it is our choice to do God's will. Here is what is important about this verse. All of us have a certain service to render, but we all play a part in praise. There is a time when we all lay aside our busyness and come together to praise together. Scripture says we are many members, joined together to form the body of Christ, *Romans 12:5 So we, being many, are one body in Christ, and every one members one of another. I Corinthians 12:12-27* would be another good place for you to read about the body and its importance. We have established that we are all an important part of the body of Christ. In considering praise and service and being a part of the body of Christ, you must know that every part of the body is an integral part. When we come together as is suggested in this Psalm are we doing our part in praise? It does not matter where you fall as far as responsibility in the leading of praise. What matters is the heart attitude of our praise. If you lead praise, are you leading in the flesh or in the Spirit? If you are following the leading of praise, are you following in the flesh or following in the Spirit? Do not sell yourself short, you and I are an important part of the body when the body praises together. A body that praises together, stays together.

May 1

Psalm 138:1
A Psalm of David. I will praise thee with my
whole heart: before the gods will I sing praise unto thee.

King David records his sincerity he has toward praising God. Look back and read *Psalm 111:1* and you will see how the heart is tied to praise. Some may appear to be praising God outwardly, but are they? Remember how the Pharisees liked to pray out in the open to be seen of men, *Matthew 6:5 And when thou prayest, thou shalt not be as the hypocrites are: for they love to pray standing in the synagogues and in the corners of the streets, that they may be seen of men. Verily I say unto you, They have their reward.* We do not decide on our own what others are doing for praise. I am simply pointing out that just because someone's mouth is moving does not mean praise is coming out. That is why there is no sense in trying to fool anyone with phony praise. It is not those around us we disappoint, it is God. For your sake, let me retype that thought; it is not those around us we disappoint with phony praise, it is God. He is the one who knows our inward thoughts. He is the one who knows what the heart is dealing with, especially concerning sin. He is the one who knows if there is praise, (joyful noise), coming forth or a lot of noise. David, the Psalmist, wants to praise God with his whole heart. If anything, go to God by way of prayer, and ask Him for help in the area of praise. Pray and strive that you would not fall short in your worship to Him. Do you ever need instructions for anything? Be sure and use the word of God for the answers. Praise is included in God's instruction manual, (Bible). Pray the Holy Spirit would teach you more about praise from the word of God. Here are three things to consider; learn to praise, live to praise, and love to praise. For the heart, God knows when we are hurting as well, and praise Him for His comfort during those times.

May 2

Psalm 138:2
I will worship toward thy holy temple, and praise thy name for thy lovingkindness and for thy truth: for thou hast magnified thy word above all thy name.

In the beginning, only the high priest serving entered the innermost part of the tabernacle. This naturally kept the people worshipping toward the holy temple instead of worshipping at the very center of the tabernacle. I have more good news for us. Christ gave His life that I might enter the Holy of Holies. We no longer worship toward the temple. We worship the temple, which is Jesus Christ. We should look toward Jesus, (our temple), with a sense of awe, admiration, and thanksgiving, which should result in praise. In this verse we are to praise the name of the Lord with lovingkindness. In order to express lovingkindness to our Saviour we need to get to know Him better. We normally do not walk up to someone and in an instant treat them with lovingkindness. We may be respectful and courteous, but that is different. The only way to treat someone with lovingkindness is to intimately get to know them. How do you propose getting to know Jesus Christ in such a manner? It is not going to be through the radio, television, or newspaper. You get to know Jesus Christ by spending time with Him, reading the word of God, and spending some quiet time with Him. We have a complete book, (Bible) that tells us everything we need to know about Jesus that we might learn more about Jesus. The more knowledge we gain of Jesus Christ the more we love Him. Do you desire to love

Him more? Then you need to get to know Him more. When you get to know Jesus more you will praise Him and serve Him. You will do all that with the same lovingkindness David records in this verse. Maybe doing a word search and devoting yourself to it will be an encouragement. I started with one page on praise and ended up with this book of devotions. If I can do it, anyone can do it.

May 3

Psalm 138:4
All the kings of the earth shall praise thee,
O LORD, when they hear the words of thy mouth.

We continue to *Psalm 138*, which is another Psalm of King David. David is convinced that the kings of the earth will praise the Lord when they hear the word of his mouth. I am not sure there is a greater testimony to be shared than that of someone in a very high leadership position praising the Lord. Many times, people learn not only by repetition, but by examples that are on display before us. David had a lot of power and authority, and it was ultimately his choice of how he would use it. When he came to the place in his life where he had acquired a lot of wisdom, his choice was to promote glory to the Lord. His goal was to preach of the Lord with hopes that the kings of the world would accept what he said and praise God right alongside him. Here is something we can both consider. When we speak, is it honoring to God? We promote Jesus, and He is the one who changes us through accepting Him as our Saviour. By how we act at home, church, and our job, do others want what we say we have? Have you ever met someone who professes to be a Christian and they live and act like the lost? I do not question their salvation, but would I want to praise the same Saviour they say saved them. I will share a true example of showing the joy of the Lord. A fellow employee came to work as bubbly as one can get. Another employee declared he wanted that same joy in his life. He wanted to know what happened? I shared that he had just given his life to Jesus the day before. His response? I want some of that! The following Sunday the one with the question submitted to the Savior and he got saved. Your testimony is so powerful. Guess what, the joy the one had was due to accepting Jesus Christ the day before. The other employee reached out and grabbed a hold of Jesus and is now a saved and a baptized member of a bible believing church as well. I praise God for allowing me to play a part in both of their lives. In testifying of God, what do others see in us? Are we frowning all the time or do smiles come easy to us? Remember, it takes fewer muscles to form a smile for Jesus than it does to form a frown with the world. Can we solicit praise from others to join in and praise God? You can if you are painting a life well lived for Jesus Christ. David thought it was possible and so do I.

May 4

Psalm 139:14
I will praise thee; for I am fearfully and wonderfully made: marvellous are thy works; and that my soul knoweth right well.

What a thing for David the king to recognize. You can almost sense tears of joy when David records in this verse he is fearfully and wonderfully made. Be certain that God does not make or create any junk. If He had a hand in it, then it is good. Do not look around and say, "Well I would not want to be in that person's condition or circumstances". You would be guilty of comparing things with what man deems good and not with what God deems good. Remember what Samuel had to be reminded of when he had to anoint a new king. Samuel looked upon Eliab and thought surely because of his looks he will be king. Look what the Lord told him in *I Samuel 16:7 But the LORD said unto Samuel, Look not on his countenance, or on the height of his stature; because I have refused him: for the LORD seeth not as man seeth; for man looketh on the outward appearance, but the LORD looketh on the heart.* King David knew God monitored his reins, which are our thoughts or emotions. Therefore, it is important to praise God as David desired with the whole heart. David's soul knew of the omniscience of God Almighty. God's wrath will be felt with an everlasting fire that cannot be quenched for those rejecting Jesus Christ as their Saviour. The other side of the coin is when we mess up, (sin), God knows if Jesus is your Saviour, and He will never forget that. He knows when and where you got saved. David mentions a marvellous work performed by God. Can you think of a more marvellous work than God sacrificing His son for us? When we accepted Jesus Christ as our Saviour another marvellous work takes place. That is the transformation that takes place in the life of born-again believers. Praise God for the marvellous work that He can perform in our lives. We were wonderfully formed to serve Him, praise Him, and to love Him. I just listed three things for you to consider. All three are important and worthy of logging down for future reference. By the way, there is no transformation without confirmation of Jesus as your Savior. You cannot be transformed unless you are ready to be conformed into His image.

May 5

Psalm 142:7
Bring my soul out of prison, that I may praise
thy name: the righteous shall compass me about; for
thou shalt deal bountifully with me.

The only type of prison I want to deal with is the prison of sin that we were in bondage to before we accepted Jesus Christ as our Saviour. We were all in bondage to sin. We were all shackled to sin. God sent His only begotten son with a key to unlock the chains of bondage to sin. That key was like no other key you would ever recognize. The key was shaped like a body, a grave, and an empty tomb. The key was and could only be Jesus Christ. Jesus is the only one who can take a person who is literally locked up in the jail of sin and set them free. It does not mean we are free to go outside the walls of justice, as there is a price to pay for sin. It does mean they can be set free from sin and never commit whatever act they had committed. With that settled, they too can praise God for their freedom in Jesus Christ. Hell is the prison that will contain a wide variety of human beings with one thing in common. God called and they still refused to accept God's righteous plan for their life and rejected Jesus Christ. Heaven will contain a wide variety of people with one thing in common. God called and they had enough good sense to answer the call and accept Jesus Christ as their personal Saviour. We had a prison staring us right in the eye. Are we praising God because He called us, saved us, and will preserve us for all eternity? If you have not trusted Jesus for you salvation, I truly hope you will do so soon.

May 6

Psalm 145:1
David's Psalm of praise. I will extol thee, my God,
O king; and I will bless thy name for ever and ever.

What a fitting start for this *Psalm 145*, {King David's Psalm of praise}. This is David's personal Psalm. It is important to praise in the congregation. It is important to promote the importance of praise. The most important thing to do is to make praise personal. Ask yourself, "how am I praising God"? David gives us the answer in this verse in how we are to praise God. He says he will extol thee, <u>my</u> God. First, God is personal to him. He labels God as <u>MY</u> God. Second, he will extol him with praise. To extol is to praise highly and glorify. When we praise Him, is it praises of the utmost high and glorifying? Let me give you something to consider. If you were to buy a new car you would really baby that thing. There is absolutely no food or drinks allowed in it. You carry a soft towel with you so you can wipe the dust off from it. The car finally gets a little age on it, and you do not eat in it, but you do wash it if it rains or is really dirty. Finally, you have had it a little while, and you can probably find enough food to feed a small army. There may even be around a dollar in various coins underneath every seat. Praise is not cared for like a car, home, motorcycle or etc. It does not get worse with age it gets better. We do not need to carry a soft towel to wipe the dust off our praise. Dust never collects on praise when we exercise it consistently.

May 7

Psalm 145:2
Every day will I bless thee;
and I will praise thy name for ever and ever.

There is one thought that is woven into every devotional that I have shared with you about praise. The first two words of this verse explain that thought. They are the words "*every day*" and that is to be the standard by which we praise and serve God. Our key verse for this entire book on praise is *Psalm 34:1 I will bless the LORD at all times: his praise shall continually be in my mouth.* Praise will be the normal throughout all of eternity. When Jesus Christ returns, and physically establishes His new kingdom, praise will be a way of life for us. Are we to wait until then to perfect our praise? No, it is to be a way of life now. Every day we are to be praising the Lord. Our verse continues by including praising His name forever and ever. You do not have to wait until Sunday to praise the Lord. Start praising the Lord consistently regardless of where you are at. God blesses us daily, so consistently return His blessings back to Him. I do not want to leave here until I remind you of the little word "I" in the text. It is your decision to accept Jesus as your Savior. It is your decision to follow Him as the Lord of your life. It is your decision to praise Him, and my prayer for you is that you will praise Him right, as He is so worthy of it. So, what is right? Giving God the Father, God the Son, and God the Holy Spirit our very best praise "every day". The result? Joy like you may have never experienced before!

May 8

Psalm 145:4
One generation shall praise thy works
to another, and shall declare thy mighty acts.

Now here is a verse to give careful consideration to. One generation is going to praise the works of the Lord to another. With all the mighty acts of God we are familiar with, we are to pass that on to the next generation. If you are not too familiar with any mighty acts of God, you should start with the book of Genesis and continue through to the book of Revelation for a little memory refreshing. Please include the mighty act the Lord performed in your life also. The mighty act of saving you for all of eternity. The mighty work he performed in changing your character. We need to pass on the word of God to the next generation. It is critical that kids today do not see some phony religion taking place. A phony religion to a kid is mom and dad look holier than thou in the pew and then live like they are possessed by the devil at home. Our relationship with Jesus needs to be real to you and to our children, (the next generation). Praise is not just singing a song; it is sharing how God can continue to change humanity through the accepting of Jesus. Have you ever heard the following phrase used, "if it were not for the grace of God there go I"? We pass on from generation to generation how beautiful and faithful God has been and that it will continue to be. The next time someone pays you a compliment for some good and kind act repeat the following, "thank you very much and praise God He could use me to do it".

May 9

Psalm 145:10
All thy works shall praise thee,
O LORD; and thy saints shall bless thee.

King David certainly has dedicated *Psalm 145* in its entirety to personal praise. Back in verse 1 of this same *Psalm 145* it is labeled as David's Psalm of praise. If we were to commit some time to prayer, sat down with pen and paper, and recorded everything we could think of concerning the works of God in our own lives, we would have our own personal Psalm. It would be a Psalm that would not make it into our King James bible, but God would indeed inspire us to write it just the same. In our devotional verse today, David says, *"all thy works shall praise thee, O Lord"*. Even the inanimate things God has created will sing out praise to the Lord. For example, *Psalm 96:11-12 11) Let the heavens rejoice, and let the earth be glad; let the sea roar, and the fulness thereof. 12) Let the field be joyful, and all that is therein: then shall all the trees of the wood rejoice.* Everything God has created will praise Him. If something inanimate will praise the Lord, what should we be doing? We continually hear the following: praise the Lord; make a joyful noise; sing out brothers and sisters, and on and on and on. It would appear we need to be coached to praise. In our example of *Psalm 96:11-12*, did you see any coaxing by anybody of the sea, the field, the heavens, the earth, and the trees rejoicing in their creator? Do not feel bad, as I did not see it either. That is exactly the point I am trying to make. Praise should be a natural thing for us. I am all for a song leader on Sunday mornings. Actually, I would go so far as to say a song leader is a necessity for the flock when we gather. God is a God of order and there is nothing wrong with order during the song service. What I am driving at, is no one should have to work their tail off trying to persuade us to praise the Lord. Let it become a natural part of our life. Write your own personal Psalm to the Lord and then rejoice in it. Before going on to another verse look how this one ends. I have alluded to trees, seas, and so on, but the saints are included at the end. What a day of praise it will be when nature and all mankind sing out to the Lord in unison. Will you participate or stand on the sidelines?

May 10

Psalm 145:21
My mouth shall speak the praise of the LORD:
and let all flesh bless his holy name for ever and ever.

This verse is for the few that are terrified to sing out to the Lord for fear someone will ask them to not sing. To the ones who boldly declare, "I cannot carry a tune in a basket", David has good news in this verse. David is still our Psalmist here and he simply pens the following, *"My mouth shall **speak** the praise of the Lord"*. Back in one of our earlier devotional verses I came across a word for praise, and I was surprised at some of the other possible uses of the word. The devotional verse was *Psalm 145:10* and it ended by saying all the saints will bless thee. The word bless is the Hebrew word barak, pronounced baw-rak. It is translated 302 times as bless such as it is in *Psalm 145:10*. It is also translated curse four times. I understand bless is the most popular rendering of the word, but the word curse is also used. Look at what the book of James says about the capabilities of our mouth. *James 3:10 Out of the same mouth proceedeth blessing and cursing. My brethren, these things ought not so to be.* To wrap things up, what will we speak for the Lord?

Will it be blessings or an occasional cursing? Praising God is not a location or an event. It is a personal choice and a personal lifestyle.

May 11

Psalm 146:1
Praise ye the LORD. Praise the LORD, O my soul.

The Psalmist wastes no time getting to the point. He does not say you praise the Lord by yourself, he includes his own responsibility to praise, *O my soul, praise the Lord.* From the innermost part of his being, his desire is to praise the Lord. I had a thought while sitting at this keyboard typing this up and I will share it with you. Picture yourself sitting in the congregation and the praise service is about to commence. As you drive to church from home you need to be expecting God to do some awesome things when you get there. You stand there prior to the praise service with one thing on your mind before the leader signals to the musicians to begin. It is the same thought the Psalmist just shared in this verse. *"O Lord help those around me to praise you"*. "O Lord help me to praise you with those I am surrounded by". It is the only thing you desire at that moment, and you will not let anything distract you from it. You are a cup running over with the filling of the Holy Spirit and you cannot wait for that first note to signal the start. That is exactly what God wants from us in our praise to Him. A desire to praise the Lord that is beyond explanation. Others cannot understand by words how your soul longs to praise the Lord. It cannot be explained it can only be experienced. The only way to experience praising the Lord is by participating in it. Here is the final consideration for both of us. Are we a spectator or a participant?

May 12

Psalm 146:2
While I live will I praise the LORD:
I will sing praises unto my God while I have any being.

Here is a verse to jump start us to praise. The writer not only will praise the Lord while he has breath, but his desire is to praise the Lord with his last breath. So then who is eligible to praise the Lord? Anyone born again, those washed in the blood of Jesus. Those who have been sanctified by Jesus Christ if you have trusted in Him as your Saviour. If you can still fog a mirror, you can praise the Lord. I will continue to fall on our key verse for praise. *Psalm 34:1 I will bless the LORD at all times: his praise shall continually be in my mouth.* If I compare *Psalm 34:1* with *Psalm 146:2,* it becomes very apparent that if we wonder what we can do with our free time then fill in the dead places with praise. Better yet, fill in the times of praise with things you must get done. Do not put praise in a Day Planner and schedule time to praise or serve the Lord. Both those things for the Lord are to be done continuously. Use a Day Planner for items that you need to be reminded of. No believer should need to be reminded to praise and serve God. Right?

May 13

Psalm 146:10
The LORD shall reign forever, even thy God,
O Zion, unto all generations. Praise ye the LORD.

Eventually, Jesus Christ is going to be sitting on His throne as our King for eternity. This *Psalm 146* gives us examples of how the Lord will take care of all. Darkness will never again be able to penetrate through the light of Jesus Christ. In the past, Israel would turn their back on God and the kingdom would be stripped from them and the city destroyed. Israel experienced freedom and independence only to go right back into captivity because of their disobedience. In this verse here, Jesus will reign forever, and we can praise God for it. Sit back and wonder what it will be like at that time. There will be a day when there is no sickness, sin, or death. This verse is clear on Jesus reigning over all generations. It does not say He will reign from generation to generation. That would indicate a passing away over time of one generation and onto the next. What will happen is all those throughout all generations who have trusted in Him for salvation will be under Jesus' reign. Do you ever watch the news and get just plain sick of what is going on around the world? Praise the Lord, and in God's timing, it is coming to an end. If Jesus is your Saviour, you can take part in His kingdom. If you have not trusted Him as your Saviour, then there is another kingdom awaiting you. Everyone not fit for the Kingdom of Heaven will be there. Who is not fit for the Kingdom? Anyone who has not accepted Jesus Christ and "fit" HIM into their heart. Praise the Lord for He has made a way of escape. If a lake of fire sounds more promising or enlightening to someone, may God help them before time runs out! According to God's word, time as we know it will cease to exist. In eternity, time will be no longer be measured. Why? Because you will never run out of time.

May 14

Psalm 147:1
Praise ye the LORD: for it is good to sing praises
unto our God; for it is pleasant; and praise is comely.

Tired of the countenance of your face? Try praising the Lord for a change and see what happens. It says here, praise is pleasant and comely. Pleasant means agreeable or you are marked by a pleasing behavior. My preference would be to have a pleasing behavior and I trust that would be your choice. The word comely means to be good looking or handsome. Are you tired of your old looks? Do you desire a change in your appearance? Do you want to take on a fresh look and want everyone to notice? This verse says you can have good behavior and be good-looking or handsome. Our nation spends billions of dollars each year on trying to look good, and all we needed to do was praise the Lord and He will change our looks. This verse starts out by telling us praise is good because it is pleasant and comely. Praise not only pleases God but it can be pleasing to us. Here are a couple of choices we have. We can praise the Lord and let our countenance be changed for the better, (to look comely, which is handsome or good-looking). We can refuse to praise the Lord and look the opposite of good looking or handsome and be satisfied with those looks. I would have to choose the first of the two. What will you choose? The beauty and the result of our praise we have for Jesus internally will shine forth from us externally. People want to have hope, and they can find that hope in people with a positive attitude, that exude the love of Jesus Christ that we have and show for Him!

May 15

Psalm 147:7
Sing unto the LORD with thanksgiving;
sing praise upon the harp unto our God:

We have more than once had this thought repeated throughout scripture. The thought is to praise the Lord using a harp, which of course is a musical instrument. There are a lot of people who believe it is wrong to use any kind of an instrument to praise the Lord. Their belief is that it was only acceptable in the Old Testament and has since died by the wayside. I wonder how many will not allow musical instruments to be used in their song service at church, but will go home and practice secular songs on the old guitar. Wonder who they are praising then? If an instrument cannot be used to praise God, then who are they praising? Not only can we use whatever means to reverently praise the Lord, but He wants us to do it with thanksgiving. I know Thanksgiving rolls around every November just like clockwork. I know in our churches we will sing songs of thanksgiving and we should keep on doing that. I do want to make sure that I am not just thankful for my blessings from God one day out of the year. I am not blessed on just one day of the year, but every single day. Thankfulness comes in many sizes, shapes, and colors. I think we all just have to slow down and meditate on how God has changed our life. We must think about what God has brought into our life, and how He is continually a part of our life. Praise God that there is no one or nothing that loves you like God does.

May 16

Psalm 147:12
Praise the LORD, O Jerusalem; praise thy God, O Zion.

We have two cities that are to praise the Lord. The first is Jerusalem, (a holy city), and Zion, (a holy hill). I hate to repeat myself so soon, but eventually Jesus Christ is coming back to establish His kingdom, and praise is going to come from this place. *Revelation 3:12 Him that overcometh will I make a pillar in the temple of my God, and he shall go no more out: and I will write upon him the name of my God, and the name of the city of my God, which is new Jerusalem, which cometh down out of heaven from my God: and I will write upon him my new name. Revelation 21:2 And I John saw the holy city, new Jerusalem, coming down from God out of heaven, prepared as a bride adorned for her husband.* Where else can praise be offered to God but on His altar. For now, we are to be content with where we are. A New Jerusalem has not arrived yet, but that in and of itself is no excuse not to praise the Lord in the cities we do have. At our own personal church, what do visitors see and hear when they come in? It is estimated that you only have about five minutes to win over a visitor. Praise may be showing yourself friendly to someone new to your church. Praise might be going the extra mile to welcome a new employee. Praise might be making your new neighbor know they are welcome. Laying all that aside, we are to be patient as we will be a part of the future New Jerusalem. In the meantime, praise Him like it was already here. Consider that we have an altar to praise God and He is always present. That altar does not have to be in a church. An altar may be a simple drop to your knees in praise right in your home. Your altar can be anywhere you happen to be. It is up to us to determine what we will lay up at that altar.

May 17

Psalm 147:20
He hath not dealt so with any nation: and as for his judgments, they have not known them. Praise ye the LORD.

Israel is reminded of how God has gone out of His way to bless them. They are reminded of how God has set them apart from all other people. Israel is to praise the Lord for His mercy and His goodness to them. It is very clear how Israel has been a chosen nation to God, but I have more good news for you. God came in the flesh, (Jesus Christ), and the partition between Jews and Gentiles has been removed. It does not mean that Israel is not a chosen nation to God, but it does mean that because of Jesus Christ that all nations have reason to praise the Lord. The same mercy and goodness God has shown to Israel is the same mercy and goodness God gave to us through Jesus. I cannot speak for a lot of nations as I have not visited too many. I have been in the United States long enough to know that most of us have not been deprived of too many of the essential things. The bottom line is praise is not reserved for the Jews only. It is not reserved for the Gentile living wherever. Praise is reserved for those who are willing to acknowledge His grace, mercy, and perfect judgment through Jesus Christ our Lord.

May 18

Psalm 148:1
Praise ye the LORD. Praise ye the LORD
from the heavens: praise him in the heights.

There are fourteen verses in this *Psalm* and praise appears thirteen times. The Psalm starts out with simple and specific instructions, *Praise ye the LORD*. The Psalmist also selects an area that is to praise the Lord. He says to praise the Lord from the heavens. If we consider the heavens in scripture, we will find three. The first heaven surrounding our earth. The second heaven holding and containing the stars and planets. The third heaven is the throne room of God. That pretty much covers everything from our level to God's level. The Psalm continues and says, *praise him in the heights*. You cannot get any higher than God as He is the utmost and the highest. The only place I can praise God in is the first heaven, but the praise that occurs in the first heaven must pass through the second heaven and into the third. So in a sense, our praise passes through two heavens to get to God in the third heaven. With praise in mind, our voices can be heard from a long way off. For the record, when our mouth offers up something other than praise it passes through all three heavens as well. We might be surprised when we say something derogatory, just how far it carries to other people around. We must harness what we are thinking or saying. *Matthew 12:36 But I say unto you, That every idle word that men shall speak, they shall give account thereof in the day of judgment.*

May 19

Psalm 148:2
Praise ye him, all his angels: praise ye him, all his hosts.

Right or wrong we look at most things from a human perspective. Those taking part in praise in this verse are angels. The word for angel is mal'ak, (mal-awk') and is translated as messenger or ambassador. I would suppose that an angel would be considered an ambassador for the Lord. I do not understand completely what all angels do. I do know what it says in *Hebrews 13:2 Be not forgetful to entertain strangers: for thereby some have entertained angels unawares.* It would be awful to be here on earth doing our own thing, throwing a good old-fashioned fit while an angel took it all in. I am only trying to stretch your imagination at this point. If there were an angel attending our song service, what would they see and hear us doing? Are there times when we do things or act differently around certain people? God is the one who recognizes our praise and service or whatever else we are doing. Do not worry about angels being present, be mindful that God is in our presence. With God present, we can present Him with a present of pouring out our adoration for Him. As one song says, "I'm drinking from my saucer because my cup has overflowed".

May 20

Psalm 148:3
Praise ye him, sun and moon:
praise him, all ye stars of light.

This *Psalm 148* starts breaking down the three different heavens once again. It is the sun, moon, and stars that will be praising God in this verse. I do not even begin to understand how God could receive praise from a planet made of dirt and rock. I am positive that man was originally formed from the dust of the earth and is able to praise the Lord. I wonder if the planets wonder how man could praise the Lord? After all, we were originally created from the dirt on the face of this planet. If we consider that, then why couldn't the planets praise God? My place is not to determine how planets can praise God. My place is to join them with my praise. Some things do not require my figuring out. This verse says the planets will praise God and that is good enough for me. This verse ends with talking about stars, but I am not one hundred percent convinced that all those stars are simply planets. Many times we are compared as the stars, and I think there is good reason to believe that we may be the stars of light mentioned here. When we give our life to Jesus we are to illuminate Him because of a changed life. We accepted Jesus and are changed because of Jesus, and we are to shine and praise Jesus. Sounds pretty simple, but I think all of us at times fail and may do just the opposite of praising Jesus or anybody. We all need to slow down and evaluate self, to make sure we have our priorities straight. For the record, we cannot keep our priorities straight if we do not have any priorities. Serving God and praising the Lord should be at the top of every one of our lists.

May 21

Psalm 148:4
Praise him, ye heavens of heavens,
and ye waters that be above the heavens.

We move from the heaven holding the planets to the heaven above all heavens. The third heaven is where God lives. We are painted a picture of the praise going on in *Revelation 4:8 And the four beasts had each of them six wings about him; and they were full of eyes within: and they rest not day and night, saying, Holy, holy, holy, Lord God Almighty, which was, and is, and is to come.* The verse in Revelation says there is no rest, so the praise is nonstop. The four beasts are not forced to praise but are more than happy to praise. May we make such an effort to praise the Lord when we are awake? These four beasts never rested day or night. You would think our praise would even be sweeter, as we rest at night with hopes of waking up fresh in the morning. Praise God before your feet hit the floor. Do not ask God for one thing. Simply let God know how much you love HIM. That is praise.

May 22

Psalm 148:5
Let them praise the name of the LORD:
for he commanded, and they were created.

This verse is a closing to the previous four verses of *Psalm 148*. Everything created in *Psalm 148:1-4* is to praise the Lord. The reason for the praise is if God had not commanded their creation, nothing in the heavens would have been created. *John 1:3 All things were made by him; and without him was not anything made that was made.* Isn't it amazing how something we would consider lifeless could praise the Lord? Take the stars and planets for instance. How could a big rock praise the Lord? In our own finite minds we think there is no way something with no intelligence could do such a thing. Look at what Jesus said to the Pharisees about rocks and his disciples. *Luke 19:40 And he answered and said unto them, I tell you that, if these, (disciples), should hold their peace, the stones would immediately cry out.* It is obvious everything created by God contains some form of praise. It would be wise to use that praise in giving thanks to God. It would appear that anyone who would not praise the creator is the unintelligent one. Have you ever heard the expression; "he or she is dumber than a rock"? For those who refuse to praise the Lord it is probably a fitting analogy. Here is something to consider; are you dumber than a rock, or smarter than a rock? Let your praise be your answer. I doubt you will offend the rock, but the wrong answer could offend your Creator.

May 23

Psalm 148:7
Praise the LORD from the earth,
ye dragons, and all deeps:

Here is our final heaven mentioned in Psalm 148. We moved from the throne room of God, on to the planets, and now we are down on the earth. Take the time to read from our verse *7* to verse *12* of this same Psalm. Everything within our grasp on this earth is to praise the Lord. No one or nothing is excluded. The Psalmist makes sure that man knows none are excluded from praise. In twelve verses of this Psalm 148 he makes mention of the young and old, men and women, rulers, and judges. Whether you are leading or following is not what is relevant when praise to God is the issue. We should all be leaders in praise. We all may not be gifted with the ability to do solos or lead music, but we can still praise God and be an example to those around us. How important is it to be an example to an unbeliever or a baby Christian when we praise? If praise is not important to someone grounded in the Bible, why would the unbeliever or baby

Christian find it necessary? When we disciple new church members or new believers we should include a lesson on praise. This verse specifically mentions the earth so take note of that. This planet is far from being the biggest planet and is actually very small in comparison to most. However, this earth is plenty big enough for every one of us to have the space to praise the Creator of the earth. Every one of us is not too big that we cannot find a place large enough where it is just God and self. I am the first to admit there is a place where we should all come together collectively to worship. I am equally convinced that we need to have our own personal time with God and no one around to bother, disrupt, or hinder us in praise. Praise can be choreographed through song leaders, or it can be choreographed by God to us. When we are still and know that He is God it is a wonderful experience.

May 24

Psalm 148:13
Let them praise the name of the LORD: for his name alone is excellent; his glory is above the earth and heaven.

This verse 13 wraps up what took place from verse 7 through 12. All are to praise the name of the Lord, for his name alone is excellent. The Lord's glory is above all and cannot be equaled nor surpassed. Nothing should excite us more than the name of the Lord. What did it take to be saved? *Romans 10:13 For whosoever shall call upon the name of the Lord shall be saved. Acts 4:12 Neither is there salvation in any other: for there is none other name under heaven given among men, whereby we must be saved.* All of us recognize certain celebrity names from movies or television shows they have been in. No matter how popular their name, you cannot be saved by it. Billy Graham's name is probably as recognized as any, but his name is not the name you can call upon for salvation. The trees, fire, hail, mountains, storms, beasts, creeping things, and fowls of the air can praise God. If creation can do that, I would think it would not be a problem for His children to do the same. Did you notice the order of the list of who is to praise in Psalm 148:7-12. Man was created in Genesis chapter one after all other things were created, and he is the last to be listed here. God is a God of order, and His desire is for man to praise Him, and that will never change or go away.

May 25

Psalm 148:14
He also exalted the horn of his people,
the praise of all his saints; even of the children of
Israel, a people near unto him. Praise ye the LORD.

God the Father has, will, and continues to exalt Israel and His children. It was God who heard Israel's cry for deliverance and sent Moses to be His ambassador. It was God who led them through forty years of wilderness and fed them while they were there. It was God who defeated their enemies for them. It was God who dried up the waters and took Israel into the promised land. It is God who is their horn, their strength or their place on the altar. God sends praise to His children and what should He expect in return? The last four words of this verse tells us: *{Praise ye the LORD}*. I mentioned Israel several times, but there came a time when Jesus Christ came and died for all. For salvation was not only for the Jew, but for the Gentiles as well, as Jesus died for all. *Galatians 3:27-28 For as many of you as have been baptized into Christ have put on Christ. 28) There is neither Jew nor*

Greek, there is neither bond nor free, there is neither male nor female: for ye are all one in Christ Jesus. The Psalmist instructs us to praise ye the Lord. It seems to be a very simple and understandable request. If it is simple and easily understood, then what keeps us from it? Israel had more than enough reason to praise God for the countless times He delivered them from many enemies. It should be a simple request for Israel to praise their Deliverer. It is a simple request for us as well. You and I should be as grateful for the salvation we received through faith in Jesus Christ as Israel was while wandering. By the way, many were wandering hopeless and helpless before finding Jesus as well. I was one of those wanderers. Eternity will never end for us, and my soul and spirit will never wear out thanks to Jesus. His death on the cross, and my believing that His death paid the penalty for my sins, are grounds to celebrate. What an unbelievable act of love Jesus painted for me. Thank you Lord is all I can say and pray.

May 26

Psalm 149:1
Praise ye the LORD. Sing unto the LORD a new song, and his praise in the congregation of saints.

You may have to stop here and go back and read *Psalm 148* in its entirety. *Psalm 148* gave us a list of God's magnificent works and now in this *Psalm 149* Israel is to praise Him for those wonderful works. I want you to consider *Psalm 148* and verse 2 of our verse today from *Psalm 149*. Israel will praise Him first. The church will praise Him second. The children of Zion will praise Him third, *Psalm 149:2*. What is the order in scripture of who God sought after? First, Israel is God's chosen people, and He went and delivered them out of the hand of Pharaoh, (*Exodus 5 to Exodus 14*). In the scheme of things God delivered Israel first and they should be the first to praise. Second, Jesus Christ, (incarnate God), came and died for the world, *John 3:16*. Christ gave up His life for mankind. His death resulted in the birth of the church, (the body of Christ). So now the church should be praising the Lord. Third, when Jesus sets up His kingdom in a New Jerusalem the saints will be gathered together and praising the Lord. Let me list in one sentence the order of how praise has been and will be. Israel started us off, the church joined in, and all the saints reigning with Jesus will follow. Let me state the same thing a different way. Israel started us off with praise, the saved Gentiles chimed in, and the saved saints of the world will bring the grand finale. The verse we are looking at mentions praise in the congregation of saints. In my opinion, we probably have many good choirs at many of our churches. There will be a day when every ethnic group of the world will gather in one place for the sole purpose of praising Jesus. The saved of all time will gather in one place praising the Lord with a new song that the lost will never sing and will never hear.

May 27

Psalm 149:3
Let them praise his name in the dance:
let them sing praises unto him with the timbrel and harp.

We just finished looking at the praise that is coming down the road when Jesus sets up His kingdom. The praise will be for the final victory over death, the grave, and Satan is no more. Now there is praise for His name in the dance as the verse says. The dance indicates a complete celebration due to the victory Jesus brought to the world. The praise and the "dancing" here is what we should be practicing now. It is praise filled with the spirit of rejoicing. Why would we not praise in this manner now? After all, we have received God's favor and His salvation was poured out to as many as will claim it. Have you claimed God's favor by asking for salvation? If you have then I would trust you are praising Him for it. If you are not praising Him, then I trust you have not asked Him for eternal salvation. Some probably do not feel like praising the Lord. Maybe they have had a bad hair day or something. Well let me remind you that Jesus probably did not want to be beaten and crucified, but He did it anyway because He loved us. Every now and then we need to lay aside the cares of this world and focus on Him. Do not allow circumstances to dictate when and where you will praise the Lord. I am not one who would advocate the entire church running up and down the aisles dancing, jumping over pews, or carrying on. When we praise God that probably ought to be what we feel like on the inside. My advice to both of us is to work at harnessing our praise for the sole purpose of directing it back to where it belongs. Our praise, service, and worship belongs to the one who loved us, died for us, and saved us. God Almighty in the person of Jesus. If that thought does not cause you to want to dance a jig, nothing will.

May 28

Psalm 149:9
To execute upon them the judgment written:
this honour have all his saints. Praise ye the LORD.

We continue on once again in *Psalm 149*. Please be sure and back up to verse 4 of this same Psalm and read through to this verse 9. We can praise the Lord now, for what is going to take place in the future. The saints will be so filled with joy that they will be praising the Lord upon their beds, *Psalm 149:5*. *Psalm 149:6* tells us we will have praise in our mouth and a two-edged sword, (word of God), in our hand. Is that not what we are to employ now? Are we not to join the congregation with a Bible in one hand and praise in the other? When you go back as I indicated to *Psalm 149:4-9* and read it, you see things are going to be put in their proper place. Vengeance will be rendered to the lost and the lost will be punished. Kings and nobles who once imprisoned or put people in bondage, will now receive the same justice. In our devotional verse for today, the saints will have honour because God has rendered judgment by what was written in the word of God. God will put sin in its proper place when the time comes to do so, and He will do that for all of eternity. We will praise the Lord when that happens and we should praise the Lord now because it will happen.

May 29

Psalm 150:1
Praise ye the LORD. Praise God in his
sanctuary: praise him in the firmament of his power.

We have been in the Psalms for a long time looking at praise and trying to apply it personally. It is no wonder since the word praise appears 160 times in just the book of Psalms. It is only fitting that our final *Psalm 150* contains six verses and praise appears in every verse. This *Psalm 150* is the doxology of all the Psalms and it is only fitting that praise is the subject at hand. The first word used in this Psalm is praise and we are commanded to do so. Some would say that this Psalm was only used to excite the Levites to carry out their responsibility in leading praise. I would say that God's word devotionally is good for all ages and we are just as responsible to praise the Lord as the Levites. The verse says we are to praise Him in His sanctuary. When we come together collectively, we are to praise the Lord in what we call our sanctuary or place of worship. We call our church the house of the Lord, so we should praise Him in His house. Here is something else to consider about this sanctuary. When you received Christ as your Saviour, what does your body become? Look what Paul said in I *Corinthians 3:16 Know ye not that ye are the temple of God, and that the Spirit of God dwelleth in you?* Are we a temple or sanctuary of God? If that is true then we should be praising Him in our temple, in our sanctuary, in our body where the Spirit of God dwelleth? God is also to be praised in the firmament of His power. Let us look at this in two ways. The first, that even the angels in the firmaments will praise God for His power. Two, we are to look at the awesomeness of the firmament,{heavens}, and rejoice over its splendor. Look at the power it must have took to create a universe so big we cannot even see the end of it. Power so mighty we cannot even begin to understand it, yet it was probably nothing for God to create. Consider all the power that was used to create the wonders of heaven and then consider that all that power is within the reach of your fingertips. We can ask for that power every time we preach, pray, and praise. Are you praising the Lord for His power? Are you not praising the Lord as you feel God has no power? Maybe we should praise God in order to experience His power?

May 30

Psalm 150:2
Praise him for his mighty acts:
praise him according to his excellent greatness.

Scripture points out that we are to praise the Lord for His mighty acts. If we had to make a list of all the mighty acts of God, we could not come up with enough paper or ink to write it down. Look at what John wrote in *John 21:25 And there are also many other things which Jesus did, the which, if they should be written every one, I suppose that even the world itself could not contain the books that should be written. Amen.* We will never know on this side of eternity what all the Lord has done. Start at Genesis *1:1* and read through *Revelation 22:21* and record all the mighty acts God performed for the world in the written word of God. Recall your own personal book about yourself. What has God performed in your life? The mightiest act done for all mankind is when God sacrificed His Son on the cross that we might be saved. Whether you accept that or not is up to you. You see, even if you reject the plan of salvation, it was still a mighty act. We are to praise Him for His **_excellent_** greatness. Not just greatness, but excellent greatness. Excellent in a sense of it cannot get any better or cannot be surpassed in any way. Satan himself tried to exalt himself above God and he was put in his place for it. That alone is worthy of our praise. I have tried after several devotions to leave you with something to think about and this is no exception. Will you praise God for His mighty acts and His excellent greatness because you truly believe in them? Do you not praise God because you do not think much of His mighty acts or His excellent greatness? Usually the reason God cannot do something wonderful in the life of a believer is not because God will not do them. It is a lack of willingness on our part to let Him use us. Praise God when we are in His will and He performs mighty acts and excellent greatness in and through us.

May 31

Psalm 150:3
Praise him with the sound of the trumpet:
praise him with the psaltery and harp.

We are back again to praising God with musical instruments. Let us look briefly at these two particular instruments. The trumpet can put out a very loud sound. That is good, we want God to hear our praise. Other than a lot of noise what has the trumpet been used for in scripture? In *Exodus 19* the trumpet was used to indicate when it was time to come to the base of Mt. Sinai where God would meet with the people. In *Leviticus 25* the trumpet was used to indicate the year of jubilee when all the people were set free from bondage or slavery and were returned with their possessions to their families. In *Numbers 10* trumpets were used for communication. The sound of the trumpet indicated who should gather. It could mean the entire congregation was to assemble, only the princes were to assemble, or a particular camp was to gather. Remember in *Joshua 6* where the trumpet was used to get everyone shouting at the same time. The people all shouted in unison and the walls of Jericho came tumbling down. There are lots of examples of the trumpet. The psaltery is translated as more than one instrument. A psaltery may be a stringed instrument such as a lyre to a harp. The psaltery and the harp are both mentioned as preceding prophesy in I Samuel 10. The harp has been used for various occasions. In I Samuel 16 the harp was used to get rid of an evil spirit in Saul. The harp was used to soothe others and to praise the Lord because of its sweet melodious sound. There is quite a contrast in our devotional verse between trumpets, psalteries, and harps. You go from a very loud instrument to a very soft sounding instrument. Not everyone can pick up these three instruments and play them. Only those who have been trained and practice can use them for how they were intended. People are a lot like instruments as we are all different. The key to praising the Lord is not the instrument we use, but how we use the instrument. God desires our praise, so as His instrument, allow yourself to be used for praise and for His glory. God will keep you in tune!

June 1

Psalm 150:4
Praise him with the timbrel and dance:
praise him with stringed instruments and organs.

We continue on with more musical instruments aiding in the praise of God. Only now there is dance mixed in with it. If you read *Psalm 150* in its entirety you can sense the enthusiasm, and with every verse the excitement heightens. I can remember going to a jail ministry with a friend. We took hymnbooks along just in case our "captive" audience wanted to sing. The first song we sang there were only two people singing. The second song you could faintly hear a couple of prisoners singing along. The third song you could actually hear several singing out. By the time we finished singing everyone had joined in. That is exactly what it should be like when we come together for praise with music. Maybe the song starts out soft, then little by little other instruments join in, and finally the people start singing. Last of all the cymbals come crashing together at the end. I guess praise is like music that has been composed. Every instrument has its part to play, but if it is not done at the right time it would sound awful. The instruments need to keep rhythm and stay in time. As a human how can we keep time? By praising all the time. How do we maintain rhythm? By living a life that is pleasing to God. Keep rhythm, stay in time, and praise God.

June 2

Psalm 150:5
Praise him upon the loud cymbals:
praise him upon the high sounding cymbals.

Here is the grand finale of the instruments in this *Psalm 150*. The musicians have really stepped it up for the Lord. There are dancers with timbrels indicating the presence of the Holy Spirit. The praise has reached its peak and it cannot get any better than this. For good measure, the Psalmist includes the high sounding cymbals. I would suggest that the musicians began to bang them together even louder. The event happening here in *Psalm 150:4* is what ought to happen at our own church and in our own home. People should participate and start applauding. The applause is not for the song leaders or the musicians, but for God. There is nothing wrong with giving someone a hand for a song that was played or sung beautifully. The person performing knows who the praise goes to, but there is nothing wrong with applauding a gift being used to praise the Lord. I do not know if anyone has truly arrived in the area of praise, but some do try and work on their praise every chance they get. It would be wonderful if at the climax of a song we could grasp that feeling of praise and hang on to it.

I know of only one way we could get to that point and that would come through participating. Instruments and musicians are the same way. An instrument left alone can do nothing, as they require someone's hands to play them. Musicians can use an instrument for praise or for other reasons. Turn on the television or radio and you would see that not all music is for the praise of God. We are in the same boat as an instrument. Our bodies as an instrument can be used for praise or we can allow ourselves to be used for things not to be spoken of or mentioned in this book. Make a decision to only listen to Christian music for just thirty days and see if it does not have a profound affect on you. I did just that and it makes a difference. Our grandson asked us once, "Grandma does your radio only play Jesus music"? Our answer was, "Yes our radio will play anything, but we choose Jesus"!

June 3

Psalm 150:6
Let every thing that hath breath
praise the LORD. Praise ye the LORD.

The entire book of the Psalms is filled with praises to God. *Psalm 150* is the closing of the Psalms. It is only fitting that the last verse in the book of Psalms devotes itself to the praise of the Lord. I have mentioned this previously, but everything that can still fog a mirror needs to praise the Lord. I do not understand how beasts, cattle, and creeping things can do so, but it is not up to me to figure it out. I think the bottom line is to take this verse and read it alongside *Psalm 34:1 I will bless the LORD at all times: his praise shall continually be in my mouth.* Tie the two verses together and see that everything that breathes is to praise the lord continually. To continually be in praise to the Lord requires a starting point. You cannot continue to praise if you have never started to praise. I can only offer up suggestions to help you praise the LORD. Is there anything you need to ask forgiveness for. He just might give a lengthy list if we stop and ask. Stay prayed up, (repentant), as to be clean in His sight. Praise is to be offered up willingly and with a clean heart. The final four words of the book of the Psalms are very fitting to close out on, *{Praise ye the Lord}*. He will bless you for it!

June 4

Proverbs 27:2
Let another man praise thee, and not thine
own mouth; a stranger, and not thine own lips.

This Proverb is pretty clear in what it is saying here. We would be better off if we received the praise of men instead of boasting of ourself to other men. Be certain of what you are being praised for. I am sure Satan has on more than one occasion thought someone committed a particular sin and was worthy of applause for it. Let me list some scripture that touches on wanting the praise of men over the praise of God. *Matthew 6:2 Therefore when thou doest thine alms, do not sound a trumpet before thee, as the hypocrites do in the synagogues and in the streets, that they may have glory of men. Verily I say unto you, They have their reward.* Other references are *Matthew 6:5 and 6:16*. Even when you do the work of God it is better to be silent about it. If someone praises you for a job well done and it is pleasing to God, then praise God for the praise. I did not say throw a tickertape parade and get on a soap box and declare you just did something good. *Matthew 6:4* says God will reward you openly so do not worry about making what you do a public matter. Concentrate on praising God for the praise we sometimes receive. Another verse shows what the religious leaders chose over God. *John 12:43 For they loved the praise of men more than the praise of God.* The praise of men and fifty cents may or may not buy you a cup of coffee. There is nothing wrong with a pat on the back, but do not make that your reason to serve and to praise. Praise is really reserved for the one that received <u>stripes on His back</u> over the one who received a <u>pat on the back</u>.

June 5

Proverbs 27:21
As the fining pot for silver, and the furnace
for gold; so is a man to his praise.

As most of you know there is only one way to purify silver and gold. You must put the heat to it and bring the impurities to the surface. The comparison of a fining pot for silver and the furnace for gold is used to compare a man to his praise. If a man does a job well and receives praise for it, how does that affect his attitude and actions? Does he pass the praise on to God, or does he take the glory on to himself? When a man is praised and he becomes more thankful to God, more respectful to his friends, more watchful against what can blemish his reputation, diligent about improving himself, and doing good for others, he is considered a wise and a good man. Not a wise and good man compared to the world but compared to the word of God. If we are mindful of what we are doing and accept the praise of men, we must quickly pass it on to God. Be thankful for praise you may receive for a job well done. May you hear at the end of this life, *"well done thou good and faithful servant"*.

June 6

Proverbs 28:4
They that forsake the law praise the wicked:
but such as keep the law contend with them.

I understand we do not have to keep the law in order to receive salvation. The word law in this verse is torah, meaning instructions or directions, not salvation. Jesus said, *"if ye love me keep my commandments", John 14:15*. There are some instructions in God's word that are for our good and need to be followed. For example, God's word says to lay aside several things in order that it would benefit us. *Colossian 3:8-9 But now ye also put off all these; anger, wrath, malice, blasphemy, filthy communication out of your mouth. 9) Lie not one to another, seeing that ye have put off the old man with his deeds.* If we fail one of these simple requests listed in *Colossians 2:8-9* it does not mean we will lose our salvation. We do however, lose our witness for Jesus Christ by disobeying what God's word says. When we willingly disobey God's word the verse says we praise the wicked. It sounds harsh, but that is the way it is. The wicked do not have any trouble praising one another over a sin they have committed perfectly. The problem is when those who are saved by the blood of Jesus Christ participate in the same sin. We not only make a fool of ourselves, we mock God. Let me give you a verse about mocking God. *Galatians 6:7 Be not deceived; God is not mocked: for whatsoever a man soweth, that shall he also reap.* Are you having trouble praising the Lord? Consider who you are hanging around with or hanging on to. If you spend all your time with those who love to break the laws of God then there is a possibility that is what your life will consist of. If you spend a lot of time with the brethren, discussing the things of God, then your life will probably be more fruitful. We all must decide whom we will serve. What says it best is *Matthew 6:24* and *Luke 16:13 No servant can serve two masters: for either he will hate the one, and love the other; or else he will hold to the one, and despise the other. Ye cannot serve God and mammon.* Are you clinging with the ungodly? It is very possible to turn out just like who you follow. Are you following Jesus Christ, living His commandments, and praising the Lord? Do not be guilty of running with dogs that you should not be running with. Doing the same thing over and over again and continually getting bad results, yet expecting good results, is the definition of insanity.

June 7

Proverbs 31:31
Give her of the fruit of her hands;
and let her own works praise her in the gates.

This is the description of a virtuous woman of **those days**, but inspirationally is suited to every woman of every age and nation. On a side note, when you see the two words **those days**, you have a glimpse of the tribulation period that is coming for unbelievers. This woman is careful to give herself over to her husband's love and affection, to know his mind, and is willing that he rule over her. She can be trusted, so he will trust such a wife to manage for him. She makes it her constant business to do him good. She takes pains in her duties and takes pleasure in them. She is a redeemer of time as she rises early. When is a better time to seek God than early? She does what she does to the best of her ability. She is also given over to providing well for her house. Above all, she fears the Lord. Beauty on the outside does not indicate wisdom and goodness, but it has probably deceived many men who made his choice of a wife because of her outward looks. The fear of God reigning in the heart is the beauty of the soul and it lasts forever. She is a great blessing to all those who are around her. The book of James is filled with comparisons of those who talk about doing good and those who do good. Talk is cheap, but good works are of eternal value. *James 2:18 Yea, a man may say, Thou hast faith, and I have works: show me thy faith without thy works, and I will show thee my faith by my works.* We have an awesome description of a special and virtuous woman. This special woman should be an example of what the body of Christ should be like. A body of believers praising the Lord by their actions and conduct, and not with vain and foolish talking. Let me paraphrase what James said, "You say you have faith, but I will show thee my faith. You say you have works, but you can see me working". My wife Beverly is not only a believer, but she is also a picture for me of this very same virtuous woman in this *Proverbs 31*. Praise God for virtuous women and men. Praise the Lord every chance you get for who you are in Jesus. May your actions speak a whole lot louder than words.

June 8

Isaiah 12:1
And in that day thou shalt say, O LORD,
I will praise thee: though thou wast angry with me,
thine anger is turned away, and thou comfortedst me.

This is about as sober of a verse as we can probably find. What a sad state of affairs of God being mad at us. We need to evaluate our life daily and make sure there is no reason why God should be ticked at us. We should never have any cause to be mad at God for what He does and refuse to praise

Him. As the verse puts it, God's anger is turned away and then the Father does the comforting. There are many things that take place that none of us will ever understand. The issue is not that we do not understand what God is doing, but there are certain things God may choose not to reveal to anyone. Our lack of understanding does not dictate what God does. It would be awful if there was something God needed to do and couldn't. Did God think we would not understand? Look at what scripture says about the wicked and their lack of understanding, *Isaiah 55:8 For my thoughts are not your thoughts, neither are your ways my ways, saith the LORD.* Praise God that His ways can only be spiritually discerned. Praise God as the Holy Spirit allows us spiritual insight into what is going on. The important issue of this verse is God's continual act of extending grace to us through His comfort. We praise God because of His grace that resulted in a pardon of sin, a turning away of His anger, and finally ending in comfort. The kind of comfort God gives is what the world will never understand. *Philippians 4:7 And the peace of God, which passeth all understanding, shall keep your hearts and minds through Christ Jesus.* The theme is praise so please consider if God's comfort, mercy, and grace He extends to us daily makes Him worthy of our praise, service, and attention.

June 9

Isaiah 12:4
And in that day shall ye say, Praise the LORD,
call upon his name, declare his doings among the people,
make mention that his name is exalted.

Eventually we will be living in a time when Jesus Christ is sitting on the throne as our King for eternity. And in that day, we shall say, *"praise the Lord, call upon his name, declare his doings among the people, make mention that his name is exalted"*. When two or more believers come together to fellowship, the topic usually turns to the Lord in some way or another. When someone asks what the Lord is doing in your life, we ought to be able to give an answer. I have found that the best of relationships between a believer and a non-believer can only go so deep. The relationship between the two reminds me of a countertop in any given kitchen. Once you get beneath the vinyl, ceramic, wood, or tile covering there is not much to look at or talk about. Praise God that we can proclaim the goodness of His name to each other. Praise God we can exalt the works He has performed in and through us. Praise God we can even call upon His name at any time and for any reason. I fully trust that God is monitoring everything going on right here on earth. It has to be especially pleasing to God as our Abba, (Daddy), to hear His children praise Him. It is not like God speaks audibly and says, "it's time to praise me, drop whatever you are doing and say nice things about me". God desires our praise, but it must be genuine, and I think even spontaneous would be good. I mention spontaneous because we do not always need a song leader in front of us to praise God. There is a time for structured praise and there is a time to praise without any structure. Some of the best praise from me comes when I am driving down the road and all alone in the car or on my motorcycle. On a motorcycle I would suggest not opening your mouth too wide. Consider why you should praise God and then praise Him for those reasons. Let me make your list easier to make and shorter. The only item you need to record on your list is Jesus Christ. That alone merits our praise for our "Abba", our DADDY.

June 10

Isaiah 25:1
O LORD, thou art my God; I will exalt thee,
I will praise thy name; for thou hast done wonderful things; thy counsels of old are faithfulness and truth.

The last verse of the chapter preceding this one, *Isaiah 24:23*, tells of the Lord Jesus Christ reigning on the throne in Zion and Jerusalem. It also points to the deliverance of the Jews out of captivity, which would solicit praise from Israel to God. For us, we look ahead at what is coming down the road. We will do just as this verse says, *we will praise his name for the wonderful things He has done*. God will have spiritual victory over our enemies. He has been a comforter from *Genesis 1:1* and He will be a comforter until *Revelation 22:21*. Many times we talk of the deliverance God provided for Israel from their enemies. We need to remember the deliverance from God in our own individual life. God sent His son who died for us that we could be delivered from Hell. The key word in this verse is "things" making it plural. I want to pause and remind you of a verse I have already used in this book, *John 21:25 And there are also many other things which Jesus did, the which, if they should be written every one, I suppose that even the world itself could not contain the books that should be written. Amen.* If we had all the books that recorded everything He has done, I wonder how many chapters would be yours or mine? It is best said in our verse for today. We are to exalt God and praise His name. Our praise is offered up to God for victories over spiritual enemies, and the comfort that He has provided. There are no "things" that God cannot deliver us from!

June 11

Isaiah 38:18
For the grave cannot praise thee,
death cannot celebrate thee: they that go down
into the pit cannot hope for thy truth.

King Hezekiah is the man who appreciates praise here in this verse. He had some things to be grateful for. First, he was sick unto death and God gave him fifteen more years to live. Second, his enemy Assyria surrounded him, and God told him through the Prophet Isaiah, I will deliver you from your enemy. Compare the situation of Hezekiah with ours today. One, we have an enemy also, (the grave), where praise will not be. Two, a pit is mentioned, and I cannot help but to think anyone thrown in a pit was not celebrating triumphantly. We praise God today because death no longer has a hold on anyone who has trusted in Jesus Christ. The grave has lost its sting for the believer, *I Corinthians 15:55-57 55) O death, where is thy sting? O grave, where is thy victory? 56)The sting of death is sin; and the strength of sin is the law. 57)But thanks be to God, which giveth us the victory through our Lord Jesus Christ.* The verse mentions death and celebration. For all who have rejected Jesus Christ and accepted Hell as their home with Satan as their king, there is no celebrating and no hope. There is celebration only in life and not in death. Only a life filled with Jesus Christ can bring praise to God. The lost are not praising the Lord, it is reserved for the believer. Are you praising God because your life is abundantly filled with the Holy Spirit? If praise is not a part of your life, then you will have to decide what else you may be filled with? Those who have trusted Jesus as their Saviour will never see death and that merits praise.

June 12

Isaiah 38:19
The living, the living, he shall praise thee,
as I do this day: the father to the children shall make
known thy truth.

This is the only place in scripture where the words "the living" are repeated back-to-back. King Hezekiah is the subject at hand in this verse. Do you sense the excitement in this verse? This is not a verse that was spoken in monotone. I would say by the time this verse is finished there is no doubt that Hezekiah is filled with jubilee. Picture a King in his royal apparel and rejoicing over the fact that he would be praising his King, (God the Father). Hezekiah thought he was going to die. He prayed to God and God gave him fifteen more years. Is all this hype and commotion over the fact he was given fifteen more years? I told you, *Psalm 34:1 I will bless the LORD at all times: his praise shall continually be in my mouth,* must be the key verse for this book. The key to praise is living to continually praise the Lord. We live for the Lord so we can praise the Lord. If enthusiasm is what you lack, then consider how Jesus took your place on the cross, bearing all your sins, dying, and spending three days in the grave for you. If that does not bring immediate jubilation, then spiritually there is something major wrong. Please head directly to *John 3:16, Romans 10:9-10,* and on to *Romans 10:13*. After those 3 references take a stop at *Ephesians 2:8-9*. Consider all the verses you just read and then pray to be saved if you do not believe you are. If what Jesus did for you does not motivate you, then my friend you are not saved, you are LOST! Hezekiah rejoiced because he had more time to praise the Lord and live. Does anyone out there know exactly how much longer they will live? Every breath we have is only borrowed. No one knows when they leave the house or get out of bed just how many minutes or seconds they have left. I would hope that while I am still living, that some of my time is reserved only for God, Jesus, and the Holy Spirit.

June 13

Isaiah 42:8
I am the LORD: that is my name: and my glory will I not give to another, neither my praise to graven images.

Exodus 34:14 For thou shalt worship no other god: for the LORD, whose name is Jealous, is a jealous God: I could think of no other way to get into our devotional verse today without going to *Exodus 34:14*. God's desire is that we praise Him. We do not need to go to any graven image to get the praise to the Lord. Any image whether gold, silver, wood, or plastic cannot receive praise because they are dead things. None of God's glory is to be placed upon any statue. The only glory God placed upon anything or anyone else was His son Jesus. What good would it do for God to shine upon an idol? God's desire is for us to praise Him and in return He sends the praise back to us. Why would He allow praise to rain on His people? One, because He loves us and two, because the praise we receive from Him is praise we can send back to Him. We are to be Christ-like, and Jesus Christ lived to serve, honor, and praise His Father. Christ had the opportunity to bow down to Satan and receive all the kingdoms of the world. What was Christ's reply you ask, *Matthew 4:8-10 8) Again, the devil taketh him up into an exceeding high mountain, and showeth him all the kingdoms of the world, and the glory of them; 9) And saith unto him, All these things will I give thee, if thou wilt fall down and worship me. 10) Then saith Jesus unto him, Get thee hence, Satan: for it is written, Thou shalt worship the Lord thy God, and him only shalt thou serve.* Jesus would not bow down to Satan and neither should we. Do not give Satan any answer other than "it is written". Christ would not worship or praise any idols, and neither should we. Christ reserved his praise for His Father alone and so should we. If praise for God alone was good enough for Jesus it is good enough for us.

June 14

Isaiah 42:10
Sing unto the LORD a new song, and his praise from the end of the earth, ye that go down to the sea, and all that is therein; the isles, and the inhabitants thereof.

Let me start your thinking by pointing out that the same word used for new is also translated as fresh. New is correct here, especially if you consider the new song that the Gentiles can and will sing. Not only can the Jews celebrate being God's children, but us good old Gentiles can celebrate right alongside of them. We have a NEW song we can sing because we have a NEW TESTAMENT! Praise will be from one end of the earth to the other, across the deepest sea, and every island along the way. All inhabitants can praise the Lord if they choose to. The reason for mentioning the word fresh, is it comes from the same word translated new. We have a fresh new song to sing, because when Jesus came and died for the entire world, we received a fresh new song. Jesus Christ is the fresh new song we can sing about. Another thought to consider is that we have a fresh new song to sing because until Jesus Christ came and revealed God's plan for salvation through Him this new song was not being sung. The Old Testament points out over and over again to the coming of Jesus Christ. It points to the King coming and reigning. The rubber met the road when Jesus Christ was born. Here is another example possibly easier to understand. The same Bible points over and over to the Second Coming of Jesus Christ. Believers all over the world know it and preach it. However, until Christ raptures out the Church, and sets up His kingdom, the rubber has not completely met the road. We know it will happen, and we should look expectantly for it to happen, but it still needs to happen. In the meantime, praise God for His book that revealed to all of us a new song that we can sing because of what Jesus did on the cross. If He can willingly die, we can willingly sing. Jesus did not come yesterday, but He might come today or tomorrow!

June 15

Isaiah 42:12
Let them give glory unto the LORD,
and declare his praise in the islands.

The best way I know how to start out here is to figure out who the "them" is in this verse. Back in verse 11 of this same chapter the villages of Kedar are mentioned and now in this verse the islands are mentioned. Kedar is located to the east of Jerusalem. The islands would be to the west of Jerusalem. That being the case, then praise would begin at the rising of the sun, and would not stop till the setting of the sun. We have already touched on verses where everything that has breath will praise the Lord in some way. Inspirationally the whole world should be praising the Lord during the waking hours of the day. Are you working nights? That is okay, God will accept your praise anytime you choose to offer it up. Let me give you something to picture in your mind. Most people have seen what is called a "wave" taking place in a stadium during some type of sporting event. One group of people jump to their feet, raise their hands in excitement, sit down, and is followed by the person to their right doing the exact same thing, and continues until everyone in the stadium has participated. Imagine praise around the world being done in the same way. The praise starts in the USA, heads to Europe, over to Australia, on to China, over to Russia, and right back to the USA. The praise does not stop until it goes completely around the world and reaches America again. Then that same wave is repeated and that is what God desires. Praise must start somewhere. Wouldn't it be nice to know praise started with you?

June 16

Isaiah 43:21
This people have I formed for myself;
they shall show forth my praise.

Let us look at "this people" as it is recorded in two different manners. The first people I mentioned is Israel. God initially chose them to be His people. The Jews were to praise Him for that. Israel has a Bible that records everything God did for them in bringing them from under the captivity of Pharaoh to a land He had promised them. A land that was flowing with milk and honey. A land they would eat from, be nourished by, and yet they had never planted a seed to grow the food. God's word here says they shall show forth my praise. Are the Gentiles off the hook then when it comes to praise? God formed another group of people along the way. They were called the people of the church. God formed the church when He offered up His Son to die on the cross. People from countless generations have had the opportunity to accept Jesus as their Saviour and become a responsible member of a New Testament Church that God instituted. In considering all that, eventually Jew and Gentile alike will come together in one place and unite in praise to the King. We will see a New Jerusalem and a New Heaven where Jew and Gentile alike will come together and praise God.

June 17

Isaiah 48:9
For my name's sake will I defer mine anger, and for my praise will I refrain for thee, that I cut thee not off.

Israel had turned their back on God, and they were put under Babylonian captivity. If Israel had received what they deserved God would have never let them return to rebuild Jerusalem. They would have stayed in Babylon, rotted and died, if it were not for the mercy and grace of God. God deferred His anger according to our verse here and cast forth what He casts forth best. He extended mercy to the fullest. God could not cut them off because He loved them. They were His chosen people and God did not want them in captivity. He wanted them to praise Him. They were placed in captivity because of their constant disobedience and for the purpose of changing them. I would like to think that when Israel was removed from captivity there was some praise going on. That is what happens when the chains that restrain us are removed. Not to beat up on Israel alone, we must look at our own bondage. Before we met Jesus, we had chains on us. The chains that held us in bondage to sin, the grave, and ultimately hell. The good news is God broke those chains that held us. We are so blessed that God did not give us what we deserve. He extended the same grace and mercy to the Gentiles as He did for the Jews. God came to the earth in the flesh, (Jesus Christ), and placed all past, present, and future sins upon Jesus and took them to the cross. When Jesus Christ gave up the ghost, spent three days in the grave, and then rose again, the chains of bondage were broken for all who will accept His death for atonement of sin. Here is the deal, picture Christ as a key. You can accept Him as Lord, (Saviour), and let Him remove the lock and chain of sin. You can reject Him and be burdened with sin and carry it by yourself. The only one who has a key to the lock of your sin is Jesus. It is a master key and only He possesses it. Here are a couple of thoughts for your final consideration of praise. Are you praising the Lord because He has set you free from bondage? Are you not praising the Lord because you have never been set free? Have you asked to be set free through Jesus Christ, yet you have allowed sin to drag you down where you cannot praise? Saved or not, God still extends mercy and grace. Simply ask for it and then praise Him for it. Back in Israel's time of captivity it would not be uncommon to be stripped naked, chained together in a row, and a hook placed through your nose to get your attention. Ever had a hook run through your nose to get your attention? It would definitely have a way of bringing about submissiveness. God's desire is to remove the hook and gain our obedience. What would be easier? Fighting a hook in your nose or praising the Lord for the removal of the hook through Jesus. Sounds like a simple question but look around. There are a lot of people fighting the hook and not praising God. For those of you who enjoy fishing, you may know some who remove the barb from their hooks so they can release the fish unharmed. Without a barb on a hook it can be easily removed. In some places when fishing for trout it is even required you remove the barb. Not to go on, but that same hook is what God wants to remove if you are lost or have not been born again. Accepting Jesus Christ is painless. Accept Jesus Christ today and God will remove the barbs off the hook. What I have pictured for you is the fact that the sin we cling to is the barb on the hook. Let God remove the barb of sin by way of Jesus Christ with your repentance today.

June 18

Isaiah 60:18
Violence shall no more be heard in thy land, wasting nor destruction within thy borders; but thou shalt **call thy walls Salvation**, and thy gates Praise.

I have seen enough in the news about Israel to know that they are not experiencing this kind of peace yet. I do not know the exact time this peace will take place, but I do know it is coming. Look to the east expectantly for it. Let me ask you a question; do you ever get sick and tired of the violence taking place around the world? I know I get to the place where I hate to turn the television or radio on. You know it will be ninety-nine percent bad news and one percent sports and weather. There is a day coming for the body of Christ, (the Church), when there is no violence. Christ will have set up His throne and the walls of Salvation will stand for eternity to protect us. There are walls named Salvation, and these walls can never be torn down. When God puts something up it is perfect, and it is forever. We have walls of Salvation and gates of praise. What other kind of gate could there be on the walls of Salvation? There cannot be sin swinging on the walls of Salvation. I always believed there is an attachment of gratefulness to salvation as you grow in Jesus Christ. You enter the gates of praise to worship the Lord of the walls of Salvation. I always go back to a particular thought. How can you be saved and not appear to have an ounce of praise or service? I try and understand how, but I have not been successful yet. Let me share a personal note with you. I still remember when Jesus Christ really became Lord after I was saved. I was in a pickup headed south on Highway 71 out of Grandview, Missouri. God laid on my heart to consider everything Jesus Christ went through during His last twenty-four hours before going to the cross. I still remember crying in gratitude for what Jesus did and it lasted for the next seventy miles. My friend, that is when my walls of salvation became real and my gratitude for His suffering became gates of praise. Picture this, the Holy city has been established and Jesus Christ is on the throne, and nothing but believers in your presence. It will be paradise like we cannot imagine. We may have some head knowledge of what we think it may be like, but head knowledge is simply head knowledge. There is nothing like personal experience to fully know what something will be like. The day is fast approaching so let us all begin to praise Him today. Our homes have gates we call doors. Does praise permeate your doors?

June 19

Isaiah 61:3
To appoint unto them that mourn in Zion,
to give unto them beauty for ashes, the oil of joy
for mourning, the garment of praise for the spirit of
heaviness; that they might be called trees of righteousness,
the planting of the LORD, that he might be glorified.

There are a lot of things to look at in this verse, but I want to stick with the issue of praise. Praise is attached to a garment this time. God gives us a garment of praise when our spirit is heavy. He wraps His garment, (Holy Spirit), around us to comfort us. Jesus said he would send a Comforter in *John 16:7 Nevertheless I tell you the truth; It is expedient for you that I go away: for if I go not away, the Comforter will not come unto you; but if I depart, I will send him unto you.* All of us should understand that there are times when things are just not going to go the way we would want them to. The thing we need to do is harness our feelings and maintain control of them. Do not let feelings harness and dictate how we act. Job had tribulation more than any of us will. He lost everything near and dear to him. Look how Job handled his situation in *Job 1:21 And said, Naked came I out of my mother's womb, and naked shall I return thither: the LORD gave, and the LORD hath taken away; blessed be the name of the LORD.* In the worst possible affliction of his life, he praised the Lord. Did he hurt clear to the depth of his soul? More than likely, but he knew who to put his trust in. We are so fortunate to be living in New Testament days. In Old Testament days the Holy Spirit came **upon** man and was temporary. In New Testament days that we now live in the Holy Spirit permanently **dwells in** the believer. We always have a Comforter dwelling within us. We need to call upon Him and then bask in His comfort. Please do not misunderstand me by thinking I believe there will not be a time when things may get very difficult or hectic for us physically and spiritually. What I do want you to understand is how much worse it must be for unbelievers in similar situations and having to deal with problems on their own. They have no garment, no protection, no comfort, and no praise. Even a baby or young child has a favorite blanket, and they take it everywhere they go. We are to approach God's throne with a child-like faith. Everywhere a believer goes, he brings a garment, a blanket of security, and the Holy Spirit wrapped around you. Praise God for the garment. Consider that there was a high price paid for your garment.

The garment you received because you asked Jesus to save you is not from a cheap clearance rack. This garment is clean and righteous because of Jesus Christ. Be reminded that there was a day when it was covered with the blood of Jesus because He loved us. Adam and Eve were covered with the glory of God in the garden, and they chose sin over it. The blood of Jesus Christ, (my garment of praise), covers me. Are you praising and serving the Lord for covering you with His garment? Praise God early and at the end of the day for the garment He freely gave, and we can freely accept. When is the last time you stopped everything you did, for the sole purpose of telling God I love you and thanks for the garment?

June 20

Isaiah 61:11
For as the earth bringeth forth her bud, and as the garden causeth the things that are sown in it to spring forth; so the Lord GOD will cause righteousness and praise to spring forth before all the nations.

It is important to go back and read *verse 10* of this Psalm before continuing. The issue is salvation in verse ten and that is important to understand before going over *verse eleven* today. We just finished up on the garment of praise and now in the same chapter we have more clothing listed for our adorning. In *Isaiah 61:10* we have a garment of salvation and a robe of righteousness. We are looking good in *verse 10*. We are compared in looks to a bridegroom all decked out with his ornaments and a bride with her jewels. On someone's wedding day, maybe that is the best someone looks. The bride strives for beauty in the eyes of her groom. The groom wants to be the most handsome man she has ever seen. With that out of the way turn your attention back to

Isaiah 61:11. Salvation is still the issue and God's word in *verse 11* compares it to the earth or a garden bringing forth new life. There will be a newness of life because of salvation, and it is offered to every nation with the results of praise springing forth from every nation. The word for nation can also be translated as people. Every nation, (person), can walk in newness of life by receiving God's salvation, and they can praise Him for it. I like the wording of this verse. God is going to cause righteousness and praise to spring forth. Before going any further let us look at *II Corinthians 5:17 Therefore if any man be in Christ, he is a new creature: old things are passed away; behold, all things are become new.* Only believers in Jesus Christ can understand the transformation process that takes place in one's life. You cannot explain a changed life you must experience it. No matter how mean a person is, Jesus Christ can change them. No human is too good or too bad that God cannot save them. The reason I use bold print for the word **cause** is because that is exactly what God does in the life of a new convert. You may not be able to explain the change, but God **causes** the transformation, and it should result in service and praise. Salvation was offered to every nation of the world. Christ did not just die for Israel. The United States is one of the greatest nations on the earth, but Christ did not just die for us living here. Every nation can praise because every nation has been offered salvation. What can be a better witnessing tool for Jesus than our praise? People need to see our praise spring forth and wonder why we are so happy. The alternative is to let a bad attitude spring forth all the time and let them witness that. Hopefully, people enjoy being around us. The only way for that to happen is to have some praise on our lips instead of an attitude on our face. By the way, it takes fewer muscles to praise the Lord than to frown with the world. Is your preference to praise or to frown? God already knows the answer. God already knows if we have been taking part in praise or not. Here is more good news; it is never too late to start to praise the One who saved us, so pass it on! God has allowed us to spring forth with a newness of life in Christ and be joyful for the change that is occurring in you. As flowers bloom in spring and are so beautiful, you can be that flower of beauty by how you reflect or illuminate Jesus Christ.

June 21

Isaiah 62:7
And give him no rest, till he establish,
and till he make Jerusalem a praise in the earth.

We think we get tired. How would you like to be in the Lord's shoes for a while. He requests in this verse that we give Him no rest. We are looking at Isaiah *62* and I would encourage you to go back and read the first seven verses together. Until we no longer have breath in us, we are to witness for the Lord. God's word tells us in *Isaiah 62:6 that there are watchmen upon the walls*. Watchmen of the walls in Isaiah's day had better not fall asleep doing their job. If someone approached a wall, they were usually the first to receive the message before it was passed on to a porter/gatekeeper. Ministers of the gospel are like watchmen upon a wall. Any time the gospel can be preached we are not to keep silent. Any time we can share the gospel we are not to be found sleeping. No one knows for certain when Jesus Christ is going to return. We do know that the Lord is not going to rest until praise is placed upon Jerusalem. That praise will not be placed fully upon Jerusalem until Jesus returns with His saints and establishes Himself on the throne as King. Eventually Judah, Jerusalem, and the Gentiles will be gathered around the throne of Jesus Christ praising Him for the New Jerusalem He has established. All that is the good news and here is the bad. If you have never trusted Jesus as your Saviour, you will not be there to witness it. You will be in a kingdom, but there will not be any praise. Instead of an excited "Wow" over Jerusalem, you will be screaming "Woe" in hell. Here is a little advice for anyone who has never prayed and asked Jesus to save their soul. The rapture of the church has not occurred yet, so you still have time to become a part of it. Hell is already done, and should you refuse to accept Jesus Christ you will become a part of it. The one requires a response, (accept Jesus Christ) as your Savior. The second requires you to do nothing, (reject Jesus Christ and accept a lake of fire), *Revelation 20:15 And whosoever was not found written in the book of life was cast into the lake of fire.* I leave you with two choices; you can praise, or you can perish. Sounds like a simple choice accepting Jesus, but sadly many will put it off until it is too late.

June 22

Isaiah 62:9
But they that have gathered it shall eat it
and praise the LORD; and they that have brought it
together shall drink it in the courts of my holiness.

We need to back up to the verse preceding this one and include it in our reading of our verse for today. Israel had a history of prospering, only to turn their back on God and worship everything except Him. The result was their enemies would take them down and remove everything of value from them including their food. Back and forth it would go. God would lead them out of captivity, Israel would mess up and go right back into captivity. Israel would again cry out in desperation when they realized God was the only One who could save them. The result was God would bail them out. If someone did us like we do God at times, we would not trust them for anything. God is a God of forgiveness and love. God is a God of mercy and forgiveness. God is a God that supplies all our needs. God is a God who can give abundantly more than we could ever hope or ask for. In time, we are not going to have enemies robbing us of what we have worked for. We are going to praise the Lord for the blessings He has given us. Speaking of blessings, I want to share something that came by way of E-mail to me and no clue who wrote it.

"I asked God to take away my pain. God said, No. It is not for me to take away, but for you to give it up. I asked God to make my handicapped child whole. God said, No. Her spirit was whole, her body was only temporary. I asked God to grant me patience. God said, No. Patience is a byproduct of tribulations, it isn't granted, it is learned. I asked God to give me happiness. God said, No. I give you blessings. Happiness is up to you. I asked God to spare me pain. God said, No. Suffering draws you apart from worldly cares and brings you closer to me. I asked God to make my spirit grow. God said, No. You must grow on your own, but I will prune you to make you fruitful. I asked for all things that I might enjoy life. God said, No. I will give you life so that you may enjoy all things. I ask God to help me LOVE others, as much as he loves me. God said...Ahhhh, finally you have the idea.

THIS DAY IS YOURS SO DON'T THROW IT AWAY
May God Bless you abundantly. Remember, to the world you might be just one person, but to one person you just might be the world." I only included the short story as a reminder that God knows what we need even before we ask, but we are to ask. Do not confuse wants with needs. God

unconditionally loves us and continually takes care of us. Is He worthy of your praise yet?

June 23

Jeremiah 13:11
For as the girdle cleaveth to the loins of a man, so have I caused to cleave unto me the whole house of Israel and the whole house of Judah, saith the LORD; that they might be unto me for a people, and for a name, and for a praise, and for a glory: but they would not hear.

Not every verse we have looked at has happy results and this verse is one of them. Make sure that you understand this girdle Jeremiah was to put on. What was this girdle made of and what could it have looked like? First off, both men and women from the east wore a girdle. It was commonly made of leather for durability. Examples of leather girdles are *II Kings 1:8* and *Matthew 3:4*. A finer girdle was made of linen, *Jeremiah 13:1* and *Ezekiel 16:10*. It was not uncommon to be embroidered with gold and silver thread, *Daniel 10:5, Revelation 1:13 and 15:6*. They were often studded with precious stones or pearls. When one girded up the loins it was commonly used to prepare for battle or active exertion. Did some things jump out at you of the description of a girdle? Does the gold and silver woven in the threads remind you of the deity of God, (gold), and the redemption of Jesus Christ, (silver)? Do the precious stones remind you of rewards given by God for a job well done for Him? Congratulations, it reminded me of the same thing. I went on about the girdle because it is the emphasis of *Jeremiah thirteen*, which is where we are. Jeremiah was to go and hide the girdle at the river Euphrates. Later God told him to dig it up and check it out. The girdle was marred to the point of uselessness. The Lord told Jeremiah that His people had become like that marred girdle. Now we go back to the description of the girdle and use what we have learned. Girdles can be intertwined with gold and silver. Those who trust in the Lord are intertwined with gold and silver, (God's deity and redemption). Girdles can be studded with precious stones or pearls. Every time someone rejects Jesus as their Saviour, they throw away the precious stones and pearls. Every time we reject rendering service for Jesus, we pluck off one of the stones and pearls and cast it down and lose rewards. God's desire for the entire human race is that we would accept Him, hear Him, and obey Him. We are girded up as believers with the Holy Spirit. God wanted Israel to be recognized and respected by the entire world. He wanted to rain His praises upon them. Israel missed the praises from the Lord by worshipping idols and turning away from Him. Israel became a marred girdle of no use. What a sad state of affairs for an entire race of people. God turned to the Gentiles by way of Jesus Christ. Many times, Christians have been no better than Israel in Jeremiah thirteen. There have been a lot of people who have rejected Jesus Christ and kept wearing a marred girdle. There have been believers who have compromised their walk with the Lord and turned to sin. A beautiful linen and silk girdle became marred, and the praise of God stopped with it. There is good news for someone who has backslid into sin. Repent and God will clean up your girdle. For the lost, repent, and God will give you a clean girdle. In both cases we can wear our girdle the same way a soldier would. It would be girded up so we can serve easily and actively participate in God's plan for our life. When a soldier girded up his loins, he was serious about what he was doing. He was preparing for battle. As believers we are to stay prepared for battle, and it is a spiritual battle. Are there occasional casualties? There are casualties only if God allows it.

June 24

Jeremiah 17:14
Heal me, O LORD, and I shall be healed;
save me, and I shall be saved: for thou art my praise.

Let us look first at the word heal. The word for heal is rapha', pronounced raw-faw. It means to mend by stitching, to cure, heal, repair thoroughly, and to make whole. What does God do when He saves us? He does everything I just listed. Jeremiah does not say heal me so-and-so. He says heal me O Lord. Jeremiah says heal me O Lord, and I shall be healed. Is it just me or is their confidence in Jeremiah's words here? Jeremiah says, "*save me and I shall be saved*". Are you thinking we might have a glimpse of the salvation of the New Testament in front of us? For me it sounds like Jeremiah is saying, "*Lord heal me and save me because I love thee*". Have you ever said, "*Lord heal me and save me because I love thee*"? Jeremiah says it because the Lord is his praise. You must think that when someone gets healed of sin and saved from hell that praise is forthcoming. How can we not praise God when we were offered forgiveness of sin and deliverance from hell. How in the world, (if you have any kind of an idea of what hell will be like), could anyone not praise God for rescuing you from it? I want to share another thought with you about praise. Back in verse 8 of *Jeremiah 17* trees are mentioned. They are described as flourishing if they are planted by the water. As an avid hunter, I have walked many a creeks and streams, and noticed tree roots down in the water. Even in the driest of times if a tree can get those roots in the water it will flourish.

With water as an example of the word, (Bible), we can plunge our roots into the living word of God, and we will flourish, and we will praise God for it. You take a tree away from water, especially an oak tree, and beetles will bore into the bark and destroy it. Those beetles are a type of sin. We stay away from the water, (the word), and there will be no flourishing and no praise.

June 25

Jeremiah 17:26
And they shall come from the cities of Judah, and from the places about Jerusalem, and from the land of Benjamin, and from the plain, and from the mountains, and from the south, bringing burnt offerings, and sacrifices, and meat offerings, and incense, and bringing sacrifices of praise, unto the house of the LORD.

People from all over were coming to offer up sacrifices in the house of the Lord. The sacrifices came when people sought forgiveness for sin. People in Old Testament times sought forgiveness through a sacrifice. People in the New Testament seek forgiveness for sin as well, but a different sacrifice. There is a difference between the Old Testament and the New Testament sacrifices for sure. Old Testament people used a four-legged lamb with wool that they raised, and we use the Lamb of God that God raised. Let me share an interesting note about sacrifices being attached to praise. I like looking in a Strong's concordance or other sources in order to see other uses of a word. This sacrifice of praise is also associated with confession. With that in mind read the verse over again. People came to bring a sacrifice of acceptance to the Lord. Would anyone think that by simply bringing a lamb or a bullock for a sacrifice with the wrong motives would be acceptable? They could have killed lambs until there were none left to sacrifice, but if no one asked for forgiveness of their sins, it could not be an acceptable sacrifice. Right animal, wrong motive, *II Corinthians 9:7 Every man according as he purposeth in his heart, so let him give; not grudgingly, or of necessity: for God loveth a cheerful giver.* There is one big obstacle in every believer's life that will hinder bringing their praise into the house of the Lord. It is bringing sin into the camp and trying to praise. The time to confess sin is not right before the song leader strikes the first note. The time to confess sin is before we ever leave the house and enter the parking lot of the house of the Lord. God wants us to bring our sacrifice of praise, but we are to bring it in a clean vessel. I am not alluding to a car or shiny motorcycle. That clean vessel is your body being used by God. The Lord did not think much of a cup that was clean on the outside, but dirty on the inside, *Luke 11:39 And the Lord said unto him, Now do ye Pharisees make clean the outside of the cup and the platter; but your inward part is full of ravening and wickedness.* Consider the religious Pharisees here. Would any sacrifice at this time have been acceptable? Absolutely NO! We can praise God as a Pharisee, or we can praise Him as one concerned with our relationship with Him. If you are not sure if you are prayed up about sin in your life, ask God to bring it to mind. If you do not want to know, do not ask as God will tell you everything you need to repent of.

June 26

Jeremiah 20:13
Sing unto the LORD, praise ye the LORD: for he hath delivered the soul of the poor from the hand of evildoers.

Jeremiah experienced some tough times in his service to God. He reminds me at times of what Paul the apostle went through. Jeremiah was locked up and placed in stocks. I am certain that Jeremiah was abused and got a little down a few times, which is understandable. None the less, God's word burned inside him, and he had to preach the truth. No matter what it would cost him he had to preach the truth. From those of the poorest of life and on to kings he would preach the truth. I wonder if he also understood what Paul wrote in *I Corinthians 9:22-23 22) To the weak became I as weak, that I might gain the weak: I am made all things to all men, that I might by all means save some. 23) And this I do for the gospel's sake, that I might be partaker thereof with you.* Jeremiah laid aside any possible pleasantries and concentrated on what God wanted him to do. Jeremiah knew there would be a day of deliverance from God, and he would praise Him for it. Look at what is said by Jesus in *Luke 12:5 But I will forewarn you whom ye shall fear: Fear him, which after he hath killed hath power to cast into hell; yea, I say unto you, Fear him.* It will be God in the Day of Judgment who will deliver the souls of the poor and oppressed out of the hands of evildoers, and they will praise Him for it. Here is what should be done. The poor and the wealthy should be praising God now for the deliverance from evil they have received. We have the word of God that tells us the way some things are going to be. We are going to be spending eternity praising God in a place of no sin and where time is no more. Praise God now for what is coming soon.

Praise God now for what is going on presently. Praise God for what He has already done, is doing, and will do in your life. Permanent deliverance is available only because of the hands of Jesus Christ. Wouldn't it be awesome to be praising God when the rapture takes place? Better start praising now as it could be today?

June 27

Jeremiah 31:7
For thus saith the LORD; Sing with gladness for Jacob, and shout among the chief of the nations: publish ye, praise ye, and say, O LORD, save thy people, the remnant of Israel.

I will look at this verse as a prayer of the saints that could be used today. One of the most important prayers we can make is for the souls of the unbelieving. Do you ever find yourself asking God to save those who are around you? Do you pray for your family members to come to a saving knowledge and acceptance of Jesus Christ? I understand that the context of this verse is God in relationship to Israel, but we can be inspired by every verse of the Bible. God offered up His Son to everyone who would receive Him as their Saviour. Here the conversation is about a remnant of Israel being saved, but there is a large remnant of Gentiles in the world who are not saved. We need to pray for the lost and praise God for the answers. The vilest of all men can come to a saving knowledge of Jesus Christ. Remember Legion, the man in the gospels filled with many devils. Look how quick Jesus saved him. **The introduction to Jesus is** *Luke 8:30 And Jesus asked him, saying, What is thy name? And he said, Legion: because many devils were entered into him.* **The result is** *Luke 8:35 Then they went out to see what was done;*

and came to Jesus, and found the man, out of whom the devils were departed, sitting at the feet of Jesus, clothed, and in his right mind: and they were afraid. Praise the Lord for His ability to save and clean up anyone at any time. I want to point out two words in this verse other than praise. The two words are **publish ye**. Publish what God is doing in your life. Publish what you see God doing in other people's lives. Publish it and then praise Him for it. If we live this Christian life the way we should, we can be an open book for the world to recognize.

June 28

Jeremiah 33:9
And it shall be to me a name of joy, a praise and an honour before all the nations of the earth, which shall hear all the good that I do unto them: and they shall fear and tremble for all the goodness and for all the prosperity that I procure unto it.

Jeremiah receives counsel again from the Lord while he is still in prison. To make a long story short, God will bring praise to His people. It is a shame that He has to place Judah and Israel back into captivity in order to get their focus back on Him. It is a shame God has to do the same thing to believers as well. God must remove us from time to time out of our comfort zone to get our attention back on Him. He does not do it simply because He can, He does it because He loves us. The verse says God wants to bring praise on His people. He cannot bring praise to those who are disobedient to Him. We have seen praise attached to many things and here praise from God is tied to obedience. Eventually God would bring Israel back out of captivity and a fear of the Lord would develop. People would fear the wrath of God, love the deliverance, and bring forth praise. We know the fear of the Lord is the beginning of wisdom according to *Psalm 111:10*. Our wisdom should remind us to be obedient. Our obedience results in a life that is pleasing to the Lord. Our pleasing the Lord results in our praise. Let me rephrase that again. Wisdom brings obedience, which brings about godly living, which ushers in praise. If you are wise, you will praise the Lord. If you are living a godly life, you will praise the Lord. It would be safe to say that if you are not wise you are not praising the Lord. If you are not living as God would have you, then there is no praise for Him. Be wise, obey God, and praise Him for how He brings praise to you. God's desire is to bring His people praise, and our desire must be to receive the praise and then offer it back to Him. Praise is not just what we sing and say, it is what we do.

June 29

Jeremiah 33:11
The voice of joy, and the voice of gladness, the voice of the bridegroom, and the voice of the bride, the voice of them that shall say, Praise the LORD of hosts: for the LORD is good; for his mercy endureth for ever: and of them that shall bring the sacrifice of praise into the house of the LORD. For I will cause to return the captivity of the land, as at the first, saith the LORD.

We just left Israel and Judah going into captivity, but now we get to read of the joy they will be receiving. In time, both nations will be restored and praise will be upon all the land. Those who have long been in sorrow shall again be filled with joy. There probably was a common belief among the people that they were stuck in captivity, and they were never going home again. Only God could deliver them, and that is exactly what God ultimately did. They finally recognize that God's mercy endureth forever. It is a good thing, or they would have stayed in captivity. I want to consider not just Israel here, but I want to move onto the Gentiles. This verse says the bridegroom and the bride are rejoicing. The bridegroom is none other than Jesus Christ. The bride is the church, (the body of Christ), born-again believers. In time, we the church, which is the bride, will meet up with the bridegroom, who is Jesus for a marriage ceremony. Everybody is going to be singing praises to the Lord for He is good. Everybody is going to be taking part in praise in the house of the Lord. Everybody will take part because everybody there will be a born-again believer. Everybody there will want to participate. Consider this if you will; everyone there is saved and will be praising the bridegroom who is Jesus. What is the difference between praise then and praise now? We will be praising in the future a bridegroom who is our Saviour Jesus Christ, and we will forever be in His presence. Why would we not praise Him now as He is always present with us? The bridegroom will never change, it will always be Jesus. Our praise does not have to wait for the actual ceremony. We are to honor our King Jesus long before He walks down the aisle.

June 30

Jeremiah 48:2
There shall be no more praise of Moab:
in Heshbon they have devised evil against it; come,
and let us cut it off from being a nation. Also thou shalt
be cut down, O Madmen; the sword shall pursue thee.

It is only fitting to record a verse out of the Old Testament before going any further. *Ecclesiastes 11:9 Rejoice, O young man, in thy youth; and let thy heart cheer thee in the days of thy youth, and walk in the ways of thine heart, and in the sight of thine eyes: but know thou, that for all these things God will bring thee into judgment.* Let me paraphrase what you have just read. You can do whatever you think is right for you, but eventually you will answer to God. Look at *Judges 21: 25 In those days there was no king in Israel: every man did that which was right in his own eyes.* Having our own way all the time is not necessarily a good thing. In Jeremiah 48:1-2 there are some cities that are fixing to be mowed down and God is the lawn mower. I am sure everyone thought how awesome and powerful those cities were. Sometimes those who are in power forget who placed them there and **why** they were placed there. To move on, these stronghold cities lost the praise of men and were looking at utter destruction. Compare that same scenario in a personal manner. We can begin to think we are something special, (pride), and God must humble us. The greatest tragedy in this verse is praise was removed. I think it equally tragic to have God remove His praise from any of us. I want God to rain praise on me and I know He wants it returned. Moab had opportunity as a city to rely on God as their Father. They chose Chemosh an idol as their god for protection and God showed them who is in charge. Praise God because He is in charge. The destruction of these cities is our warning. They found out that they could be knocked off their pedestal they had created. God does not need you and me running His show.

July 1

Jeremiah 49:25
How is the city of praise not left, the city of my joy!

It has not been too uncommon for me to start you out with a different verse to get your thinking cap working. *Psalm 20:7 Some trust in chariots, and some in horses: but we will remember the name of the LORD our God.* Where do we place our trust for protection? Let me paraphrase *Psalm 20:7 "You can put your trust in whatever you choose, but it is the Lord who I will trust for my protection".* In *Jeremiah 49*, (where we are at today), Damascus is the city in question. It was recognized by all for its ability to defend itself against any enemy. People praised Damascus because of the carnal abilities it possessed. Whether you lived there or were a stranger, both praised the city for what it could do on its own. The leaders of Damascus trusted in chariots and horses instead of the name of the Lord our God. We have a classic example of what money and power can do. A city with too much power and too much wealth becomes self-sufficient and sees no need for God. The end result is always the same. You may receive praise for a season, but it will all come to pass. We can be just like the city of Damascus in a spiritual manner if we are not careful. We must concentrate on keeping the focus from ourselves and putting it on Jesus Christ. The greatest tragedy is Damascus did not have the praise of God. What a terrible spiritual state to be in. Never come to the place spiritually where you are of no use to God. I have been mentioning a city, but it takes people to make up a city. We could say that the people of Damascus were relying on what they could do and not on what God wanted to do for them. How easily God can dispirit those nations that have been celebrated for valor! Damascus waxes feeble, but was a city of joy, having all the delights of the sons of men. We deceive ourselves when we place our happiness in carnal joys. Let us lay aside the chariots and horses and praise God wholeheartedly. Our theme is praise, but our attitude must be pleasing. When our attitude is pleasing, then what follows will be praise. Let there be praise of God and not of self. Any blessing man comes up with is for a season of time. Blessings from God are eternal. Self-gratification is based on self, but how much better when we have "victories" in the LORD.

July 2

Jeremiah 51:41
How is Sheshach taken! and how is the praise of the whole earth surprised! how is Babylon become an astonishment among the nations!

Jeremiah uses two different names for the same place. Sheshach is also Babylon under another alias. At first glance you would wonder why Jeremiah would use two different names for the same place. This is not the first time as he uses a third name back in *Jeremiah 50:21*. Let us look at the meanings of those names and then apply them personally. The first name is Merathaim in *Jeremiah 50:21* meaning "double rebellion". It was from rebellion that they were founded under. The second name of Sheshach is thought to mean "thy fine linen". Third, the original name used of Babylon meaning confusion. Let us apply the three names in order as they appear. First there was double rebellion resulting in great wealth for a season. People saw the wealth, (fine linen), and praise was given to those who were rebellious, but prosperous. Third, Babylon relied on her own power and wealth instead of the Lord, and God took them down a notch. The praise Babylon so eagerly accepted was no more. You can only trust in the riches of this world for so long, *Matthew 6:19 Lay not up for yourselves treasures upon earth, where moth and rust doth corrupt, and where thieves break through and steal:* When our affections are set on things we can see, feel, taste, or touch we jeopardize our relationship with Jesus Christ. I am not saying wealthy people cannot get close to the Lord. I am saying the wealthy and the poor can lose blessings because their affections are on the physical and not the spiritual. Paul recorded it perfectly in *Colossians 3:2 Set your affection on things above, not on things on the earth.* Affection to things that are carnal brings carnality. Affection to God, Jesus, and the Holy Spirit brings praise. The praise of men will only endure for a little while. The praise of men to the Lord is for eternity. Here is where Babylon made their biggest mistake. Babylon was proud of what they had accomplished and loved the praise for it. Babylon should have recognized God for what He could do for them and then praised Him for it. We can be just like Babylon spiritually if we are not careful. We can strive for recognition of all our successes. We can strive to be recognized as someone who wants to praise God. We can be a Babylon or a New Jerusalem. If that is confusing, then let me make it simpler. Satan will be the king of Babylon, but Jesus will be the King of a New Jerusalem. If you are saved, then you have a New Jerusalem coming and Jesus on the throne forever. Hallelujah and Amen!

July 3

Daniel 2:23
I thank thee, and praise thee, O thou God of my fathers, who hast given me wisdom and might, and hast made known unto me now what we desired of thee: for thou hast now made known unto us the king's matter.

Daniel has petitioned God for His help. Just as King Solomon requested wisdom, Daniel was asking for the same thing. The issue here was Daniel needed some spiritual insight to interpret King Nebuchadnezzar's dream. Daniel could have claimed the glory for revealing to the King what God had revealed, but he did not do that. Instead, he would praise God for trusting him with truth. Look at the wisdom we have right at our fingertips, and I am referring to the Word of God. We have the thoughts of God and the mind of Jesus Christ right under our nose. We have a book that can fill us with wisdom that no lost man can ever possess. Daniel asked for wisdom and so can we. Daniel requested God's insight for help and so can we. We request God's help through the Holy Spirit to teach us. Daniel praised God for the wisdom he received. Do we praise God every time He reveals something to us? We learn the Bible a bite at a time as we could not handle understanding it to its fullest at one time. We need to give God praise every time He points out a new truth to us. If we will praise God for the truth He reveals, it may keep us from getting puffed up at what we think we know. Another thing Daniel was praising God for was that he could petition God for help at any time and for anything. As a believer, feel free to make a list of what you cannot pray to God for. The answer to all your requests will either be yes, no, or not right now. Either way you can still petition God for whatever. *Philippians 4: 6 Be careful for nothing; but in everything by prayer and supplication with thanksgiving let your requests be made known unto God.* God not only wants to hear from His children through prayer, but he wants to hear from them in praise. Here would be a fitting prayer to commemorate this book. Pray God would help you to be more diligent, faithful, regular, and responsible in your praise to Him. I believe the more we praise God the sweeter our petitions to God.

July 4

Daniel 4:37
Now I Nebuchadnezzar praise and extol and honour the King of heaven, all whose works are truth, and his ways judgment: and those that walk in pride he is able to abase.

The key to praise in this verse is the first word "**now**". It is this entire chapter of *Daniel four* that Nebuchadnezzar had to be humbled. He was at the point in his reign where he was puffed up over everything he had accomplished. He had no clue who had allowed him to even be king. God put Nebuchadnezzar to the test in *Daniel 4:33* and he was broken in *Daniel 4:34*. He had to have everything removed that was near and dear to him before he could get to the place of praise to God instead of himself. Nebuchadnezzar resorted to eating grass like an ox, his hair was like that of eagle's feathers, and his nails turned to bird-like claws. Does not really sound like a man in his right mind does it? There was one thing that was a stumbling block to the king's praise. His eyes were on what he had accomplished and not on what God could accomplish. When Nebuchadnezzar got his pride in order he turned to praise. Nebuchadnezzar lost seven years while living a life of total degradation before he came to his senses and recognized God for who He is. Some believers do not have a problem with praising the Lord and are more than ready to participate. Some may have issues that need to be dealt with before the praise can begin. The bad news is losing all that precious time and allowing God to mold them into the image He desires for them. The biggest tragedy is for those who never turn loose of pride and never turn toward God. Nebuchadnezzar was finally at the place in his life where he could say, "Now, I will praise the Lord".

July 5

Joel 2:26
And ye shall eat in plenty, and be satisfied, and praise the name of the LORD your God, that hath dealt wondrously with you: and my people shall never be ashamed.

The context of *Joel 2:26* is the restored nation of Israel. There is coming a day when Israel will be gathered up into one kingdom with all born-again believers. Then we will all be satisfied and praise the Lord. The satisfied here is the satisfaction of the Lord, not a satisfaction to self. We are told here that Israel shall eat in plenty, will be satisfied, and will praise the name of the Lord. A couple of verses earlier our Prophet Joel makes mention of wheat, wine, and oil. Those three foods ought to satisfy us. Look at wheat first; wheat is an analogy to speak of God's judgment. Wine that is unadulterated, unfermented, and pure is used to represent the blood of Jesus Christ. Oil is used to represent the Holy Spirit. Combine the three and you have the Father, Son, and the Holy Ghost. What more could make us complete? What more could satisfy us? What more could bring us to the place of praise for God Almighty? Our Prophet Joel says the people will praise the name of the Lord. We touched on praise for the name of the Lord several times in this book.

Check out every name used to represent the name of God and you will not find one that is used in a negative sense. Praise God because He is everything good. Praise God because what He wants for us is everything good. Praise God because there will be a day when sin and death are conquered. The only thing present will be things that are perfect and righteous because God is completely perfect and righteous.

July 6

Habakkuk 3:3
God came from Teman, and the Holy One
from mount Paran. Selah. His glory covered the
heavens, and the earth was full of his praise.

There are times when we need to look back at what God has performed throughout history and simply dwell on those things. The writer Habakkuk looks back at when God delivered Israel out of the hands of Pharaoh and brought them through Teman and Mount Paran. We can only try and picture the scene that must have taken place when Moses was up on Mount Sinai receiving the law of God on tablets of stone. It says in this verse that His glory covered the heavens, and the earth was full of His praise. It does not say the people were full of praise, it says the earth was full of His praise. Let me jog your memory of what Israel witnessed in the book of Exodus. *Exodus 19:16-18 16) And it came to pass on the third day in the morning, that there were thunders and lightnings, and a thick cloud upon the mount, and the voice of the trumpet exceeding loud; so that all the people that was in the camp trembled. 17) And Moses brought forth the people out of the camp to meet with God; and they stood at the nether part of the mount. 18) And mount Sinai was altogether on a smoke, because the LORD descended upon it in fire: and the smoke thereof ascended as the smoke of a furnace, and the whole mount quaked greatly.* If necessary, close your eyes and picture what Israel just witnessed. Israel witnessed the power, majesty, and glory of God through creation. There were thunders, lightnings, thick clouds, and an earthquake. When God is present and doing something, all nature and creation will praise Him. I do not fully understand how things of nature can praise the Lord. I do understand that if God says it can praise then it can praise. Jesus told the Pharisees what would happen if His disciples held their peace concerning Him, *Luke 19:40 And he answered and said unto them, I tell you that, if these should hold their peace, the stones would immediately cry out. Isaiah 55:12 For ye shall go out with joy, and be led forth with peace: the mountains and the hills shall break forth before you into singing, and* **_all the trees of the field shall clap their hands_**. We do not have to understand everything the earth is able to do. We only need to accept God's word for what it says. Let us apply this lesson of creation to ourselves. In the beginning God created man and praise was a necessary part of their being. Sin entered the picture, and we are a result of that sin. Because sin entered the world does not mean that praise left the world. Stated another way; sin can interfere with praise, but praise can also distinguish sin. Can you sin and praise at the same time? I really doubt it. I can sin and sing, but I cannot sin and praise. Nature will praise the Lord in its own way and so can you and I.

July 7

Zephaniah 3:19
Behold, at that time I will undo all that afflict thee:
and I will save her that halteth, and gather her that was
driven out; and I will get them praise and fame in
every land where they have been put to shame.

There is no doubt that what we have here is a future Messianic prophecy. For years Israel has been dispersed to the four corners of the world and has not been a nation that has praised Jehovah together. It is true Israel was restored May 14, 1948, but a lot of Jews have not gathered back in Jerusalem to worship their King. Israel has been through its share of persecutions and has experienced plenty of shame. The Bible is filled with examples of Israel being under captivity for disobedience to God. Look in our own history books under World War II and read what Hitler did to those who were Jewish. Sometimes Israel brought on its own misery because of disobedience to God. Here is where the praise enters our topic. In this verse we are looking at God's word and it says He will bring praise and fame in every land where they have been put to shame. We have a familiar thought here. While we should be praising God, He is raining praise on His people. We do not know the exact day and the hour when the saints will be gathered together with Jesus Christ, but we know the season. The season to be gathered with Jesus is now. The time to render praise should be a current event and not just history. Praise should have already filled our mouth. When I mention our mouth, it includes Jews and Gentiles alike. Praise and fame are now and future. Jesus Christ's return is coming soon. Wouldn't it be great to be in the middle of praise when Jesus Christ takes the church out in the rapture? The only way you can get caught in the middle of praise is if you are one who praises. Israel is not the only one who has been persecuted. Read Fox's Book of Martyrs and you will see another group who gave their life because they praised the Lord through preaching and serving. They may not have been famous in the eyes of those who killed them, but they were famous in the eyes of God. We are living in a generation right now where most places cannot display things of God. We are on the brink of living in a society where being a Christian is an awful thing to testify of. We are on the brink of living in an age where testifying of being a Christian may cost you your rights. We are living in a time where there is no king, (Jesus), and every man is doing that which is right in his own eyes. The last verse of the book of Judges records that last sentence. Rejoice and praise God because He loves you. In time, your praise will be perfected for all of eternity.

July 8

Zephaniah 3:20
At that time will I bring you again, even in the time that I gather you: for I will make you a name and a praise among all people of the earth when I turn back your captivity before your eyes, saith the LORD.

In the previous devotional verse we looked at, the Lord was going to bring praise and fame to His people. In this verse He is going to bring praise and He includes a name among all the people of the earth. Have you ever heard the expression, "making a name for yourself"? That expression can carry a negative or a positive connotation. In simpler words, people that know your name attach a reputation to it. That reputation can be good, or it can be bad. We receive the praises of man or the insults of man. We need to make sure that when we receive the praise of men that we send the praise on to God. When we receive the insults of man, we need to make sure that the insults do not stick or are false. All that is for the here and now. In the future God will bring praise and a name recognized by all the earth to His people. God has a name above all names, and He is going to give us a name above all upon the earth. Let me give you something to think about for a while with closed eyes. Jesus is sitting on the throne and the entire world is gathered around listening to Him. Praise and a name above all names is coming for you. God already has a name above all names. Are we sending Him praises now and making a name for Him by our lifestyle? We must make sure that our living testimony points to the glorious name above all names, Jesus Christ.

July 9

Matthew 21:16
And said unto him, Hearest thou what these say? And Jesus saith unto them, Yea; have ye never read, Out of the mouth of babes and sucklings thou hast perfected praise?

With a baby you just naturally see the innocence in them that is missed in adults. I am not saying it does not exist in adults, we just tend to not look for it. It is that child-like praise that we all ought to strive for. I do not claim to have arrived in the area of praise, but I know which direction to go to get there. Lay aside the crying of a baby and look at their other qualities. A baby is content with just taking in their surroundings. Everything is new and fresh for them. Take a baby outside and watch their eyes take in what God has created. As we get older, we get set in our ways of doing things and start taking things around us for granted. We need to look for joy in everything we do and in everything we see. If you are married, do you see how precious your spouse is? Do you have kids and are they the most special kids on this earth to you? Do you have a job and are you grateful to be working? If your parents are still living, have you thanked them for your life? Are you saved and are you grateful to have a Saviour? For most, the day you were saved was a very memorable day. It is a day to be cherished and not forgotten. Have we lost some of the praise we had? Look at the day you were saved like it was fresh today. If you think about it, your salvation is just as fresh today as it was when it happened. Keep the salvation experience like the innocence of a newborn baby discovering something new. Praise God today like you did when you were first saved. Praise God now like we will be praising Him in the future and for eternity. We are His children, so let us act like it. *II Corinthians 5:17* says we are a new creature and that all our old habits have been laid aside and we have taken on new and improved qualities. I paraphrased all that to say this; when we were first saved, we were spiritually a new baby in Christ. That enables us to approach His throne of grace with the same innocence that a baby would approach its mother's breast. A baby feeding on its mother's breast should be a very beautiful and natural thing to do. That my friend is the same innocence we should possess when we praise our Saviour. Approach His throne in a manner that is incredibly beautiful to hear, see, and a natural thing to do.

July 10

Luke 18:43
And immediately he received his sight,
and followed him, glorifying God: and all the people,
when they saw it, gave praise unto God.

You all know this story. Jesus was heading to Jericho and a blind man just kept on calling for Jesus to take away his blindness and restore his sight. First off, how did the blind man know it was Jesus, he could not see? If you backed up to *verse 36* of this same chapter, you would read where there was a multitude of people passing by and they told him Jesus of Nazareth was passing by. How did he know what Jesus could do? He could not see the miracles. He knew because he had heard of the miracles. It is vital to proclaim the name of Jesus Christ to all. Guess what, the blind man heard, and he reached out to Jesus. Many wanted him to hold his peace, but Jesus said, "bring him to me that I might hear his petition". Jesus heard and then He healed. The result was the blind man glorified God. When the blind man glorified God, the crowd joined in and praised the Lord. Praise tends to multiply praise. The story here was of a blind man who physically had no sight. All of us were spiritually blind to the truth of salvation. We suffered from spiritual blindness because we did not know Jesus as our personal Savior. We were blind for a season to the truth that we needed a Saviour. Most of us have sang John Newton's song "Amazing Grace". Most know the lyrics, "I once was lost but now am found, Was blind but now I see". Our eyes were opened to the truth that without Jesus Christ there is no hope in our eternal future. When our eyes were opened spiritually did we glorify God by a changed lifestyle? Just as others saw the blind man rejoicing over his newfound sight, do others see us rejoicing over our newfound spiritual insight? Praise brings praise and you can lead the way.

July 11

Luke 19:37
And when he was come nigh, even now at the descent of the mount of Olives, the **whole** multitude of the disciples began to rejoice and praise God with a loud voice for all the mighty works that they had seen;

The key here is the word whole as in the whole multitude of disciples praised God with a loud voice. It says they praised Him for all the mighty works that they had seen. The exciting news is the disciples saw what the Lord did, but we can read and visualize it. Even if we did not have it recorded, (but we do), we can still look around at the mighty works of God and praise Him for it. Look at the countless lives that have been changed because of Jesus Christ's saving power. We need to be cautious not to put blinders on and miss when God is at work in someone's life or in our own life. Did you notice that the disciples are praising God and they are not in a church, sanctuary, or synagogue? I cannot help but think that Jesus Christ found joy when His disciples broke out in praise to Him. I believe Jesus still finds joy when those who love and have trusted Him as Lord break forth in praise. We praise not just on Sunday morning, but whenever the occasion arises. Praise and worship does not consist in just singing a song, but by how we live. We do not need to limit our praise to what He has done only in our life. We praise God for what He will do in the lives of those closest to us, and to those we have never met. I have been to El Salvador and Honduras on evangelism trips a few times. In leading a group to Honduras, we saw God work in many people's lives. People we had never met or would never meet on this side of eternity showed up for a movie. Over nine hundred people stayed around **after** watching the Jesus movie with us. Hundreds watched and listened to the preaching of Jesus. Over nine hundred people testified that they had just received Jesus Christ as their personal Saviour. We serve a living God that is always at work. Because we do not see something going on does not mean God is not at work. Praise God that He never sleeps and never tires of working with His children and working in the lives of unbelievers to bring them to a place of repentance.

July 12

John 9:24
Then again called they the man that was blind, and said unto him, Give God the praise: we know that this man is a sinner.

This verse is part of a story of a man who had been blind since birth. His parents were called forth to testify of their son. Their response was, "yes, this is our son, and yes he was blind, but he can answer for himself he is of age". They did not want to be thrown out of a religion by going against the religious leaders with the truth of Jesus Christ. The Pharisees wanted the blind man to give God the praise. We all know that Jesus Christ is God and when he praised Jesus, he was praising God. The Pharisees saw Jesus Christ as an enemy, not as God come in the flesh. The blind man saw Jesus Christ as someone who had compassion on him and healed his eyes. The Pharisees wanted a religion based on laws they had drummed up. The blind man had a relationship with Jesus based on Jesus alone. Look at *Luke 9:38 And he said, Lord, I believe. And he worshipped him.* The blind man's response for being kicked out of the synagogue was praise to the Lord. He was not concerned about a building made of bricks and stones to develop his relationship. His relationship with the Lord was based on the Lord. We were once like the blind man with no spiritual sight of the truth of salvation. Our eyes were opened to the gospel, and we saw the truth. Here is our comparison. Did we do the same thing in Luke 9:38 that the blind man did? *Luke 9:38 And he said, Lord, I believe. And he worshipped him.* Are we continuing in that worship? Our salvation is good every day and we can never lose it. Never lose your praise to God!

July 13

John 12:43
For they loved the praise of men
more than the praise of God.

The context of this verse is of those who were the chief religious leaders. It says *they loved the praise of men more than the praise of God*. How about that? They desired the praise of men, were fearful of losing a position in a synagogue, and forsook Jesus. Let me record the verse right before this one. *John 12:42 Nevertheless among the chief rulers also many believed on him; but because of the Pharisees they did not confess him, lest they should be put out of the synagogue.* I want to give you one more scripture reference before moving on. *Romans 10:9-10 That if thou shalt confess with thy mouth the Lord Jesus, and shalt believe in thine heart that God hath raised him from the dead, thou shalt be saved. 10) For with the heart man believeth unto righteousness; and with the mouth confession is made unto salvation.* What a trade-off; five minutes of the praise of men in exchange for an eternity in hell. Here is a good reason for us who have confessed Jesus as Lord to praise Him. We praise Him because we were allowed of God to accept Him. We could have said "no" as the chief rulers did, but by the grace of God said "yes". Isn't it amazing what we will trade for five minutes of pleasure? The chief rulers would reign for a short season and born-again believers will be reigning with Jesus for eternity. Hell and heaven are both attainable. Hell requires you to reject Jesus. Heaven requires you to accept Jesus. All around the world people have made decisions to choose hell and reject Jesus. People by default will go straight to hell when they do not accept Jesus as their Savior.

July 14

Romans 2:29
But he is a Jew, which is one inwardly; and circumcision is that of the heart, in the spirit, and not in the letter; whose praise is not of men, but of God.

The issue here is not whether you are a Jew or a Gentile. Back up and read *Romans 2:28* and the first few words are, *"for he is not a Jew"*. We are talking about praise here. God is not looking at the outward appearance of a Jew or Gentile. He looks at the inward appearance of the heart. The circumcision of the flesh, (foreskin), may be pertinent to the Jew, but the cutting of the skin will not save you. If it could, then there would not be many saved women would there? One other thing that cannot be hid from God is genuine praise. God knows who His children are, and He knows who is praising Him. God knows who is just singing to be singing. God knows who belongs to Him and who does not. God knows if those saved are in sin and are singing words of vanity and not praise. God is not impressed by the circumcision of the flesh, but He adores the genuine praise of His children. God does not need us to be recognized by a ritual to testify of who we are by circumcision. God recognizes us because we belong to Him through our faith in Jesus Christ for salvation. May our outward appearance reflect an inward change because of the gift of the Holy Spirit we received. We will always reflect something, but be sure you believe God is pleased with that outward reflection. I wrote some lyrics down years ago and they are about our reflection. "Just who was the one who nailed this man to a tree? Then I caught my reflection and I saw it was me"!

July 15

Romans 13:3
For rulers are not a terror to good works, but to the evil. Wilt thou then not be afraid of the power? do that which is good, and thou shalt have praise of the same:

Those in power were only granted that position because God allowed it. Most know what laws need to be obeyed. There should be no fear of punishment if we observe the laws of the land providing it does not contradict the commandments of God. Not only is it good to maintain a good testimony by being law-abiding, but it may render praise to your name. I can remember one time at work where one man wanted to witness to a welder. He wanted permission to tell the welder how Jesus had changed his life. The problem was the welder knew him very well, as did I. He was told to hit the road. You see the welder as a lost man lived a cleaner life than the so-called saved one who wanted to witness. There is honor in not shafting your co-workers or your neighbors. The one wanted to witness, (which is right), but he had nothing to witness about, (which was wrong). He had never received recognition of praise for a godly lifestyle. He had received condemnation from those who had seen at times his debauchery. The praise of men is not a mandate as a Christian, but we do not want to receive scorn either. We praise God by our lifestyle. What kind of picture are we painting to the lost around us? One of admiration, (recognition of Jesus in your life), or one of zero respect, (either no Christ or no morals)? We only get one chance to live a life pleasing to God and there are no do-overs.

July 16

Romans 15:11
And again, Praise the Lord,
all ye Gentiles; and laud him, all ye people.

There was a time when God was addressing the Jewish people only. There also came a day when God addressed the Gentiles as well. That specific day was when Jesus Christ willingly died for all of humanity. Here in *Romans fifteen* Paul is reminding the Jews that the Gentiles will also be praising the Lord. If a Jew would not allow a Gentile to praise the Lord in the same place, then I would guess that is something that a Jew would have to answer for. God is no respecter of persons, *Acts 10:34 Then Peter opened his mouth, and said, Of a truth I perceive that God is no respecter of persons.* Let me also include God's desire for all, *II Peter 3:9 The Lord is not slack concerning his promise, as some men count slackness; but is longsuffering to us-ward, not willing that any should perish, but that all should come to repentance.* Consider all those things God desires for the world and then praise Him for it. Think about it, God did not have to send His son to die. God did not have to turn to the Gentiles. God did not have to be willing that none should perish. Actually, He did have to do all of the above as God is love, *I John 4:8 He that loveth not knoweth not God; for God is love.* Ponder this for a while. He that loves God will praise Him, and he that does not love God will not praise Him. Some disagree and say, "well you do not know my circumstances". You are right, I do not know your circumstances, but I know the circumstances God placed His Son in. He placed Him in a world that hated, despised, and then killed Him. If God can put Jesus in that situation for us, then surely we can look at our own situation no matter what it might be and praise God. Look at Paul and Silas when they were locked up in prison, *Acts 16:25 And at midnight Paul and Silas prayed, and sang praises unto God: and the prisoners heard them.* This was after they had been beaten and then put in stocks. Most of us have never been beaten and then put in stocks for Jesus Christ. Most of us will never be in that position and praise God for that. Jesus died for all, (and stocks or not), we ought to be praising Him for it.

July 17

I Corinthians 4:5
Therefore judge nothing before the time, until the Lord come, who both will bring to light the hidden things of darkness, and will make manifest the counsels of the hearts: and then shall every man have praise of God.

For believers, reading their Bible daily is probably not a new revelation. Jesus is coming back, and when He does all the hidden things of our heart will be made manifest. He will make known any sin because He is aware of every sin. Every sin has been dealt with on the cross, but every sin of the believer will be brought to light and an account will be given of it. *II Corinthians 5:10 For we must all appear before the judgment seat of Christ; that every one may receive the things done in his body, according to that he hath done, whether it be good or bad.* Good news: any time sin is dealt with and put in its place there is a cleanness brought forth. When we have cleanness within us then the praise will exude from us. The greatest deterrent to praise is sin. It is amazing what some will sacrifice in their walk with Jesus Christ for a moment of pleasure? A few moments of pleasure can result in a loss of several hours, days, or years when it comes to praise. Consequences of sin can have so much impact on an individual and a family. God forgives us of our sin if we confess it according to 1 John 1:9. I am 100% convinced that if we spent more time praising God, it would lead to less time doing things we should not be doing. Let me end this thought with five little words: **praise more and sin less**. Or better yet, **praise more and be "sinless"**?

July 18

I Corinthians 11:2
Now I praise you, brethren, that ye remember me in all things, and keep the ordinances, as I delivered them to you.

Paul was a follower of Jesus Christ, and it was easy for him to praise other brethren. His praise here was in recognition of their following him as he was following Jesus. Paul obviously had a heart for being in the midst of God's people who were as active in ministry as he was. Remember, this is quite a statement to make when you consider Paul is addressing the Corinthian church. Up to now he has been reproving or rebuking them. We are not to desire the praise of men over God's, but there is nothing wrong with commending someone for a job well done. After all, that is what we should be longing for Christ to say to us. Do we not want to run a good race and fight a good fight for Jesus? *II Timothy 4:7 I have fought a good fight, I have finished my course, I have kept the faith:* Jesus told us of a master who commended two of his servants for a job well done and the third was called wicked. Which category would you want to be found in? Look at what Peter wrote in *I Peter 1:22 Seeing ye have purified your souls in obeying the truth through the Spirit unto unfeigned love of the brethren, see that ye love one another with a pure heart fervently:* We are to do good unto all men, but let us look forward to spending time with and loving the brethren. *Galatians 6:10 As we have therefore opportunity, let us do good unto all men, especially unto them who are of the household of faith.* We will be spending eternity with other believers, so how about giving a little praise when praise is due. When we praise the brethren, we are not just praising a man or a woman, we are praising God's children.

July 19

I Corinthians 11:17
Now in this that I declare unto you I praise you not, that ye come together not for the better, but for the worse.

Paul's words have changed rapidly in only fifteen verses. I would encourage you to read all of *I Corinthians 11* before going on. Paul lists some things that the Corinthian church should not be guilty of. He declared that you should not come together for the wrong reasons in your church. The reason for reading all of chapter eleven of this book is that I will be pointing out a few of the things Paul mentions that should not happen in the house of the Lord. All verse references will be from I Corinthians 11. First, there cannot be divisions within the ranks of the people, (v.18). There needs to be a set of rules, orders, and doctrine and all need to be obeyed, followed, and carried out. Second, (v.19), there are heresies within these walls. You cannot have someone teaching the truth and then another teacher instructing in something else. It wreaks havoc and chaos, and God is not the author of confusion. Third, (v.21), there is a bad case of selfishness among you. You are all quick to eat, devour your supper, and the poor are left hungry. Fourth, (v.22), the members were guilty of misusing the church. Jesus ran off the moneychangers and said they had turned His father's house into a den of thieves. Fifth, (v.22), there was the shaming of the poor. Paul mentions in this verse that there are some that have nothing to eat and you could care less. This happens to be the second time in this chapter that Paul says with much emotion, "I PRAISE YOU NOT"! Sixth, (vs.27-30), many were partaking unworthily of the Lord's Supper and taking advantage of its benefits. We should appreciate the clarity of Pastors when we partake of the Lord's Supper. Everyone gets time to pray and search their own heart for unconfessed sin. Everyone gets time to search their heart and know if they are saved or not and should they participate or not. Here at Corinth it was obviously nothing more than a piece of bread and some wine. Seventh, (vs. 31-34), some of you have failed to judge yourself. Paul knew when we judge ourselves with righteous judgment that there is a better chance of not receiving the condemnation of others. Praise God if you are a part of a church that will address sin. We need to know what can be expected by choosing sin and not adhering to the Word of God. It's called consequences.

July 20

I Corinthians 11:22
What? have ye not houses to eat and to drink in? or despise ye the church of God, and shame them that have not? What shall I say to you? shall I praise you in this? I praise you not.

We touched on this verse a little in our devotional verse yesterday and that is not going to stop us from looking at it further. Let me give you Webster's definition of church. It is the Lord's house, a building especially for Christian public worship, denomination, congregation, and finally a place to display divine public worship. I like all those definitions, so let me expound upon a couple. First off it is the Lord's house. How would you act if you were physically in the presence of God, in His house, in the third Heaven? The same way we ought to act when we come into the doors of our perspective church. It is a place to be respected and revered for the sole purpose of bringing glory to God. It is a building for Christians to come together and publicly worship. The building is made of bricks, stones, and wood, but it is to be used by those who would seek, find, and want to praise the Lord. It is a place where you declare the doctrine of Jesus for eternal salvation. Proclaiming Jesus for salvation is imperative and cannot be compromised. Any doctrine different than that and I would suggest you find you another church that believes in the truth. Finally, it is a place where we can publicly participate in the worship of the one who created all and wants to save all. Let us praise one another, lift up one another, and use this building we call a church for the divine purpose God has intended for it.

July 21

II Corinthians 8:18
And we have sent with him the brother,
whose praise is in the gospel throughout all the churches;

I will not concern myself with who was sent with Titus. What I will spend time on with you is the fact that someone was found of like faith and compassion as that of Titus. Someone whose praise was in the gospel. What an acknowledgment to make of another believer in Jesus Christ. This praise was not just recognized in one church, the verse says he was recognized throughout all the churches. What a perfect example of what we are to be like. No matter where you are at, people wonder what it is about you that makes you different. Everywhere you go you are a living example of the gospel and a changed life through Jesus. Titus was happy to be ministering with someone who found praise in the gospel. In otherwords, to be with someone who would preach at every opportunity and found their peace in sharing the gospel of Jesus everywhere they went. Their awesome tendencies have a good chance of rubbing off on you. Many times we become who we are around the most. Many times we can evaluate where we are at spiritually by who we run with continually. Praise God for the faithful brethren who can be an example. Let us pray to God that we could be that kind of person. Let us praise God for allowing us to be a Paul in someone's life. I think it is healthy for all to have a Paul and a Timothy in their life. Someone we can lift up spiritually or someone to lift us up when we are down. Praise God we can complement and encourage one another.

July 22

Ephesians 1:6
To the praise of the glory of his grace,
wherein he hath made us accepted in the beloved.

This epistle was written when Paul was a prisoner at Rome. Paul appears to be strengthening the Ephesians in their faith of Jesus Christ. Paul pens these words to give us an exalted view of the love of God that God had for the world. Paul shows that they were saved by grace, and that however wretched they once were, they now had equal privileges with the Jews, (the beloved). We are to praise the glory of God's grace. Think about the splendor of Heaven that God left to come in the form of a man and to die for us. That is when we are to praise the glory of His grace. It was a glorious thing that God performed for us. Even in our everyday life God extends His grace in some way or another. Watch the news sometime and see what is going on around the world. Maybe there will be a day when tragedy fills our life. It will be the grace of God we will praise as He delivers us through it. Ever won someone over to Jesus Christ? We praise the grace of God because He could use us for soul winning. Have you ever had the opportunity to preach the word of God? Praise the grace of God that He could save a wretch like me and then allow me to share the word of God with others. God knows every single situation we have ever been faced with or will be faced with. Praise the glory of God because nothing can get past His watchful eyes. God does not sleep or get tired, and He is always right on time. Praise the glory of God for His hand of protection, answered prayers, and His faithfulness. When everything around you seems to be letting you down, look up so He can lift you up. Praise the glory of God, His goodness, and His grace! Praise God that as Gentiles we have been accepted because of the sacrifice of His Son Jesus Christ. You can now be "His" beloved if you will only believe in Jesus for salvation.

July 23

Ephesians 1:12
That we should be to the praise
of his glory, who first trusted in Christ.

You need to go back in this chapter and read a few verses. At least go back to verse 7. We have promises made to us that can lead us to praise His glory. Those who have placed their trust in Jesus Christ are those who should be praising the Lord. Back in verse 7 of this chapter we have been redeemed and forgiven by the richness of His grace. We can use the word richness as what kind of price tag could you put on the life of Jesus? *Verse 8* of the same chapter says God has given us an abundance of wisdom and prudence meaning things that are sensible. In the word of God, we have the thoughts of God. God has made known His very thoughts through scripture of what is to be done and what will be done, verse 9. *Verse 10* is coming down the road. A time when those who have gone on before us by death and those who are alive at God's rapture of the church will be gathered together. We have a promise of God that He will bring us all together in time to spend eternity with the Lord Jesus Christ. *Verse 11* says we have an inheritance coming for us. When God leaves an inheritance you can rest assured that it is going to be one fine gift. God can only do what is the absolute best. Now in our devotional verse for today we are to be the praise of His glory. If we can live and commit to this verse today, we will be forever changed. Not just because we are His children, but are we living a life that is showing the praise of

His glory? Jesus was God's glory by what He did and for who He was. Are we God's glory by who we are and by what we do? We are God's children by spiritual adoption and His spirit seals us for all of eternity, but are we living a life that shows forth the praise of His glory? Are we like Job when Satan appeared before God? *Job 1:8 And the LORD said unto Satan, Hast thou considered my servant Job, that there is none like him in the earth, a perfect and an upright man, one that feareth God, and escheweth evil?* Sometimes it is good to acknowledge that we are a child of God and that should please us. It is equally good to acknowledge God as our "daddy" and consider if He is pleased with us. Let me leave you with a few words of an old hymn. The title to the song is "Satisfied with Jesus". The words I want you to meditate on are in the ending chorus. They are as follows; *I am satisfied, I am satisfied, I am satisfied with Jesus, But the question comes to me, As I think of Calvary, Is my Master satisfied with me?*

July 24

Ephesians 1:14
Which is the <u>earnest of our inheritance</u> until the redemption of the purchased possession, unto the praise of his glory.

You must include the first thirteen verses of this chapter to see **_what is the earnest of our inheritance_**. Verse 13 says we were sealed by the Holy Spirit of promise. Combine the promise of being sealed by the Holy Spirit with hearing the truth of the gospel. By accepting the truth and applying it to your life personally you have a sealed inheritance to come. The word earnest is defined as money put down until full payment is made. When you accepted Jesus' death on the cross as sufficient for your salvation, the Holy Spirit sealed you as one of God's children until the day of reckoning when your inheritance will be waiting. We never lose our salvation as we are sealed, but we have not yet received all the benefits and rewards. Those rewards are coming, but we cannot lay hold on them yet. With all that said, consider the final words of the verse, *"unto the praise of His glory"*. The word glory is also translated as splendor, majesty, brightness, excellence, preeminence, or a thing belonging to God. God's glory is His son Jesus Christ. Our greatest inheritance is not streets of gold in a New Jerusalem, seeing a crystal sea, or not having to deal with sickness or death. Our greatest inheritance will be our privilege of standing in the presence of God, (Jesus Christ), and He is reigning as our King on the throne for all of eternity. The glory we praise for eternity is Jesus Christ. We thank others for gifts we receive. Sometimes we are downright excited about them. The greatest material gift, however special, will never compare to the gift of salvation. How are we thanking Jesus Christ for the gift of what He had to go through for you and for me? Are you praising Him for the gift? Are you not praising Him because you have not received the gift of salvation? There is an inheritance that is for all who want it. Jesus Christ covered all of our sin debt and has already paid the earnest money. If it is one thing I know, it is that Jesus has never written a bad check. What kind of a spiritual inheritance do you prefer? One with Jesus Christ in His kingdom, or eternity with Satan in hell? Jesus Christ is coming soon so do not delay in accepting Him. There is only one bail bondsmen for freedom from hell and that is Jesus.

July 25

Philippians 1:11
Being filled with the fruits of righteousness, which are by Jesus Christ, unto the glory and praise of God.

We have all probably been accused of being filled with a lot of things other than the fruit of righteousness. As believers, God has filled us with the fruit of righteousness. Let me list the fruit, (singular) from *Galatians 5:22-23 love, joy, peace, longsuffering, gentleness, goodness, faith, meekness, and temperance.* You did not get just one or two fruits on that list; you received them all. We were filled with the fruit of righteousness, and they are through and from Jesus Christ. God gave them to us for the glory and praise to be given back to Him. I wonder if we let the fruit of righteousness control everything we do if the world would notice? You better believe they would. An attitude and a lifestyle that shows us as a peculiar people set apart for use by God himself. We praise God when others see Jesus Christ in us. We were saved by Jesus and filled with the fruit of righteousness through Him. Jesus gave the fruit, in order that we can praise Him, who is the glory of God. Another example of receiving praise from God is enabling us to send praise back to Him. It says it best in *John 15:5 I am the vine, ye are the branches: He that abideth in me, and I in him, the same bringeth forth much fruit: for without me ye can do nothing.* Without Jesus Christ we can produce no fruit. We can do some wonderful things in the flesh on our own, but to produce fruit comes by abiding in Jesus Christ and praising God for it. After all, what do you imagine God thinks of those who refuse to praise His Son Jesus Christ? Probably the same thing you and I would think. Fortunately, God shows more mercy and grace than we do. To the honor and glory of God let us praise His honorable and glorious Son Jesus Christ.

July 26

Philippians 4:8
Finally, brethren, whatsoever things are true, whatsoever things are honest, whatsoever things are just, whatsoever things are pure, whatsoever things are lovely, whatsoever things are of good report; if there be any virtue, and if there be any praise, think on these things.

Is it your desire to keep your mind right and your life in order? If so, this has to be one of the best verses there is to maintain a life that is pleasing and acceptable. Paul is addressing believers and he calls them brethren right from the start. He gives them a list of things to think on and closes by saying if there be any praise, think on these things. Have you ever been reading the word of God and then realized your mind had wandered a hundred miles from where you are reading? I have done that as well and had to back track and read the same scripture over. The main thing is to get back on track and re-read where you have just been. Here is the deal; how can we possess the mind to praise God if all we place in it is filth and trash. There is a popular saying about having balance in your life. Well that is just fine, but what are you balancing? Where in the word of God does it say to have a balance of filth, profanity, or drunkenness alongside some sort of life with the Lord? Please feel free to bring me a chapter and a verse that says I can watch all the dirty movies I want, drink all the alcohol I want, spew profanities out of my mouth, commit adultery every other day, and then read God's word an equal amount of time and be okay. I wonder sometimes if that is why some cannot praise God on Sunday morning because of what they did Monday thru Saturday. There is a church in the town I lived in that after Church is over on Saturday night, most raced down to the local bar to have a couple or several so-called cool ones. By my calculations, if they were in church an hour and a half then they should stop drinking in an hour and a half to maintain balance. Right? It is not going to happen. The balance we need is spending time in the Word of God, ministering to others, rendering service for God, and being faithful to God. Praise God that He has provided some good things for us to think on. Watching television or going to movies is not what makes us balanced. If you want to see a clean movie with your family it is okay, I do it myself. We do not become balanced by comparing our time in the world or movie theater with our time with God. You become balanced when you start applying this verse personally. Take time to think on good things, and if there is praise in the midst send it on to the Father, Son, and Holy Ghost.

July 27

Hebrews 2:12
Saying, I will declare thy name unto my brethren,
in the midst of the church will I sing praise unto thee.

The key thought in the text of Hebrews chapter two is the unity of Jesus Christ. For those who have accepted Jesus Christ are not ashamed to declare them as His brethren. For those who have accepted Him we should have no shame to declare Him as Lord. With that thought in mind, we can gather in our churches and sing praise unto Him. I think that there are times when we forget that Jesus is our brother. We are God's children by adoption and Jesus is God's child by the virgin birth through Mary. If Jesus is God's Son and we are His children, then we need to acknowledge Jesus Christ as our brother. Let me show what the word of God says about what one brother did for another brother. *John 15:13 Greater love hath no man than this, that a man lay down his life for his friends.* Jesus was the brother that laid down his life for His friends. His friends are those who have trusted Him as their Saviour. Jesus died in order to save the world. He did not die to save the saved. He died to save those who were lost. At one time we were among the lost. Praise God for His grace and His calling that saved us. We all have a family tree and I pray that Jesus is the root that keeps us standing for Him. Are you proud Jesus is your brother? Let Him hear you sing about it when you are at your church, home, or in the car. By the way, a church is a body of believers and not a building made with hands. Next time you are hanging with a body of believers might be a good time to praise your brother. That is of course your brother and Saviour Jesus!

July 28

Hebrews 13:15
By him therefore let us offer the sacrifice
of praise to God continually, that is, the fruit of
our lips giving thanks to his name.

If we only read the first half of this verse, we might wonder what is the sacrifice of praise? If we read the last half, we would be told the sacrifice of praise is the fruit of our lips giving thanks to his name. We lay aside all the cares of the world to go to the Saviour who died for us. Something to consider is that Israel as a nation during the tribulation period is going to read the book of Hebrews to try and figure out what in the world is going on. People everywhere have disappeared, (**rapture of the church**), and Israel will be looking for some instruction. Israel will come to the place where the truth of Christ's death is accepted and for those who are wise, they will head to the wilderness to be under God's protection. Those of us who are saved are already under the protection of God. If anything happens that causes our death, we will be present with the Lord, *II Corinthians 5:8 We are confident, I say, and willing rather to be absent from the body, and to be present with the Lord.* May the fruit of our lips continually praise the name of the Lord. Remember the key verse to praise is *Psalm 34:1 I will bless the LORD at all times: his praise shall continually be in my mouth.* We are to offer up praise to God through Jesus Christ. Whether it be prayer, thanksgiving, rejoicing, or a song of praise, offer it up through Jesus who will send it to the Father. There will be a day when it will be too late to offer up praise to God through Jesus Christ because they never accepted Jesus.

July 29

I Peter 1:7
That the trial of your faith, being much more precious than of gold that perisheth, though it be tried with fire, might be found unto praise and honour and glory at the appearing of Jesus Christ:

Gold can be tried in fire and all the impurities removed, but the best it can buy will perish in time. Gold in its purist earthly form will last a season, but the trials of your faith will be found to praise, honour, and glory for eternity. Let me insert a quote from Matthew Henry that would be fitting.

Matthew Henry

Let this reconcile us to present afflictions. Seek then to believe Christ's excellence in himself, and his love to us; this will kindle such a fire in the heart as will make it rise up in a sacrifice of love to him. And the glory of God and our own happiness are so united, that if we sincerely seek the one now, we shall attain the other when the soul shall no more be subject to evil. The certainty of this hope is as if believers had already received it.

No matter what is going on or has gone on in your life you are to look to the future of Jesus Christ's return. We will be found praising Him with honor and glory or we will not. I would hope for all of us that we would be found faithful at His coming. *I Corinthians 4:2 Moreover it is required in stewards, that a man be found faithful.* The way to be found faithful when Christ raptures us out is to be found faithful in everything we do and not get caught off guard. *Mark 13:33 Take ye heed, watch and pray: for ye know not when the time is. Mark 13:35 Watch ye therefore: for ye know not when the master of the house cometh, at even, or at midnight, or at the cockcrowing, or in the morning*: ARE YOU READY? Better yet, ready or not here HE comes!

July 30

I Peter 2:14
Or unto governors, as unto them that are sent by him for the punishment of evildoers, and for the praise of them that do well.

We have touched on the responsibilities of a Christian for those who have been in power. God has allowed certain individuals to reach certain offices and we are not to usurp authority or slander that position. I personally have not had anyone in a government position call or stop by and praise me for keeping the law. Those who are in government offices in the town where I live can be sure that if something malicious has taken place the culprit will not be at my house. I guess them knowing that is unspoken praise. We praise God through Jesus Christ when we are found blameless. *Philippians 2: 15 That ye may be blameless and harmless, the sons of God, without rebuke, in the midst of a crooked and perverse nation, among whom ye shine as lights in the world;* Whether we are in the midst of a crooked and perverse nation should not dictate our actions. As *Philippians 2:15* says *we are to be lights in the world*. We bring praise to God through Jesus Christ when we are seen as lights in the world. Christians must attempt in all relations to behave in a manner that is right in the eyes of the Lord. We cannot make our liberty in Christ a cloak for wickedness. We are servants of God, and our lifestyle must be pleasing and acceptable to Him. Living for God is praise to God.

July 31

I Peter 4:11
If any man speak, let him speak as the oracles of God; if any man minister, let him do it as of the ability which God giveth: that God in all things may be glorified through Jesus Christ, to whom be praise and dominion for ever and ever. Amen.

God has given us gifts and they differ one from another. *Romans 12:5-6 5) So we, being many, are one body in Christ, and every one members one of another. 6) Having then gifts differing according to the grace that is given to us.* God gives us gifts to minister unto others for Him, but it is our duty to exercise those gifts in the way God intended. Some have the gift of singing, but they do not praise God with that gift. Some have the gift of teaching, but they do not study to teach. Some have the ability to preach, but refuse to open their Bible and prepare. Some have the gift of giving, but are filled with greed or selfishness. Some have the gift of discernment, but could care less about what they discern. We use our gifts for the purpose of manifesting Jesus' name to the world. We are to use our gifts to believers and unbelievers. We use our gifts to the lost to bring them to a saving knowledge of Jesus. We use our gifts to those saved that they might be edified and lifted up spiritually. Let God in all things be glorified through Jesus Christ our Savior to whom be praise and dominion for ever and ever. Praise is eternal, God is eternal, the Holy Spirit is eternal, and Jesus Christ is eternal. Could it be possible that how we exercise the free gifts God has given us may be eternal? Absolutely Yes! God's desire is that we have the best gifts possible, in order to serve Him the best. Let us be good stewards of His gifts and bring praise to Him through Jesus Christ where praise and dominion will be forever. You and I may not be gifted for every calling of God, but God will provide every gift we need every time He calls.

August 1

Revelation 19:5
And a voice came out of the throne, saying, Praise our God, all ye his servants, and ye that fear him, both small and great.

This is the verse I have waited for as far as the word praise goes. The specific word praise appears for the last time right here in the book of Revelation. The day mentioned above will be the greatest day of praise any believer has ever experienced. We will praise our God as we are about to participate in the marriage of the church with Jesus Christ. All those who died for Jesus, lived for Jesus, and accepted Jesus will finally be singing together in one accord to God the Father. Believers of all ages will be singing together. Think on this; the Apostle Paul is on your left and maybe Moses is on the right. All the old prophets written about in our Bible singing together for the first time in the same place and at the same time. There will not be one person who will not hit the right note when we sing Amen and Hallelujah. I wonder if when we start to praise God if we will be astounded at the sound of our voice. We will be focused on God and nothing around to distract us. We will sing at the top of our voice. We will lift holy hands to the one we are about to be married to. On this day, we will fully understand praise in its best form. On this day, there will be one praise, from one body to one Saviour, and not one sin to be found. My prayer is that we might develop praise today that resembles the praise coming on the day of the marriage to the Lamb. Praise God He has saved us from the wrath to come that we might praise Him eternally.

August 2

Deuteronomy 6:5
And thou shalt love the LORD thy God with all
thine heart, and with all thy soul, and with all thy might.

Let us dissect this verse together for today's devotional. Look at the word "thou" first off. It is an individual choice to love the Lord. You cannot force love on anyone, and you certainly cannot fake love towards God. He knows our heart and mind and there is no fooling Him. The word for love here is (ahab, pronounces aw-hab), or to love like a Friend. How can you not love a friend like God? Watch the news sometime, and I think it is obvious that people reject loving God every day, hour, minute, and second. God does not want a little bit of love. He wants our whole heart. God does not want our leftovers, but our everything. We must be careful due to what is written in *Jeremiah 17:9 The heart is deceitful above all things, and desperately wicked: who can know it?* The question from Jeremiah is, "who can know it"? God the Father knows our heart a lot better than we do. The next thing to catch my attention is the use of the word soul. The word for soul comes from a word meaning to refresh. If you and I will love Him with our soul, we will feel refreshed. It is about not being too busy to love Him and letting the junk of the world take us over. He ends the verse with a challenge to not just give Him a little love, but to love Him a lot. With every ounce of energy, we are to love God with a child-like love. A sweet innocence for God who loved us first. Concentrate loving Him more and just maybe a little less focus on self.

August 3

Deuteronomy 7:9
Know therefore that the LORD thy God, he is God, the faithful God, which keepeth covenant and mercy with them that love him and keep his commandments to a thousand generations;

I would like to spring-board off the thought of how much pagan worship was going on by Israel and their neighbors around them. This verse says the Lord is "the" faithful God. It always makes me wonder why Israel would turn to an idol when their history pointed to an alive and well God who brought them out of Egypt. Who am I to talk about Israel's shortcomings? Egypt in scripture is a type of the world. When I was lost, I was of the world as well. How could I possibly be guilty of worshipping a god or an idol as well. An idol may be money, house, car, motorcycle, friends, success, traveling, etc. When you and I attach ourselves to, or set our attention on worldly things, we become unfaithful to Him. We may spend so much time with our attention on wrong things that eventually our vision becomes cloudy, and we do not even realize how far we have drifted from God. The verse declares that God keeps His covenant and mercy. The only covenant I need to keep is staying faithful to God and worship him with the first of my time instead of my leftover time. I am grateful when it comes to mercy that God does not give me what I deserve. God is a big God, but so very approachable to His children. With God we can expect anything and everything, but what can He expect from us? If God does all this for a thousand generations, can we offer up our love and affection towards HIM?

August 4

Deuteronomy 10:12
And now, Israel, what doth the LORD thy God require of thee, but to fear the LORD thy God, to walk in all his ways, and to love him, and to serve the LORD thy God with all thy heart and with all thy soul,

The same thing the LORD desired of Israel is still desired of you and me. He wants us to fear Him for who He is. We do not walk around with fear and trepidation for what God can do to us. We fear Him for what He does for us. I am not suggesting that there is not anything God will not do when it comes to chastising us for disobedience/sin. The verse simply says to fear Him, and we are to walk in His ways. What exactly are God's ways and how do we know His thoughts. According to *Isaiah 55:8 For my thoughts are not your thoughts, neither are your ways my ways, saith the LORD*. We learn about God and His thoughts through the Word of God. Once we start learning, meditating, and memorizing God's word we learn how to walk in His ways. We then realize just how healthy walking in His ways is for us and our love will grow for Him. We are to fear Him, walk with Him, love Him, and serve Him with every ounce of our being. God expects us to carry out what He says. We have one short span of time called life to do things right. My question is, "How are we measuring up to God's expectations"? Are you happy with where you are spiritually? If yes, then you should rejoice! Not happy with where you are at spiritually? Maybe some confessing and repenting is necessary and long overdue. Repentance brings rejoicing, and rejoicing brings praise to a deserving and Almighty God.

August 5

2 Chronicles 19:7
Wherefore now let the fear of the LORD be upon you; take heed and do it: for there is no iniquity with the LORD our God, nor respect of persons, nor taking of gifts.

This verse is really the first verse where a man instructs the people to have this quality. It is not the first time the phrase appears. It is the first time that a leader of Israel says, *"The fear of the Lord must be in your life"*. Jehoshaphat is the head Judge here. Here is what Jehoshaphat knew. Judges had to be set up for law and order to determine right and wrong among people. He also knew there were Judges, but the Judges neglected the people, or the people ignored the Judges. *Judges 21:25 In those days there was no king in Israel: every man did that which was right in his own eyes.* Jehoshaphat sends preachers to instruct the people of the law. Put another way, it is for them to know right from wrong. Right is no problem, but when something is wrong, there will be a price to pay for disobedience. What were the main responsibilities for the Judges & Preachers? To keep man in the worship of God. What is worship? Worship is right living for the Lord. When anyone is hiding in sin God knows what has been going on. There is a difference between just singing a hymn and worshipping God. I find it hard to believe that any man or woman can praise the LORD and be in sin. Praise is not sitting in a pew with Satan holding your left hand and Jesus holding your right hand. You cannot live in a house with Jesus and pay rent to the devil. You cannot rest in Jesus and sleep with Satan. Amen!

August 6

2 Chronicles 19:7
Wherefore now let the fear of the LORD be upon you; take heed and do it: for there is no iniquity with the LORD our God, nor respect of persons, nor taking of gifts.

Do not take the fear of the Lord as a grain of salt as it is very serious. Consider often just what you are thinking and how you should want to avoid making silly mistakes. As they say, "Ponder long; Ponder wrong". Ignorance of the Bible does not make sin "Acceptable". Let the fear of God be upon us to prevent us from wrongdoing. As I stated, "Ponder Long, Ponder Wrong". I would also add that "Haste makes Waste" in making decisions. Jehoshaphat knew the Fear of the Lord was greater than any decision a Judge could make. The best Judge we have should be ourselves. Who knows better than us the areas that need to be corrected? No one knows how much an individual fears the Lord except the individual. Our testimony is a dead giveaway to that. We are to fear what God can do over what man can do. God's judgment is perfect, and He does not make any mistakes. Here is what I do know, and I will end with this thought. God's word is perfect and if we will apply His truths to our life then our personal judgment will be perfected. God wants us to judge righteously and that cannot be done outside the confines of the Word of God. Judging righteously is not reserved for others, but for self as well. May the verdict you make of yourself, (concerning sin), be "Not Guilty"!

August 7

2 Chronicles 19:9
And he charged them, saying, Thus shall ye do in the fear of the LORD, faithfully, and with a perfect heart.

We have just read specific instructions to the Levites, Judges, Preachers, and Priests. Because of the fear of the Lord, you will be faithful in your decisions. If fear causes faithfulness to God, then no fear must cause unfaithfulness to God. Not everyone in positions of Leadership or Authority did what was right then or now. Discipleship lessons to some are nothing more than recommendations. Many do not have "The Fear of the Lord" and give no thought to God's condemnation. Judging ourself is not something done sporadically or on a whim, but a daily reckoning of how our day was. The Bible, in the book of Jeremiah, talks about our heart being desperately wicked and who can know it. Two people know what is in our heart. One, God knows exactly what is going on and two, so do we. We may not want to admit our faults, but I am fairly sure we know when we are at fault. I hate that feeling you get in your stomach when you know you are pondering messing up or have messed up. What God wants us to do is to be faithful in judgment to self before tackling the world with their problems. There really is no sense in trying to solve the world's problems if we cannot even fix our own foolish ways. Long story short, do the right thing even if it is difficult. The right thing may not always be easy, but it is always right.

August 8

Job 28:28
And unto man he said, Behold, the fear of the Lord,
that is wisdom; and to depart from evil is understanding.

What exactly is wisdom? It is putting into practice what we know about the Word of God. It is trusting that God knows what is best and obedience gives us perfect results for living. *Proverbs 10:14 Wise men lay-up knowledge: but the mouth of the foolish is near destruction.* Telling someone to do as I say, and not what I do, has made Christianity very phony. If you asked many kids today, where did you learn to do something so awful? Their answer may be, "from my mom and dad". Here is the problem when there is a disregard of wisdom about sin. Some may see shortcomings in others, but not their own. The gossip that others have may be gossip, but is it gossip that is true? Sin should embarrass a Christian. If there is no conviction of sin in someone, it will be difficult for anyone to believe they are wise "OR" a child of God. Sin betrays, belittles, and discredits how Jesus can change a life. Completely opposite of someone wise in Christ. The verse says to depart from evil is understanding. To stay in evil must mean you have no understanding. It is obedience to the devil. Would someone wise or unwise stay in evil? Understanding is taking something we know and applying it personally. If we do not depart from evil, then we are either unwise or in rebellion. Scripture says rebellion is as witchcraft. Staying in sin is unwise and foolish. Can a believer have the fear of the Lord and live in sin? Would be hard convincing anyone of that including yourself.

August 9

Psalms 19:9
The fear of the LORD is clean, enduring forever: the judgments of the LORD are true and righteous altogether.

We are clean spiritually because sin is not being practiced. We can be clean physically as well. Doing what is right will keep our bodies clean and healthy. If I fear the Lord, it will guide my spiritual decisions. If I fear the Lord, my decisions may affect how I treat my body and guide my decisions. *1 Corinthians 3:16 Know ye not that ye are the temple of God, and that the Spirit of God dwelleth in you?* It is amazing how many Christians due to overeating are obese and can quote this verse. I understand medical conditions can cause obesity as well. However, to continue to eat and eat and eat is not taking care of your body. Do we treat our body like a temple or an old rag? Physically we are the judge of self, and spiritually we are judged by God. Are you taking care of your body? Find a full-length mirror and you can see for yourself. The fear of the Lord is clean, so the goal is to be clean physically and spiritually. How long is fearing the Lord clean? The verse says forever, and we both know how long forever is. The part of the verse about judgments of the Lord being true and righteous, let me put that in my own words.

The *"Perfect Law"* of the Lord Jehovah is stable, faithful, perfect, and morally right, which will keep us cleansed from all evil". Repentance is the greatest thing any of us can submit ourselves to. It is humbling, *Proverbs 15:33 The fear of the LORD is the instruction of wisdom and before honour is humility.* Walking in sin should be humiliating, and humiliation not resolved brings zero honor to Jesus. Walking away from sin is humility, and brings honor to Jesus. Humility is someone living right physically and spiritually according to the word of God.

August 10

Proverbs 8:13
The fear of the LORD is to hate evil: pride, and arrogancy, and the evil way, and the froward mouth, do I hate.

Evil – That which is contrary to the Word of God and Satan wants us to do this. Pride comes before a fall and places self before all else and others. Satan tried this and it is called arrogancy. Arrogancy is feeling superior to everyone and everything and Satan tried that with God. An Evil Way is a direction that leads away from God instead of to God. Satan took one third of the Angels with him and we can take others down the same path by them observing us. The verse mentions a froward mouth, and in it dwells no good thing. Satan will only give us a mind and a mouth that is evil towards God. Let me rewrite this verse with no fear of the LORD used. *No Fear is to love evil; pride, arrogancy, an evil way, and to have a crooked or forward mouth.* Take a look at the different definitions of what I just read in a negative context. Evil is to be in agreement with Satan and in opposition to God's word. Pride is thinking I have a better plan than God's Word. Arrogancy is when I thank God that

I am not doing what they do, but may be doing worse. The Evil Way is when I try and communicate a lifestyle that will take others down the same path of evil. Froward Mouth - Sometimes it is not what we are saying, it is what we are doing. A froward mouth is when someone says, "What, I cannot hear you, your sin is too loud"! I do not know anyone who could not stand some self-improvement including the one writing these devotionals. We are all in the same boat when it comes to hating evil. We are to love God and all that is good according to the truth of the Word of God. I say this a lot, but we only get one chance at doing life right according to the word of God and we should not blow it.

August 11

Psalms 36:1
To the chief Musician, A Psalm of David the servant of the LORD. The transgression of the wicked saith within my heart, that there is no fear of God before his eyes.

King David is the writer and concludes that some are wicked because they have no fear of God. David knows if they did fear God that sin would not be long lasting. King David knew the wicked may not verbally renounce God, but their works would. Many will live their life as if there is no Fear of God and repercussion of sin. Satan has deceived many to believe they fear God, but live contrary to the Bible. You cannot serve God and Mammon. Satan says, "Do whatever makes you feel good, so thereby it must be good". *Romans 3:18 There is no fear of God before their eyes.* **How can you tell?** *Romans 3:10-18 10) As it is written, There is none righteous, no, not one: 11) There is none that understandeth, there is none that seeketh after God. 12) They are all gone out of the way, they are together become unprofitable; there is none* *that doeth good, no, not one. 13) Their throat is an open sepulchre; with their tongues they have used deceit; the poison of asps is under their lips: 14) Whose mouth is full of cursing and bitterness: 15) Their feet are swift to shed blood: 16) Destruction and misery are in their ways: 17) And the way of peace have they not known: 18) There is no fear of God before their eyes.* At a glance you would think this is about someone just plain EVIL. At a second glance we must realize not to put a point system on sin. Sin is sin and God does not want us in sin, acknowledging sin, partnering with sin, or for one second entertaining sin. Sin is not an Olympic event with a score card. I know some sins are worse than others, but for a born-again believer, sin is sin.

August 12

Proverbs 9:10
The fear of the LORD is the beginning of wisdom:
and the knowledge of the holy is understanding.

Need a place to start getting wisdom? The fear of the Lord is the start. The beginning of wisdom is an interesting thought. The word beginning is a commencement. It would be the equivalent of trumpets in your life going off to learn wisdom. It is the exact moment in time when someone digs in their heels and quotes *Joshua 24:15 "As for me and my house we will serve the LORD"*. The fear of the LORD is the "ORIGIN" of Wisdom. The fear of the LORD is the "FIRST" of wisdom. It appears to be impossible to please God and not be wise. If the fear of the Lord is the beginning, then is No fear the end? When we acquire wisdom through the fear of the Lord, other things are acknowledged with it. *Proverbs 9:10 The fear of the LORD is the beginning of wisdom: and the knowledge of the holy is understanding.* Knowledge of the "HOLY" is something sacred. The Word of God and how we apply it to our life brings a holy lifestyle. Morally pure is taking the Word of God and applying it to our life. If someone is lacking in both areas, then there is an ignoring of the word of God. When we know what scripture says and defy it, we agree with Satan as well. Satan tried a different plan and where exactly did that get him? It got him thrown out of Heaven. To understand is to figure out what is right or wrong based solely on the Bible. It is not to determine what is right based on popularity, but on TRUTH. Understanding is dealing wisely with others as well as ourselves. God's word is truth and is a lot better than a boatload of opinions. Any opinion that is in opposition to the truth of the word of God should be discarded. An opinion and a quarter will not buy anything.

August 13

Proverbs 10:27
The fear of the LORD prolongeth days:
but the years of the wicked shall be shortened.

The Fear of the Lord "can" prolong days through bodily health. We do not know how many days, but it would appear the fear of the Lord can add days to our life. How many people kill themselves by what they do with their body? We have really tainted the blood from Adam, and we are paying for it today. Spiritually speaking, some will die sooner because of their stand for Jesus and be martyred. However, I would rather die standing for Jesus than to kill myself with drugs, alcohol, and etc. People have two decisions in this verse. One, to live according to the Bible and God can bless with additional days. Two, is to live outside the confines of the Bible and days can be shortened with shame. One of the saddest verses for a human regarding shame and dishonor is for Jehoram in *2 Chronicles 21:20 Thirty and two years old was he when he began to reign, and he reigned in Jerusalem eight years, and <u>departed without being desired</u>. Howbeit they buried him in the city of David, but not in the sepulchres of the kings.* Look at the wicked and death by association, *Numbers 16:26 And he spake unto the congregation, saying, Depart, I pray you, from the tents of these wicked men, and touch nothing of theirs, lest ye be consumed in all their sins. Psalms 7:11 God judgeth the righteous, and God is angry with the wicked every day. Psalms 10:4 The wicked, through the pride of his countenance, will not seek after God: God is not in all his thoughts.* We must determine according to scripture what is good and what is wicked and go in the right direction.

August 14

Malachi 3:8
Will a man rob God? Yet ye have robbed me. But ye say, Wherein have we robbed thee? In tithes and offerings.

Seems to be a simple question, yet there are a lot of different ways to rob God. If God has called me to a specific ministry, but I refuse to obey, I have robbed God. If God gives me a divine encounter to share the gospel of Jesus Christ, and I do not, I have robbed God. I also rob that person of the opportunity to receive Jesus. In this verse, the answer is given at the end. It says, *"you have robbed God in your tithes and offerings"*. I am a strong advocate of a minimum of 10% to be given to your local Bible-believing New Testament church. I could also assert that after that, you should give to special causes, events, and missionaries. Look at the first time the word "tithe" is used. It is in *Leviticus 27:30 And all the tithe of the land, whether of the seed of the land, or of the fruit of the tree, is the LORD'S: it is holy unto the LORD.* The verse does not say part of the tithe, it says all the tithes. The verse also shows that God does not want our leftovers, but He wants what we earn first. Many people then argue with themselves about tithing on the gross or the net. My response is that it depends on what do you want blessed on? Tithe means 10%, but that is probably just a good start. I love how people say, "It is all God's anyway". I would challenge those that declare that, to reveal the ledger of their checkbook and prove it. Now, does God really need our money in order to accomplish anything? The answer is no as God has done just fine long before you and I came into existence. God owns the cattle on a thousand hills so He can afford to do anything He wants. We do not tithe to get a blessing. We tithe to be in harmony with God and financially support His work. Whether in your house or your church it takes money to run things. It is unfortunate that as prosperous as America is, we spend more on chocolate, flowers, cigarettes, drugs, and alcohol than we do on Jesus. There is a bible study rule called "The Law of First Mention". I mentioned already the first use of the word tithe. If God does not give new instructions, then the first mentioned use is not void. The New Testament never says that tithing was to stop. Tithing for the work of the ministry is one more way of how we praise the LORD!

August 15

Psalms 100:2
Serve the LORD with gladness:
come before his presence with singing.

Let us start out this verse with the first word "*serve*". Serve means to be in bondage to the Lord. Serve meaning to stay <u>compelled</u> serving Jesus Christ. Serve as in being like a husbandman of a field, a piece of property, or one that protects the interests of an Almighty God and the work He has for you. Serve here also means to be a "worshipper". One who worships God by the service they give. We are to serve the "LORD", the Eternal One. We are to serve Him with gladness. Gladness means taking on unmistakable joy, rejoicing, or pleasure. There is no pleasure like knowing you are in the will of God as you serve wherever He has called you to. The second half of the verse reminds us of coming to His presence with singing. We must always remember that a person saved is always in the presence of God. When you prayed and made Jesus your Savior, you received the gift of the HOLY SPIRIT that dwells within you forever. Any time you feel the call of God you are in His presence. Any time you feel convicted of sin you are in His presence. Any time you recognize the blessings of God you are in His presence. No born-again believer can run from the indwelling of the Holy Spirit. It is a wonderful thing to know that twenty-four hours a day you are in God's presence. The verse says we are to come into His presence with singing. Singing can be a shout for joy as well as a triumphant prayer of victory in Jesus. God never focuses on just those with a beautiful voice. God focuses on an obedient heart and a grateful attitude.

August 16

Matthew 6:24
No man can serve two masters: for either he will hate the one, and love the other; or else he will hold to the one, and despise the other. Ye cannot serve God and mammon.

This may be one of the more popular verses in the Bible when it comes to good old-fashioned pulpit preaching. This verse does not say some men can, but it says no man can serve two masters. Satan has his victories as well. If we extend a hand or a foot to him, he will suck you in and destroy your testimony. Here is how this ultimately works with going back and forth between good and evil. There may be a time when someone jumps into sin and leave God to do their own thing. They recognize their shortcoming, supposedly repent, and here they come back to church looking all religious and holy. What next you ask? Another sin or the same sin shows up and off they go again. Time goes by and they see the errors of their way. What next you ask? They recognize their shortcoming, supposedly repent, and here they come back to church all religious and holy looking. This is exactly why the world looks at Christianity like we are a bunch of buffoons. For crying out loud, would it not be easier to pick what team you want to be on or what Captain you would prefer to follow? If you are for God, then give yourself to God fully. If Satan is your master, then I would guess you would do your best to serve him. "Serving God is not a game, it is a lifestyle". If there has never been a time in your life where you have completely sold out to God, then let today be the start of a brand-new day.

August 17

2 Corinthians 5:17
Therefore if any man be in Christ, he is a new creature: old things are passed away; behold, all things are become new.

The first word is *"Therefore"*, and we need to see why the word therefore is there for. In the previous verse of this same chapter, it is mentioned that a believer should not be living according to the flesh. Not to be confusing using the word flesh, I could have said we are not to live like the world and be enamored or partner with sin. Remember, one moment of pleasure in sin is temporary, but serving Jesus is joy eternal. You and I have a responsibility to live up to what the word of God teaches. I did not write any of the Bible, but I believe all of the Bible. I do not claim to know the Bible and its truths to the fullest, but I understand more of it daily. I fully believe that if we obey the Bible, we can live in a glass house for all the world to see. I believe the Bible contains truths that will transform, conform, and reform every single one of us. I believe that the transforming power of the Holy Spirit to believers will convict us to a life of clean living. I believe that the power of the Holy Spirit will not only convict us of sin, but will keep us out of sin. I once was lost, but now I am found, was blind, but now I see. Every hurt, habit, and hang-up can be done away with by accepting Jesus as your Savior and living for Him. We are all responsible for witnessing to people about how Jesus has changed our life. People know if you live a life that points to the risen Savior Jesus Christ. They also know if you do not look any different than the world and the lost as well.

August 18

1Samuel 15:22
And Samuel said, Hath the LORD as great delight in burnt offerings and sacrifices, as in obeying the voice of the LORD? Behold, to obey is better than sacrifice, and to hearken than the fat of rams.

King Saul gets called on the carpet by God through Samuel. Saul just completed a great victory over the Amalekites and at first glance it appears everything is as it should be. If you back up to *verse 3* of this same chapter, he was told to slay everything and to take nothing. I do not know what take nothing means to everyone, but to me it means "take nothing". What does Saul do? He does what "he" believes God wants him to do. Obviously, God must have made a mistake, so Saul is correcting the matter. Saul does not destroy everything as God had instructed him. God knew that those things Saul refused to destroy would eventually destroy all of Israel. God declares to Samuel that Saul had disobeyed and there would be a price to pay. Saul kept the best, (**in his eyes**), and we will never have the best until God "gives" us the best. What is best for us is to obey God's word to the letter. Nothing in this chapter was too confusing to understand. What is confusing is why Saul took matters into his own hands and destroys what he wanted to destroy and kept what he wanted to keep. If we are not careful, we will be in the same boat. The sacrifice God wants from us is our life. God does not want us to pick and choose what areas of our life is His and what area we retain to do our own thing. He desires that we submit fully to His Lordship over us. We must surrender to a perfect King who has a perfect plan.

August 19

1 Samuel 16:7
But the LORD said unto Samuel, Look not on his countenance, or on the height of his stature; because I have refused him: for the LORD seeth not as man seeth; for man looketh on the outward appearance, but the LORD looketh on the heart.

Many times, we do not know what someone is like on the inside and it takes time to figure that out. We are not like God the Father who is all knowing. We cannot always run on our first impression as we could be right, or we could be wrong. *1 Thessalonians 5:21 Prove all things; hold fast that which is good.* We may not be able to prove things immediately as to someone's character and you must be patient. These two verses explain part of what I am trying to convey to you. *Proverbs 14:33 Wisdom resteth in the heart of him that hath understanding: but that which is in the midst of fools is made known. Luke 8:17 For nothing is secret, that shall not be made manifest; neither anything hid, that shall not be known and come abroad. 1 John 4:1 Beloved, believe not every spirit, but try the spirits whether they are of God: because many false prophets are gone out into the world.* I have been talking about how to figure out where someone is at spiritually as they might not be healthy for you to hang with. We need to be reminded of where we are at spiritually as well. God knows what kind of goofiness we will pull even before we pull it. The best we can do is a daily personal evaluation of self. If we evaluate ourselves and address any problems, people will believe that we are living for Jesus and possibly want to hear more about Jesus.

August 20

Deuteronomy 13:4
Ye shall walk after the LORD your God,
and fear him, and keep his commandments, and
obey his voice, and ye shall serve him, and cleave unto him.

The more I read and study God's word the more I see natural progressions. In *Deuteronomy 13:4* we can follow a path that will lead us to service for Him. We will go from following Him, which is good, to hanging on tight to Him, which is better. It would be like having the dust from Jesus' feet kick up in your face as you are that close. Anytime you participate in the Lord's Supper you can ponder where you are at spiritually beforehand and get things in order if they are not in order. No matter what, who is willing to stand for Jesus Christ and do whatever will please Him? *Joshua 24:15 And if it seem evil unto you to serve the LORD, choose you this day whom ye will serve; whether the gods which your fathers served that were on the other side of the flood, or the gods of the Amorites, in whose land ye dwell: but as for me and my house, we will serve the LORD.* The Flood – how about that flood, (sin), before you were saved? The Flood – are you still there, wading in the water, (sin), or repentant and clean? The Flood – If God saved us then why would we stay in dirty water? The Flood – If God saved us then why would we go back in the same water? The Flood – Get in the boat, THE ARK OF JESUS, and sin no more!

August 21

Deuteronomy 13:4
Ye shall walk after the LORD your God, and fear him, and keep his commandments, and obey his voice, and ye shall serve him, and cleave unto him.

If you just realized you are reading the same verse from yesterday you would be absolutely correct. Let us dive a little more into this same verse in Deuteronomy. The verse says, *"Ye shall walk after the LORD your God"*. With that said, take a look at Jesus' path. Where did Jesus' paths take him? He went down every path that God sent Him to proclaim salvation and to heal the sick. *John 8:4 They say unto him, Master, this woman was taken in adultery, in the very act,* {**Jesus delivered her**}. *Luke 8:30 And Jesus asked him, saying, What is thy name? And he said, Legion: because many devils were entered into him,* {**Jesus healed him**}. Have you ever heard this said about someone at a funeral, "They were fighting demons"? *Matthew 14:21 And they that had eaten were about five thousand men, beside women and children,* {**Jesus fed them all**}. *John 19:17 And he bearing his cross went forth into a place called the place of a skull, which is called in the Hebrew Golgotha,* {**Jesus sacrificed it all**}. Can we not do the same thing with our life? Who will stand with Jesus Christ no matter what? Jesus said it repeatedly, *"Go and sin no more"*! Every path Jesus went down was to fulfill the will of God. Every path Jesus took was to minister and serve people. *Mark 10:45 For even the Son of man came not to be ministered unto, but to minister, and to give his life a ransom for many*. Jesus came to serve and if we are to be Christ like, what do we do? This world is not all about us. It is all about God, family, and then the church. One thing will steal your joy, trip you up on your path, and ruin your testimony. It is a three-letter word known as "SIN".

August 22

Luke 24:46
And said unto them, Thus it is written, and thus it behoved Christ to suffer, and to rise from the dead the third day:

Let us look one more time at Jesus' path and the correlation with our path. First, let us start with the path of Jesus. The end of Jesus' path appeared to the world to be death. Satan thought he had gotten the victory over Jesus. The only reason we can sing the hymn Victory in Jesus is because Jesus' path brought victory to those who will accept the victory. Jesus' path took Him to serve others and should ours be any different? We can serve others and we can serve self. If we serve others, we are serving God as well. God wants one sacrifice on our path, and it is called obedience. Look at our path and the fact that we have two choices in life. Walk a path of defeat and in bondage to sin, self, and Satan. Walk a path of victory and sold out to God who loves you. Anyone dwelling in sin will pay the piper eventually. If we pray about what God would have us do, then that is the path we should take. There are questions we must ask ourself daily. What is keeping me from repenting? What would God have me do? What is keeping me from serving? Jesus' path took him to people who were hurting, the cross, grave, and back home to His Father. May our path take us to helping those who are struggling as well.

August 23

Psalms 25:4
Shew me thy ways, O LORD; teach me thy paths.

As we go down a path we want to know where we are going. If you do not have a goal, then where will your path take you? If the person we are following has no goal set towards following Jesus, then we really would not know where we are headed either. Let me give you the key to service in my opinion. There is a future glimpse about Jesus in *Isaiah 50:6 I gave my back to the smiters, and my cheeks to them that plucked off the hair: I hid not my face from shame and spitting.* Do you think Jesus put the cross to the back of His mind? Do not take your eyes off your goal or the prize of serving Jesus. If you do, you will not see victory, you will only see obstacles. I have a sticky note that I leave on my desk. It says, "obstacles are things you see when you take your eyes off of your goal"! If you do not have a goal for serving God, then how can you accomplish anything for Him? Where will your path take you if you choose to follow Jesus Christ? *Psalms 16:11 Thou wilt shew me the path of life: in thy presence is fulness of joy; at thy right hand there are pleasures for evermore.* Sin may bring joy for a moment, but Jesus' joy is eternal. Some paths may look good, but are they good for us? Christians hook up with the wrong person and the path is jagged at best. Following Jesus will bring peace and joy to your path. May your walk be consistent and sweet as you walk with Jesus. You cannot walk down a path with Jesus and hold hands with the devil. You cannot have a home filled with joy and pay rent to Satan. I will really shorten and paraphrase what *Joshua 24:15* says. Choose at this exact moment of time who you are going to follow. It does not matter what others will do, what will you do today for God?

August 24

Psalms 27:11
Teach me thy way, O LORD,
and lead me in a plain path, because of mine enemies.

The word "plain" in our verse today literally means a place of uprightness and righteousness. Can you have sin in your life and appear upright and righteous? I guess we could phony our way through life. We can pretend we are upright, but God knows. When we are in a place surrounded by evil and enemies, you want to be in a place of uprightness. Do not go down or stay on a path where you should not be. I believe it is just as easy to repent as it is to sin. It is as easy to stay in sin as it is to get out of it. Some will say, "Well I just could not get out of there". *1 Corinthians 10:13 There hath no temptation taken you but such as is common to man: but God is faithful, who will not suffer you to be tempted above that ye are able; but will with the temptation also make a way to escape, that ye may be able to bear it.* Not only is being at the end of a bad path not good, but the journey along the way is not too pretty either. The end of a bad path just might be the last place you would want to be and possibly too late to turn back. It is more than likely that you just might hate what is waiting at the end because of poor choices. Your path is only plain, upright, and righteous because of Jesus. He did His part, and we must do ours. *Isaiah 64:6 But we are all as an unclean thing, and all our righteousnesses are as filthy rags; and we all do fade as a leaf; and our iniquities, like the wind, have taken us away.* Jesus' path is a good path. {**Walk with HIM**} If you are saved, surrender all and let him lead you on your path. If you are lost, surrender all and get on the path. Most people are following someone or something. Be certain the path you are on is the right path. Be certain of who you should be with. Every one of us need one Master and Shepherd and that is JESUS!

August 25

Deuteronomy 13:4
Ye shall walk after the LORD your God, and fear him, and keep his commandments, and obey his voice, and ye shall serve him, and cleave unto him.

What things do we have in common with Jesus Christ? A Cross – Jesus carried His and died. A Cross – We are to take up our cross daily and LIVE, *Mark 8:34 And when he had called the people unto him with his disciples also, he said unto them, Whosoever will come after me, let him deny himself, and take up his cross, and follow me.* A Will – Jesus and every born-again believer are to do the Will of God. For today's devotional let us move on to things required of us to enhance our spiritual walk. We can dissect this verse for clarity. We are to fear God, which is to stand in awe of, honor, and respect, or have reverence for with a godly fear. It is not like someone hiding in a corner, but rather reverently serving God. If we stay in sin, are we really reverencing God? I say ABSOLUTELY NO! *Psalms 34:9 O fear the LORD, ye his saints: for there is no want to them that fear him.* {God will take care of you} Psalms *67:7 God shall bless us; and all the ends of the earth shall fear him.* Blessings will follow reverence and obedience to God. The fear of God is not something I see a whole lot of on the news or in the newspaper. To be honest with you, and from a Pastor's perspective, there are many times I did not even see that in the church. I do not believe I ever had a lost person cause a problem, but it was common for those who claimed they were a Christian to be the problem. You want to know why? They wanted to run the church instead of God running the church. They wanted to be in charge instead of God being in charge. There is a final judgment coming, but many do not appear to be too concerned about that. Many people do not fear God and sin is running rampant even in the church. People do not appear to worry about the consequences of sin. People do not worry about eternity, but rather the here and the now. People are not concerned with when they may draw their last breath. Many could care less what they are in the middle of doing when Jesus returns. Plan like Jesus will not come back for a long time, but live like it could be today.

August 26

Matthew 10:28
And fear not them which kill the body,
but are not able to kill the soul: but rather fear him
which is able to destroy both soul and body in hell.

Fear not what others may say, but fear what God can DO! God is good all the time and all the time God is good. There is a path to follow and stay on and keep his commandments fully. Do what his Word says. Why? *Psalms 33:4 For the word of the LORD is right*; Why? *Psalms 119:11 Thy word have I hid in mine heart, that I might not sin against thee.* It creates healthy living. Why? *Psalms 119:140 Thy word is very pure: therefore thy servant loveth it.* In *Psalm 119:140* the word pure is used in the same sense as gold when it is put to the fire. After a while, the gold has no impurities, and it is priceless and perfect. Our life can head toward that process of being Christ-like. As a servant do you love God's word?

Are you daily in His word? This is why we can trust God's Word and we are to live by God's word. *Proverbs 13:13 Whoso despiseth the word shall be destroyed: but he that feareth the commandment shall be rewarded.* How do you know if you despise or fear God's word? Do a self-evaluation of where you think you are at spiritually. Does your life stack up with the Word of God? Is sin reigning in your life? When did you open your Bible last and read it? Are you consistently in God's word or whenever you can fit it in? If we do not like where we are at spiritually there are two choices. One is to fix it and the second is to live with the consequences. To sum up today's devotion please remember that there is a path. We need to live a life of reverence to God. We should keep His commandments by living a life that points to the Bible and obey His voice. Let us concern ourselves with what God thinks and not worry about what the world thinks. We will be so much the better for it. For the record, we do not have to be tolerant of sin. We are to be intolerant of sin and reject it regardless of what anyone has to say. When it comes to sin, the Lord is very intolerant. *John 2:14-15 14) And found in the temple those that sold oxen and sheep and doves, and the changers of money sitting: 15) And when he had made a scourge of small cords, he drove them all out of the temple, and the sheep, and the oxen; and poured out the changers' money, and overthrew the tables;* **The LORD is intolerant of sin**!

August 27

Jeremiah 7:23
But this thing commanded I them, saying,
Obey my voice, and I will be your God, and ye shall
be my people: and walk ye in all the ways that I have
commanded you, that it may be well unto you.

We must obey His voice and do what the Lord says to us. I believe God would first say you must Stop & Listen. Can we agree that the Bible is literally the voice and mind of God? *John 10:27 My sheep hear my voice, and I know them, and they follow me*: Are you hearing from God? Hopefully, the case is not, "I cannot hear you Lord my sin is too loud"! Is God's Word God's Voice? *I John 2:4 He that saith, I know him, and keepeth not his commandments, is a liar, and the truth is not in him*. Only two people can measure your love for God. {You & God Almighty). One question to answer is how are we measuring up with obeying God when He talks to us? For those who are simply going through the motions of Christianity, here is one incredibly sad verse. *Matthew 7:22-23 22) Many will say to me in that day, Lord, Lord, have we not prophesied in thy name? and in thy name have cast out devils? and in thy name done many wonderful works? 23) And then will I profess unto them, I never knew you: depart from me, ye that work iniquity*. Please be certain that you have really accepted Jesus by faith for your personal salvation. Be certain that you believe Jesus' sacrificial death was sufficient to pay your sin debt. Be very certain…

August 28

Romans 12:1
I beseech you therefore, brethren, by the mercies of God, that ye present your bodies a living sacrifice, holy, acceptable unto God, which is your reasonable service.

If we are to present our bodies a living sacrifice, what does that mean? You received the gift of the Holy Spirit when you prayed to receive Jesus Christ as your Savior. Your body immediately became a temple. Your body now houses the Holy Spirit permanently. So if I am going to present my body to God as a living sacrifice, what do I do? First off, do not be conformed to anything except the example Jesus gave us. What does the Christian community buy into? They will buy into abortion, drugs, alcohol, filthy language, abuse, and on and on and on. To conform means to comply with rules, standards, or laws. Another meaning of conform is the worldly view meaning to do what is socially acceptable. Sometimes pressure is used to conform someone and sometimes not. What or who are we supposed to conform to? Do you think Jesus would be a good example to shoot for? If Jesus wanted to spend a day with us, what would we do? Technically, if the Holy Spirit is residing within a believer, are we not in fact really hanging with God? Does the world laugh or make fun of "Christianity" and why is that? Because at times "Christians" look like the lost. You know the biggest difference between someone lost or saved? The lost may not justify anything they do, but simply sin. The saved will sin, but will justify or explain the sin. Can you really explain to the HOLY SPIRIT residing in you that the sin you hang on to is acceptable and He would understand. No, you cannot do that. It only sounds good in your head.

August 29

Deuteronomy 30:20
That thou mayest love the LORD thy God, and that thou mayest **obey** his voice, and that thou mayest cleave unto him: for he is thy life, and the length of thy days: that thou mayest dwell in the land which the LORD sware unto thy fathers, to Abraham, to Isaac, and to Jacob, to give them.

Obedience will bring spiritual prosperity. The more we love and obey the LORD, the more we cleave to the Lord. Why? Because it is good for the soul. The more we cleave or hang on to the Lord, the more our lifestyle will reflect it. We are going to reflect something, but what will that reflection be? When it comes to being in right standing with God, how are we doing? Right standing is Jesus being your personal Savior. Sinful behavior is resisting God and staying in sin. Staying in sin is selfishness. Selfish is when someone does something or commits an act for personal profit or pleasure. Selfish is having no regard for others including God. Selfish is taking no thought for the welfare of others. Want to tell others about how Jesus changed your life? How can we do that according to today's verse? Follow, fear, obey, and serve Him. The result will be a fulfilled life. I did not say a life without problems. I said you would feel fulfilled.

August 30

John 10:27
My sheep hear my voice,
and I know them, and they follow me:

God has a desire for all to follow Him. God's desire for His children may be different than the reality of what His children do. God asks that we accept him, and yet many will reject Him. God asks us to Love Him, and some will Despise Him by what they do. God asks for obedience, and some will only give disobedience. God longs for loyalty and He receives betrayal. God deserves reverence, and many people spit in His face. God longs for our embrace, and yet He received a crown of thorns. God enjoys spending time with us, but we just cannot seem to fit Him into our schedule. God wants what is best for us and we give Him our worst. God wants all to avoid Hell and some will say I can party in Hell. Some will sing "I Love You Lord", and never give Him a second thought all week. Some will sing "O Victory in Jesus" and live a defeated life and in complete bondage to Satan and sin. Some will sing "Have thine own way Lord", but do not bother me with it. We have one shot at living a life that points to Jesus Christ. There are no do overs in life so strive to be the best you can be for God. I believe He is more than worthy of it, and not occasionally, but consistently.

August 31

Luke 5:26
And they were all amazed, and they glorified God, and were filled with fear, saying, We have seen strange things to day.

The context of this verse is about a man feeble or paralyzed. Maybe you and I got saved from a pretty rough background. Did your friends say to each other, "that is him, but we have seen strange things today"? "OR", do they say, "I hear what you say, but I see what you do"! Let me jump to *Acts 17:20 For thou bringest certain strange things to our ears: we would know therefore what these things mean.* This verse is

Paul on Mars hill testifying of what he had seen. People should see a changed life in us. Everyone was in disbelief over how Paul's life had turned 180 degrees towards Jesus. Paul went from wreaking havoc with the church to leading the church to Jesus. When people see a changed life, they cannot argue what they have seen. Our actions are a lot louder than our words. Our walk is what leads people to Jesus. Stay steadfast in your walk, cleave to the LORD, and you will bear fruit. Let my walk and your walk appear to some to be a "strange" walk in a good way. If Christ is not as important today as He was in times past, are you ready to fix it? Is there anything keeping you from being sold out and on a path with Jesus? Do an evaluation of where you have been physically and spiritually and address any issues. We have the ability to hear God's voice, as He is not too busy. Lost people – You want to hear from Jesus, then turn to Jesus. Saved people – Are you not hearing from God? Are you not looking to hear or is the sin in your life too loud to hear from God? Does God have to use us? No, but He desires that we would partner with Him. When we are on a path with Jesus, and serving Jesus, we will cleave to Jesus. God the Father, (Creator of the Universe), wants a relationship with every one of us. The Creator of the Universe is never too busy to hear His children, take care of His children, or steer His children in the right direction. Sometimes we struggle focusing on something silly when God is so in love with us! What a small price to pay in loving God when He so loved us and sent His Son to die for us.

September 1

Genesis 4:3-5
3) And in process of time it came to pass, that Cain brought of the fruit of the ground an offering unto the LORD. 4) And Abel, he also brought of the firstlings of his flock and of the fat thereof. And the LORD had respect unto Abel and to his offering: 5) But unto Cain and to his offering he had not respect. And Cain was very wroth, and his countenance fell.

This is the first time an offering is talked about. Cain brought fruit of the ground and Abel offered the blood of an animal. The word for Abel's offering is tsone, (tseh-one'), or used for a herd of lambs. They needed a lamb for a sacrifice in the Old Testament and it pictures Jesus. We needed a lamb for a sacrifice in the New Testament and it is Jesus. There were many different things that were offered for a sacrifice for sin, but all of it was only a temporary solution to a permanent sin problem. The system of sacrifices was God's example of grace by which humanity and God could have a restored relationship. However, the sacrifices were ultimately inadequate, and God came in the person of Jesus. A Lamb was a sin offering to pardon sin and a picture of God's grace. A Goat was a sin offering that recognized the sin. One goat was killed, and one was set free. The freed goat was a picture of God's mercy. A Bullock was also a sin offering as well and they would burn part of it outside the camp. There were times that the offering was abused by corrupt Priests. *I Samuel 2:16 And if any man said unto him, Let them not fail to burn the fat presently, and then take as much as thy soul desireth; then he would answer him, Nay; but thou shalt give it me now: and if not, I will take it by force.* Hophni & Phinehas were a couple of those bad Priests. The offering became nothing more to the Priests than something to grill and eat. Our High Priest Jesus took our sin and cast it as far as the east is from the west. There is only "ONE" High Priest that forgives permanently, and it is Jesus. All the sacrifices in the Old Testament and New Testament were a bloody mess. One would have been a four-legged animal that was cut up and burned. The other was a two-legged man, (Jesus), that was beaten up and crucified. Old Testament sacrifices had to be repeated. Jesus as our New Testament sacrifice died once. If someone by faith will accept Jesus' atoning death, burial, and resurrection for salvation it is permanent. When Jesus on the cross said, "It is finished", it meant it is finished.

September 2

Hebrews 9:11
But Christ being come an high priest of good things
to come, by a greater and more perfect tabernacle,
not made with hands, that is to say, not of this building;

When Jesus Christ came and died, we were given a New Testament. All things that were prophesied during the Old Testament came to be through Jesus. Every spiritual and eternal blessing the Old Testament promised was fulfilled when Jesus came. The New Testament is the fulfillment of the Old Testament. The Old Testament promised a Savior that would come. *Isaiah 9:6 For unto us a child is born, unto us a son is given: and the government shall be upon his shoulder: and his name shall be called Wonderful, Counsellor, The mighty God, The everlasting Father, The Prince of Peace.* The New Testament fulfilled the promise of the gift of a Savior, Jesus Christ. *Luke 2:11 For unto you is born this day in the city of David a Saviour, which is Christ the Lord*. Jesus is not a tabernacle or a church that man built physically. The Savior said that the Church would be built spiritually for those who will trust Him as LORD. Jesus said He would be the ROCK that the church would be built on, and the gates of hell could not prevail. Jesus is the "high priest" above any who call themselves a priest. We have gone from a temple made with hands that held the Holy of Holies, to a human body that is a temple that now contains the Holy Spirit if you are "SAVED". *I Corinthians 3:16 Know ye not that ye are the temple of God, and that the Spirit of God dwelleth in you?* Be mindful of taking care of your "Temple". We must guard what we put in our eyes, ears, and mouth. Once something goes in the brain it is hard to get it out of the brain. The bible says our body is a temple and that means to take care of it for use for Jesus. God let man destroy Jesus' body publicly so that we could serve Him with our body proudly and publicly. We have to look like a saint, not a sinner!

September 3

Hebrews 8:12
Neither by the blood of goats and calves,
but by his own blood he entered in once into the
holy place, having obtained eternal redemption for us.

We no longer must bring an animal for a sacrifice in order to be pardoned temporarily. Jesus became the sacrificial Lamb that redeemed us from death. If we trust him for salvation and accept him by faith it is permanent. Jesus Christ – A perfect, unblemished, and the holy Lamb of God. Look at Abraham and Isaac. *Genesis 22:8 And Abraham said, My son,* **God will provide himself a lamb** *for a burnt offering: so they went both of them together.* There is no greater picture in the Old Testament of God providing the lamb. No one can earn their salvation by doing anything. *Ephesians 2:8-9 8) For by grace are ye saved through faith; and that not of yourselves: it is the gift of God: 9) Not of works, lest any man should boast.* God saw the degradation of man and provided another Lamb, Jesus His Son. Jesus was the sacrifice, 'BUT" we cannot forget about an Empty Tomb. Every cult religion in the world will have a "god". If you dug up their grave, you would find a bag or a box of bones. Jesus, the Savior of the world, arose from the grave in a perfect and glorified body. No longer are we kept out of the Holy of Holies. When Jesus gave up the ghost the veil was rent in two from the top to the bottom. Jesus' death brought light to the Holy of Holies. Jesus' death brought light to every person that will trust Him as their Savior. This verse does not say that our redemption is temporary. It says out redemption is eternal. You and I on our own cannot attain redemption. Jesus, and only Jesus provided eternal redemption. Jesus did not offer up any blood other than His own. Jesus shed His own blood and died so that I could accept His sacrificial death and live.

September 4

Hebrews 9:13
For if the blood of bulls and of goats, and the ashes of an heifer sprinkling the unclean, sanctifieth to the purifying of the flesh:

The verse only poses a comment about an animal only purifying the flesh, but it says nothing about purifying the spirit. Only Jesus can make anyone whole or complete. The Old Testament says the Holy Spirt came upon man. The New Testament says that by trusting Jesus, the Holy Spirit dwells in man. *John 8:36 If the Son therefore shall make you free, ye shall be free indeed.* Free is used twice in John 8:36. It means you have been liberated from the penalties of death. It means you have been set free and are no longer a slave to sin. The blood of bulls and goats were offered for the sacrifices of sin and had to be repeated. Jesus was the sacrifice for our sin. Jesus said, "It Is Finished". *John 19:30 When Jesus therefore had received the vinegar, he said, It is finished: and he bowed his head, and gave up the ghost. 1 Corinthians 15:3 For I delivered unto you first of all that which I also received, how that Christ died for our sins according to the scriptures.* Would you like to go back to raising perfect unblemished livestock so you have an acceptable sacrifice? Would you rather give thanks that God raised up a perfect Son in the person of Jesus Christ? I am thankful to have been born in a time frame where I could stop and ask for forgiveness of my sin, and by faith trust Jesus to be my personal Lord and Savior.

September 5

Hebrews 9:14
How much more shall the blood of Christ, who through the eternal Spirit offered himself without spot to God, purge your conscience from dead works to serve the living God?

Jesus' blood was sufficient to cleanse us from sin and is so much more than the blood of an animal. Jesus' blood was without spot because he knew no sin. Jesus became sin for us when he died on the cross. *2 Corinthians 5:21 For he hath made him to be sin for us, who knew no sin; that we might be made the righteousness of God in him.* Jesus' blood was shed so that we could live a holy life for him and serve a "living"

God. With Jesus we have hope, and without Jesus, we are hopeless and helpless. We have some instructions in this verse as well. It says to purge your conscience from dead works. What are possible dead works? If it is not honoring to God and has no eternal significance it is probably dead works! Let me give you a nugget of truth about the difference between the blood of an animal and the blood of a human. I have cut myself before and got my own blood on my clothes. I have also hunted several animals and got a lot of animal blood on my clothes as well. Here is the distinct difference between the two. When you do laundry, human blood rarely comes out even if you treat the blood stain. I promise you one thing, plain water will wash the blood stain of an animal away. That is exactly why we needed Jesus' blood for our atonement. Jesus' blood can never be washed away. When we sing, "what can make me whole again"? The answer in that same hymn is "nothing but the blood of Jesus"!

September 6

Hebrews 9:15-16
15) And for this cause he is the mediator of the new testament, that by means of death, for the redemption of the transgressions that were under the first testament, they which are called might receive the promise of eternal inheritance. 16) For where a testament is, there must also of necessity be the death of the testator.

The world was promised an eternal inheritance in the Old Testament and Jesus fulfilled that prophecy. We needed a permanent blood sacrifice to redeem us, and Jesus gave His life to redeem us. The gospel should be considered as the last will and testament of our Lord and Saviour Jesus Christ. Jesus is the inheritance that God gave to the world.

Sometimes the word testament is the word covenant. It is an agreement that for eternity Jesus is sufficient for someone to be saved and spend eternity in Heaven. Jesus as the mediator means it was a voluntary act. No one forced Him to the cross, He willingly went. It was a single work of Jesus Christ. Jesus Christ is in fact the Mediator of the New Testament. Jesus redeems or saves unbelievers from their sin. We were indebted to God and Jesus paid the debt. We have been left an inheritance from Jesus Christ. He is the "high priest" and Savior for those who will trust his sacrificial death for sin. No one has ever left the world a greater legacy than what Jesus did. Jesus did His part and died. Someone lost must do their part and by faith receive Jesus to be their personal Lord and Savior and live. Our responsibility is to share the truth about what you know about the free gift. Those spiritually lost will either accept or reject Jesus and that choice is theirs. The world has two choices: Trust in the power of an "Empty Tomb" or Trust in self and live an "Empty Life". Whatever we do, is it glorifying God or the world?

September 7

Exodus 28:3
And thou shalt speak unto all that are wise hearted, whom I have filled with the spirit of wisdom, that they may make Aaron's garments to consecrate him, that he may minister unto me in the priest's office.

We are now talking about the Holy of Holies where only the High Priest could enter therein. This would have been one of the most protected and revered areas of the tabernacle and called the "Holy of Holies". It was covered by a heavy veil and "NO" one except the High Priest could enter. Once a year the High Priest offered the blood of sacrifice, known as the blood of atonement. Only the High Priest could enter the Holy of Holies without consequences from God. The High Priest appointed would thoroughly wash his body and wear priestly clothes. It could best be described as the inner-most sanctum. Nothing was more revered than the Holy of Holies. When Jesus died the curtain was torn from the top to the bottom. We were now provided free access to "the Holy of Holies". We now have access to God by way of Jesus through faith. *Matthew 27:51 And, behold, the veil of the temple was rent in twain from the top to the bottom; and the earth did quake, and the rocks rent; Mark 15:38 And the veil of the temple was rent in twain from the top to the bottom.* Keep in mind that the Holy of Holies would have been completely dark around the ark. The only way to shed light on it and allow us to enter the Holy of Holies was Jesus. The garment worn by the Priest was specific and you can read about it in *Exodus 28*. For us today God says, "Come as you are". *Matthew 11:28 Come unto me, all ye that labour and are heavy laden, and I will give you rest.* God will not judge because we are a fashion statement. He will judge if we know Jesus and I pray you do. A lot of people have heard of Jesus and think they know Jesus. You cannot know Jesus unless by faith you have trusted Him to be your Savior. It is then, and only then, that the Savior of the world will start revealing Himself to you. A common saying is that the distance from Heaven and hell is about 16 or so inches. That would be the distance from the top of your head to your heart. Head knowledge is not sufficient, but heart knowledge is. Heart knowledge is taking what you have heard or know and applying it personally. It is making Jesus your Savior and asking Him to save your soul. Do not let 16 inches or so send you to hell. The devils know about Jesus too and they will not be in heaven. *James 2:19 Thou believest that there is one*

God; thou doest well: the devils also believe, and tremble. Romans 5:1 Therefore being justified by faith, we have peace with God through our Lord Jesus Christ: Galatians 2:16 Knowing that a man is not justified by the works of the law, but by the faith of Jesus Christ. It is not what you know, it is who you know!

September 8

Matthew 7:3
And why beholdest thou the mote that is in thy brother's eye, but considerest not the beam that is in thine own eye?

Before Jesus' first coming there were tons of ceremonial things to do. If you do this sin, then it was your duty to offer a particular sacrifice for that sin. The Pharisees were quick to point out sin, but slow to look at their own. I cannot repent for you, and you cannot repent for me. The response from Jesus was in *Matthew 7:5 Thou hypocrite, first cast out the beam out of thine own eye; and then shalt thou see clearly to cast out the mote out of thy brother's eye.* A Hypocrite is an actor, assumed character, or you are not really who you say you are. What is certain about a hypocrite is that most already know if we are a fake or not. What happens is we will come off looking foolish, and behind our back we will be roasted and toasted. They will smile with you, but are really laughing at you. They will say, "Oh that's nice", but in their mind say, "What a phony"! There are things that must be considered such as why can't Jesus clean me up? Our personal testimony must not be, "Do as I say, not as I do". This is exactly why Christians leave a bad taste in someone's mouth. We can never believe that except for this one sin I am living for Jesus. The LORD never overlooks what you and I are doing. If we do not like where we are at spiritually, then allow God to clean up the speck.

September 9

Matthew 8:25-26
25) And his disciples came to him, and awoke him, saying, Lord, save us: we perish. 26) And he saith unto them, Why are ye fearful, O ye of little faith?

The devotional for today will invoke the thought of being fearful for assorted reasons. The Disciples are out to sea in a boat, and it is stormy. The boat is probably rocking back and forth violently. Maybe the water is getting them soaking wet from coming over the sides. The disciples wake Jesus up and say, *"Lord, save us; we perish"*. Is it not true that all would perish if it were not for Jesus Christ and a cross? In many cases it looks like people are perishing to sin and refusing to serve. Some are afraid to serve Jesus for several reasons. Are Christians afraid that their life will conform to the truth of the Bible and that scares them? Is it because their life will commit to the things of God and that is asking too much? Maybe some are afraid that their life will be consistent in what they do for God and bye-bye free time. Maybe their life will become consecrated to God and sin will be no more. Maybe some do not want their friends to think you are a holy roller and not want to be around you. Maybe some would rather be cool to the world than hot for the LORD, which is typical for today. With anything you must know who to go to that can fix a problem. If you needed a boat fixed, would you go to someone that does quilting? Why? Because your boat does not need a quilt, it needs an engine. If you go for help you must apply the advice, or it is all wasted. I have heard this said, "I know what to do, but I just don't do it". If you were drowning and someone threw you a life jacket, would you refuse to use it because it is just not your color? Jesus Christ, as far as delivering from sin and self, is that life jacket. Look at Peter, he at least got out of the boat and walked on the water to Jesus. Peter never went under until he took his eyes off Jesus. Why are people perishing in sin and not delivered? Because their eye is off the Lord, and they are focusing on obstacles. For the disciples getting soaked, the water is a symbol of the word of God. I would suggest that if there is a problem with sin that you need to get soaked by the word of God. Many do not want to get wet with the word, they only want a sponge bath. Sponge baths I guess are sometimes necessary, but do that for days, weeks, and months and see how that works for you. We stink spiritually because we are not letting God soak us with His word. If God deals with a sin, we cannot be quick to grab a towel and dry off so the word does not soak in too deep. There is no storm that Jesus cannot deliver us from. The storm you cannot be delivered from is the one you do not want delivered from. Many times people will be in a storm, but love the sin, (storm). Maybe it is because some believe they have a better plan than God does. Turn loose of sin and hang on tight to God. If Jesus can calm the wind and the waves, He can calm you and me.

September 10

Matthew 9:28
And when he was come into the house, the blind men came to him: and Jesus saith unto them, Believe ye that I am able to do this? They said unto him, Yea, Lord.

It is difficult to have someone come "into" your house if you will not open the door. If someone knocked, would you say,

"Just a minute, I will unlock the basement window for you". Every one of us should have a continual need for Jesus, so never shut the door. What is the issue in this verse? These blind men wanted to see. I kind of think it is interesting that there was not just one blind man, but multiple blind men. If you or I have a problem, we must know who to go to. If someone was completely blind, would you go to the store to buy them some glasses? They have no eyes to see, but do we insist that they try on a pair of readers? Someone born with no ear drums, and we get them a hearing aid. Someone born with no legs probably does not need roller blades. Here are some guys with a legitimate need going to the ONE who can heal them. Do we really want to "SEE" the truth? We know what the problem is, but refuse to deal with it? We have perfect physical sight, but we are blind spiritually. What born again believer does not recognize when they are in sin? Born again believers can recognize sin and still refuse the deliverance. Just because we do not confess truth, does not mean we do not know the truth. Do you know why some keep Jesus at arm's length? I do not have an answer either. *John 8:36 If the Son therefore shall make you free, ye shall be free indeed.* There is freedom and liberty being set free from sin. The opposite is staying in bondage to sin and a horrible place to live. *Galatians 4:3 Even so we, when we were children, were in bondage under the elements of the world.* The context is being under the law and pre-Jesus. Christians today are under the same bondage to the elements of the world and refuse to be released from sin. Many times, Christians know the truth, but refuse to deal with the truth. The Bible is not much GOOD if it is not used to make us BETTER and to be at our BEST.

September 11

Matthew 16:13-15
13) When Jesus came into the coasts of Caesarea Philippi, he asked his disciples, saying, Whom do men say that I the Son of man am? 14) And they said, Some say that thou art John the Baptist: some, Elias; and others, Jeremias, or one of the prophets. 15) He saith unto them, But whom say ye that I am?

Two Questions to consider right off the bat. Who do men say that I am and who do you think that I am? One may address a bunch of opinions about Jesus and the other is "personal". Does who we say He is match up with "WHO we really are"? Peter had two testimonies. <u>FIRST ONE</u>: *Matthew 26:69 -74 69) Now Peter sat without in the palace: and a damsel came unto him, saying, Thou also wast with Jesus of Galilee. 70) But he denied before them all, saying, I know not what thou sayest.* **Peter did not want to identify with Jesus** *71) And when he was gone out into the porch, another maid saw him, and said unto them that were there, This fellow was also with Jesus of Nazareth. 72) And again he denied with an oath, I do not know the man.* **A little bit stronger refusal to identify with Jesus**. *73) And after a while came unto him they that stood by, and said to Peter, Surely thou also art one of them; for thy speech bewrayeth thee. 74) Then began he to curse and to swear, saying, I know not the man. And immediately the cock crew.* **Peter uses some stronger language in order to not identify with Jesus**. Peter's **second** testimony was *John 21:15-17 15) So when they had dined, Jesus saith to Simon Peter, Simon, son of Jonas, lovest thou me more than these? He saith unto him, Yea, Lord; thou knowest that I love thee. He saith unto him, Feed my lambs.* **Is it possible that Peter is identifying with Jesus because**

no one is around? It is not about being a Christian in the pews. It is about living for Jesus all the time. *16) He saith to him again the second time, Simon, son of Jonas, lovest thou me? He saith unto him, Yea, Lord; thou knowest that I love thee. He saith unto him, Feed my sheep.* **Peter for the second time identifies with Jesus. Is it still because no one else is around to condemn him for it**? *17) He saith unto him the third time, Simon, son of Jonas, lovest thou me? Peter was grieved because he said unto him the third time, Lovest thou me? And he said unto him, Lord, thou knowest all things; thou knowest that I love thee. Jesus saith unto him, Feed my sheep.* **Peter finally realizes that Jesus already knew the answer to the question**. Do we say we LOVE the Lord, but our life says something else? The Lord Jesus Christ has never been fooled. What really changed Peter's testimony for Jesus where he could write I and II Peter? *Matthew 26:75 And Peter remembered the word of Jesus, which said unto him, Before the cock crow, thou shalt deny me thrice. And **he went out, and wept bitterly**. Mark 14:72 And the second time the cock crew. And Peter called to mind the word that Jesus said unto him, Before the cock crow twice, thou shalt deny me thrice. And **when he thought thereon, he wept**. Luke 22:61-62 61) And the Lord turned, and looked upon Peter. And Peter remembered the word of the Lord, how he had said unto him, Before the cock crow, thou shalt deny me thrice. 62) **And Peter went out, and wept bitterly**. John 18:27 Peter then denied again: and immediately the cock crew.* The book of John does not record the crying or the repenting. The book of John only records the denial. Peter's repentance required an action. We can do one of two things. Lord, I love you please deliver me, or Lord, I love you, but not enough to change. Does it really matter what the world thinks about Jesus? Jesus' question one more time is: Who do you say I am?

September 12

Matthew 16:13-15
13) When Jesus came into the coasts of Caesarea Philippi, he asked his disciples, saying, Whom do men say that I the Son of man am? 14) And they said, Some say that thou art John the Baptist: some, Elias; and others, Jeremias, or one of the prophets. 15) He saith unto them, But whom say ye that I am?

Today is a repeat of using the same verse from yesterday, but I do not want to leave out things that can make a difference for both of us. Let us start out with "what matters"? **WHAT MATTERS IS "WHO IS HE TO YOU"?** Is Jesus really a deliverer? Is Jesus really a Comforter? Is Jesus really the Savior? Is Jesus really the Master? Is Jesus really running our life? Is Jesus really a Redeemer? Is Jesus really a Sustainer? How do you know? By the willingness to open the door and surrender your life to Him. Jesus ultimately says, "Feed my Sheep". You cannot feed sheep that do not want your food! For you and me, **WHO IS THIS JESUS**? Is Jesus an acquaintance that I will give a shout out to when all else fails? Is Jesus the Savior and I need Him for hell insurance only? Is Jesus the Lord and Master and I go to Him with every detail of my life? That is exactly what Jesus wants from us. He wants every intricate detail confessed. Who is this Jesus? Good and evil answers have been given for roughly two thousand years and they are as follows. I have heard of Him. I know a little about Him. I know Him personally. I deny He exists. I curse the thought of Him being in my life. Better yet is to think, "I want to repent right now and allow Jesus to be a part of my life". I repent and by faith receive Jesus as my Savior. I repent and turn my whole life over to Jesus Christ today. Or is it, "I repent of everything, but this "ONE" little thing"? Jesus wants our admission of sin so we can render submission to Him. Is the Savior of the world worth turning every area of our life over to Him? Not just for safe-keeping, but for God's safe-using. It is very valuable to be honest and answer the question presented in this verse. "Who do you say that I am"?

September 13

Matthew 22:41-42
41) While the Pharisees were gathered together, Jesus asked them, 42) Saying, What think ye of Christ? whose son is he? They say unto him, The Son of David.

Today our devotional will consist of answering the question, *What Think YE of Christ*? Let's just say we are a bunch of different people gathered together today. Among us there will be many different views, thoughts, and opinions. We may get asked about our political views and we can give an "opinion". An opinion may be truth, but in reality, it is still just an opinion. In many cases an opinion is like a theory, and you cannot prove a theory. You can surmise that a theory is right based on research, but ultimately you cannot prove it. An opinion based on Bible truth is not really an opinion. An example is comparing an opinion about the Bible. Some say it is just a book and some say it is the inerrant word of God. If it is just a book, then I guess you do whatever you want with it. If it is the inerrant word of God, then how we live the Bible ought to stack up with our lifestyle. What we ultimately think of Jesus Christ will be reflected in how we live. Our testimony has already painted a picture of what we think about Jesus. Let us pretend that we are asking the news channels to go to the sidewalk and ask, What do you think about Jesus Christ? Some may say, I am an atheist and I do not believe in that nonsense. Some will say, I have heard that He was a nice person or a good man. Some might say that I heard He did a lot of miracles. Believers will say He is the Savior of the world. Some might even say they heard that Jesus died on a cross and then after 3 days arose from the grave. I would guess that the answers from the world could be endless. It boils down to what someone thinks about Jesus Christ may be described with words. What we think about Jesus Christ is really made clear through our actions, conduct, or decisions. We are all faced with this question every single day. Jesus used King David as an example to prove a point. If you asked any Pharisee what line of ancestry did the Messiah come from? They would answer that so fast as, He is the Son of David. They would have positively identified that the Messiah was coming from royalty. Jesus did in fact come from a Kingly line making Him royalty, but He came from God through Mary, which made Him identify with man. *Isaiah 11:1-2 1) And there shall come forth a rod out of the stem of Jesse, and a Branch shall grow out of his roots: 2) And the spirit of the LORD shall rest upon him, the spirit of wisdom and understanding, the spirit of counsel and might, the spirit of knowledge and of the fear of the LORD.* Jesus had all these qualities from day one. What think ye about the Messiah? *John 1:45 Philip findeth Nathanael, and saith unto him, We have found him, of whom Moses in the law, and the prophets, did write, Jesus of Nazareth, the son of Joseph.* Read *Deuteronomy 18:15* if you want to read Moses' words about the Messiah. If Philip knew all there were to know, would he have called Him the son of Joseph? Only men were put in the Jewish lineage, so Joseph was substituted for Mary. However, for today, would we say the son of Joseph or the Son of God? WHAT THINK YE OF CHRIST? Let's keep every answer about this personal. Is Jesus just my hell insurance, or a lifestyle? Do I think highly enough of Jesus Christ that He is worthy of me living a clean life? Do I think enough of Jesus Christ to serve Him? Do I think so little of Jesus Christ that I will not obey Him? Our answer will not necessarily be in our words. Our answer will be in deeds done for Jesus. Our life will show either how "little" or how "Much" we think of Jesus Christ. *Romans 6:1-2 1) What shall we say then? Shall we continue in sin, that grace may abound? 2) God forbid. How shall we, that are dead to sin, live any longer therein?* Peter said in *Matthew 16:16 And Simon Peter answered and said, Thou art the Christ, the Son of the living God. Jesus said in Matthew 23:10 Neither be ye called masters: for one is your Master, even Christ.* Either we are calling all the shots or Jesus is calling all the shots. Following Jesus on His path is positively a one-way street.

September 14

John 9:30
The man answered and said unto them,
Why herein is a marvellous thing, that ye know not
from whence he is, and yet he hath opened mine eyes.

In our devotion for today we have a Blind Man Healed. The blind guy is testifying about Jesus. He said, "This is a Marvelous thing"! Have you pondered your life before Jesus and now declare, "This is a marvelous thing". Is my life and your life a "Marvelous" thing for Jesus? When we surrendered to Jesus Christ and accepted HIM as our Savior are we: MIRACULOUS and MARVELOUS? Are we TRAGIC and RIDICULOUS? Only two people can answer that question, You and Him. The blind man is healed and now what? *John 9:35-38 35) Jesus heard that they had cast him out; and when he had found him, he said unto him, Dost thou believe on the Son of God? 36) He answered and said, Who is he, Lord, that I might believe on him? 37) And Jesus said unto him, Thou hast both seen him, and it is he that talketh with thee. 38) And he said, Lord, I believe. And he worshipped him.* This blind man chose Jesus instead of staying in the synagogue. He confessed Jesus, was thrown out, and yet he worshipped Jesus. Do we think enough of Jesus Christ to worship Him? It will be reflected in our lifestyle by what we do according to the Word of God. When you got saved your eyes should have been opened to the truth. When the eyes are open, we become responsible to how we handle the "truth". Let me repeat the blind man, "Why herein is a Marvelous thing". It is only marvelous if our physical life matches up with our spiritual sight. It is marvelous when we know what Jesus wants us to do and we do it. Who was Christ to the blind guy? Jesus was a Healer and the Son of God. When we continually see Jesus as the Son of God, we reject the Sin of Satan. Jesus Christ is only a deliverer to those who have been delivered. *1 Peter 2:9 But ye are a chosen generation, a royal priesthood, an holy nation, a peculiar people; that ye should shew forth the praises of him who hath called you out of darkness into his marvellous light.* Our praise of Him should start with our life. No one should make a mockery of what Jesus did on the cross. Did He really die for your sin? Did He pay the ultimate sacrifice for all sin? Am I willing to leave any sin on the cross or carry them everywhere? What think ye of Christ will be revealed by how we live, not by what we say. What we think about Jesus to others is already known. A Hypocrite is when we act like a Pharisee on Sunday and a lost man the other six days of the week.

September 15

Luke 6:46
And why call ye me, Lord, Lord,
and do not the things which I say?

For today we will ponder the question in Luke. "*Why call ye me, Lord, Lord, and do not the things which I say*"? Why do some call Him Lord when it just is not so? Lord as applied to Jesus is not just a term of endearment. Lord is someone having power or influence over you. It is a Master or a Ruler. It will be someone superior to you and me. Is He really the Lord and how can I assess myself? Calling Him Lord just might not be who He really is to us spiritually and personally. Our confirmation is that our life stacks up with His position as LORD of our life. *Matthew 7:21-23 21) Not everyone that saith unto me, Lord, Lord, shall enter into the kingdom of heaven; but he that doeth the will of my Father which is in heaven. 22) Many will say to me in that day, Lord, Lord, have we not prophesied in thy name? and in thy name have cast out devils? and in thy name done many wonderful works? 23) And then will I profess unto them, I never knew you: depart from me, ye that work iniquity*. Because someone calls Jesus King or LORD does not mean they are saved. *Matthew 27:29 And when they had platted a crown of thorns, they put it upon his head, and a reed in his right hand: and they bowed the knee before him, and mocked him, saying, Hail, King of the Jews! Mark 15:18 – 19 18) And began to salute him, Hail, King of the Jews! 19) And they smote him on the head with a reed, and did spit upon him, and bowing their knees worshipped him. John 19:3 And said, Hail, King of the Jews! and they smote him with their hands*. So **many** called him LORD, but are those "**many**" really saved? The QUESTION: "Why call me LORD and MASTER and then do your own thing"? If you continued reading past this verse, it is about a house built on sinking sand. It is about not having a firm foundation for your life. We say Jesus is Lord, but we decide what is best, and in reality we become the lord. Some may say, "Jesus is the Real Thing", but in reality, will do their own thing. *John 5:14 {**Lame Man**}, Afterward Jesus findeth him in the temple, and said unto him, Behold, thou art made whole: sin no more, lest a worse thing come unto thee*. When Jesus becomes someone's Savior the slate is wiped clean. I am not saying there are not consequences for sin. I am saying the slate is wiped clean and you have a fresh start. Why would anyone want to take a marker and mark up the slate? The woman at the well when asked by Jesus about who is condemning you about your sin said in *John 8:11 She said, No man, Lord. And Jesus said unto her, Neither do I condemn thee:* **go, and sin no more**. Jesus did not come to condemn the world, He came to redeem the World. Jesus came to destroy sin, not support sin. Jesus came to offer repentance from sin not acceptance of sin. Jesus came to die for our sin so we could live without sin. Big Question: Why do you not do the things I say? A few examples from scripture are: *Thou shalt have no other gods before me. Love the Lord with all thy heart, soul, and mind. Love your neighbor as yourself. Job 42:6* <u>Wherefore I abhor myself, and repent in dust and ashes</u>. When God becomes real in someone's life repenting in dust and ashes will be natural. Let your action of serving Jesus be your dust and your ashes of humility. You positively will not regret it.

September 16

Luke 8:30
And Jesus asked him, saying, What is thy name? And he said, Legion: because many devils were entered into him.

The question to consider today came from Jesus to a demon-possessed man. He simply asks, *"What is thy name"*? How many think that Jesus probably already knew who this was? Jesus did not ask because He did not know. He asked to get a response. Jesus asked, "What is your name or what are you called or recognized by"? We have a demon-possessed man that knew his name based on what or who he held internally. Devils or not, when Jesus asks a question there will be a response. The Response: My name is LEGION because there were many devils in him. A legion means many things. A Roman Legion could be dozens or thousands. If we give place to Satan in one area, we will give place to Satan in several areas. *Luke 16:15 {Pharisees}, And he said unto them, Ye are they which justify yourselves before men; but God knoweth your hearts: for that which is highly esteemed among men is abomination in the sight of God.* People will justify their sin today. People can have their reason for sin, but it is still sin. *Luke 16:15* says sin is highly esteemed among men, but an abomination to God. There are things that used to be shameful. Now those same things that are contrary to the Word of God are widely practiced and accepted. Many times kids can be messed up because of an example. They may not know what the Bible taught, but by watching others, it is what they caught. *James 4:17 Therefore to him that knoweth to do good, and doeth it not, to him it is sin.* Jesus does not want us to justify sin. He wants us to do justly about sin. Jesus does not want us to conform to sin, He wants us to condemn sin. The question from Jesus was, *"what is thy name"*? Based on what our testimony is or has been, *"what is your name"? Psalms 44:20-21 20) If we have forgotten the name of our God, or stretched out our hands to a strange god; 21) Shall not God search this out? for he knoweth the secrets of the heart.* We may have secrets from others, but God knows all. The tragedy will be like David the King. He was told that what he did in Secret, (Bathsheba), or in darkness, would be revealed to everyone around him in the light of day. It all ends up with nothing except embarrassment. One Question: By what I have going on in my life right now, what is my name? Second Question: Can I completely turn my life over to Jesus Christ? Jesus has a name above all names, but what is our name recognized as? Our name to God if you are saved is you are a child of the most HOLY KING. Ever heard this expression about someone, "they have made quite a name for themselves". That can mean prosperous or extremely poor. That can mean successful or not so much. That can mean spiritually rich or spiritually poor. You and I, based on what we do, really tell the story about who God is to us. If anyone hears our name, what is the first thing on their mind? People can linger on our past, but they cannot deny the present. When we do things for God in the present, we must make sure we keep on in the future. The world needs to see Christians that are rock-solid and committed to Jesus. The world needs to see that we will not compromise the Word of God. The world needs to see that when someone is called by the name of Christian, that we are living by the standard associated with it. We are Christians and followers of Jesus by choice. Jesus is the name above all names and by association let the world know you love Him! *Psalms 8:9 O LORD our Lord, how excellent is thy name in all the earth! Psalms 22:22 I will declare thy name unto my brethren: in the midst of the congregation will I praise thee.* **We declare our praise by how we live**.

Psalms 23:3 He restoreth my soul: he leadeth me in the paths of righteousness for his name's sake. **Are people seeing Jesus in us and through us**? *Psalms 74:18 Remember this, that the enemy hath reproached, O LORD, and that the foolish people have blasphemed thy name.* What is our name to our family, community, workplace, and church based on those that know us best?

September 17

John 18:7
Then asked he them again,
Whom seek ye? And they said, Jesus of Nazareth.

We can ask ourselves the same question, "*Whom seek ye*"? The context is a group finding Jesus in order to arrest Him in the garden. Some that were there followed Jesus and were His disciples. Some went there to arrest Jesus and turn Him over to the religious leaders for crucifixion. One group took Him captive, and another group ran as fast as they could to get away. Not sure that isn't how it is today. Some will follow fully Jesus. Some will follow Jesus half-heartedly. Some will not follow Jesus at all. Honest question from Jesus about who or what were they looking for? The Bible is current and are we seeking Jesus of Nazareth? Through life we answer that question through various means. I love the word "seek" in the verse and there are two different meanings. Seek, as in to worship. Seek, as in to plot against or destroy. The eleven Disciples sought to worship and learn from Him and one betrayed Him with a kiss. If I am seeking Jesus, what do I do, and what does it look like? What will be noticeable as I seek Jesus Christ? *Romans 12:2 And be not conformed to this world: but be ye transformed by the renewing of your mind, that ye may prove what is that good, and acceptable, and perfect, will of God.* There will be unity among the brethren *Philippians 1:27 Only let your conversation be as it becometh t.he gospel of Christ: that whether I come and see you, or else be absent, I may hear of your affairs, that ye stand fast in one spirit, with one mind striving together for the faith of the gospel*; As we all seek God individually and corporately we will have unity of the Spirit. It would be hard to work together in unity corporately without seeking Jesus as an individual first. **Wise men** - *Matthew 2:1-2 1) Now when Jesus was born in Bethlehem of Judaea in the days of Herod -the king, behold, there came wise men from the east to Jerusalem, 2) Saying, Where is he that is born King of the Jews? for we have seen his star in the east, and are come to worship him.* The wise men had the Word of God and a star to "follow" to Jesus. We have the Word of God and the Holy Spirit to "guide" us to Jesus. *Colossians 3:1 If ye then be risen with Christ, seek those things which are above, where Christ sitteth on the right hand of God. Matthew 6:20 But lay up for yourselves treasures in heaven, where neither moth nor rust doth corrupt, and where thieves do not break through nor steal: Colossians 3:2 Set your affection on things above, not on things on the earth. Matthew 10:37 He that loveth father or mother more than me is not worthy of me: and he that loveth son or daughter more than me is not worthy of me.* Humanly that sounds very mean to even ask of us. Spiritually it sounds like nothing should come before Jesus. Seeking Jesus consistently will bring spiritual blessings. *John 18:5 -6 5) They answered him, Jesus of Nazareth. Jesus saith unto them, I am he. And Judas also, which betrayed him, stood with them. 6) As soon then as he had said unto them, I am he, they went backward, and fell to the ground.* A group is sent on a mission to find and arrest Jesus. The group finds Jesus and then they go backward and fall to the ground. The group still arrested Jesus and turned Him in. When they fell down to the ground to Jesus it was short-lived. That is the kind of world we live in. I will just sprinkle a little of Jesus on me today to look good. Remember that old phrase; "If I were arrested for being a Christian, would it stick"? It is always a good time to fall on our face before God. There is no greater feeling than to bow the knee to the King as we seek Him. To the world Jesus is just an acquaintance they do not seek after. To the body of Christ, Jesus is our Savior, and who we must follow. There will be a day when everyone will bow the knee to Jesus Christ. *Romans 14:11 For it is written, As I live, saith the Lord, every knee shall bow to me, and every tongue shall confess to God. Philippians 2:10 That at the name of Jesus every knee should bow, of things in heaven, and things in earth, and things under the earth.* If you do take some time to fall down in worship, do not be too hasty to jump back up.

September 18

John 18:7
Then asked he them again,
Whom seek ye? And they said, Jesus of Nazareth.

I wanted to use the same verse from yesterday and continue the thought of how we are seeking Jesus. Are we seeking Jesus with a passion? I believe there is only one time in the King James Bible where the word "Passion" is used. *Acts 1:3 To whom also he shewed himself alive after his **passion** by many infallible proofs, being seen of them forty days, and speaking of the things pertaining to the kingdom of God*: Passion as in Jesus showed himself alive after His suffering. Passion as in showing Himself alive after His beatings. If you and I seek Jesus with the same passion that

He endured His sufferings, you and I will never be the same. Some may be in good standing with the world, but will go to Hell without Jesus. I am fully convinced that many in our world do not even realize that they are lost and that makes it difficult to win them over to Jesus Christ. If lost people do not see us seeking Jesus, why would they? People will notice our commitment to Jesus, "IF", it has made a change in us. Seeking Jesus should not be when we have nothing better to do. Seeking Jesus should be a natural thing that does not require planning. We do not write out a plan to include Jesus into our daily routine. When others see us pursuing Jesus, they just might grab on to our coat tails and follow.

September 19

Hebrews 9:11
But Christ being come an high priest of good
things to come, by a greater and more perfect tabernacle,
not made with hands, that is to say, not of this building;

When Jesus Christ came and died, we were given a New Testament or a New Covenant. Every good thing that was prophesied in the Old Testament has now come to pass through Jesus. All spiritual and eternal blessings the Old Testament promised were fulfilled when Jesus came. The New Testament is the fulfillment of the Old Testament. The Old Testament **promised** a Savior that would come. *Isaiah 9:6 For unto us a child is born, unto us a son is given: and the government shall be upon his shoulder: and his name shall be called Wonderful, Counsellor, The mighty God, The everlasting Father, The Prince of Peace.* The New Testament **fulfilled** the promise of the gift of a Savior, Jesus Christ. *Luke 2:11 For unto you is born this day in the city of David a Saviour, which is Christ the Lord.* Jesus is not a tabernacle or a church that man built physically. Jesus the Savior is what the Church would be built on spiritually for those who will trust Him as LORD. Jesus is the "high priest" above any who call themselves priests. Because of Jesus we now have a perfect tabernacle that can be accessed by faith in Jesus. Jesus is not a stone for a building, but rather the "Cornerstone" that we build upon. Jesus is the way, the truth, and the life and we cannot get to God without going to Jesus. This is why today's church does not need several cornerstones of what they believe. Contrary to some, there is only one way to get to Heaven and that is through faith in Jesus Christ. We have gone from a temple made with hands that held the Holy of Holies, to being a human body that is a temple, that now holds the Holy Spirit if you are "SAVED". *I Corinthians 3:16 Know ye not that ye are the temple of God, and that the Spirit of God dwelleth in you?* Let us be mindful of taking care of our "Temple". God is not asking us to be body builders. He is telling us to take care of our bodies. Once again, which is easier? Driving "to" the gym or going inside and exercising? We also must exercise our minds by putting the Word of God in it. Remember, what we put in our mind may be easier to put in that it is to get out. A memory can be a good gift of good things. A memory will also recall things we should not have done. Praise God we can be forgiven, but do not add things to the memory of what we should not do. Jesus Christ is the perfect tabernacle made without hands. May we be a reflection of everything Jesus is to us personally. May our memory always remind us of what Jesus did for us on the cross!

September 20

Hebrews 9:12
Neither by the blood of goats and calves,
but by his own blood he entered in once into the
holy place, having obtained eternal redemption for us.

Praise the Lord we no longer must bring an animal to sacrifice in order to be saved. Jesus became the sacrificial Lamb that redeemed all from death for those who will trust him for salvation and accept him by faith. Jesus Christ, a perfect, unblemished, and holy Lamb of God. Something to consider: The High Priest would be appointed once a year to offer the sacrifice of Atonement. It would not always be the same High Priest, but it still had to be repeated yearly. Jesus was appointed by God to be the New Testament sacrifice and it will never have to be repeated. Jesus' death, burial, and resurrection will never be repeated and is good for eternity. Look at Abraham and Isaac, *Genesis 22:8 And Abraham said, My son,* **_God will provide himself a lamb_** *for a burnt offering: so they went both of them together.* There is no greater picture in the Old Testament of God providing himself as the lamb. No one can earn their salvation by doing anything. God saw the degradation of man and provided another Lamb, Jesus His Son. However, Jesus was the sacrifice, 'BUT" we cannot forget about an Empty Tomb. For me, the key to what I believe are the words "eternal redemption". Many run around wondering if they lost their salvation or not. What did they do? Did they misplace it? Goodness gracious if Jesus says we received eternal redemption, then they should look at the word eternal. We received a free gift and did not deserve it. Everything regarding salvation points to Jesus. We cannot lose what we did not earn. We accept by faith what Jesus offered and no one can pluck us out of His hands. *Romans 8:38-39 38) For I am persuaded, that neither death, nor life, nor angels, nor principalities, nor powers, nor things present, nor things to come, 39) Nor height, nor depth, nor any other creature, shall be able to separate us from the love of God, which is in Christ Jesus our Lord.*

September 21

Hebrews 9:13
For if the blood of bulls and of goats, and the ashes of an heifer sprinkling the unclean, sanctifieth to the purifying of the flesh:

This verse poses a comment about an animal only purifying the flesh. The verse says nothing about purifying the spirit. Only Jesus can make anyone whole or complete spiritually. Only Jesus can make us a "permanent quickening" spirit or made alive. *1 Corinthians 15:45 And so it is written, The first man Adam was made a living soul; the last Adam was made a quickening spirit.* The Old Testament says the Holy Spirt came upon man temporarily. The New Testament teaches that by trusting Jesus the Holy Spirit dwells in man permanently. *John 8:36 If the Son therefore shall make you free, ye shall be free indeed.* Free is used twice in *John 8:36*. Once it means you have been liberated from the penalties of death. The other time means you have been set free and are no longer a slave to sin. No one has to live a defeated life with Jesus. Blood of bulls and goats were offered for the sacrifice of sin and had to be repeated. Jesus was given as a sacrifice for our sin and Jesus himself said, "It Is Finished". *John 19:30 When Jesus therefore had received the vinegar, he said, It is finished: and he bowed his head, and gave up the ghost. 1 Corinthians 15:3 For I delivered unto you first of all that which I also received, how that Christ died for our sins according to the scriptures;* Only through Jesus can anyone be justified, sanctified, purified, and glorified. What do we do with all that? I leave you with this; "Live your life so the Pastor does not have to lie at your funeral".

September 22

Hebrews 9:14
How much more shall the blood of Christ, who through the eternal Spirit offered himself without spot to God, purge your conscience from dead works to serve the living God?

What are the Key words in this verse for today? **How much more**! The Old Testament lamb sacrifice would be repeated. The New Testament Lamb Jesus Christ died once, and it is forever. *Hebrews 7:22 By so much was Jesus made a surety of a better testament.* Surety means to be a slave. Surety can be one who stands behind a business deal. Jesus, the Lamb of God, committed to God's plan of being "the" sacrifice. Jesus sealed the deal and is behind the promise of eternal life to those who will believe. Jesus' blood was sufficient to cleanse us from sin permanently. Jesus' blood was without spot as He knew no sin, but became sin for us when He died on the cross. *John 1:47 Jesus saw Nathanael coming to him, and saith of him, Behold an Israelite indeed, in whom is no guile!* There was absolutely no deviousness in Jesus Christ. *2 Corinthians 5:21 For he hath made him to be sin for us, who knew no sin; that we might be made the righteousness of God in him. 1 Peter 2:22 Who did no sin, neither was guile found in his mouth: 1 John 3:5 And ye know that he was manifested to take away our sins; and in him is no sin.* A sacrifice had to be pure and unblemished and Jesus was the perfect Lamb of God that died for the world. *2 Corinthians 5:21 For he hath made him to be sin for us, who knew no sin; that we might be made the righteousness of God in him.* Jesus' blood was shed so we could live a holy life and serve a "living" God. With Jesus we have hope and without Jesus we are hopeless and helpless. Jesus' sacrifice was "SO MUCH MORE" than the sacrifice of an animal, yet He was treated shamefully, beaten relentlessly, and hung to die on a cross.

September 23

Hebrews 9:14
How much more shall the blood of Christ, who through the eternal Spirit offered himself without spot to God, purge your conscience from dead works to serve the living God?

I did not want to sell short the verse from yesterday so you can pick right back up where we left off. When someone accepts Jesus by faith the slate is wiped clean. Are there consequences to things we did before meeting Jesus? That is a positive yes. However, we have had our conscience purged from dead works. To purge our conscience is to kill off any works of the devil that we had going on. Learn the Word of God, and serve the living God, to the best of God's ability. *2 Corinthians 5:17 Therefore if any man be in Christ, he is a new creature: old things are passed away; behold, all things are become new. 1 Thessalonians 1:9 For they themselves shew of us what manner of entering in we had unto you, and how ye turned to God from idols to serve the living and true God.* Our verse today is from the book of Hebrews, and it was written to the Jews. Hebrews is going to be one of the books of the Bible they will turn to during the tribulation period. The book of Hebrews will have a profound effect for those who missed the rapture of the body of Christ. Many will miss the rapture of the church. Many will look diligently for an answer to what happened when so many people are instantly gone. During the tribulation period you cannot turn back the clock, and your only hope is that you endure to the end. Many will realize the truth of Jesus Christ and the regrets will be many. The bottom line is when we got saved, we now have the mind of Christ. It is up to us to learn, meditate, and memorize the word of God so as to put on the Lord Jesus Christ according to *Romans 13:14*. We have been purged from dead works so let us take on new works for Jesus Christ. For the record, the rapture of the church has not happened yet, or I would not be sitting here typing. Make sure you are ready for Jesus to call you home!

September 24

Hebrews 9:15
And for this cause he is the mediator of the new testament, that by means of death, for the redemption of the transgressions that were under the first testament, they which are called might receive the promise of eternal inheritance.

The world was promised an eternal inheritance in the Old Testament and Jesus fulfilled that prophecy. We needed a permanent blood sacrifice to redeem us, and Jesus gave His life to do just that. The gospel should be considered the last will and testament of our Lord and Saviour Jesus Christ. We would say Jesus is our inheritance that God gave to the world to those who will believe. Sometimes the word testament is the word covenant. It is an agreement that for all of eternity Jesus is sufficient for someone to be saved and to spend eternity in Heaven. Jesus as the mediator means it was a voluntary act. No one forced Him to the cross he willingly went. It was the act of a single person, and that was Jesus Christ. Christ is the Mediator of a New Testament. Jesus redeems and saves unbelievers from their sin. We are all indebted to God and Jesus paid the debt. We have been left a legacy or inheritance from Jesus Christ. Jesus is our "high priest", and our Savior if we will just trust his sacrificial death for sin. No one has ever left the world a greater legacy than what Jesus did when he declared on the cross that He loves us. Nothing has caused more controversy in the world. Jesus did His part and died. Someone lost must do their part and by faith receive Jesus to be their personal Lord and Savior. Our responsibility is to share the truth about what we know about the free gift. For the lost, their responsibility is to either accept or reject Jesus and that choice is theirs. The world has two choices to either trust in the power of an "Empty Tomb" or trust in self and live an "Empty Life". Let me really paraphrase this verse 15 for understanding. Follow along in your Bible as I will change it just a little bit for your edification. My paraphrase of *Hebrews 9:15 is, "And for this exact reason, is why Jesus reconciled us to God and gave us a brand New Contract, and because of Jesus' death it paid our ransom that we owed God for violating His word. Some were under the Old Testament or an old Contract, but now God is calling out to the world to grab on to Jesus and receive God's divine assurance and possession of eternal life.*

September 25

Genesis 4:3-5
3) And in process of time it came to pass, that Cain brought of the fruit of the ground an offering unto the LORD. 4) And Abel, he also brought of the firstlings of his flock and of the fat thereof. And the LORD had respect unto Abel and to his offering: 5) But unto Cain and to his offering he had not respect. And Cain was very wroth, and his countenance fell.

This is the first time an offering is mentioned. Cain brought fruit of the ground and Abel offered the blood of an animal. The word for Abel's offering is *tsone, tseh-one'*, and could be used for a flock of lambs. They needed a lamb for a sacrifice in the Old Testament and it pictured Jesus. We needed a lamb for a sacrifice in the New Testament and it was Jesus. A lamb, goat, bullock, turtledove, pigeon, or even wheat could be a sin offering. The offering by some priests became a joke and abused. The account of that is in *I Samuel 2:16 And if any man said unto him, Let them not fail to burn the fat presently, and then take as much as thy soul desireth; then he would answer him, Nay; but thou shalt give it me now: and if not, I will take it by force*. Hophni & Phinehas were bad and evil priests. The offering became nothing more to the priests than something to grill and eat. "ONE" High Priest takes our sins and casts them as far as the east is from the west. There is only "ONE" High Priest that forgives permanently, and that is Jesus. A blood sacrifice has always been required of God for cleansing. Both sacrifices would be a bloody mess. One would be an animal on an altar cut up. One would be Jesus on a cross, beaten, and nailed to a tree. Some may be in good standing with the world, but will go to Hell without the Lamb of God. Keep on promoting

Jesus to others and if necessary, use words. Your testimony is a powerful thing, so keep on serving and witnessing about Jesus!

September 26

Ezekiel 42:14
When the priests enter therein, then shall they not go out of the holy place into the utter court, but there they shall lay their garments wherein they minister; for they are holy; and shall put on other garments, and shall approach to those things which are for the people.

Let us give thanks to Jesus for His willingness to die as our sacrificial Lamb. His death allowed us to enter the Holy of Holies, receive the free gift of salvation, and the permanent indwelling of the Holy Spirit. The Holy of Holies was the most protected and revered area of the tabernacle. It was covered by a veil and "NO" one except the High Priest could enter. Even the High Priest could enter only once a year to offer the blood of sacrifice known as the blood of atonement. The High Priest appointed thoroughly washed himself and would wear priestly clothes. It could best be described as the inner-most sanctum. Nothing was more revered than the Holy of Holies. No one could enter that area unless you were "Chosen" to serve as "the high priest". When Jesus died, was buried, and arose from the grave the curtain was torn from the top to the bottom, and we were now provided free access to "the Holy of Holies" We now have access to God by way of Jesus through faith. *Matthew 27:51 And, behold, the veil of the temple was rent in twain from the top to the bottom; and the earth did quake, and the rocks rent; Mark 15:38 And the veil of the temple was rent in twain from the top to the bottom.* Keep in mind that the Holy of Holies would have been completely dark around the ark. The only way to shed light on anything and allow us to enter the Holy of Holies was because of Jesus' death, burial, and resurrection. Jesus is the "LIGHT" of the world and we display that light by right living.

September 27

Hebrews 9:11
But Christ being come an high priest of good things to come, by a greater and more perfect tabernacle, not made with hands, that is to say, not of this building;

The Old Testament had a place that could only be entered if you were chosen. I am referring once again to the Holy of Holies. God has given us through Jesus a New Covenant. For us today God says, "Come as you are". *Matthew 11:28 Come unto me, all ye that labour and are heavy laden, and I will give you rest.* God will not judge because we are a fashion statement. He will judge if we know Jesus. We cannot make light of what was expected in the Old Testament for offerings. We cannot make light of what Jesus did by being "The" offering giving us a New Testament. I would like to take you back and forth between the Old and the New Testament. Old Testament, one man selected by man to go into the Holy of Holies once a year. New Testament, Jesus is sent by God to open the Holy of Holies and tore the veil from top to bottom. Old Testament, one man was required to wear specific clothing when he entered. New Testament, Jesus gave His life and wants us to come as we are. Old Testament, one man would offer up the sacrifice of Atonement. New Testament, Jesus offered up His life and became our Atonement. Old Testament, the sacrifice was a temporary solution for sin and had to be repeated. New

Testament, those who claim Jesus as their Savior now have a permanent solution from sin. Old Testament, the Holy Spirit came upon man and it was temporary. New Testament, the Holy Spirit dwells in men that are saved permanently. Old Testament, men would decide who will enter the Holy of Holies next year. New Testament, when Jesus said it is finished, sacrifices of animals were no longer required. This New Covenant given by God was not a building of sticks and stones. It was a building built by the blood of Jesus and will never rot, fall down, or decay.

September 28

Matthew 9:13
But go ye and learn what that meaneth,
I will have mercy, and not sacrifice: for I am not
come to call the righteous, but sinners to repentance.

Many religious leaders then and now may think they are perfect in and of themselves. Our thoughts should be that we know we are not perfect, but that we want Jesus to perfect us. I believe one of the best verses that depicts humility instead of pride would be found in *Luke 8:10-13 10) Two men went up into the temple to pray; the one a Pharisee, and the other a publican. 11) The Pharisee stood and prayed thus with himself, God, I thank thee, that I am not as other men are, extortioners, unjust, adulterers, or even as this publican. 12) I fast twice in the week, I give tithes of all that I possess. 13) And the publican, standing afar off, would not lift up so much as his eyes unto heaven, but smote upon his breast, saying, God be merciful to me a sinner.* One left justified in his own mind and the other left justified with God's blessing. I understand that we are not perfect and a work in progress. I also get that because we are prone to make mistakes that this is not a license to do what we want, and God will forgive us. Yes, God will forgive us, but we are to strive to live a life where we do not need forgiven for bad choices we make. This verse mentions mercy and that is simply not getting what we deserve, which is death and hell. The opposite is God's grace, which is receiving what we do not deserve and that would be eternal life and Heaven. If Jesus is your Savior rejoice that when God called you to salvation you answered the call. I am convinced that I would rather be a repenting Publican than a religious symbol. A religious symbol is nothing more than someone looking like they are holier than thou and not one trace of Jesus in them. If the leader of any church does not believe the Bible is necessary to read, study, and meditate you better run away from that. It has never been about a religion. It has always been about a relationship. Because you belong to a specific church will not save you. Because a church gives you multiple choices of how to be saved will not save you. There is only one way to get to God and that is through Jesus. Anything besides those few things I just listed makes it no better than a cult group.

September 29

Mark 10:51-52
51) And Jesus answered and said unto him, What wilt thou that I should do unto thee? The blind man said unto him, Lord, that I might receive my sight. 52) And Jesus said unto him, Go thy way; thy faith hath made thee whole. And immediately he received his sight, and followed Jesus in the way.

If there is one thing I know, it is that Jesus knew who could see physically and who could give or restore sight. He not only knew then, but Jesus knows now who is spiritually blind to the truth. Jesus knows who struggles with sin and only Jesus Christ can make anyone whole. I am not talking about being perfect. I am talking about allowing God to perfect us. When you and I decide that we want insight to God's truth, He will teach us as we are ready to receive it. Being spiritually blind is when someone lost does not recognize they are lost or who has rejected Jesus from being their Savior. This blind man's sight was restored because Jesus said, "thy faith has made thee whole". The more we trust Jesus with every detail of our life the more our faith will grow. Our faith may waiver at times, but when we run back to the Savior, He can and will put us back on track. There is a consistent path in this verse that has not changed. The first is when Jesus asks a question, it required a response. The blind man's response was, "I want to see". Jesus' response was, "according to your faith let your sight be restored". I always wondered what would have happened if the blind man would have had just a little faith. Would he have needed corrective lenses? OR, did he have the faith as a grain of a mustard seed and his sight was restored because that was enough to have his sight restored. Ultimately, when you and I pray or request something from God, do we pray and then expectantly await an answer? Faith is praying for rain, but never leaving the house without an umbrella. Spiritual insight for anyone will require the intervention of Jesus Christ as He takes our requests to God. *1 Timothy 2:5 For there is one God, and one mediator between God and men, the man Christ Jesus.*

September 30

John 5:6
When Jesus saw him lie, and knew that he had been now a long time in that case, he saith unto him, Wilt thou be made whole?

Here we have a man that has been crippled for thirty-eight years. Just how bad did this man want to be healed? For thirty-eight years he could not walk and probably struggled even moving. Can you imagine what it would be like to struggle just to get to the bathroom? Can you imagine as an adult submitting to someone just to get you on and off the toilet? I know some have this struggle, but I know that Jesus is still healing. I also wonder what if the crippled man had said, "No I do not want to be healed". That last comment is based on the fact that every person has a choice to make with their personal walk with the Lord. I can walk in front of Him and run into a lot of problems. I can walk beside Him, and unless I turn my head towards Him, I will miss His directions. Finally, I can walk behind Him, and let Him move obstacles out of the way and this is obviously the best place to be. The worst is not to follow Jesus at all and step in a cesspool of sin and no hope. We are all at different ages in life and we all have our own individual walk. If it has been some time since you followed close to Jesus, it is never too late to start. If you have never followed Jesus, He is only a prayer away from getting on board and on His path. Our path will be filled with disappointment and failure. Jesus' path will be filled with satisfaction and success. Will our walk always be without problems? No, but I would rather have a problem crop up with Jesus than to have a problem without Him.

October 1

Luke 8:50
But when Jesus heard it, he answered him, saying,
Fear not: believe only, and she shall be made whole.

We now have a little dead girl who Jesus raised from the dead. Before any of us accepted Jesus to be our personal Lord and Savior we were all incomplete spiritually. Only Jesus can make us whole spiritually. I did not say we are suddenly perfect, but rather we are made whole spiritually. When Jesus saved us, we were made a quickening spirit or made alive. The exact second you received Jesus, you also received the permanent indwelling of the HOLY SPIRIT. For those who have rejected Jesus, they are nothing more than dead men walking, and spiritually they cannot harm you in any way. I have never come across anything that Jesus cannot deliver us from and make us whole. What hurt, habit, or hang-up, can Jesus Christ not rescue us from? If you and I cling to sin, we look to the world as no better than they do. This little girl had her life breathed back into her. This little girl received and felt the personal touch of the Master's hand. Person after person has been touched by the LORD Jesus Christ and made spiritually whole. I am not sure what this little girl died of. I only know that she was raised to new life. How much rejoicing did her family and friends experience when she started breathing again and walked? Never forget what it was like when you received Jesus as your Savior and were pardoned of all your past, present, and future sin. I am sure of what I struggled with before Jesus. Like this little girl, I have been raised to new life to walk with Him. I do not care how good someone thinks they are in this life. Without Jesus they are incomplete spiritually, and their final destiny is a Lake of Fire. I was made whole spiritually when I accepted

Jesus and He does not turn anybody down. Blessings to you as God gives you opportunities to share of how accepting Jesus Christ as your Savior has **significantly** changed you.

October 2

John 19:30
When Jesus therefore had received the vinegar, he said, It is finished: and he bowed his head and gave up the ghost.

The phrase from Jesus "It is finished", appears only one time in the book of John and Jesus said it on the cross. A new work began, and God echoed the call for sinners to come to repentance. Part of that work is to mold born again believers into His image through the gift of the Holy Spirit. There will be a day when this life is over and there will be another brand-new day. Let me reference for you a passage out of the book of Revelation. *Revelation 21:1-4 1) And I saw a new heaven and a new earth: for the first heaven and the first earth were passed away; and there was no more sea. 2) And I John saw the holy city, new Jerusalem, coming down from God out of heaven, prepared as a bride adorned for her husband. 3) And I heard a great voice out of heaven saying, Behold, the tabernacle of God is with men, and he will dwell with them, and they shall be his people, and God himself shall be with them, and be their God. 4) And God shall wipe away all tears from their eyes; and there shall be no more death, neither sorrow, nor crying, neither shall there be any more pain: for the former things are passed away.* Satan wants us to believe that what Jesus did was just a lie and never really happened. Satan lost his battle when he said, "if you are who you say you are, come down off that cross". The last thing Jesus was going to do was to come down off the cross and not die for humanity. God's will was for Jesus to be a sacrifice for the world. God's will for humanity is to come to a saving knowledge of Jesus Christ as your personal Lord and Savior. When you and I got saved, Satan occasionally gets a win as he is the accuser of the brethren. For salvation purposes, "IT IS FINISHED", are Jesus' words and Satan cannot stop anyone coming to Jesus for salvation. Death and Hell no longer have any strongholds or victory on believers. When we hear, "come up hither", and the rapture occurs nothing can stop that event. *1 Corinthians 15:57 But thanks be to God, which giveth us the victory through our Lord Jesus Christ.* Hallelujah and Amen! When it is finished, the church age as we know it is over and the tribulation period begins. For those who have never accepted Jesus to be their Savior, this will be a time like they have never experienced before. It will literally be 7 years of hell on earth in a physical sense. Very few will make it through this dispensation of time, but no one has to experience it. Just trust you soul to Jesus.

October 3

Romans 1:1
Paul, a servant of Jesus Christ,
called to be an apostle, separated unto the gospel of God,

Paul mentions the Gospel of God in this verse. Gospel meaning good news. *Matthew 4:23 And Jesus went about all Galilee, teaching in their synagogues, and preaching the gospel of the kingdom, and healing all manner of sickness and all manner of disease among the people.* It should not surprise us that the first time the word gospel is used is by Jesus. He preaches the gospel of the kingdom. Jesus already knew what the people understood about the scriptures as He is all-knowing. Jesus is God and the Word is Jesus, God, and the Holy Spirit. Jesus wanted them to know what they should know right now and in the future. Jesus preached the kingdom of Heaven where Jesus is the King of Kings and Lord of Lords. When we became a Christian, someone told us about Jesus. We heard the gospel and we either accepted or rejected it. Some might say I did not reject or accept Him. When there is no answer it is "NO". For those that are saved we have a Christian legacy. Someone is your spiritual Father. Someone told you, someone told them, and on and on. We must be diligent about continuing that legacy to others. Do we pray for divine appointments to share the good news of Jesus? When someone hears the gospel of God, they hear the good news about Jesus. They will either accept or reject the good news that will save their soul from hell. No matter what someone does with the good news, it is still personal. Do not take someone rejecting Jesus as your burden to bear. They are not rejecting you, they are rejecting Jesus. We have a responsibility to tell everything about Jesus. Matthew 11:5 The blind receive their sight, the lame walk, lepers are cleansed, the deaf hear, the dead are raised up, and the poor have the gospel preached to them. They may not be poor due to a lack of money. More than likely, they are poor because of a lack of Jesus. No matter how wealthy someone is monetarily, if they do not know Jesus, they are spiritually bankrupt. Here is Jesus' message. *Luke 4:18 The Spirit of the Lord is upon me, because he hath anointed me to preach the gospel to the poor; he hath sent me to heal the brokenhearted, to preach deliverance to the captives, and recovering of sight to the blind, to set at liberty them that are bruised.* Any one lost is spiritually bruised and broken. Only Jesus can take a lost soul and make it whole and of use to God the Father. You can choose Jesus and heaven or reject

Jesus and accept the consequences of hell. Both places are for eternity.

October 4

Romans 1:1
Paul, a servant of Jesus Christ, called to be an apostle, separated unto the **gospel of God**,

You were at Romans 1:1 yesterday and we will continue with the same verse today. Be encouraged to share the good news of Jesus. The gospel of God is powerful, and we are to take it to the uttermost ends of the earth according to *Matthew 28:19-20*. As far as sharing the good news of the gospel we are to mimic Jesus. Jesus preached to the poor of the world so they could understand He was all the wealth they needed. He preached to the poor in spirit, the meek, and the humble. He preached to those who were sorrowful for their sin. You can be the wealthiest person on the planet, and be poor in Spirit. It is like an itch you cannot scratch. I remember reading a story about a very wealthy man on his death bed who said, "I wish I would have had just one good friend". The number one question I was faced with as an unbeliever was, "Is this all there is to this life"? I finally realized that when we died, I did not just go poof, and life was over. I could grasp that there is an eternity somewhere. I knew that Jesus wanted to heal the brokenhearted and that was me. Accepting by faith, the gospel of God, is so much more of a benefit than just salvation. Salvation is beyond wonderful, but the gospel of God daily transforms people. Did you ever believe it could not get any worse in your life, but it did. Have you ever been wronged beyond your wildest imagination by someone that was close to you? God not only gives us hope, but He helps us cope with anything that is difficult. God desires to become all things to all men that we might win some. The Jesus we possess internally, is to be shared with the world externally. May Jesus be revealed through what you do daily. People will recognize your faith.

October 5

Romans 1:4
And declared to be the **Son of God**
with power, according to the spirit of holiness,
by the resurrection from the dead:

Yesterday we looked at the gospel of God in order to be saved, and now what? Through spiritual adoption you became a son of God. Not "THEE" Son of God, but a son of God. We become new creatures when we get saved and are gifted with the power of God. Check out *Luke 3:38 Which was the son of Enos, which was the son of Seth, which was the son of Adam, which was the son of God.* This verse is telling us about the genealogy of Adam. Adam was a son through creation, and we become a son through adoption. We are adopted into God's family because of a personal faith in Jesus. *Hwee-os* is the word for those who are born again, angels, and of Jesus Christ. *Luke 20:34-36 34) And Jesus answering said unto them, The children of this world marry, and are given in marriage: 35) But they which shall be accounted worthy to obtain that world, and the resurrection from the dead, neither marry, nor are given in marriage: 36) Neither can they die any more: for they are equal unto the angels; and are the children (Hwee-os) of God, being the children of the resurrection.* Son of God or {*hwee-os* of God}, is used of those God esteems as sons who He loves, protects, and benefits. In the Old Testament it is used of the Jews, (God's chosen race), and in the New Testament of

Christians. The Lord loves us the same way or He would not have sacrificed His Son for any of us. Had there been no sacrifice then no one could be a son of God. As a son of God we are to be reverent to an Almighty God. I am not talking about being reverent in a sense of always staying quiet and doing nothing. I am talking about being reverent, staying still, and listening for the still small voice of God to direct you.

October 6

Romans 1:4
And declared to be the **Son of God**
with power, according to the spirit of holiness,
by the resurrection from the dead:

We are at the same verse as yesterday as there is much to consider in this verse. We are a son of God according to the spirit of holiness. This holiness is in a sense of moral purity and yet so much more. Moral purity is set according to God's standard, the Word of God. All the world has a standard or what they believe to be acceptable. What the world says is acceptable, and what is morally pure according to God's Word, are two different things. As a son of God, is everything acceptable behavior? We are a son of God according to God's majesty and holiness. How majestic and holy do we think God is? If I am to be holy, is that when it is easy, or all the time? Does the Bible apply only to clergy or to everybody? The name in and of itself, "son of God" has responsibilities. We are a son of God because of the resurrection from the dead. I can assure you that if Jesus' tomb contained His bones, you or I could not be a son of God. If God could not raise His Son from the dead, then He could not raise us up from the dead. Do we honestly think the church could keep a secret for 2000 years that Jesus did not really rise from the dead? The church knows when Aunt Sally burnt the roast last Sunday. If something is verbalized, I guarantee it will be passed on by many. The grave could not hold Jesus and it cannot hold a born-again believer. If the grave could not hold Jesus, Satan cannot hold you from being a son of God. Satan was defeated the day you trusted Jesus Christ as your Savior. Satan cannot keep you down now, and the proof will be when God raptures us out of this world, to meet Jesus in the clouds. Gravity will have no hold on those who belong to God through Jesus Christ.

October 7

Romans 1:7
To all that be in Rome,
<u>beloved of God</u>, called to be saints: Grace to you
and peace from God our Father, and the Lord Jesus Christ.

I would like for us to focus on three little words in this verse and that is "beloved of God". Through faith in Jesus Christ for salvation we are now the "beloved of God" and we ought to rejoice. I will give to you some cross-reference verses for your own personal daily devotion. First, look at the word Agape along with *Romans 5:8 But God commendeth his love toward us, in that, while we were yet sinners, Christ died for us*. Keep in mind that born again believers are the beloved of God and God did not commend His love for us because we were perfect. God commended His love towards us because of *Romans 3:23 For all have sinned, and come short of the glory of God.* Because of God's love for us He offered up His Son Jesus. The word beloved is a form of the agape love God had for the world. God's love is agape, and if by faith you accepted the gospel, you are a son of God, and are now the "Beloved" of God. Beloved is the word *ag-ap-ay-tos'* and is translated as beloved, well beloved, dearly beloved, and dear. No matter what word is used, God loves us unconditionally. The word *ag-ap-ay-tos'* for beloved is used in two ways. Jesus the Messiah according to the verses you just read, and Christians being reconciled to God through Jesus Christ. If God uses the same word beloved for Jesus, then we are mightily loved. Here is Satan's tactic to those who claim Jesus as Lord. You accepted the gospel of God, became a Son of God, and you are now the beloved of God. Satan will mess with your mind and try and convince you that you are not worthy to serve God. The word beloved means, "Of Christians being reconciled to God". Those saved are worthy because they have been reconciled because of Jesus. As the beloved of God do not let Satan steal your joy. Rejoice daily because when you became the beloved of God, He wants to enlarge your joy through Jesus.

October 8

I Peter 5:8
Be sober, be vigilant; because your adversary the devil, as a roaring lion, walketh about, seeking whom he may devour:

I want you to leave Romans for today. We left being the beloved of God devotional and have declared that you are worthy of service to the King. Be aware because we have a nemesis. Satan will try and mess you up if you give him half a chance to do so. He will try and convince you that because of some sin you should not serve God. As far as serving God, God may not call the perfect, but God will perfect the called. Satan says stay clear of Jesus and God says, "Come as you are". Satan will say you are unfit for duty and God says, "let me fit you for duty". With all our imperfections God says, "I love you, died for you, so come to me as you are". You should say to Satan, "In the name of Jesus get thee behind me Satan". We all should witness to make sure someone is really the beloved of God. I read my Bible every day, prepare messages, and I pray. That is all good, but that is not all there is. I cannot spend all my time on those three things and not get out into the community. People do not get saved because I read, study, and prepare. People get saved because God called them, and we witnessed to them. We cannot live in a bubble while the world goes to hell in a handbasket.

October 9

Romans 1:10
Making request, if by any means now at length I might have a prosperous journey by the **will of God** to come unto you.

So now that we are the beloved of God we can walk in the "will of God". Only as a child of God can we experience the will of God. The word for the Will of God is *thel'-ay-mah*. The word simply means when you or I predetermine to accomplish something. God's will is to accomplish something for yourself, others, or for God. Doing things that God has called us to do carries eternal significance. The "Will" of God can be a specific purpose that is designated only for you. The "Will" of God is active and will require action on your part. A tragedy is suspecting God's calling to something, but ignoring it. If we look to the will of God, the result will be verses 8 & 9 that precede this verse for today. *8) First, I thank my God through Jesus Christ for you all, that your faith is spoken of throughout the whole world. 9) For God is my witness, whom I serve with my spirit in the gospel of his Son, that without ceasing I make mention of you always in my prayers.* If we determine to be in the Will of God, everyone around is going to know it. God's will dictates everything we do. Everything we do will either point to the glory of God or the word of God. Both will go hand-in-hand. Let me stop and really define in simple terms the Will of God. It is what one wishes or has determined shall be done as led by an Almighty God. The purpose of God is to bless mankind through Jesus Christ. With God's will in mind what purpose do we have in this life? What calling has God placed on you? God calls, but the question is will the call be answered? God calls people to salvation, repentance, and to service. If you are not sure of God's will, find a quiet place and listen. One thing to pray about, is do I have any sin that needs to be repented of. I caution you, do not ask God unless you are prepared to listen. Pray for the still small voice of God to speak to you according to *Psalm 46:10 Be still and know that I am God.* Pray that when you hear his voice you will follow His direction. Do not let the fear of serving keep you from the Will of God for your life. I promise, you are the perfect person to do what God will call YOU to do.

October 10

Romans 1:10
Making request, if by any means now at length I might have a prosperous journey by the will of God to come unto you.

I would like to continue with another day of devotion looking again at *Romans 1:10*. We have been looking at the will of God. You can hear from God in many ways. A good friend of mine heard a message about trusting your leadership and he became my right-hand man. What does God desire to do through us? God's "Will" is for us to feel fulfilled or satisfied because of service to Him. *2 Timothy 4:7 I have fought a good fight, I have finished my course, I have kept the faith*: There is no long-term satisfaction without direction from God. There will be no direction without obedience to God. The first place to start is by submitting to Jesus and asking to be saved. Submit to baptism if you have never done that. Baptism is as an act of obedience to God. By the way, biblical baptism is complete immersion in water. It is not a few sprinkles of water thrown on you. There is absolutely no example of that in scripture. Everyone that was baptized in the Bible was immersed in water. From the head to the toes, everything gets wet! Submit to the authority of the body of Christ if you never have. Submit to the teaching of the Word of God. If the word says do not do this or that, then do not do this or that. If the word says do this, then do it. Here is the Common Sense of it all. If we do not seek God's will, we will probably not find it. On the other side of the coin, Satan has a will for us as well. If you have not heard it already, he will tell you that you are not worthy, so you cannot be in God's will. He may tell you that God's will is not for you, it was only for Jesus. Satan may try and convince you that God's will is not for you it is only for the Pastors. Satan says, "I know what you have done". God says, "I know what you can do". Satan will say, "You have done bad things with me". God will say "I know what great things you can do for me". Satan tells you how big your sin is. Tell your Sin/Satan just how big your God is. God's will is having the ability to do or achieve what you never thought possible. It may be that you can be what you never thought you could be. In life there are two types of people. They are "Dreamers" and "Doers". Dreamers may never do, and Doers will fulfill their Dream. Those in God's will say, "I never thought God would use me in this capacity". Only you and I limit what God wants to do in and through us. Satan will try and convince you that you are not equipped for anything. God can equip you to do anything.

October 11

Romans 1:16
For I am not ashamed of the gospel of Christ: for it is the **power of God** unto salvation to every one that believeth; to the Jew first, and also to the Greek.

As a child of God, we can fully experience the "power of God". I will remind you that there is no power greater than God's power. Let us examine the power of God, and this power will sound great to you. The word for power here is *dunamis (doo'-nam-is),* and where we get our word dynamite. It means strength, power, and ability. It is the power Jesus used when performing miracles. Isn't it amazing that the power Jesus used to raise people from the dead, is the same word used for the power we have as a son of God. Think of the potential within every one of us to do remarkable things for God. Think of the things we do not carry out because we do not trust in His power to do it. Truth is, we cannot do anything in and of ourselves, but God can use us. As a son of God, has God called you to something in order for Him to pour a little of His power on you? Here is the sad side: If you do not know Jesus, you do not have the power. This power is used to battle armies, forces, or any evil host. We have an army and it is being led by the Lord Jesus Christ. We have an army and it is called the body of Christ. You have the power to do great things under the influence of the Holy Spirit. We have the power, (*dunamis*) to be used. When you let God get a hold of you, (it is boom), a power above all power. Have you claimed it yet? When God created the heavens and the earth, BOOM it was done. Want to serve the Lord? BOOM it can be done. Look at a few verses about the power of God? *Psalm 49:15 But God will redeem my soul from the power of the grave: for he shall receive me.* The grave has power over our soul without Jesus. Here is the verse that protects us with Jesus. *1 Corinthians 15:55 O death, where is thy sting? O grave, where is thy victory?* You see the grave has no power over your soul with Jesus Christ. *2 Corinthians 5:8 We are confident, I say, and willing rather to be absent from the body, and to be present with the Lord.* Paul knew that when he drew his last breath he would wake up in the presence of the Lord Jesus. If you have trusted Jesus as your Savior, you will also wake up in Jesus' presence. The lost will go to hell alone, and end up kicking and screaming. Those saved will be carried by angels to Jesus Christ and will never be alone in perfect paradise. *Luke 16:22-23 22) And it came to pass, that the **beggar died, and was carried by the angels** into Abraham's bosom: **the rich man also died, and was buried; 23) And in hell he lift up his eyes, being in torments**, and seeth Abraham afar off, and Lazarus in his bosom.*

October 12

Romans 1:16
For I am not ashamed of the gospel of Christ:
for it is the **power of God** unto salvation to every one
that believeth; to the Jew first, and also to the Greek.

Take one more look at *Romans 1:16* that we used for our verse yesterday. I want you to consider some things when it comes to the power of God. All on your own you are limited, but under the influence of the power of God there is nothing you cannot do for God. The power of God transforms people for any kind of service. The power of God defeated death for those who have trusted Jesus Christ with their soul. There is no power of God if you do not know Jesus as your Savior, You will wake up without Jesus Christ because you did not have the power of God to rescue you. The good news is the word of God tells us we can know for sure. *John 20:31 But these are written, that ye might believe that Jesus is the Christ, the Son of God; and that believing ye might have life through his name.* The power of God is the power unto salvation if someone wants it. Some do not want the power of God according to *1 Corinthians 1:18 For the preaching of the cross is to them that perish foolishness; but unto us which are saved it is the power of God.* We will tell some about Jesus, and they will think we are silly or maybe even bonkers. The good news is we are going to tell some and they will believe. *1 Peter 1:5 Who are kept by the power of God through faith unto salvation ready to be revealed in the last time.* We are going to have times as a believer when there will be trials. It will be the power of God that will get us through it. An unbeliever will have trials as well, but will have to deal with it on their own. I have been on both sides of the fence, and I will absolutely trust the Power of God to get me through the difficulties that come up. I have done it on my own and I have done it with the Lord, and it is a very easy decision. *Philippians 4:7 And the peace of God, which passeth all understanding, shall keep your hearts and minds through Christ Jesus.* When you do not have peace, it is God that offers you peace. Like any gift such as the power of God or the peace of God you have to receive it. The power of God was offered by the shed blood of Jesus, but you must reach out and receive the free gift.

October 13

Romans 1:17
For therein is the **righteousness of God** revealed from faith to faith: as it is written, The just shall live by faith.

Because we are living under the power of God in the preceding verse, *Romans 1:16* we can experience the *righteousness of God.* To recap part of Romans 1 again and for your edification it is as follows and in this order. We heard the gospel of God. We accepted Jesus Christ and became sons of God. We are sons of God so that makes us the beloved of God. Now that we are the beloved of God we can walk in the will of God. If we walk in the will of God, we will experience the power of God. We are living under the power of God, so we can now experience the righteousness of God, which is where we are at today. This verse 17 says the righteousness of God and it is not mine and it is not yours. It is God's righteousness you can experience. The word righteousness is also translated as character. Do I show forth the character of God to some degree? Have you ever heard the expression, "He or she is quite a character"? Is it my desire to mimic the kind of character Jesus laid out for us? In verse 16 of this same chapter, Paul says he is not ashamed of the gospel. Paul loved the gospel and said in *Romans 1:17 it is the gospel where the righteousness of God is revealed.* Consider the gospel of God that leads to the righteousness of God. The gospel is beautiful if you consider the love it took to carry it out. The gospel is not beautiful if you consider what Jesus had to endure for us. By accepting Jesus, God transforms the worst of the worst to something beautiful. What is the worst? Anyone who has not named the name of Jesus as their Savior. What exactly is Righteousness? Righteousness is the spiritual state of an individual. Righteousness is a condition acceptable to God. Righteousness is the way in which man obtains approval of God. It is integrity, virtue, purity of life, rightness, or correct thinking. My favorite is correct thinking. Have you ever had bad thinking? We all will make bad choices when we harbor bad thinking. Am I going to do this or not do this? Some will choose to stay on one side of the fence and walk in a state of unrighteousness. You can only get and stay on the side of righteousness by accepting Jesus. Righteousness is not in what you do, it is only through Jesus. Our works has nothing to do with it. God is a righteous and Holy God and only the righteous can stand before Him. You do not become righteous because you are such a good person. The righteous are those who have trusted Jesus as their Savior. If you are a saved person, Jesus is your righteousness, justification, and sanctification. Praise God for those who know they will never be good enough on their own. Praise God for those who by faith have bowed the knee to Jesus willingly and obediently.

October 14

Romans 1:18
For the **wrath of God** is revealed from heaven
against all ungodliness and unrighteousness of men,
who hold the truth in unrighteousness;

We are still in Romans chapter one, and I will again recap in order where we have been the last few days and then continue on to verse 18. We heard the gospel of God. V. 1. We accepted Christ and became sons of God. V. 4. We are sons of God so that makes us the beloved of God. V. 7. Now that we are the beloved of God we can walk in the will of God. V. 10. If we walk in the will of God, we will experience the power of God. V. 16. We are living under the power of God, so now we can experience the righteousness of God. V. 17. Some will never accept or want the righteousness of God and will receive free the **wrath of God**, V. 18. Romans chapter one just changed directions. All have the opportunity to trust God before the entire world, but many will not. The gospel of God is given and it is either rejected or accepted. Spiritually, there are only two spiritual fathers in the Bible. One is God and the other is Satan. Only the saved are the beloved of God. Only those saved can look for and find the will of God. Only those in the will of God will experience the power of God. Jesus is the righteousness of God, and if you are saved, He is your righteousness. If someone does not want a Savior then forthcoming will be the wrath of God, which is the topic of today. Do not confuse man's wrath with God's wrath. Man's wrath may be someone out of control. God's wrath is controlled and already planned out. Paul informs the world through his writings that there is a price for rejecting Jesus. This *Verse 18* starts us out with a warning of the *wrath of God* to come. This is exactly why it is so important to be a good and bold witness to others. I do not know anyone that I would want to experience hell or try and get through the tribulation period. Paul begins to show that all mankind needs the salvation of the gospel because none could obtain the favour of God or escape His wrath by their own works. Please note that the "wrath" of God will not take place before the rapture. *John 3:36 He that believeth on the Son hath everlasting life: and he that believeth not the Son shall not see life; but the wrath of God abideth on him.* The wrath of God will come down on those who have had the truth of God revealed and said, "Nah, I don't need that stuff, religious stuff is just not for me". The word of God is the truth, but it is an individual choice as to how it is handled. Here are some Cross-References of the Wrath of God.

John 3:36 He that believeth on the Son hath everlasting life: and he that believeth not the Son shall not see life; but the wrath of God abideth on him. Romans 1:18 For the wrath of God is revealed from heaven against all ungodliness and unrighteousness of men, who hold the truth in unrighteousness, Man will not and cannot release the wrath of God. God will reveal and unleash His wrath. Unbelievers only have death to look forward to and then on to a Lake of Fire for eternity. Many on TV will tell you there are multiple ways to get to Heaven. Not true if you read *John 14:6 Jesus saith unto him, I am the way, the truth, and the life: no man cometh unto the Father, but by me.* Just how bad will the wrath of God get at the end? Those left behind will experience Revelation chapter 16. *Revelation 16* is just one of the chapters of God's wrath for those who have decided that they just do not need the Lord Jesus Christ. God's wrath is not reserved for believers, but for unbelievers. Do not confuse God correcting us because He loves us, with God's wrath to those who rejected Jesus Christ. For those saved you have the power of God for the good. For the lost they will experience the power of God better known as the wrath of God and it will be to lost man's demise. The decision an individual must make is to either experience the wrath of God or accept the love of God. Praise God if you know Jesus as your Savior as you will avoid a wrath that the world has never experienced. KNOW Jesus and NO Wrath or NO Jesus and KNOW wrath. Man can go either direction, but it will be a whole lot easier with Jesus.

October 15

Romans 1:19
Because that which may be **known of God**
is manifest in them; for God hath shewed it unto them.

You are still in the book of Romans today and still considering Chapter One. We heard the gospel of God, V. 1. We accepted Christ and became sons of God, V. 4. We are sons of God so that makes us the beloved of God, V. 7. Now that we are the beloved of God we can walk in the will of God, V. 10. If we walk in the will of God we will experience the power of God, V. 16. We are living under the power of God, so now we can experience the righteousness of God, V. 17. Some will never accept or want the righteousness of God and will receive the wrath of God, V. 18. The wrath of God will come because of what can be *known of God* has been clearly revealed and many have rejected the truth, V. 19. When God created the earth and man He has never been without a witness. ELIJAH - *1 Kings 19:18 Yet I have left me seven thousand in Israel, all the knees which have not bowed unto Baal, and every mouth which hath not kissed him.* John the Baptist - *John 1:15 John bare witness of him, and cried, saying, This was he of whom I spake, He that cometh after me is preferred before me: for he was before me.* We are to be an Elijah, John the Baptist, Paul, or a bold witness for Christ. Verse 19 starts out "That which may be known of God". How is the truth revealed? *Romans 1:19-23 19) Because that which may be known of God is manifest in them; for God hath shewed it unto them. 20)For the invisible things of him from the creation of the world are clearly seen, being understood by the things that are made, even his eternal power and Godhead; so that they are without excuse: 21) Because that, when they knew God, they glorified him not as God, neither were thankful; but became vain in their imaginations, and their foolish heart was darkened. 22) Professing themselves to be wise, they became fools, 23) And changed the glory of the uncorruptible God into an image made like to corruptible man, and to birds, and fourfooted beasts, and creeping things.* People will worship everything except God. People will adore cars, motorcycles, jobs, homes, and on and on. The problem with Christianity is worshipping everything and God at the same time, and possibly equally. Israel jumped all over worshipping idols before they hit the Promised Land. Mankind sits right smack dab in the middle of everything God has created and either miss it or reject it. No one can say I have never heard the gospel, so I am not responsible. Creation says, There is something greater out there than a single-cell amoeba that reproduced itself into everything we can see, taste, touch, or experience. There have been tribes discovered in the deepest parts of Africa that were worshipping a Creator and an evangelist or preacher had never been there. They trusted what they had. Creation points to something Supreme and then worship follows. That which is *known of God* or knowable concerning God. The expression implies that there may be things concerning God which cannot be known in this lifetime. Two lines of thinking on what I just said. You cannot contain God in a box or in a book. Everything you need to know about God is in the Word of God. We have finite understanding and cannot perfectly know an infinite being. However, I can know exactly what I need to know about God through God's WORD. What can we know about God through the word of God? We can know of His character, qualities, power, wisdom, justice, likes, and dislikes. We can know exactly how to live and make good sound judgment for ourselves. Paul's wording of that which may be *known of God* only meant that we learn about God from scripture. With that said, there is no excuse for rejecting Him. There were plenty of witnesses that saw the work of God. From Moses and the Prophets we can see God clearly. Paul wrote in *1 Corinthians 15: 1-8 1) Moreover, brethren, I declare unto you the gospel which I preached unto you, which also ye have received, and wherein ye stand; 2) By which also ye are saved, if ye keep in memory what I preached unto you, unless ye have believed in vain. 3) For I delivered unto you first of all that which I also received, how that Christ died for our sins according to the scriptures; 4) And that he was buried, and that he rose again the third day according to the scriptures: 5) And that he was seen of Cephas, then of the twelve: 6) After that, he was seen of above five hundred brethren at once; of whom the greater part remain unto this present, but some are fallen asleep. 7) After that, he was seen of James; then of all the apostles. 8) And last of all he was seen of me also, as of one born out of due time.* You have access to the HOLY Scriptures to tell you what you need to know. You have the Holy Spirit permanently residing in you to lead, guide, and direct you closer to God. You have enough scripture and your own personal experience to know God. You may not understand everything perfectly, but you must believe everything in the Bible is perfect. We have more than enough information to make an educated decision as to what is best for our life. Jesus is what I need, or Jesus is not what I need. We have had enough light revealed to us through scripture and personal testimonies to know what God has, can, and will do. We have enough information in God's word that we can know exactly what He wants us to do and the desire of His heart. If scripture and personal testimonies are not enough, He says look at nature. There was no big Bang and it happened. God is the "Creator" of the heaven, heavens, and the third heaven. Nature is enough to lead someone to the "Creator". What I know is *2 Peter 3:9 The Lord is not slack concerning his promise, as some men count slackness; but is longsuffering to us-ward, not willing that any should perish, but that all should come to repentance.* I will close with a thought I have already mentioned before. The Bible has all the information you need to know God, and it will be as intimate as the effort you put into knowing Him.

October 16

Romans 1:19
Because that which may be **known of God**
is manifest in them; for God hath shewed it unto them.

It is a different day, but the same devotional verse as yesterday. There is a little more to help inspire you to the phrase, "*KNOWN OF GOD*". God has shown to the world His intentions. (*He has made it known*). It started with Adam and then Eve. Until the fall of Adam there was perfect harmony between God and man. After the fall of man, sin had to be dealt with through animal sacrifices for roughly four thousand years. Man had to deal with and be under the law. The law is nothing more than a tool to condemn the fallen state of man. God had to bridge the gap between man and Himself. God came in the form of a man, (Jesus), and witness after witness saw the miracles of Jesus. They saw the beatings of Jesus. They saw Jesus on the cross. They saw him taken down from the cross and laid in a tomb. They saw him after 3 days arise from the grave. They saw him ascend to the Father. There is nothing about God's plan of eternity that should cause anyone to reject it. As an individual, how are we managing what we know? Everyone has a different walk with God. We must handle correctly what we know about God. The word manifest in this verse is also translated as *is known* or *is understood*. It means that we have had knowledge revealed, or it has been communicated to us. Most of us here at one time or another had the truth of God told to us. Those reading this book are hearing the truth of God. Paul knew there were enough witnesses of who Jesus healed, or who he had raised from the dead, to confirm what God had done. Look at the Apostles who walked with Jesus, slept with Jesus, and ate with Jesus. The religious leaders and philosophers of the day had the knowledge of God and what had taken place. Their denial meant nothing. You can deny something, but that does not mean it is not so. God manifested himself in the form of man, Jesus Christ. Whether Jesus was rejected or not is not relevant. The *truth of God* has been revealed and it was known and is known. There is no denying, (only lying), that God came to the earth in the form of a man. If all that is not enough read verses 20-24 of this chapter again. Man can corrupt the truth with a lie, but the truth is still the truth. Man can worship what he will worship, but God is still God. Man can say that what Jesus did was a lie, but it does not change that fact that Jesus did what He did. Man can say, "I do not believe the word of God is the word of God". It does not change the fact that it is the Word of God. If that is not enough to convince us, God says, "Look around and then tell me if everything you see in nature just happened"? There comes a time in the life of every person that they must ask themselves a very simple question: "Is this all there is to this life, and it is over"? No, we are all going to spend eternity somewhere. The question looming before some is "where"? Heaven or Hell?

October 17

Romans 1:25
Who changed the **truth of God** into a lie,
and worshipped and served the creature more
than the Creator, who is blessed forever. Amen.

To keep us in line with the truth, I want to recap clear back to the start of Romans chapter 1. We learn by repetition so I will recap where we have been the last few days for our benefit. We heard the gospel of God. We accepted Christ and became sons of God. We are sons of God so that makes us the beloved of God. Now that we are the beloved of God we can walk in the will of God. If we walk in the will of God, we will experience the power of God. We are living under the power of God, so now we can experience the righteousness of God. Some will never accept or want the righteousness of God and will receive the wrath of God. The wrath of God will come because what can be known of God has been clearly revealed and some have rejected the truth. God has revealed himself to us so now we have to handle the truth of God. God has revealed himself to us, so we must handle the **truth of God**. Someone may know the truth, BUT for devious reasons will change the truth. God cannot lie: *Titus 1:2 In hope of eternal life, which God, that cannot lie, promised before the world began*; We need to let scripture define truth for us. Before turning Jesus over to be beaten and condemned Pilate asked this in *John 18:38 "Pilate saith unto him, What is truth? And when he had said this, he went out again unto the Jews, and saith unto them, I find in him no fault at all.* John chapter 18 has Jesus arrested and condemned, but in John chapter 17, Jesus had already answered his question, *John 17:17 Sanctify them through thy truth: thy word is truth. Malachi 2:6 called it the law of* *truth or the "Torah" of truth.* The Bible of truth for us. *Psalm 33:4 For the word of the LORD is right; and all his works are done in truth. Psalm 69:13 But as for me, my prayer is unto thee, O LORD, in an acceptable time: O God, in the multitude of thy mercy hear me, in the truth of thy salvation.* In *Psalm 69* David is speaking of just how bad his enemies were condemning him. You may have already discovered that some may make fun of you for your faith. Even though some may make fun of us for our faith, we must not let that deter us from our faith. BACK TO TRUTH: The world has heard the truth, but it does not always fit what the world wants to do. *Romans 1:19-25 19) Because that which may be known of God is manifest in them; for God hath shewed it unto them. 20) For the invisible things of him from the creation of the world are clearly seen, being understood by the things that are made, even his eternal power and Godhead; so that they are without excuse: 21) Because that, when they knew God, they glorified him not as God, neither were thankful; but became vain in their imaginations, and their foolish heart was darkened. 22) Professing themselves to be wise, they became fools, 23) And changed the glory of the uncorruptible God into an image made like to corruptible man, and to birds, and fourfooted beasts, and creeping things. 24) Wherefore God also gave them up to uncleanness through the lusts of their own hearts, to dishonour their own bodies between themselves: 25) Who changed the truth of God into a lie, and worshipped and served the creature more than the Creator, who is blessed forever. Amen. Psalms 135:15-18 15) The idols of the heathen are silver and gold, the work of men's hands. 16) They have mouths, but they speak not; eyes have they, but they see not; 17) They have ears, but they hear not; neither is there any breath in their mouths. 18) They that make them are like unto them: so is every one that trusteth in them.* In two different Psalms

King David addressed the issue of the truth of God: *Psalms 14:1 To the chief Musician, A Psalm of David. The fool hath said in his heart, There is no God. They are corrupt, they have done abominable works, there is none that doeth good.* {**A fool will worship a statue**}. *Psalm 53:1 To the chief Musician upon Mahalath, {Sickness}, Maschil {Instruction}, A Psalm of David. The fool hath said in his heart, There is no God. Corrupt are they, and have done abominable iniquity: there is none that doeth good.* It takes more faith to be an Atheist than a follower of Jesus. This is why April 1st is celebrated as April Fool's Day. Unbelievers can have a holiday as well. I am amazed at how humanity could build something and then think it will have special or mystical powers. Maybe in cartoons, but not in real life. THE TRUTH: Jesus has never forced himself on anyone. Jesus died for the world so that man could look forward to the rapture of the church, the 2nd coming of Jesus, and eternal life with God the Father. *Romans 5:18 Therefore as by the offence of one judgment came upon all men to condemnation; even so by the righteousness of one the free gift came upon all men unto justification of life.* Adam passed on a sinful nature and condemnation. Jesus gave opportunity for a new nature and justification. Some will still pawn off their own truths as if it is God's truth. This is exactly why you check out your Bible when someone attempts to tell you something NEW. Living the truth of God's word is easier and healthier, but many choose something else. How contrary is the world to the *"Truth of God"*? *Romans 1:29-31 29) Being filled with all unrighteousness, fornication, wickedness, covetousness, maliciousness; full of envy, murder, debate, deceit, malignity; whisperers, 30) Backbiters, haters of God, despiteful, proud, boasters, inventors of evil things, disobedient to parents, 31) Without understanding,* *covenantbreakers, without natural affection, implacable, unmerciful*: People have been justifying their actions for years. Everything God despises some men will choose. Sin may satisfy for the moment, but Jesus satisfies for eternity. Have you ever had someone tell you they did not want to be saved because it was fun doing their own thing? God gave us truth so that we could live in "HARMONY" with Him and with others. When others are against God they are going to be at odds with you! Living a Christian life is easier and healthier. God's Truth is like *Genesis 1:1, "In the Beginning God"*. Getting saved through Jesus is our beginning, middle, and ending. Want a changed life? In the beginning, middle, and end God must be in charge, and you must allow the truth of God to prevail!

October 18

Romans 1:30
Backbiters, **haters of God**, despiteful, proud, boasters, inventors of evil things, disobedient to parents,

To keep us in line with the truth, I want to recap clear back to the start of Romans chapter one. We all learn by repetition, so repetition I will use for the benefit of both of us. We heard the gospel of God. We accepted Christ and became sons of God. We are sons of God so that makes us the beloved of God. Now that we are the beloved of God we can walk in the will of God. If we walk in the will of God, we will experience the power of God. We are living under the power of God, so now we can experience the righteousness of God. Some will never accept or want the righteousness of God and will receive absolutely free the wrath of God. The wrath of God will come because of what can be known of God has been clearly revealed and some reject the truth. God has revealed himself to us, so now we have to handle the truth of God. Today we will look at the phrase, "***haters of God***". If you have not noticed by now, Romans chapter one takes you from hearing the gospel, and eventually ending at the judgment of God. For today we will concentrate on "***haters of God***". For me, (haters of God), is one of the strongest statements you read in the Bible. Some words describe a man's qualities, "both good and bad". ***Haters of God*** creates a sense of finality for someone's life. At death we draw our last breath as a "Lover of God" or draw our last breath as a "Hater of God". Either way is secured by accepting or rejecting Jesus Christ as Savior. I will give you two schools of thought. I love the truth of God and it is reflected in how I love and live for God. I hate the truth of God and it is seen by how much I do not love or live for God. Today's devotional of "***haters of God***" is intertwined with a whole bunch of bad qualities such as is found in *Romans 1:25-29 25) Who changed the truth of God into a lie, and worshipped and served the creature more than the Creator, who is blessed forever. Amen. 26) For this cause God gave them up unto vile affections: for even their women did change the natural use into that which is against nature: 27) And likewise also the men, leaving the natural use of the woman, burned in their lust one toward another; men with men working that which is unseemly, and receiving in themselves that recompence of their error which was meet. 28) And even as they did not like to retain God in their knowledge, God gave them over to a reprobate mind, to do those things which are not convenient; 29) Being filled with all unrighteousness, fornication, wickedness, covetousness, maliciousness; full of envy, murder, debate, deceit, malignity; whisperers*, We must recognize and understand the judgment of God in *Romans 1:32*. Is the judgment of God just for those in these verses we just read? It is if they do not know Jesus as their

Savior. Read the next two verses with me as well. Read about Man's potential qualities recorded in *Romans 1:29-31*. Everything contained in these verses are an internal problem. What is internal becomes very external. What we experience externally may influence what we do internally. The bottom line is to guard your heart, soul, and mind through Christ Jesus. *Matthew 22:37 Jesus said unto him, Thou shalt love the Lord thy God with all thy heart, and with all thy soul, and with all thy mind.* If we are struggling, what do we do? *1 John 1:9 If we confess our sins, he is faithful and just to forgive us our sins, and to cleanse us from all unrighteousness. Ezra 9:5 And at the evening sacrifice I arose up from my heaviness; and having rent my garment and my mantle, I fell upon my knees, and spread out my hands unto the LORD my God, 1 Kings 8:54 And it was so, that when Solomon had made an end of praying all this prayer and supplication unto the LORD, he arose from before the altar of the LORD, from kneeling on his knees with his hands spread up to heaven. 2 Kings 19:14 And Hezekiah received the letter of the hand of the messengers, and read it: and Hezekiah went up into the house of the LORD, and spread it before the LORD.* For those who are **haters of God** they must recognize that there is a problem. Recognize that God is bigger than any problem. Recognize that we do not tell God bits and pieces, but all the problem. You do not have to be in a Church building to open up to God. *1 Corinthians 10:13 There hath no temptation taken you but such as is common to man: but God is faithful, who will not suffer you to be tempted above that ye are able; but will with the temptation also make a way to escape, that ye may be able to bear it.* Paul understood the potential problems or God would not have had him pen *Romans 7:15-20 15) For that which I do I allow not: for what I would, that do I not; but what I hate, that do I. 16) If then I do that which I would* *not, I consent unto the law that it is good. 17) Now then it is no more I that do it, but sin that dwelleth in me. 18) For I know that in me (that is, in my flesh,) dwelleth no good thing: for to will is present with me; but how to perform that which is good I find not. 19) For the good that I would I do not: but the evil which I would not, that I do. 20) Now if I do that I would not, it is no more I that do it, but sin that dwelleth in me.* What is the main cause of someone being a "***hater of God***"? When someone takes their eyes off God, or have never had their eyes on God, anything is possible. When someone keeps their eyes on God, anything is possible. As a Christian we have a boatload of potential, but what is the reality? No matter the list, if it was not for the grace of God there go I. Does it seem more important as to why we need to promote the gospel? Jesus has, can, and will continue to save souls and we can be the tool he uses to do it. Pray for your family, friends, and community and God will honor that prayer. A **hater of God** has rejected Jesus. A lover of God has accepted Jesus. You cannot know where someone stands with Jesus Christ unless you ask.

October 19

Romans 1:30
Backbiters, **haters of God**, despiteful, proud, boasters, inventors of evil things, disobedient to parents,

You probably noticed that we are right back at *Romans 1:30* as there is more to share about "haters of God". To keep us in line with the truth I recap clear back to the start of Romans chapter one "again". We heard the gospel of God. We accepted Christ and became sons of God. We are sons of God so that makes us the beloved of God. Now that we are the beloved of God we can walk in the will of God. If we walk in the will of God, we will experience the power of God. We are living under the power of God, so now we can experience the righteousness of God. Some will never accept or want the righteousness of God and will receive the wrath of God. The wrath of God will come because what can be known of God has been clearly revealed and some have rejected the truth. God has revealed himself to us so now we have to handle the truth of God. After a wordy introduction, our topic will be "**haters of God**" again. Some will say that just because Jesus is not my Savior does not mean I am a "**hater of God**". To reject Jesus gets someone, (by default), labeled as a hater of God spiritually. *Matthew 10:33 But whosoever shall deny me before men, him will I also deny before my Father which is in heaven.* Question: Do people normally cling to those they love to be around? Cling to God! *Matthew 6:24 No man can serve two masters: for either he will hate the one, and love the other; or else he will hold to the one, and despise the other. Ye cannot serve God and mammon.* Who exactly is their master? Who is their master on Sunday, and who is their Master the rest of the week? In discipleship lessons there are only two spiritual fathers recorded. God the Father or Satan the father of lies. Here is where the rubber meets the road. If we do not love the Lord, then we are giving ourselves over to the wiles of the devil. Is the love of God prevalent in our life as seen by the world? In service – do we devote time to Him? The Bible, do we set aside time to study and meditate upon His word? In Prayer, are you praying for the souls of the people you know? Prayer. are you lifting up your Pastor and his family? In Service, what are you willing to do or not do for God? With regards to Tithes & Offerings, God wants what is first, not what is left. Question: what would a hater of God do in the area of tithes and offerings, service, bible reading, and prayer? I am pretty sure it is nothing and God will bless accordingly. If someone is ever a Pastor of a church and sees just what it costs to keep the doors open many would be surprised. God does not love us for what we do, He just plain loves us. However, we express our love for Him by what we do. *James 2:18 Yea, a man may say, Thou hast faith, and I have works: shew me thy faith without thy works, and I will shew thee my faith by my works.* These are hard things to say, and many will not, but as sons of God we need to be honest about ourselves. Either what we have is all HIS, or it is all our ours. I answer for me and you answer for you.

October 20

Romans 1:32
Who knowing the **judgment of God**, that they which commit such things are worthy of death, not only do the same, but have pleasure in them that do them.

We moved from "haters of God" and on to "*judgment of God*". To keep on track with the truth and to follow an order of events in Romans one I will recap clear back to the start of Romans chapter one. We heard the gospel of God. We accepted Christ and became sons of God. We are sons of God so that makes us the beloved of God. Now that we are the beloved of God we can walk in the will of God. If we walk in the will of God, we will experience the power of God. We are living under the power of God, so now we can experience the righteousness of God. Some will never accept or want the righteousness of God and will receive absolutely free the wrath of God. The wrath of God will come because what can be known of God has been clearly revealed and some have rejected the truth. God has revealed himself to us so now we have to handle the truth of God. For the haters of God, there will be a "**Judgment of God**", and what we will consider today. Some will not care about the truth of God and will be haters of God as we read in Romans 1:30. Now when someone is a "hater of God" by rejecting Jesus, and leaves this earth in that spiritual condition, they will face the *judgment of God* as recorded in this verse 32. What is the judgment of God? It is a righteous judgment. It is a perfect judgment. It is a judgment that when it occurs there will be no arguments from anyone. No one will smart off and the judgment will be swift, and it will be eternal. *John 12:48 He that rejecteth me, and receiveth not my words, hath one that judgeth him: the word that I have spoken, the same shall judge him in the last day.* Who will experience the final Judgment of God? Anyone who has rejected God's plan of accepting Jesus as their Savior. God could positively say, "You judged yourself not needing Jesus and now you will be judged by Me for doing just that"! Here is my fear for every single denomination on the planet. Some serve faithfully everywhere and depend on their service for salvation, but we are not saved by works according to *Ephesians 2:8-9.* They may not say that, but serving does not save you. Only Jesus saves. A person must accept Jesus as their "Personal Lord and Savior". *Romans 10:9-10 9 That if thou shalt confess with thy mouth the Lord Jesus, and shalt believe in thine heart that God hath raised him from the dead, thou shalt be saved. 10) For with the heart man believeth unto righteousness; and with the mouth confession is made unto salvation.* We preach Jesus died, was buried, and after 3 days arose from the grave. Our responsibility is to make sure when afforded the chance to ask, "Have you by faith asked for forgiveness of sin and received Jesus as your Savior"? The *judgment of God* will be for anyone that has rejected Jesus. Even if a person knows of the judgment coming it still may not change their mind. The judgment of God must be carried out as the Bible says and nothing or nobody can stop it. The verse also says they not only had pleasure in their sin, but had pleasure watching others perform their sin. What happens when people love their own sin and the sin of others? There becomes a confederacy or union with Satan himself. Most in sin will not only stay in their sin but will justify it to the fullest. Why do we witness through our lifestyle? So others just might notice a difference and maybe want what we have in Jesus. Then maybe they will repent and avoid the *judgment of God*. Our testimony is one that should point to Jesus at all times of the day. My heart for the community is that all would completely sell out to Jesus. We should want everyone to recognize that they do not have to live like a dog and return to its own vomit. The ultimate judgment of God is *Revelation 20:11-15 11) And I saw a great white throne, and him that sat on it, from whose face the earth and the heaven fled away; and there was found no place for them. 12) And I saw the dead, small and great, stand before God; and the books were opened: and another book was opened, which is the book of life: and the dead were judged out of those things which were written in the books, according to their works. 13) And the sea gave up the dead which were in it; and death and hell delivered up the dead which were in them: and they were judged every man according to their works. 14) And death and hell were cast into the lake of fire. This is the second death. 15) And whosoever was not found written in the book of life was cast into the lake of fire.* This is not where we want anyone to end up! In the book of life, make sure that one of those chapters has your name recorded. Jesus will never run out of ink in that book.

October 21

Romans 1:32
Who knowing the **judgment of God**, that they which commit such things are worthy of death, not only do the same, but have pleasure in them that do them.

I want to commit one more day to the discussion of the "*Judgment of God*". We heard the gospel of God. We accepted Christ and became sons of God. We are sons of God so that makes us the beloved of God. Now that we are the beloved of God we can walk in the will of God. If we walk in the will of God, we will experience the power of God. We are living under the power of God, so now we can experience the righteousness of God. Some will never accept or want the righteousness of God and will receive absolutely free the wrath of God. The wrath of God will come because what can be known of God has been clearly revealed and some have rejected the truth. God has revealed himself to us, so now we have to handle the truth of God. For all the haters of God there will be a *judgment of God* and what we will consider again today. Man will never be justified by his actions for righteousness or get out of God's judgment. Man will never repent unless he believes he has something to repent of. Repentance is not turning away for a moment or feeling bad. Repentance is a permanent turning away of that which is in complete defiance of God's word. Complete defiance is found in this *Romans 1:20–31*. I want to make sure you understand that God's ultimate judgment will be the rejecting of Jesus Christ as your Savior. God at times may spank his children for disobedience, but that is not the ultimate and final judgment of God. Let me give some examples of God's judgment so we understand its finality. *Genesis 6:13 And God said unto Noah, The end of all flesh is come before me; for the earth is filled with violence through them; and, behold, I will destroy them with the earth. Genesis 7:23 And every living substance was destroyed which was upon the face of the ground, both man, and cattle, and the creeping things, and the fowl of the heaven; and they were destroyed from the earth: and Noah only remained alive, and they that were with him in the ark. Genesis 18:20-21 20) And the LORD said, Because the cry of Sodom and Gomorrah is great, and because their sin is grievous; 21) I will go down now, and see whether they have done altogether according to the cry of it, which is come unto me; and if not, I will know. Genesis 19:24-25 24) Then the LORD rained upon Sodom and upon Gomorrah brimstone and fire from the LORD out of heaven; 25) And he overthrew those cities, and all the plain, and all the inhabitants of the cities, and that which grew upon the ground.* Those are just a few examples of God getting fed up and dealing with people. Now the final judgment of God will be a whole lot worse. If someone thinks they are going to heaven without Jesus, read *Matthew 10:23 But whosoever shall deny me before men, him will I also deny before my Father which is in heaven. Matthew 10:28 And fear not them which kill the body, but are not able to kill the soul: but rather fear him which is able to destroy both soul and body in hell.* Is hell the final judgment of God? That answer is NO! *Revelation 20:14 And death and hell were cast into the lake of fire.* This is the second death, and no repentance is available for anyone here and the ***judgment of God*** is final. Those who die lost will gather at the Great White Throne for their "Final Judgment". This judgment will be a perfect, righteous, eternal, and the final demise for those who did not want anything to do with Jesus. No one will smart off or be surprised. The Great White Throne is where unbelievers will stand before God for final judgment. The punishment will be harsh, and it will be eternal. Some say, "If God is so loving why would He send anyone to hell"? He does not send anyone to a lake of fire, but God will honor their choice. The judgment seat of Christ for believers is found in *2 Corinthians 5:10*. Man used a judgment seat as well to deliver the verdict to those guilty. Man could render judgment to an innocent man based on false witnesses. Jesus was judged guilty and sentenced to be crucified. The judgment seat of Christ will have no false witnesses: Jesus will run this courtroom. *2 Corinthians 5:10 For we must all appear before the judgment seat of Christ; that every one may receive the things done in his body, according to that he hath done, whether it be good or bad.* Believers will appear at the judgment seat of Christ and there is no hiding from it or avoiding it. The Great Judge is Jesus Christ and praise God that Jesus is also your defense attorney. If Jesus is your Savior, you are going home to your real home in heaven. This life is just a coffee break and you are just passing through. Know Jesus, No final judgment of God. No Jesus, A final Judgment of God and by God. *Romans 10:13 For whosoever shall call upon the name of the Lord shall be saved. 1 Corinthians 15:57 But thanks be to God, which giveth us the victory through our Lord Jesus Christ.* "**Victory over death and the grave**"! That ought to be worth two hallelujahs!

October 22

1 Corinthians 2:1
And I, brethren, when I came to you,
came not with excellency of speech or of wisdom,
declaring unto you the testimony of God.

Today we are going to change books and go on to 1 Corinthians chapter two. We can study together and consider each of the sixteen verses in this chapter and see just how God can inspire us. If anything, the entire chapter can tell us about dependence on the Holy Spirit, true gospel preaching, and the divine power we can possess through God the Father, God the Son, and God the Holy Spirit. Have you ever had to rely on the Holy Spirit? Did you hope and pray that the Holy Spirit would intervene and get you onto the subject of God with somebody? Have you ever had to rely on the Word of God for counseling for yourself or to help others? Has God ever reminded you of a particular verse that you needed at just the exact moment in time when you really needed it? We do not always understand how the Holy Spirit works, but we know He works. The Holy Spirit builds our faith and confidence in our self as we submit to Him. Our faith and confidence becomes stronger the more we rely on the Holy Spirit. I know you read our verse for the day, but here it is again: *And I, brethren, when I came to you, came not with excellency of speech or of wisdom, declaring unto you the testimony of God.* Excellency of speech or wisdom is not a declaration of arrogance here. It is saying that I am not coming to you feeling or promoting my superiority to you. I do not outrank you because I am an Apostle to the Gentiles. Paul declares, "I am coming to you with simple words of truth about Jesus". Wisdom is the word "Sophia" and can mean worldly and spiritual wisdom. Worldly in a sense of I have common sense like you. Spiritual is I can take the worldly wrongs and stay away from them. Spiritual as Paul could take a worldly example and give it a spiritual application. Jesus called this a "Parable". An earthly story with a heavenly application. As we dissect this chapter you will see that Paul does not use a lot of twenty-dollar words. He conveys the truth of Jesus in simplicity, and it will be understandable. The greatest way to convey the truth of Jesus is a "Good" testimony. People can question the word of God, but they cannot question a life turned over to God. Someone's testimony may be the most readable thing on the planet. As we declare how Jesus changed our life some may ask, "Did He now"? I live my life for Jesus. Do you now? I will sacrifice anything for Jesus. Then why were you out fishing when church was going on? Paul wants to win the Corinthians over to God. We want to win over the county, state, nation, and the world. Paul will not try and impress them with anything, but will boast of one thing in *1 Corinthians 2:2 For I **determined** not to know anything among you, save Jesus Christ, and him crucified.* Determined meaning to decide mentally what to do. It is to reach a conclusion for something you are about to say or do. It is to know you are ordained to do something. Every born-again believer is ordained to share the truth of who Jesus is. One of the two most forsaken things are 1)The word of God and 2) the church of God. If you or I live a life that does not point to the word of God or a local New Testament church, then why in the world would someone lost want what we do not live? Paul as his own personal judge had condemned himself to preaching Jesus to everybody and I pray you and I follow suit.

October 23

1 Corinthians 2:2
For I determined not to know any thing
among you, save Jesus Christ, and him crucified.

For your edification and simplicity, Paul is saying, "I really do not need to know anything other than Jesus Christ". Paul knew that Jesus selflessly submitted to humiliation and ultimately hung on a cross. Paul had determined not to cultivate or encourage any other knowledge, or esteem any other doctrine as worthy of notice. All of the Bible is good for us, but only one name contained in its pages could save us, and that is the name of JESUS. For someone to be saved they need to hear or see the truth. *Romans 10:14 How then shall they call on him in whom they have not believed? and how shall they believe in him of whom they have not heard? and how shall they hear without a preacher? 2 Timothy 4:2 Preach the word; be instant in season, out of season; reprove, rebuke, exhort with all longsuffering and doctrine.* Paul's example of fortitude can change us forever if we fully commit to Jesus. The Bible will become real. Going to church is not something we have to think about, it is something we do. I have never had anything happen to me like what happened to Paul, but I can read about it in verses 3 and 4 of this same chapter 2. *3) And I was with you in weakness, and in fear, and in much trembling. 4) And my speech and my preaching was not with enticing words of man's wisdom, but in demonstration of the Spirit and of power.* The most powerful passage I know of concerning what Paul went through and yet it did not stop him. *Acts 14:19–21 19) And there came thither certain Jews from Antioch and Iconium, who persuaded the people, and, having stoned Paul, drew him out of the city, supposing he had been dead. 20) Howbeit, as the disciples stood round about him, he rose up, and came into the city: and the next day he departed with Barnabas to Derbe. 21) And when they had preached the gospel to that city, and had taught many, they returned again to Lystra, and to Iconium, and Antioch.* They thought he was dead, and the next day Paul is preaching and promoting Jesus. Would you like to raise your hands toward God right now to testify that this is what you want to be like? You must depend on the Holy Spirit in ministry, or you will operate in the flesh. Pray to God for His divine providence and protection as you testify of Jesus, and for Jesus.

October 24

1 Corinthians 2:3-4
3) And I was with you in weakness, and in fear, and in much trembling. 4) And my speech and my preaching was not with enticing words of man's wisdom, but in demonstration of the Spirit and of power:

I will start out today with a cross-reference passage to coincide with our text verses today. *2 Corinthians 10:10 For his letters, say they, are weighty and powerful; but his bodily presence is weak, and his speech contemptible.* Paul may have been little in stature, maybe his voice was not pleasant, or they just plain hated what he had to say. Was Paul weak and broke down because of the stoning, beatings, or other sufferings? Bad Weakness: When we think we do not need anything or anybody. Good Weakness: An expression of utter dependence upon the Holy Spirit of God. Verse 3 talks about his fear and trembling and possibly the state of mind Paul was in because of what he had been through. *2 Timothy 1:7 For God hath not given us the spirit of fear;*

but of power, and of love, and of a sound mind. If we knew we could be beaten like Paul, would we share the gospel? Despite any possible fear, Paul did not let that stop him from preaching Jesus. Paul also had a message of confidence. *Romans 15:29 And I am sure that, when I come unto you, I shall come in the fulness of the blessing of the gospel of Christ.* Remember, Corinthians is a book of rebuke for repentance and Romans is written to Christians simply to edify Christians. Here are some things that the Apostle Paul knew and spoke of. I come with all the gifts I need from the Holy Spirit to present His case. We do not need to defend God, but we do need to stand up with God. Paul knew any man or woman could be filled with the Holy Spirit. Paul knew that if you needed a gift, God could grant the gift. Paul knew, and we should know, that we can do nothing for God without God. Paul knew that he could become all things to all men that he might win some, *1 Corinthians 9:22 To the weak became I as weak, that I might gain the weak: I am made all things to all men, that I might by all means save some.* May we consistently represent Jesus to the entire world.

October 25

1 Corinthians 2:3-4
3) And I was with you in weakness, and in fear, and in much trembling. 4) And my speech and my preaching was not with enticing words of man's wisdom, but in demonstration of the Spirit and of power:

I want to pick back up on the last reference verse from yesterday and what Paul was all about. *1 Corinthians 9:22 To the weak became I as weak, that I might gain the weak: I am made all things to all men, that I might by all means save some.* **May we do the same**? It is not just becoming all things to all men, but striving to show your identity in Jesus Christ. Not everyone is going to like your stories about the saving grace of Jesus. Not everyone is going to like your straight and narrow path. We all have a CHOICE: walk on a narrow path with Jesus "OR" a wide path with the world. We do not share truth with only those who like it, but with any who will watch & listen. A CHOICE: Hopeful or Hopeless and it depends on whether one is lost or saved. Do I think Paul tried to come across as somebody he was not? NO! Paul refused to rely on anything other than the truth of Jesus in what he taught. Keep Jesus where He should be in your life and the rest will fall into place. I do think Paul spoke modestly, but he also spoke with authority. You and I have the authority as born-again believers to promote the name of Jesus. We MUST live a life that points to Jesus without words. I pray that the communities we live in would see that those who claim to be Christians are in fact living a more blessed life than those who do not. Why would someone want what I have if I am living like they do or worse? If a believer does not share truth or need the body of Christ, then why would an unbeliever? Some Christians, (if they are), are a laughingstock to the world because of their behavior. We gain spiritual maturity through Jesus, truth, and being an active part of the body of Christ. What sign can I see when someone gets saved? They will strive to obey the truth of scripture as the Holy Spirit reveals it. Revelation will come by studying, teaching, and preaching. If the Holy Spirit is revealing nothing, then you have none of the Holy Spirit. I have always struggled with someone saying they are saved, yet knowingly and consistently disobeying the truth of the Word of God. I do not question whether or not they lost their salvation as I believe in eternal security. I do question whether or not they ever had salvation.

October 26

1 Corinthians 2:3-4
3) And I was with you in weakness, and in fear, and in much trembling. 4) And my speech and my preaching was not with enticing words of man's wisdom, but in demonstration of the Spirit and of power:

You would be correct in seeing that we may have changed the date for this devotional, but are still considering the same verses. Yesterday we looked at how Paul did not get distracted from doing what is right. Only death could stop him from preaching and serving Jesus. It appears at times to take very little to turn someone away from God, the truth, and His church. We can be victorious for God because we have access to the power of God. How we handle it remains to be seen, but we have free and unlimited access to Him! When you and I made Jesus our Savior we were set free to serve Him anyway He calls. *John 8:36 If the Son therefore shall make you free, ye shall be free indeed.* It is time to reread the verses for today one more time. *3) And I was with you in weakness, and in fear, and in much trembling. 4) And my speech and my preaching was not with enticing words of man's wisdom, but in demonstration of the Spirit and of power*: What demonstration was there of the Spirit and of power? How many people were healed by the power of God through Paul? How many people were saved by the words of Paul about Jesus? How many people were converted because Paul was converted? How many people are healed and delivered because of our prayers? The demonstration of the Spirit and power is a testimony that points to Jesus with no words. Only one thing can stop the saving power of grace from an Almighty God and that is the individual. Paul went from killing people and sending some to hell, to rescuing men from Hell. Are we committed to know nothing first, save Jesus the Savior of the World? God does not send anyone to hell, but He will honor their decision to go there. Let me ask again, "Anyone want to raise up holy hands or kneel on the floor right now and make a stand for Jesus"? Believers have the Spirit and Power permanently. God's Holy Spirit is what changes someone spiritually for the good. The Holy Spirit teaches us what the Bible says, we apply it, and we are changed. The power of God will change one internally and it will be reflected externally. May your internal change be a powerful influence on the world around you.

October 27

1 Corinthians 2:5
That your faith should not stand in the
wisdom of men, but in the power of God.

So this verse 5 pretty much sums the verses of *1 Corinthians 2:1-4.* The wisdom of men can be what someone has been taught, but never applied. The wisdom of men may have absolutely nothing to do with the truth of the Word of God. Knowing what the Bible says may be knowledge, but applying it is wisdom. Knowing what the Bible says, and obeying what it says, is two different things. The wisdom of men can be hearing and talking about Jesus as the Savior, but never accepting Him as "their" Savior. The wisdom of man can be traditions, or how someone was brought up, and even taught as biblical. We do not trust in man's truth, but in God's truth. I will leave you with at least one example of heresy. Some will tell you that they will just sprinkle you for baptism, but the Bible says to completely immerse. The following verses spell that thought out.

*Acts 8:36-39 36) 36) And as they went on their way, they came unto a certain water: and the eunuch said, See, here is water; what doth hinder me to be baptized? 37) And Philip said, If thou believest with all thine heart, thou mayest. And he answered and said, I believe that Jesus Christ is the Son of God. 38) And he commanded the chariot to stand still: and **they went down both into the water**, both Philip and the eunuch; and he baptized him. 39) And **when they were come up out of the water**, the Spirit of the Lord caught away Philip, that the eunuch saw him no more: and he went on his way rejoicing.* For baptism, have you ever tried to get in or out of a four-to-six-inch bowl of water? Me either. Some may say the Bible is a good book, but man wrote it. They leave out that the Word of God was written entirely while under the inspiration of the Holy Spirit. *2 Timothy 3:16 All scripture is given by inspiration of God, and is profitable for doctrine, for reproof, for correction, for instruction in righteousness: 2 Peter 1:21 For the prophecy came not in old time by the will of man: but holy men of God spake as they were moved by the Holy Ghost.* Some will declare that you do not need to read your Bible and they will tell you what it says. However, according to *2 Peter 1:20 Knowing this first, that no prophecy of the scripture is of any private interpretation.* That last thought about not needing to read your Bible is right out of the pit of hell. Some religious leaders will tell you to keep on repeating those memorized prayers and you will be fine, but that is not what Jesus said in *Matthew 6:7 But when ye pray, use not vain repetitions, as the heathen do: for they think that they shall be heard for their much speaking.* Be led by the Holy Spirit and not the spirit of man. Do not look for a **religion,** but look to Jesus for a **relationship**.

October 28

1 Corinthians 2:5
That your faith should not stand in the
wisdom of men, but in the power of God.

The Bible does in fact have plenty to say if we will just listen and obey its truth. As far as thinking that a born-again believer cannot experience the power of God is foolish thinking. We do not need to get caught up in the traditions of men, but the truth of God. We left off yesterday with some thinking that we cannot even pray a personal prayer to God because we have to recite what some religion told us needed to be recited. *Ephesians 5:6 Let no man deceive you with vain words: for because of these things cometh the wrath of God upon the children of disobedience.* So how do you define vanity? It would be vain as in lying words. Vain as in empty and not a lick of truth with the Word of God. Vain as in people memorize a prayer and no idea what it even means. I believe God wants prayer that is honest, personal, and current. I believe God wants prayer that we do not even know how to submit. God does not need prayers we have memorized. He needs our prayers under the influence of the Holy Spirit. God wants us to experience His goodness and to pray in the power of God. Even though we have the power of God we should stick with the simplicity of Jesus came, died, was buried, and arose from the grave. We can get into deeper things after someone confesses Jesus as LORD. Stick with Jesus' death conquered death for those who will believe. Hang on to the fact that the gospel is preached, and God is glorified by the one speaking of Jesus. Believers have the power of God and can boast of the power of God, which is Jesus. God is glorified in our words and in our actions. If the Bible says something, then say it. If the Bible says we should do this, then do it? Why? Because God knows it is absolutely what is best for us. How can anyone outdo or overwhelm us as we operate under the "power" and influence of God?

October 29

1 Corinthians 2:5
That your faith should not stand in the
wisdom of men, but in the power of God.

Once again, we may have changed the day of the year, but not the verse for the day. Our wisdom should come from the Word of God, and sometimes even our personal experience. Why is our wisdom from the Word of God? *1 Corinthians 3:19 For the wisdom of this world is foolishness with God. Psalms 14:1 The fool hath said in his heart, There is no God. They are corrupt, they have done abominable works, there is none that doeth good. 1 Corinthians 1:18 For the preaching of the cross is to them that perish foolishness; but unto us which are saved it is the power of God.* We must rely on the power of God to lead us every second of the day. The wisdom of God is supported by the word of God, and we are empowered by the power of God. For us today: *Romans 1:16 For I am not ashamed of the gospel of Christ: for it is the power of God unto salvation to everyone that believeth; to the Jew first, and also to the Greek.* The power of God can move mountains. The power of God can make the vilest of the vile whole and useful for service. The power of God can transform any man or woman. No one can be transformed without wanting to be reformed. When clay gets hard you add water to it and it becomes malleable again. Water is likened to the word of God. If we get hardened, get back to the water, the word of God and soften back up to the truth and that still small voice of God. In staying with this verse 5 I want to briefly touch on three little words. That your faith should not stand in the wisdom of men, but in the **power of God**. *1 Corinthians 1:24 But unto them which are called, both Jews and Greeks, Christ the power of God, and the wisdom of God. Christ is our Mediator and power of God.* What can the power of God do? *Luke 9:42-43 42) And as he was yet a coming, the devil threw him down, and tare him. And Jesus rebuked the unclean spirit, and healed the child, and delivered him again to his father. 43) And they were all amazed at the mighty power of God. Philippians 3:21 Who shall change our vile body, that it may be fashioned like unto his glorious body, according to the working whereby he is able even to subdue all things unto himself. Philippians 4:13 I can do all things through Christ which strengtheneth me. Romans 8:35-39 35) Who shall separate us from the love of Christ? shall tribulation, or distress, or persecution, or famine, or nakedness, or peril, or sword? 36) As it is written, For thy sake we are killed all the day long; we are accounted as sheep for the slaughter. 37) Nay, in all these things we are more than conquerors through him that loved us. 38) For I am persuaded, that neither death, nor life, nor angels, nor principalities, nor powers, nor things present, nor things to come, 39) Nor height, nor depth, nor any other creature, shall be able to separate us from the love of God, which is in Christ Jesus our Lord.* The word power, from the phrase power of God, comes from the word Dunamis, where we get our word dynamite. You possess the power of God through Jesus as the mediator and onto an Almighty God as directed by the Holy Spirit of God. Satan will tell you that you have no power, and you say, "Maybe not, but my Savior does"! Because of the power of God, you have the authority to say, "Get thee behind me Satan". We have the power of God to serve Him to the best of "His" ability that He so freely grants us. Embrace the fact that you have the POWER OF GOD at your fingertips and use it to glorify Him.

October 30

1 Corinthians 2:6-7
6) Howbeit we speak wisdom among them that are perfect: yet not the wisdom of this world, nor of the princes of this world, that come to nought: 7) But we speak the wisdom of God in a mystery, even the hidden wisdom, which God ordained before the world unto our glory:

Just a couple of days ago we touched on wisdom and what it is. Wisdom can be worldly or spiritual. Spiritual wisdom is perfect or morally correct according to the word of God. Wisdom is perfect and sinless such as Jesus was, but wisdom must be applied personally. For us, perfected is in having a form of godliness or maturity. We cannot get too high and mighty because of what it says in *Isaiah 64:6 But we are all as an unclean thing, and all our righteousnesses are as filthy rags; and we all do fade as a leaf; and our iniquities, like the wind, have taken us away.* How do you evaluate yourself? Obedience to the truth of the Word of God. I promise you that if someone will disobey one thing, they will disobey a hundred things. Fortunately, if we fall out of the circle of perfect, we can fall back into the circle of grace. *1 John 1:9-10 9) If we confess our sins, he is faithful and just to forgive us our sins, and to cleanse us from all unrighteousness. 10) If we say that we have not sinned, we make him a liar, and his word is not in us.* These two verses are not a get out of jail card to sin freely or consistently. Let us stop and reread verses 6 and 7 one more time before moving on. *6) Howbeit we speak wisdom among them that are perfect: yet not the wisdom of this world, nor of **the princes of this world**, that come to nought: 7) But we speak the wisdom of God in a mystery, even the hidden wisdom, which God ordained before the world unto our glory*: Princes can be those such as demons, judges, rulers, and believe it or not politicians. Two different thoughts about who Jesus was as "thee" Prince. Read what they thought about Jesus in *Matthew 9:34 But the Pharisees said, He casteth out devils through the prince of the devils*. Religious leaders thought He was nothing more than a tool or servant to Satan. Look at the verse in *Acts 3:14-15 14) But ye denied the Holy One and the Just, and desired a murderer to be granted unto you; 15) And killed the Prince of life, whom God hath raised from the dead; whereof we are witnesses.* Jesus' followers knew Jesus was the Savior of the world. Jesus is either a "prince" with a small "p" or a "Prince" with a capital "P". The goal is to not go back and forth, but to completely submit to the truth and service. Why? Because the wisdom of the world will be judged perfectly by the wisdom of God. Man says do what feels right and it is probably right. In most cases, how is that working for them? Some might say, "You do not understand why I do what I do or why I disobey when I disobey"? You would be right. I do not understand disobedience to the word of God. We have the power of God in order to obey the word of God. Anything less than that raises the question of, "How's that working for you"?

October 31

1 Corinthians 2:6-7
6) Howbeit we speak wisdom among them that are perfect: yet not the wisdom of this world, nor of the princes of this world, that come to nought: 7) But we speak the wisdom of **God in a mystery**, even the hidden wisdom, which God ordained before the world unto our glory:

We will continue the thought process from *1 Corinthians 2:6-7* for one more day. We have the phrase, *"God in a mystery"*. Believers in Jesus can now know the hidden wisdom of God as verse 7 says. What is "God in a mystery". A scriptural mystery is a previously hidden truth that has been revealed. The mystery of scripture was always going to be revealed as God says in verse seven. It is has been ordained or predestined to be revealed to those who will trust, believe, and obey. Nothing can be revealed if I do not open the curtain to His truth. The truth is behind the cover of His book, which is your bible. Verses 6 and 7 *6) Howbeit we speak wisdom among them that are perfect: yet not the wisdom of this world, nor of the princes of this world, that come to nought: 7) But we speak the wisdom of God in a mystery, even the hidden wisdom, which **God ordained before the world** unto our glory*. Only God could have a plan before the world began of a Savior going to the cross. Only God could tell men hundreds of years in advance what would happen, and it happened. If Paul heard of it, then why did he kill so many believers? Paul was lost before He was found on the road to Damascus. I do not care how smart Paul was, he had to have the gift of the Holy Spirit for discernment. He was brought up at the feet of Gamaliel, but we can be trained and brought up at the feet of the Holy Spirit. If religious leaders knew it, then why did they crucify Jesus? Because their desire was to have a place of prominence in the church. As a Pastor, I have had to deal with those who want to be in charge instead of God. They want to run the show instead of God running things. They may look religious, but looking religious is not the key. Being spiritual for God by the power of God is what we all need. The religious leaders had a desire to be in charge, instead of Jesus as the King. They were lost men and ignorant of the truth. For us, the truth is still revealed, and man is still rejecting Jesus. For us, the Holy Spirit reveals what we should do, but we still fight it. In the Old Testament the Prophets searched for truth, but few went to Bethlehem to find the King. If the truth is readily preached then why doesn't everyone come to repentance, which is a reasonable question. The answer is because many would rather obey Satan and the world than God and a Savior. I did not mention the Holy Spirit because if you are lost you do not have the Holy Spirit. I was asked on more than one occasion if I thought you could lose your salvation? My answer was no, and I passed on some scripture that supports that. However, I do not think you can lose your salvation, but I question whether someone ever had it. "The Fruit in someone's life is the key". Many will not give up the tradition of men or a religion. Many prefer life in the world and onto hell than an eternal life with Jesus and heaven. Many will not look any farther than what they can see or put their hands on. Life is short and death is inevitable so we must point our life towards Jesus, and live for Jesus. God has ordained you as a child of God to promote His kingdom. After all, the theme of the Bible is about a King and a Kingdom. It is about Jesus reigning as we worship Him for all of eternity.

November 1

1 Corinthians 2:6-7
6) Howbeit we speak wisdom among them that are perfect: yet not the wisdom of this world, nor of the princes of this world, that come to nought: 7) But we speak the wisdom of **God in a mystery**, even the hidden wisdom, which God ordained before the world unto our glory:

We are looking at the same verses, but a different day. We have talked about the "Mystery" of scripture. It was a mystery, but it has been revealed to those who are born again via the Word of God. It was a mystery because a few events had not happened yet. Many mysteries became a reality such as Jesus' birth. Some mysteries have been told so we can understand, but they have not happened yet. Some mysteries as far as when they happen, we will not know until it happens. Eventually, every event in scripture that has been foretold will come to fruition. You see, a mystery can be revealed, but you may not be around to see it firsthand. I do not need to see something happen to believe the Bible's accuracy. If God's word says something "will be" then it "will be". Back to the mystery or the truth of the word of God. Truth is hidden from the lost not the saved. God gave Israel many verses pointing to the Messiah coming and He did come. God gave verses pointing to the death, burial, and resurrection of Jesus and it happened. What else does God's word say will happen, but has not happened yet? God has given us verses that He will rapture us out and it "WILL" happen. God says there will be a horrible time on earth known as the tribulation period. God says there will be a thousand-year reign of Jesus setting up His kingdom and nothing can prevent it. God said JESUS will return, sit on a throne for eternity, and nothing or nobody can stop it. The gospel has been revealed, the word of God given to all to understand, and every future prophecy has been revealed. We simply wait for it all to come true. No matter how powerful someone is, they cannot stop what God says is inevitable. Why? *Titus 1:2 In hope of eternal life, which **God, that cannot lie**, promised before the world began*; So let us head on back to God's truth and our responsibility. *2 Corinthians 11:10 As the truth of Christ is in me, no man shall stop me of this boasting in the regions of Achaia.* Do our **words** boast of Jesus? Does my **life** boast of Jesus? We are like the guard at a castle where we are to blow the trumpet. We are to warn people of impending danger or events so they can avoid the disaster of hell. God loves us, but does our life point back to a love to God? I think we all must daily evaluate all areas of our life. *Colossians 1:10 That ye might walk worthy of the Lord unto all pleasing, being fruitful in every good work, and increasing in the knowledge of God. 1 Thessalonians 2:4 But as we were allowed of God to be put in trust with the gospel, even so we speak; not as pleasing men, but God, which trieth our hearts. 2 Corinthians 4:2 But have renounced the hidden things of dishonesty, not walking in craftiness, nor handling the word of God deceitfully; but by manifestation of the truth commending ourselves to every man's conscience in the sight of God.* What the Bible is saying is that we are not to justify sin through wrong thinking. If we take verses out of context we can make scripture say what it does not say. God's word says what it means, and it means what it says.

November 2

1 Corinthians 2:8
Which none of the princes of this world knew: for had they known it, they would not have crucified the Lord of glory.

We have touched on a few thoughts about why anyone would have crucified Jesus. If they knew that He was the Savior of the world, why would they do that? Nonetheless, I will add to it anyway. If they had **really known** Jesus, they would not have crucified the Lord of glory. If they had really known Jesus, they would not have disobeyed the Lord of glory. FOR US TODAY: If someone really knows Jesus would they disobey His word? If someone really knew Jesus would they have _____? You fill in the blank. When we disobey Jesus, it is as if we crucify Him all over again. It is one thing to know we need some improving, but it is another to submit to changing. Read again Verse 8: *Which none of the princes of this world knew: for had they known it, they would not have crucified the Lord of glory.* We look back at the "they" of this verse as it is in a past tense timeframe. What about the timeframe we are in today? Question: Will we serve the Lord part of the time, most of the time, or all the time? For many believers, they need to do as Earl Pitts would say, "Wake up America". Wake up Christian, as it appears that many Christians are literally living two lives. Christians living two lives is exactly what was said in *Revelation 3:15-16 15) I know thy works, that thou art neither cold nor hot: I would thou wert cold or hot. 16) So then because thou art lukewarm, and neither cold nor hot, I will spue thee out of my mouth.* By the way, those previous verses here in Revelation is written in red as Jesus is the one talking. The word spue in Revelation 3:16 is ***em-***

eh'-o and literally means Jesus will hurl or vomit them out. I think I honestly know how Jesus feels as it is so applicable today. Doctrinally, we are in the Laodicean church age, and it definitely shows. I am praying I overcome my ill thoughts towards Christianity, but it does not appear that will happen anytime soon. So many of my old friends have fallen away from serving God and are now serving sin. However, if Jesus did not get over it then why would I? I believe for the first time in my Christian life I fully understand what righteous indignation is. No one can force someone to live for Jesus because it is a personal choice. Two choices to ponder: Two choices Christian: Wake up to Serve, or Sleep-In and do nothing.

November 3

1 Corinthians 2:8
But as it is written, Eye hath not seen,
nor ear heard, neither have entered into the heart of man,
the things which God hath prepared for them that love him.

This verse 9 actually comes from *Isaiah 64:4 For since the beginning of the world men have not heard, nor perceived by the ear, neither hath the eye seen, O God, beside thee, what he hath prepared for him that waiteth for him.* First off, things which God hath prepared is for them that love him. It is not prepared for the lost. It is prepared for those that love Him. How can anyone gauge where someone is at spiritually? Give it time and it will be revealed. Over time a lost man or woman will almost always turn their back from what the Bible says to do. I did not say Christian, because if someone is born again, how can they disobey God "consistently"? *John 14:23 Jesus answered and said unto him, If a man love me, he will keep my words: and my Father will love him, and we will come unto him, and make our abode with him. Revelation 3:15-16 15) I know thy works, that thou art neither cold nor hot: I would thou wert cold or hot. 16) So then because thou art lukewarm, and neither cold nor hot, I will spue thee out of my mouth.* God through Jesus had done something new and marvelous, and we enter the "Age of Grace". Men still cannot conceive what all could be received through Jesus Christ, and we are to convey that same message of hope for what is to come. Eternal Security – Nothing can separate you from the love of God which is in Christ Jesus. Romans 8:38-39 is about the gift of the Holy Spirit for eternity. *John 14:16 And I will pray the Father, and he shall give you another Comforter, that he may abide with you forever.* We will be escorted by angels at death to our real home in heaven. *Luke 16:22 And it came to pass, that the beggar died, and was carried by the angels into Abraham's bosom: the rich man also died, and was buried.* We will receive a new incorruptible body that will never perish. *1 Corinthians 15:52 In a moment, in the twinkling of an eye, at the last trump: for the trumpet shall sound, and the dead shall be raised incorruptible, and we shall be changed.* The older we get the more we change and not necessarily in a good way. It is a fact that we are dying a little bit every day. We will get to live and reign with Jesus for eternity. *Revelation 20:6 Blessed and holy is he that hath part in the first resurrection: on such the second death hath no power, but they shall be priests of God and of Christ, and shall reign with him a thousand years.* We will be reunited with other believers who have gone on before us. *1 Thessalonians 4:13-14 13) But I would not have you to be ignorant, brethren, concerning them which are asleep, that ye sorrow not, even as others which have no hope. 14) For if we believe that Jesus died and rose again, even so them also which sleep in Jesus will God bring with him.* We have the gifts of the Spirit given for service to those who believe in God's plan regarding Jesus. What a blessing to gain new life in Jesus. All the junk is put away and a life transformed, *2 Corinthians 5:17 Therefore if any man be in Christ, he is a new creature: old things are passed away; behold, all things are become new.* What I see way too often is a lack of transformation. I see more disobeying the Word of God than I see those honoring the word of God. A life <u>deformed</u> by sin, can be <u>transformed</u> only because someone wants to be <u>reformed</u>. Being reformed will result in being conformed into the image of Christ little by little. You and I have been given the opportunity to render service for Jesus. We can have a Church family to belong to and partner with. We no longer have to fear death or the grave. You can kill the old spiritual nature you were born with and live a new nature through the acceptance of Jesus. *Ephesians 2:10 For we are his workmanship, created in Christ Jesus unto good works, which God hath before ordained that we should walk in them. Revelation 4:11 Thou art worthy, O Lord, to receive glory and honour and power: for thou hast created all things, and for thy pleasure they are and were created.* John's vision allowed him to see into Heaven, and he is seeing the wonderful majesty of God. While here on earth, do people see the majesty of God by how we live? If we were arrested for being a Christian would there be enough evidence to convict us? We have the liberty or "free will" to do whatever, but liberty is intended to be used to serve Jesus. Liberty according to the word of God has never been for sin, self, or satisfaction.

November 4

1 Corinthians 2:9
But as it is written, Eye hath not seen, nor ear heard, neither have entered into the heart of man, the things which God hath prepared for them that love him.

We are going to spend one more day going over the verse from yesterday. 1 Corinthians 2:9 ends in **_love_**, the greatest gift of all. This verse promises us that God has some extraordinary things for **us**. When I use the word **us**, I am referring to those that love Him. For those that love Him is exactly what this verse says. It takes God's love and the Holy Spirit to understand God's secret wisdom. The bottom line for a believer is you will receive truth when you are ready to receive truth. A tragedy in Christianity is many will not find God, search for God, or obey God. *Matthew 7:14 Because strait is the gate, and narrow is the way, which leadeth unto life, and few there be that find it.* Few there be that find it, and I have seen many fall from His path, or were never on His path. God's path is not wide with sin, it is very narrow and fenced in with righteousness. People must get off their path of sin and turn to the narrow path with Jesus. Why do I think many may be lost that think they are saved? Jesus said in *Matthew 7:16 Ye shall know them by their fruits*. I have seen too many so-called saved people worse than the lost. *Isaiah 53:6 All we like sheep have gone astray; we have turned everyone to his own way; and the LORD hath laid on him the iniquity of us all*. God had a plan and not because we loved Him first, but because HE loved us. *1 John 4:19 We love him, because he first loved us.* I believe all of God's word because of the first five words of this verse 9, "But as it is written". You and I will either do what the Bible says, or we will pick and choose what we want to obey. If I refuse to obey, then I ought to be questioning my own salvation. Who will stand up with holy hands or kneel and proclaim, "I will stand with Jesus, and I will obey whatever the Word of God says"? Be careful before you raise those hands, as God will deal with your witness. If you need to make amends with God, He is always listening, and just a prayer away. The beauty of calling out to God is there is never a busy signal.

November 5

1 Corinthians 2:9
But God hath revealed them unto us by his Spirit: for the Spirit searcheth all things, yea, the deep things of God.

So what else is on the horizon as we look at this verse 9? First off, the word for God is the word Theos. He is the supreme, most holy, and Divine God. He is the perfect Judge on a throne and the ultimate magistrate of all things. In moving on, Pneuma is the word for Spirit. I like how this is used to describe a breath or current of air, as God's Spirit is everywhere. Sometimes Pneuma is a blast of air and I have experienced that blast from the Holy Spirit. I have experienced when God allows something new to be discovered as we read His word. Pneuma is the divine intervention of God in a believer's life to understand truth. Pneuma is the word for Spirit, as in Holy Spirit, that an unbeliever will receive when they repent and accept Jesus by faith. Man can be broken down into two basic categories. 1) There is a **_saved, (or better put), spiritual man_**, whose body now contains the Holy Spirit upon receiving Jesus by faith. We can now know about God, the thoughts of God, and all about Jesus. We can be guided to truth by the Holy Spirit. 2) If you are **_lost you are simply a natural man with no Holy_**

Spirit indwelling within you, and you merely have know-how of Jesus, or you have heard about Jesus. A natural man can never reach anything beyond the conscience of what is plain and ordinary humanity. Let me break this down to more understandable terms. There are two spiritual fathers in the Bible. One is Satan and if you are lost, he is your daddy. The second is God if you have trusted Jesus to be your Savior. Then and only then God becomes your daddy. I have always wanted to say this, "Who's YOUR Daddy? So if you do not want Satan to be your daddy then do something about it. You might want to put this book down and pray to receive Jesus if you have not done so already. Then please consider telling your family about Jesus. Hell is real and so is spiritual stupidity. Spiritual stupidity is hearing and knowing you need Jesus but refusing the offer. Some will ask, "why would a loving God send someone to hell"? God does not send anyone to Hell as He made a way of escape through Jesus. However, God will honor their choice to reject Jesus and choose hell. *John 14:6 Jesus saith unto him, I am the way, the truth, and the life: no man cometh unto the Father, but by me.* A person is either lost or saved. A person is either bound for heaven or bound for hell, and that is based on an individual's choice to accept Jesus. Where are you at spiritually and where are you headed? Keep in mind, if you have children, they will be accountable for their own sin as well. Have you taken the time to spell out to your kids why they need to accept Jesus by faith? Kids or grandkids will spend eternity somewhere, and you can influence their decision.

November 6

1 Corinthians 2:10
But God hath revealed them unto us by his Spirit: for the Spirit searcheth all things, yea, the deep things of God.

You have arrived at a brand-new day and a brand-new thought. When a believer is ready for a particular Bible truth God will reveal the truth through guidance from the Holy Spirit. How do I know that? We can look at an example or two from the Bible. *Daniel 2:47 The king answered unto Daniel, and said, Of a truth it is, that your God is a God of gods, and a Lord of kings, and <u>a revealer of secrets</u>, seeing thou couldest reveal this secret. John 14:26: But the Comforter, which is the Holy Ghost, whom the Father will send in my name, <u>he shall teach you all things</u>, and bring all things to your remembrance, whatsoever I have said unto you.* Because scripture was given by the inspiration of God it can only be understood by the influence of God the Holy Spirit. *2 Peter 1:20-21 Knowing this first, that no prophecy of the scripture is of any private interpretation. 21) For the prophecy came not in old time by the will of man: but holy men of God spake as they were moved by the Holy Ghost.* Believers can speak by inspiration of the same Holy Spirit. You and I can be led in our words by God if we will allow it. We can have truth revealed in the same manner Paul had it revealed. There is no end to the depth of understanding we can have of God's word. God will not keep us hanging for truth, and just as He taught the disciples and prophets, He will teach you and me. God reveals understanding and truth so we can share the truth. It is amazing how you can sit down and pray for God's divine intervention and experience God leading you to truth. You cannot explain that, you can only experience it. There are two choices in the life of a Christian.

One is to allow God to lead us to the deep things of truth that only He can reveal. The second is to wallow in the shallow things of the world that have zero spiritual benefits. You and I determine what we desire from God spiritually and HE will bless accordingly. It is like tithing, serving, or worshipping; God can only bless what we are willing to give.

November 7

1 Corinthians 2:11
For what man knoweth the things of a man, save the spirit of man which is in him? even so the things of God knoweth no man, but the Spirit of God.

First off, the Bible is clear about the fact that man is a three part being. Why do I think that? *1 Thessalonians 5:23 And the very God of peace sanctify you wholly; and I pray God your whole **spirit and soul and body** be preserved blameless unto the coming of our Lord Jesus Christ. Hebrews 4:12 For the word of God is quick, and powerful, and sharper than any two-edged sword, piercing even to the dividing asunder of soul and spirit, and of the joints and marrow, and is a discerner of the thoughts and intents of the heart.* The body is used to allow us to function. The body is the mechanism that will either lead us to Church on Sunday, or to the lake and golf course. The soul is the part that holds our senses such as things we may desire or crave. With no Holy Spirit connected to a lost soul, the soul is always in unrest. We could say that a lost soul is earthly, and a saved soul is heavenly. By the way, for those saved, we are already seated in the heavenlies. The soul is the part of us that will either connect us to God or reject God. I like to separate the spirit and soul for clarity, as the spirit thinks, but the soul knows. What the bible is very clear about, is that until someone receives Jesus, the soul is dead and headed to hell. By accepting Jesus, we are then made a quickening or "alive" spirit. *1 Corinthians 15:22 For as in Adam all die, even so in Christ shall all be made alive.* An easier term would be to say the spirit is the innermost, surrounded by a soul, and encapsulated with a body. If you or I want to know anything spiritual, why would we look any farther than God? We can on occasion hear from God through a message preached, personal study of the Word of God, meditation of scripture, or maybe praying scripture right back to God. Perhaps the right Christian song will move you to know something. It could be a conversation about Jesus with someone else and that will teach you. What I know is that God is all-knowing, and when you and I are ready He will reveal truth. God the Holy Spirit can and does bear witness with our spirit so we can discern truth. None of us can think like God unless we let God guide our thinking. *Isaiah 55:8 For my thoughts are not your thoughts, neither are your ways my ways, saith the LORD.*

November 8

1 Corinthians 2:11
For what man knoweth the things of a man,
save the spirit of man which is in him? even so the
things of God knoweth no man, but the Spirit of God.

We left off yesterday talking about how we can let God guide our thinking. Let us pick right back up on that thought. *John 14:26 But the Comforter, which is the Holy Ghost, whom the Father will send in my name, he shall teach you all things, and bring all things to your remembrance, whatsoever I have said unto you.* In talking about the Spirit of God, remember that in the Old Testament the Spirit of

God came **upon** man. In the New Testament the Spirit of God dwells **in** man when he accepts Jesus by faith. The Spirit of God is powerful enough to conquer all things. *Matthew 12:28 But if I cast out devils by the Spirit of God, then the kingdom of God is come unto you. Romans 8:9 But ye are not in the flesh, but in the Spirit, if so be that the Spirit of God dwell in you. Now if any man have not the Spirit of Christ, he is none of his. Ephesians 4:30 And grieve not the holy Spirit of God, whereby ye are sealed unto the day of redemption.* The bottom line is that if you want a thorough knowledge of God, you must be led by the Holy Spirit. If you or I did not have a mind, where would we be, and how could we function. The same thing holds true for rejecting Jesus and not receiving the free gift of the indwelling of the Holy Spirit. We cannot function without a mind, and we cannot function correctly without the Holy Spirit indwelling in us. Our mind connects us to our body, and the Holy Spirit connects us to God. As we are ready God will communicate or reveal to His children the truth of the Word of God. For someone lost they can only look at life objectively by how they were raised or their opinion. Someone saved can look at life objectively through the mind of God as He instructs through His word. The soul and spirit are internal and by injecting the word of God we can reveal externally what He has revealed to us internally. We must witness to people by actions that we are different than the world. 1 John 4:4 Ye are of God, little children, and have overcome them: because greater is he that is in you, than he that is in the world. Learn the word and make God's thoughts your thoughts. Turn every area of your life over to God and let His ways be your ways. *Matthew 11:28 Come unto me, all ye that labour and are heavy laden, and I will give you rest.* Christians must let scripture lead them to doing what is right and following God faithfully. *Romans 7:23 But I see another law in my* *members, warring against the law of my mind, and bringing me into captivity to the law of sin which is in my members. 2 Corinthians 10:5 Casting down imaginations, and every high thing that exalteth itself against the knowledge of God, and bringing into captivity every thought to the obedience of Christ; 1 Corinthians 2:16 For who hath known the mind of the Lord, that he may instruct him? But we have the mind of Christ.* The phrase "mind of Christ" appears only "one" time and here it is. May God richly bless you as you seek the truth of His word and His will for your life. May everyone around you see Jesus in and through you, and want what you have to offer. Your offer of Jesus and discipleship is all they need to be changed forever.

November 9

1 Corinthians 2:12
Now we have received, not the spirit of the world,
but the spirit which is of God; that we might know
the things that are freely given to us of God.

We do not need a whole lot of explanation for this verse. It is addressing what a Christian has received. The word for received is <u>*lam-ban'-o,*</u> and it is a verb meaning that it is and was an active word. It means we have accepted, obtained, or caught because it was offered to us by God, and we had to either accept or reject the Holy Spirit. The gift of God, His Spirit requires a decision. Yes I want it, or No I don't. Yes, I want Jesus and you receive the Holy Spirit, or no I do not want Jesus and you do not receive the gift of the Holy Spirit and you remain a dead spirit. The spirit of the world is not a positive thing to possess or hang on to. No matter who may be the wisest man on the planet, the world's wisdom does not compare with God's wisdom. No matter who is the greatest leader of all ages they will never attain the wisdom of God. Look at a few examples from *1 Kings 4:29–30 29) And God gave Solomon wisdom and understanding exceeding much, and largeness of heart, even as the sand that is on the sea shore. 30) And Solomon's wisdom excelled the wisdom of all the children of the east country, and all the wisdom of Egypt. 1 Kings 10:24 And all the earth sought to Solomon, to hear his wisdom, which God had put in his heart. 2 Chronicles 9:23 And all the kings of the earth sought the presence of Solomon, to hear his wisdom, that God had put in his heart.* You want wisdom, look to the source of wisdom, the word of God. *1 Corinthians 2:12 Now we have received, not the spirit of the world, but the spirit which is of God; that we might know the things that are freely given to us of God. Ephesians 2:2 Wherein in time past ye walked according to the **course** of this world, according to the prince of the power of the air, the spirit that now worketh in the children of disobedience*: In time past, as an unbeliever, this is more than likely how I walked. What is interesting about this verse is the word **course**, which is the word **ahee-ohn'**, **Ahee-ohn** simply means "in the past". It implies the beginning of the world and I find that interesting. By implication and before accepting Jesus, we walked in a course that was never going to connect us to God. I do not care how nice somebody is, they will be eternally separated from a Holy God without a personal relationship with Jesus. Stay on course with Jesus, not the world.

November 10

1 Corinthians 2:12
Now we have received, not the spirit of the world, but the spirit which is of God; that we might know the things that are freely given to us of God.

As mentioned in the devotion yesterday you can only be connected to God through Jesus. *John 14:6 Jesus saith unto him, I am the way, the truth, and the life: no man cometh unto the Father, but by me.* No matter how wise a lost guy is, he is still lost, or better put, a lost unwise guy. I would question anyone's wisdom that has determined to reject Jesus. Look at Solomon for example and how quickly things can change if we do not guard ourselves. SOLOMON: WHAT HAPPENED WHEN HE TOOK HIS EYES OFF OF GOD? *1 Kings 11:4 For it came to pass, when Solomon was old, that his wives turned away his heart after other gods: and his heart was not perfect with the LORD his God, as was the heart of David his father.* Never take your eyes off the word of God. Never take your eyes off the prize, which is your calling to serve God. You cannot receive the Spirit of God unless you receive by faith Jesus as your Savior. If you are a born-again believer, you absolutely cannot live like someone who is lost. We are a peculiar people set apart to serve an almighty God. Be wise in the things you do as God is the one we ultimately drag through the mud. Look at a few of the tragedies from some who say they are saved. There will be some who will die and never serve God. Some will die and never allow another believer to disciple them. Some will die and never attend church faithfully. Some will die and no one will know if they were saved or not. Some will die and have a zero testimony of belonging to the body of Christ. Some know about baptism, but will never submit to the ordinance of complete immersion in water. Some will die and never support financially the work of the ministry. Some will say they love God, but do not support it biblically. They love the air conditioning and the heat, but will not help pay the bills. However, they will be quick to say, "It all belongs to God". Some will say they love their Pastor, but do next to nothing to support him. Some will say this and that, but their life says something totally different. This is a pretty good definition of a hypocrite, and may we not be labeled that by others, and especially by God. I leave you with verses about hypocrites: *Matthew 7:21-23 21)Not everyone that saith unto me, Lord, Lord, shall enter into the kingdom of heaven; but he that doeth the will of my Father which is in heaven. 22) Many will say to me in that day, Lord, Lord, have we not prophesied in thy name? and in thy name have cast out devils? and in thy name done many wonderful works? 23) And then will I profess unto them, I never knew you: depart from me, ye that work iniquity.*

November 11

1 Corinthians 2:12
Now we have received, not the spirit of the world,
but the spirit which is of God; that we might know
the things that are freely given us of God.

The Spirit of God is the spirit of truth, and it is absolutely free. You will not wake up one morning with all the insight of truth without opening the pages to the truth, and then allowing God to lead you in truth. God will take His word and illuminate what you need when you are ready to receive it. TURN YOUR ATTENTION TO THE SPIRIT OF GOD: *Genesis 1:2 And the earth was without form, and void; and darkness was upon the face of the deep. And the Spirit of God moved upon the face of the waters.* Used at Creation. *Genesis 41:38 And Pharaoh said unto his servants, Can we find such a one as this is, a man in whom the Spirit of God is?* It is obvious that God had control of Moses. *Matthew 12:28 But if I cast out devils by the Spirit of God, then the kingdom of God is come unto you.* The Spirit of God can cleanse all things according to the Will of God. *Romans 8:9 But ye are not in the flesh, but in the Spirit, if so be that the Spirit of God dwell in you. Now if any man have not the Spirit of Christ, he is none of his.* Paul is talking to Christians in the book of Romans when he says, "Ye are not in the flesh, but are in the Spirit" with a capital "S". If you do not have the Spirit of Christ, you do not belong to God. Heaven is not on your horizon, but hell is. We circle right back to "Who is your Daddy"? God or Satan? *Romans 8:14 For as many as are led by the Spirit of God, they are the sons of God.* The question becomes who is leading you? If it is not God, then who are you following and why? *1 Corinthians 3:16 Know ye not that ye are the temple of God, and that the Spirit of God dwelleth in you?* Hey Christian, you are the temple of God so you must take care of it. *Ephesians 4:30 And grieve not the holy Spirit of God, whereby ye are sealed unto the day of redemption.* We are sealed for eternity and guaranteed salvation through Jesus by grace. Being sealed by God is not a license to sin. I am not saying we will not fail. I am saying we will repent from the failure, and as Jesus said to the woman at the well, "Go and sin no more". I tend to believe that Jesus positively meant, "go and sin no more".

November 12

1 Corinthians 2:12
Now we have received, not the spirit of the world, but the spirit which is of God; that we might know the things that are <u>freely given</u> to us of God.

What has been freely given and we have already covered this. *Romans 5:14-15 14) Nevertheless death reigned from Adam to Moses, even over them that had not sinned after the similitude of Adam's transgression, who is the figure of him that was to come. 15) But not as the offence, so also is the free gift. For if through the offence of one many be dead, much more the grace of God, and the gift by grace, which is by one man, Jesus Christ, hath abounded unto many. Romans 6:18 Being then made free from sin, ye became the servants of righteousness.* If someone is not the servant of righteousness, then what are they the servant of? Sin – looking like they are lost. Satan – He is really your daddy, and you cannot help yourself. What has God freely given to help us serve Him? Have we or have we not been equipped to serve and support the body of Christ? What has God called you to do, or where has God told you to go? Why does God freely give us anything? *Hebrews 13:21 Make you perfect in every good work to do his will, working in you that which is well pleasing in his sight, through Jesus Christ; to whom be glory for ever and ever. Amen. 2 Timothy 3:16–17 16) All scripture is given by inspiration of God, and is profitable for doctrine, for reproof, for correction, for instruction in righteousness: 17) That the man of God may be perfect, throughly furnished unto all good works.* God positively wants to do a work in your life that you might be perfected. A child of God is not someone going through the motions of Christianity. For those who know Jesus as their

Savior, they are the only ones who can be perfected. *Ephesians 2:10 For we are his workmanship, created in Christ Jesus unto good works, which God hath before ordained that we should walk in them.* Before the world began, God had orchestrated a plan that for those who would accept Jesus by faith, they would serve Him. We can ultimately judge how we are doing in our service to the King. Is Jesus an acquaintance, head knowledge, or is He a Savior & Friend? Is He a passing occasional thought or a committed lifestyle?

November 13

1 Corinthians 2:13
Which things also we speak, not in the words which man's wisdom teacheth, but which the Holy Ghost teacheth; comparing spiritual things with spiritual.

We have talked about being under the influence and leadership of the Holy Spirit. We have discussed not holding on to the foolishness of the world, but hanging on to the things of God. Today, if we do what we have talked about, then what will be the result? Because of what we have learned about God, we will share the truths of God. God has freely given us many spiritual things and we must stay underneath His influence. Because we are saved, now what? We cannot speak with man's wisdom, but that which the Holy Ghost teacheth. Speak is the word ***lal-eh'-o*** meaning to talk, speak or preach. We do not need a pulpit to share what the Holy Spirit has taught us. You may be able to teach someone, and it is not even in a church setting. Here is what you cannot do. You cannot share the truth if you do not have any of the truth. You and I cannot possess the truth if we leave the Bible of truth closed. I do not know of a shortcut to learning the Bible without opening its cover. If you do not know Jesus as your Savior, the Holy Spirit cannot teach you. I do know that an ordination service or bible college may not make you wiser. You may end up with a plaque on your wall, but no truth hanging in your heart. I can assure you that a lot of lost men and women graduate from seminary. In the last couple of days we have covered how even the wisest man of today's world does not hold a candle to God. You will not get a whole lot of Bible truth from any lost man. You may receive what they believe is the truth, but in reality, it is their opinion. Have you ever noticed that many people have an opinion as to what they believe the Bible says? It will be nothing more than the wisdom of the world as delivered by man. Man says abortion is okay and acceptable, yet God said, "I knew you before you were born". Man says the gay lifestyle is okay and acceptable, yet God turned them over to a reprobate mind in *Romans chapter 1* as well as in other places. Man says to eat, drink, and be merry, but do not read all of the verse. Look at what God's word says in *Luke 12:20 But God said unto him, Thou fool, this night thy soul shall be required of thee:* No one knows when they will draw their last breath. Man says to waste your money on riotous living, but God says, *"Lay up for yourself treasures in Heaven"*. Many times, man's wisdom may be in opposition to the Word of God, and that is where I believe a lot of Christians are today. A lot of Christians and lost people believe they have a better plan than God. Jesus died so we could be saved and serve, but many do not. Every single day I have this thought: Why do many Christians look like the lost? Are they backslidden or are they really lost and have no relationship with Jesus Christ? I lean towards that lost comment and here is why. *Psalms 119:115 Depart from me, ye evildoers: for I will keep the commandments of my God.* That is quite a phrase you just read: **_I WILL KEEP THE_**

COMMANDMENTS OF MY GOD. When someone refuses to do the truth of the word of God, I have to doubt God is really their God. It would be hard to convince me that God is their daddy. Many churches today are suffering spiritually and closing because "Christians" want to run the show instead of God being in charge. They do not want the Pastor to shepherd them by leadership of the Holy Spirit. They are like Pharisees that prefer their so-called place of prominence. There was one particular church that would try out a Pastor to see how he would conform or perform to them. If they did not like him, they would simply get another one. They wanted the Pastor to conform to them, instead of staying conformed to the leadership of the Holy Spirit. God help them as that mentality will ruin a lot of young men spiritually forever.

November 14

1 Corinthians 2:13
Which things also we speak, not in the words which man's wisdom teacheth, but which the Holy Ghost teacheth; comparing spiritual things with spiritual.

We are supposed to teach and preach what the Holy Ghost instructs us to teach and preach. The truth of God does not need dressed up, but rather presented as to what it says. The Bible does not need defended, but for some the Word of God makes them feel offended. Why? Because they are living a life that does not point towards the things of God. Many actually think, "Well I am a pretty good person so I must be okay with God". Are you serving God **faithfully**? Are you attending church **physically**? Are you Biblically supporting the body of Christ **financially**? Then there is only one answer to any of those questions and that is "If not, then why not"? *Proverbs 28:26 He that trusteth in his own heart is a fool: but whoso walketh wisely, he shall be delivered. Jeremiah 17:9 The heart is deceitful above all things, and desperately wicked: who can know it? Proverbs 12:15 The way of a fool is right in his own eyes: but he that hearkeneth unto counsel is wise.* So if our thinking is contrary to Bible truth, does it or does it not make us a fool? If we happen to think that our counsel is better than Gods' counsel, then we are foolish. *Proverbs 9:8 Reprove not a scorner, lest he hate thee: rebuke a wise man, and he will love thee.* You preach the truth, and some will get their little feelings offended. You know who does not get their little feelings hurt? Those who are doing right. At times we all need rebuked by God through His word. I have two choices: I will either be mad or glad that God shed some light to His truth. What will you do with the truth of the Word of God as it is taught? *Luke 11:28 But he said, Yea rather, blessed are they that hear the word of God, and keep it. Romans 10:17 So then faith cometh by hearing, and hearing by the word of God.* The Bible is filled with the glory of God and our faith will grow as we read it. Put forth a little extra time and effort and allow God to teach you His truth. It will be so worth it for you.

November 15

1 Corinthians 2:13
Which things also we speak, not in the words which man's wisdom teacheth, but which the Holy Ghost teacheth; comparing spiritual things with spiritual.

We are to compare scripture with scripture to create a complete puzzle. Every verse, chapter, or book is a puzzle piece and through study we start putting the pieces together. We start comparing spiritual things with spiritual things or verse against verse. Take a look at the Old Testament and the prophecy of things in the New Testament. Start out in *Isaiah 9:6 For unto us a child is born, unto us a son is given: and the government shall be upon his shoulder: and his name shall be called Wonderful, Counsellor, The mighty God, The everlasting Father, The Prince of Peace.* Move on for comparison to *Matthew 2:1 Now when Jesus was born in Bethlehem of Judaea in the days of Herod the king, behold, there came wise men from the east to Jerusalem,* <u>New Testament comparisons as well</u>: *1 Thessalonians 5:9 For God hath not appointed us to <u>wrath</u>, but to obtain salvation by our Lord Jesus Christ*, and reference that with *John 3:36 He that believeth on the Son hath everlasting life: and he that believeth not the Son shall not see life; but the <u>wrath</u> of God abideth on him. 1 Thessalonians 1:10 And to wait for his Son from heaven, whom he raised from the dead, even Jesus, which delivered us from the <u>wrath</u> to come. 1 Thessalonians 5:9 For God hath not appointed us to <u>wrath</u>, but to obtain salvation by our Lord Jesus Christ.* The last verse is the rapture of the Church and supporting verses that we will be taken out and meet Jesus in the clouds one day. *1 Corinthians 15:52 In a moment, in the twinkling of an eye, at the last trump: for the trumpet shall sound, and <u>the dead shall be raised</u> incorruptible, and we shall be changed.* Compare what you just read with *1 Thessalonians 4:17 Then we which are alive and remain shall be <u>caught up together with them in the clouds</u>, to meet the Lord in the air: and so shall we ever be with the Lord.* The tribulation period is for those who have rejected Jesus Christ and God gives us the discernment by way of comparing scripture with scripture to know the truth. We can go on for eternity comparing truth with truth. If God opens our eyes up to truth, then we must obey that "TRUTH". Why do I think like I do about so-called Christians in disobedience to the word of God? I see and hear of empty Churches because so-called Christians will not participate. Over thirty-seven hundred churches close every year because people will not attend. In the Baptist world we have the truth, and yet attendance is at its lowest in roughly 40 years, but we still have thousands of fewer baptisms a year. A pastor ran an ad in the paper one time and it read as follows: Funeral for the church this Saturday at two o'clock in the afternoon. Curiosity filled the building to overflowing capacity. The pastor gave a very eloquent eulogy, and everybody sat there nodding their head in agreement. When it was over, he opened the lid of the casket for viewing. One by one the curious crowd approached the casket to look inside. What was propped inside the casket was a mirror. The death of the church was because of the many reflections in the mirror. In 2014, Billy Graham statistics estimate that 85% of church members are not saved. We talk about the Pandemic of the Coronavirus every second of the day. The coronavirus will not hold a candle to how bad it will be in hell and there are no booster shots for that. The coronavirus is nothing when compared to how many will spend eternity in hell with no way of escape. What about the Epidemic of churches struggling and ultimately closing? We need to be concerned with how many have rejected Jesus instead of how many have not taken the Covid shot to supposedly help with the "Planned-Demic". The only shot to keep someone out of hell is a shot of Jesus. Christians must wake up and not let Satan be victorious in their life. I always ask myself, "what is it going to take to turn the trend around even at bible-believing churches. Maybe all churches should go by the name of "Good Intention Church". I meant to attend, I meant to participate, and I even meant to support the church financially. Pretty soon you are dead and for eternity you will live with those rewards. Jesus loved us enough to die for us. Can we not love Him enough to live for Him? The proof is in what you do and not what you think you will do. Best intentions and a quarter will more than likely not buy you a cup of coffee. The Church does not need good intentions, it needs good, loyal, and faithful servants. Let us end today's thought with *Joshua 24:15 And if it seem evil unto you to serve the LORD, choose you this day whom ye will serve; whether the gods which your fathers served that were on the other side of the flood, or the gods of the Amorites, in whose land ye dwell: but as for me and my house, we will serve the LORD.* We not only need a revival for the lost, but a revival for those who say they are saved. Pray and commit to being a slave in ministry for Jesus. Can you do it? God's word says you can.

November 16

1 Corinthians 2:14-16
14) But the natural man receiveth not the things of the Spirit of God: for they are foolishness unto him: neither can he know them, because they are spiritually discerned.
15) But he that is spiritual judgeth all things, yet he himself is judged of no man. 16) For who hath known the mind of the Lord, that he may instruct him? But we have the mind of Christ.

Since we have three verses that we need to tie together today, we will spend multiple days pondering what God would have us get out of all three of them together. We are getting towards the end of the year and Easter is behind us for this year. However, we absolutely must keep the Resurrection of Jesus as a daily thought. There should be nothing that should define who we are in Jesus Christ, except Jesus Christ. We are a child of the most- high God. *Philippians 4:13 I can do all things through Christ which strengtheneth me.* We can conquer all things through Jesus. We have the ability to serve Jesus to the best of His ability. We have eternity to worship our Creator and we must start now. We must see a revival in the Christian community so that it can spread to the lost world. Let us start dissecting this verse and go as long as length allows for today. Our first topic in this verse is the natural man and his nature. The word for natural is **psoo-khee-kos'**, meaning that a natural man is alive physically, but he is dead spiritually. You could only be considered at best a bestial form of man without Jesus. A natural man can only rely on his senses and not on the Holy Spirit for direction. The natural man receiveth not the things of the Spirit of God. This verse defines that the things of God are foolishness to him. *Psalms 14:1 The fool hath said in his heart, There is no God. They are corrupt, they have done abominable works, there is none that doeth good. Psalms 53:1 The fool hath said in his heart, There is no God. Corrupt are they, and have done abominable iniquity: there is none that doeth good.* The fool will commit iniquity or sin. I would suggest that Christians can be foolish and sin, and I have been guilty of that as well. *Proverbs 12:15 The way of a fool is right in his own eyes: Proverbs 26:11 As a dog returneth to his vomit, so a fool returneth to his folly. Proverbs 28:26 He that trusteth in his own heart is a fool: but whoso walketh wisely, he shall be delivered.* When you trust in the word of God, you will obey the word of God. Those who do not trust are foolish, and that is what I see in the Christian world today. The word for foolishness also means something that is silly or absurd. To obey God's word to some means they think it is silly. To some they will believe that what God's word teaches is absurd. Sounds harsh to a Christian, but how many Christians disobey the truth of the word? If someone disobeys, they are in essence saying it is silly, absurd, or foolish. Christian or not we are all without excuse and will be JUDGED by a perfect and Holy God. The word of God; Are we faithful or foolish with it? Do we apply it all or do we pick and choose what is easy and forget the rest? I can only judge for me, and you can only judge for you based on what the word of God says. The Bible is not like a dart board that you throw a dart at and then read wherever it sticks. Start from Genesis one and read through to Revelation 22. As of this devotion today I have read my Bible completely through 68 times. I learn something every time I read it through it and so will you.

November 17

1 Corinthians 2:14-16
14) But the natural man receiveth not the things of the Spirit of God: for they are foolishness unto him: neither can he know them, because they are spiritually discerned.
15) But he that is spiritual judgeth all things, yet he himself is judged of no man. 16) For who hath known the mind of the Lord, that he may instruct him? But we have the mind of Christ.

You have read the text for today, so jump right into another passage or two to help your understanding. John 14:26 But the Comforter, which is the Holy Ghost, whom the Father will send in my name, he shall teach you all things, and bring all things to your remembrance, whatsoever I have said unto you. *2 Thessalonians 2:12 That they all might be damned who believed not the truth, but had pleasure in unrighteousness.* Some lost people may know a few Bible facts, but they do not know Jesus as their Savior. Many who call themselves a Christian have the facts, but do not obey the facts. The Bible can only be understood through the teaching of the Holy Spirit. The Holy Spirit wants to teach, but we must want to be taught. *1 Corinthians 2:14-16 14) But <u>the natural man receiveth not the things of the Spirit of God</u>: for they are foolishness unto him: neither can he know them, because they are spiritually discerned. 15) But he that is spiritual judgeth all things, yet he himself is judged of no man. 16) For who hath known the mind of the Lord, that he may instruct him? But <u>we have the mind of Christ</u>.* Many believe we are not to judge somebody, but what does the Bible say about that? *John 7:24 Judge not according to the appearance, but judge righteous judgment.* To judge with righteous judgment means you must judge according to the word of God. Before we judge we must read *Matthew 7:5 Thou hypocrite, first cast out the beam out of thine own eye; and then shalt thou see clearly to cast out the mote out of thy brother's eye.* We may see other's shortcomings but may forsake our own sin. We comment about those who disobey God's word, but disregard our own. Sin is not necessarily on a numbering system. We should not say, "well I may have a number five sin, but his or hers is a number ten sin". Let us live *2 Timothy 4:7-8 7) I have fought a good fight, I have finished my course, I have kept the faith: 8) Henceforth there is laid up for me a crown of righteousness, which the Lord, the righteous judge, shall give me at that day: and not to me only, but unto all them also that love his appearing.* Paul was in prison when he wrote these verses. If he can have this attitude in prison, just think what our attitude can be walking around free. As a believer you have been enlightened through God the Holy Spirit. You have been enlightened internally, so you can illuminate Jesus externally. May those around you see a sold-out servant and soldier for Jesus Christ. People around you may not understand why you are what you are, but they may want what you have. There is nothing sweeter than someone asking why you are the person you are? Your answer can be short and sweet. It is because of God the Father, God the Son, and God the Holy Spirit.

November 18

1 Corinthians 2:14-16
14) But the natural man receiveth not the things of the Spirit of God: for they are foolishness unto him: neither can he know them, because they are spiritually discerned.
15) But he that is spiritual judgeth all things, yet he himself is judged of no man. 16) For who hath known the mind of the Lord, that he may instruct him? But we have the mind of Christ.

I want to continue with the same verses from yesterday, but we will go down a different road today. If we do what is right, we may be judged by others, but it may be according to nonsense or jealousy. It is even possible that you may even get called a Bible-thumper. Praise God if you look like one, and should others calling you that join your ranks. Ultimately, our Judge is a perfect Judge. *Psalms 7:11* <u>God judgeth the righteous</u>, and <u>God is angry with the wicked every day.</u> *Hebrews 10:30 For we know him that hath said, Vengeance belongeth unto me, I will recompense, saith the Lord. And again,* **<u>The Lord shall judge his people</u>**. God is the JUDGE of the quick and the dead, or more appropriately the lost and the saved. The saved will be judged by their decision to trust Jesus as their Savior and then whisked into heaven. The lost will be judged by their decision to reject Jesus and will immediately be whisked right straight to hell. Somebody is their spiritual daddy, and it can only be God and Heaven, or it is Satan and Hell? *Romans 8:5 For they that are after the flesh do mind the things of the flesh; but they that are after the Spirit the things of the Spirit.* To the

Christian, are you minding the things of the flesh, or are you minding the things of the Holy Spirit of God? This raises a question: If someone continually minds the things of the flesh and disregards the word of God, do you think they are really saved? Yeah, I do not either. *1 Corinthians 2:14-16 14) But the natural man receiveth not the things of the Spirit of God: for they are foolishness unto him: neither can he know them, because they are spiritually discerned. 15) But he that is spiritual judgeth all things, yet he himself is judged of no man. 16) For who hath known the mind of the Lord, that he may instruct him? But we have the mind of Christ.* Only a saved person has the mind of Christ. The saved cannot instruct God, but God can instruct the saved as to the truth. A lost man cannot be under the inspiration of God. Someone lost can only "**act**" spiritual in the flesh. When the lost act religious there is no power, authority, or influence from the Holy Spirit of God because they do not possess the Holy Spirit. The saved can receive instruction from the Holy Spirit as far as what he or she is to do. After receiving instructions, the believer must decide what to do with the instruction and there is not a whole lot of choices. I will obey or NO I will not obey. No decision to do anything is a NO as well. Do you want to know God's will for your life? Then seek His instruction through prayer and the Bible. The Bible has 66 books contained within one book. I am positive you will find at least one of God's instructions that you can hang on to. You might even find two if you keep reading, studying, and meditating on His word. *2 Timothy 2:15 Study to shew thyself approved unto God, a workman that needeth not to be ashamed, rightly dividing the word of truth.* All of us have to stop trying to determine what we should do and let God choose. God will either open a door of opportunity, or He will close a door when it is time. We do not always have to pick and choose what we will do. When God has a task for you to do, it will be as obvious as the nose on your face. Follow His lead and the blessings will be tremendous.

November 19

1 Corinthians 2:14-16
14) But the natural man receiveth not the things of the Spirit of God: for they are foolishness unto him: neither can he know them, because they are spiritually discerned. 15) But he that is spiritual judgeth all things, yet he himself is judged of no man. 16) For who hath known the mind of the Lord, that he may instruct him? But we have the mind of Christ.

For the context today I included all three verses again, but focus on the phrase "The mind of Christ". We are told here that we have the mind of Christ. What we must do is nurture our mind by way of the word of God. We cannot nurture our mind if we do not interject the word of God into our mind. If the mind of Christ is the mind of God, then how do I receive instruction? I would suggest that you will receive truth when you are ready. You will receive the truth from the Holy Spirit of God and from no other. The Spirit of God is the messenger or side of God that reveals what we need to know. If you want the truth about the word of God, then open the pages and search for it. You and I can be empowered by the Holy Spirit of God. We received the gift of the Holy Spirit through faith in Jesus, the Son of God. The Holy Spirit then leads us to be a servant of the most-high God. The greatest gift we possess is having an Almighty God who loved us so much He sent His Son to die for us. We have access to an Almighty Holy Spirit who loves us so much He gives us all the time we need. If I was on Jesus' mind on the cross when He died, Jesus should be on my mind as I live. God is a very patient God, and we are very fortunate for that. For today, are you lost or saved as determined by who is your Daddy? Are you lost and need Jesus? Please pray and receive Jesus to save your soul. Are you saved and wandering aimlessly? Go back to where you accepted Jesus, and you will find God right where you left Him. Are you saved and wanting to know more? Find a bible-believing Church that will teach you the truth? Do you need some spiritual guidance? You can contact someone at a Bible-believing church to help you get plugged into a discipleship program. Are you where God wants you to be spiritually? Trust God and live for God right now and forever. However, nothing or no one is better than God the Holy Spirit for receiving instructions from.

November 20

Matthew 7:3
And why beholdest thou the mote that is in thy brother's eye, but considerest not the beam that is in thine own eye?

I would like to take you for several days on a journey looking at questions Jesus gave, and the response. I will not exhaust every question in the Bible that He asked, but I will do enough of them to stimulate your thinking. The reason I shifted gears was because many times we can learn not just from comments, but rather through tough questions. We will take a tour through some of the things Jesus asked and see how to apply those personally. We will not exhaust everything Jesus asked, but rather digest fully what we do look at. The reason for these questions is to drive us to an answer. If we refuse to answer a question, it will lead to denial of where we are at. Even if we do not verbally answer the question, honesty will appear in our brain. A revival happens when we are honest with ourselves and to the

Savior. Why not be honest, as He already knows. You see repentance is not when you cry. Repentance is when you change! It really does not matter how many tears fall. It is your response to the sin. Answered or not, for every question asked there is an answer. The answer we give is either "Right", or it is "Wrong". No response does not make it "Right", it only implies we will not address the "Wrong". Consider some of the questions of Jesus, and if you do not like the question, take it up with Jesus. If you do not like your response, take it up with Jesus. And if you do not want to respond, take it up with Jesus. So, question one for today is our verse **_Matthew 7:3_**. If you need to read the verse again before moving on please do so. Before Jesus' first coming there were tons of ceremonial things to do. If you had committed a sin, then it was your duty to offer a particular sacrifice for that sin. The Pharisees were quick to point out a sin, but slow to look at their own. I cannot repent for you, and you cannot repent for me. The reference verse I am giving you now is the response from the question Jesus just presented. *Matthew 7:5 Thou hypocrite, first cast out the beam out of thine own eye; and then shalt thou see clearly to cast out the mote out of thy brother's eye.* We need to define what is a Hypocrite and it is as follows. A hypocrite is an actor, an assumed character, or you are not really what you appear to be. What makes one a hypocrite is that others know the truth about us already? We will then come off looking foolish to them. They may not respond to your face but will laugh behind your back. They will smile with you, but laugh at you. They will say, "Oh that's nice", but in their mind say, "PLEASE dude, I know better". There are some things that must be considered. Why can't Jesus clean me up? Our personal testimony must not be, "Do as I say, not as I do". This is exactly why Christians leave a bad taste in someone's mouth. Some may even say, "except for this one sin I am living for Jesus, and I am pretty sure the Lord overlooks what I am doing". If we do not like where we are at spiritually, repent and get rid of the speck. There is no speck that God cannot deliver us from. I'm sorry, there is one speck that God cannot do away with. It is the speck/sin that you want to hang on or cling to.

November 21

Matthew 8:25-26
25) And his disciples came to him, and awoke him, saying, Lord, save us: we perish. 26) And he saith unto them, Why are ye fearful, O ye of little faith?

We are on a new day and another one of Jesus' questions. Be reminded that spiritual questions demand a spiritual answer. It does not mean we will answer the question, but simply not answering kind of means we may be embarrassed to answer. Today's question will invoke the thought of being fearful for various reasons. The context of this verse is that the Disciples are out to sea in a boat, and it is stormy. The boat is probably rocking back and forth very violently. The water is getting them soaking wet from coming over the sides and they are miserable. They wake Jesus up and say, "*Lord, save us; we perish*". Is it not true that all would perish if it were not for Jesus Christ, a cross, and an empty tomb? In many cases it looks like people are perishing to sin and refusing to serve. Some are afraid to serve Jesus for assorted reasons. Is it because our life will conform to the truth of the Bible, and maybe that is scary? Our life will commit to the things of God and maybe that is asking too much. Our life will become consistent in what we do for God and bye-bye free time. Our life will become consecrated to God and sin will be no more. I do not want my friends to think I am a holy roller and not want to be around me. Some may practice that they would rather be cool with the world than hot for the LORD, which is a typical Laodicean church age problem. With anything, you must know who to go to that can fix the problem. If you needed a boat fixed, would you go to someone that does quilting? Why? Because your boat does not need a quilt, it needs an engine. If you go for help, apply the advice or it is all wasted. I have honestly heard this said, "I know what I need to do, but I just don't". If you were drowning and someone threw you a life jacket, would you refuse to use it because it is just not your color? Jesus Christ, as far as delivering from sin and self, is that life jacket. Look at the Apostle Peter, at least he got out of the boat and walked on water to Jesus. Peter never went under until he took his eyes off Jesus. Why are people perishing in sin and not delivered? Because their eye is off the Lord. For the disciples getting soaked, water is a symbol of the word of God, and I would suggest for every one of us with a problem to get soaked by the word. Many do not want to get wet with the word, they only want a sponge bath. Sponge baths are sometimes necessary, but do that for days, weeks, and months and see how that works for you. We stink spiritually because we are not letting God soak us with His word. Is it possible that if God deals with a sin, we are quick to grab a towel and dry off so the word does not soak in too deep? We lack faith as Jesus questioned them because we do not let God have an active role in our life. What storm cannot Jesus deliver us from? Is it possible that you love the storm or because you have a better plan than God does? Do not end up saying, "My life is all God's except this one little area". That one area is the rocking boat that Jesus wants to deliver you from. Your faith will grow as you trust God, Jesus, and the Holy Spirit consistently.

November 22

Matthew 9:28
And when he was come into the house, the blind men came to him: and Jesus saith unto them, Believe ye that I am able to do this? They said unto him, Yea, Lord.

We move on today to question three and based on *Matthew 9:28*. Is it safe to say that on any given day we all have needs? It is going to be food, shelter, or clothing that is essential. There are things beyond the essentials that can be essential to an individual. Maybe some have been hurt physically or emotionally and need to be healed. It is difficult for any human to address these issues without Jesus. We may have something that could be fatal if God does not heal us. If God does not heal us and we are saved, we still win. *Daniel 3:17-18 17) If it be so, our God whom we serve is able to deliver us from the burning fiery furnace, and he will deliver us out of thine hand, O king. 18) But if not, be it known unto thee, O king, that we will not serve thy gods, nor worship the golden image which thou hast set up. John 9:2-3 2) And his disciples asked him, saying, Master, who did sin, this man, or his parents, that he was born blind? 3) Jesus answered, Neither hath this man sinned, nor his parents: but that the works of God should be made manifest in him. Galatians 1:4 Who gave himself for our sins, that he might deliver us from this present evil world, according to the will of God and our Father*: Do we believe God can deliver us? Warning: God sometimes does some powerful things to get our attention. God sometimes allows tragedy due to the fact that we are a fallen race from Adam. No matter what the issue is, would we go to the one who can deliver us, or do we just stay quiet? Take all things to God who loves us the most. The key is taking "ALL" things to

God, not just some things or the leftovers. First off, it is difficult to have someone come "into" your house if you will not open the door. Every one of us has a need for Jesus, so never shut the door. The issue in this verse is that these blind men wanted to see! If you have a problem, you have to know who to go to. If someone was completely blind, would you go to the store to buy them glasses? They have no eyes to see, but do we insist that they try on a pair of readers? Someone born with no hearing drums, we would not get them a hearing aid. Someone born with no legs probably do not need roller blades. Here are some guys with a legitimate need going to the ONE who can heal them. Second, do we really want to "SEE" the truth? We know what the problem is, but refuse to deal with it? We have perfect physical sight, but we are blind spiritually. What born again believer does not recognize when they are in sin? What born again believer recognizes sin, but refuses the deliverance? Just because we do not confess truth, does not mean we do not know what the truth is. *John 17:17 Sanctify them through thy truth: thy word is truth*. There is freedom and liberty being set free from sin. *John 8:36 If the Son therefore shall make you free, ye shall be free indeed*. The opposite of freedom from sin, is staying in bondage to sin, and what a horrible place to live. *Galatians 4:3 Even so we, when we were children, were in bondage under the elements of the world*: The context of that last verse is being under the law and pre-Jesus. Many Christians today are under the same bondage to the elements of the world and refuse to be released from sin. Christians may know the truth but refuse to deal with the truth. The Bible is not much GOOD if it is not used to help us be at our BEST. Where is our faith you ask? Within the confines of 66 books that we call the Bible. Love it, Learn it, and Live it.

November 23

Matthew 9:28
And when he was come into the house, the blind men came to him: and Jesus saith unto them, Believe ye that I am able to do this? They said unto him, Yea, Lord.

We are staying at Matthew 9:28 again today for some additional thoughts to apply personally. There are some other thoughts to consider before moving on. The goal is to take God's word as 100% truth and apply it 100% personally. We have the same question as yesterday: *Do you believe that I am able to do this*? Had the blind men said no, what would have happened? Jesus could have simply walked off and said, *"So let it be"*. The blind men could have walked off and said, "He is ridiculous". The biggest "IF" is that Jesus could have said, *"as you believe so let it be done"*. That is how hanging on to sin is. We will lose a blessing and a touch from God. We will never be what God intended us to be. We will lose out on what God wants to do in and through us. Even if you know who to go to, and do not go, the problem will persist. You see Jesus could heal, but He wanted the blind men's presence and their request. As from yesterday, we cannot be in our own field and God is in another field waiting. The text is specifically talking about physical blindness, but there is also spiritual blindness. Physical blindness may be beyond our capability to repair such as a birth defect or an accident. Jesus in this text is just about to heal these men. There is nothing that Jesus Christ cannot heal according to God's will. Spiritual blindness is when you either do not see the truth or do not acknowledge what you see. It is not realistic to think that if we ignore the problem, then it is all good. Who has ever seen someone blind with a white cane? That cane is for us to know that their vision is lacking or gone. In 1921 James Biggs, a photographer from Bristol, (England), became blind after an accident and was uncomfortable with the amount of traffic around his home. Mr. Biggs painted his walking stick white to be more visible. Even though someone does not acknowledge sin, everyone around knows. And when they see us coming it is like that tap, tap, tap of the white cane. "Hey look, here comes so-and-so, and you will not believe what they are doing". Some canes have a red stripe to reinforce that the person has vision issues. Our sin is that red stripe and Jesus' desire is to remove it. The stripe is removed at salvation. Many reading this verse today know the Savior is at the door. Jesus is at the door and that requires an action on your part. You must open the door and invite Him in. Do not just invite Jesus in part of the way, but all the way into your life. Jesus asks, "Do you believe that I can do this"? Do you believe that I can give you sight? Do you commit the problem to me to heal you or do you prefer to hang on to it? Their response was not some long speech or dissertation. They answered, "Yes Lord I do". "Yes, Master I do". "Yes, Supreme Authority, I do". If we have an area that needs repentance and spiritual insight, what do we do? Open the door and let Him in. This Son, (Jesus), is not like the Sun during an eclipse as there are no special glasses needed. For many, they are letting the moon, "SIN", block out the SON, and are living a life of a total eclipse of the Son. People around will see the sin, not the person. Some will ask, "Did you hear me about Jesus"? The response is, "No, I could not hear you, your sin is way too LOUD"! *Revelation 21:23 And the city had no need of the sun, neither of the moon, to shine in it: for the glory of God did lighten it, and the Lamb is the light thereof.* Believers in Jesus are to be the Light of the Word and make an impact to the World. The body of Christ is to influence the world, but it appears the world is influencing the body of Christ. We can all make a difference by condemning sin instead of conforming to sin. The blind men were in absolute darkness and their desire was to see light. Their trust was in the ONE who could give them light. Their commitment was to the one who could permanently deliver them. As Christians are we walking in darkness? Do we commit every area of our life to Him to be a light to the world? Are we committed to Jesus with every area of our life? If we are talking about our life, it should be easy: "It's all His anyway". One eclipse in the past had some crazy happenings. I read on the good old internet that many had to go see an Ophthalmologist after it was all over. Some put their heads together and thought putting sunscreen on their eyes would work. All it did was burn their eyes. You cannot make this stuff up. The solution to sin is not sunscreen, it is SON screen. Is the sunscreen on the eyes during an eclipse a crazy idea? It is not any crazier than living in sin every day and not repenting. It is not any crazier than rejecting Jesus as your Savior and choosing eternal hell and damnation. Want a revival in your life? Start with your decision to be a light for and with Jesus.

November 24

Matthew 16:13-15
13) When Jesus came into the coasts of Caesarea Philippi, he asked his disciples, saying, Whom do men say that I the Son of man am? 14) And they said, Some say that thou art John the Baptist: some, Elias; and others, Jeremias, or one of the prophets. 15) He saith unto them, But who say ye that I am?

Today's question from Jesus is, *"Who do you say that I am"*? Preceding this question for today, Jesus addresses a few issues leading up to our text today. He says to beware of hypocrites, remember how five thousand were fed with five loaves of bread, and the four thousand that were fed with seven loaves of bread? Jesus brought up several things to consider and then He asks one simple question. *"Who Do You Say That I Am"*? I will start you off with two Questions? *Who do men say that I am? Who do you think that I am*? One may address a bunch of opinions about Jesus and the other is "PERSONAL". Does who we say HE is match up with "WHO WE REALLY ARE"? PETER'S TWO TESTIMONIES: FIRST ONE: *Matthew 26:69 -74 69) Now Peter sat without in the palace: and a damsel came unto him, saying, Thou also wast with Jesus of Galilee. 70) But he denied before them all, saying, I know not what thou sayest. Peter did not want to identify with Jesus 71) And when he was gone out into the porch, another maid saw him, and said unto them that were there, This fellow was also with Jesus of Nazareth. 72) And again he denied with an oath, I do not know the man. A little bit stronger refusal to identify with Jesus. 73) And after a while came unto him they that stood by, and said to Peter, Surely thou also art one of them; for thy speech bewrayeth thee. 74) Then began he to curse and to swear, saying, I know not the man. And immediately the cock crew.* (**Peter uses some stronger language in order to not identify with Jesus**) PETER'S SECOND TESTIMONY: *John 21:15-17 15) So when they had dined, Jesus saith to Simon Peter, Simon, son of Jonas, lovest thou me more than these? He saith unto him, Yea, Lord; thou knowest that I love thee. He saith unto him, Feed my lambs*. Peter is identifying with Jesus because no one is around. It is not about being a Christian in the pews; it is about living for Jesus all the time. *16) He saith to him again the second time, Simon, son of Jonas, lovest thou me? He saith unto him, Yea, Lord; thou knowest that I love thee. He saith unto him, Feed my sheep.* Peter for the second time identifies with Jesus. Is it still because no one else is around to condemn him for it? *17) He saith unto him the third time, Simon, son of Jonas, lovest thou me? Peter was grieved because he said unto him the third time, Lovest thou me? And he said unto him, Lord, thou knowest all things; thou knowest that I love thee. Jesus saith unto him, Feed my sheep*. Peter FINALLY realizes Jesus already knew the answer to the question. Do we say we LOVE the Lord, but our life says something else? The Lord Jesus Christ has never been, is not, or will ever be fooled. What really changed Peter's testimony for Jesus where he could write I and II Peter? *Matthew 26:75 And Peter remembered the word of Jesus, which said unto him, Before the cock crow, thou shalt deny me thrice*. **_And he went out, and wept bitterly_**. *Mark 14:72 And the second time the cock crew. And Peter called to mind the word that Jesus said unto him, Before the cock crow twice, thou shalt deny me thrice.* **_And when he thought thereon, he wept_**. *Luke 22:61 - 62 61) And the Lord turned, and looked upon Peter. And Peter remembered the word of the Lord, how he had said unto him, Before the cock crow, thou shalt deny me thrice. 62) And* **_Peter went out, and wept bitterly_**. *John 18:27 Peter then denied again: and immediately the cock crew.* John does not record the crying or the repenting, he only records the denial. Peter's repentance required an action. We can do one of two things today. We can say, "Lord I love you and please deliver me". We can also say, "Lord, I love you, but not enough to change". DOES IT REALLY MATTER WHAT THE WORLD THINKS ABOUT JESUS. Peter's question from Jesus: WHO DO YOU SAY THAT I AM? Take some time and answer that question before moving on and take your time answering. How you answer just might change your life forever.

November 25

Matthew 16:13-15

13) When Jesus came into the coasts of Caesarea Philippi, he asked his disciples, saying, Whom do men say that I the Son of man am? 14) And they said, Some say that thou art John the Baptist: some, Elias; and others, Jeremias, or one of the prophets. 15) He saith unto them, But whom say ye that I am?

We have moved nowhere from the verse yesterday as there are a few more things to consider. Jesus' question was, "Who do you say that I am"? What is so important is (Who is Jesus to you)? Is Jesus really a deliverer? Is Jesus really a Comforter? Is Jesus really your Savior and the Savior of the world? Is Jesus really my Master? Is Jesus really running my life? Is Jesus really a Redeemer? Is Jesus really a Sustainer? How do you know? By the willingness to open the door and surrender your life to Him. Jesus ultimately says, "Feed my Sheep". You cannot feed sheep that do not want spiritual food! For you and me, WHO IS THIS JESUS? Is Jesus an acquaintance that I will give a shout out to when all else fails? Is Jesus the Savior and I need HIM for hell insurance? Is Jesus the Lord and Master as we go to Him with every detail of our life? Jesus wants every intricate detail confessed. Once again, "Who is this Jesus"? Maybe it is simply I have heard of Him or maybe you even know a little about Him. Praise God if you know Him personally. There are many questions that can be composed about Jesus and presented to the world. Some will answer by cursing the thought of Him being in their life. That last sentence sounds harsh, but recently I had someone tell me that he is okay with going to hell. He believes the cards he was dealt in life is all he has and when he dies he does not care. I reminded him that his decision to choose hell was eternal. It is not simply poof and then you are gone. It is an eternal burning fiery hell. Would you like to repent right now and allow Jesus to be a part of your life? Would you repent and by faith receive Jesus as your Savior? Will you repent and turn your whole life over to Jesus Christ today? Jesus wants our admission of sin so we can render submission to Him and from sin.

November 26

Matthew 22:41-42
41) While the Pharisees were gathered together, Jesus asked them, 42) Saying, What think ye of Christ? whose son is he? They say unto him, The Son of David.

For edification reasons I would like to recap quickly the last four days of questions before moving on. What questions have we had to answer so far from Jesus? What about your own sin? Why are you so fearful? Do you believe I can do this? Who do you say that I am? For today it is "*What think YE of Christ*"? Let us just say we are a bunch of different people gathered together today. Among us there will be many different views, thoughts, and opinions. We may get asked about our political views and we can render an "opinion". An opinion may be truth, but in reality, it is still just an opinion. In many cases an opinion is like a theory and a theory cannot be proven. You can surmise that a theory is right based on research, but ultimately you cannot prove it. An opinion based on Bible truth is not an opinion. For some the Bible is just a book. To others it is the inerrant word of God. If it is just a book, then I guess you do whatever you want with it. If it is the inerrant word of God, then how we view the truth as far as what we think of Jesus Christ, ought to stack up with our lifestyle. Our testimony has already painted a picture of what we think about Jesus. Ask the news channels to go to the sidewalk and ask, *"What do you think about Jesus Christ"*? You might hear from some that they are an atheist and I do not believe in that nonsense. Some may say that they have heard that He was a nice person or a good man. Some may even declare that they have heard that He did a lot of miracles. What we declare is that Jesus is the Savior of the world. Some believe He died on a cross and then after three days arose from the grave. I would guess that the answers from the world could be endless. It boils down that what someone thinks of Jesus Christ may be described with words. Would it not be better if what we think about Jesus is made clear through our actions, conduct, and decisions? We are all faced with this question every single day. The context of this verse is Jesus mentioning King David as an example to prove a point. If you asked any Pharisee what line or ancestry is the Messiah coming from, they would answer that so fast as, *"He is the Son of David"*. They would have positively identified that the Messiah was coming from royalty. Jesus did in fact come from a Kingly line making Him fully human, but He came from God through Mary, which made HIM fully God. *Isaiah 11:1-2 1) And there shall come forth a rod out of the stem of Jesse, and a Branch shall grow out of his roots: 2) And the spirit of the LORD shall rest upon him, the spirit of wisdom and understanding, the spirit of counsel and might, the spirit of knowledge and of the fear of the LORD*; Jesus had all seven qualities in these verses from Day ONE. What think ye about the Messiah? *John 1:45 Philip findeth Nathanael, and saith unto him, We have found him, of whom Moses in the law, and the prophets, did write, Jesus of Nazareth, the son of Joseph. Deuteronomy 18:15* is where you can go if you want to read Moses' words about the Messiah. If Philip knew all there were to know, would he have called him the son of Joseph? Only men were put in the Jewish lineage, so Joseph was substituted for Mary. For us today, would we say the son of Joseph or the Son of God? *WHAT THINK YE OF CHRIST?* We need to keep every answer about this personal. Is Jesus influencing my lifestyle? Do I think highly enough of Jesus Christ that He is worthy of me living a clean life? Do I think enough of Jesus Christ to serve Him? Do I think so little of Jesus Christ that I will not obey Him? Our answer will not be in words, our answer will be in deeds done for Jesus Christ. Our life will show either how "little" or how "much" we think of Jesus and there will be no mistaking it.

November 27

Matthew 22:41-42
41) While the Pharisees were gathered together, Jesus asked them, 42) Saying, What think ye of Christ? whose son is he? They say unto him, The Son of David.

Today's question Jesus offered is the same as yesterday, just some different thoughts for you to start or end your day with. Jesus asked, *"What think you of Christ"?* Sounds like a simple question and it is, but there are many answers available. Do we think enough of Jesus Christ to live like we are "**owned**" by Jesus Christ? Our testimony will reflect how we really feel about Jesus. *Romans 6:1-2 1) What shall we say then? Shall we continue in sin, that grace may abound? 2) God forbid. How shall we, that are dead to sin, live any longer therein? Matthew 16:16 And Simon Peter answered and said, Thou art the Christ, the Son of the living God. Matthew 23:10 Neither be ye called masters: for one is your Master, even Christ.* Either we are calling all the shots or Jesus is calling all the shots. Which decision do you think will bring about the greatest results? Jesus just asked the religious leaders this question, but let me change it? Do we think enough of Jesus to get our life in order? Does anyone think that all the Pharisees got right spiritually with God? *Mark 15:11-14 11) But the chief priests moved the people, that he should rather release Barabbas unto them. 12) And Pilate answered and said again unto them, What will ye then that I shall do unto him whom ye call the King of the Jews? 13) And they cried out again, Crucify him. 14) Then Pilate said unto them, Why, what evil hath he done? And they cried out the more exceedingly, Crucify him.* When we refuse to get right with God about sin are we really any different than those who cried out crucify Him? Is crucify Him worse than telling Jesus, "NO, I will not cleanup my act"? One act killed Jesus physically, the other kills you spiritually. We answer that question not by what we say, but by what we do. No one can truly say I really love the LORD and continually hang on to sin. Sometimes we justify sin with our head when we ought to follow Jesus with our heart. You must be very careful with what your heart tells you according to the book of Jeremiah. *Jeremiah 17:9 The heart is deceitful above all things, and desperately wicked: who can know it?* We know our heart. Jesus Christ knows our heart. Look at the Pharisees' thoughts about Jesus: *Matthew 12:24 But when the Pharisees heard it, they said, This fellow doth not cast out devils, but by Beelzebub the prince of the devils.* I will say one thing, "you would have to be extremely gutsy to say that". If I paraphrased their comment it would say, "Jesus is nothing more than a demon". If people see us in sin, why would they think that Jesus Christ can deliver them? It obviously did not work in us so why would it work in them. Does what we think of the "Christ" stack up with our testimony? The Pharisees demeaned Jesus with words and actions. Were the Pharisees words and actions really any different than today? You can take many Christians, put them in a bag with lost people, shake them together, and in many cases, you cannot tell which one rolled out. Jesus said, "What think ye of Christ". May your answer reflect your life in Jesus.

November 28

Matthew 22:41-42
41) While the Pharisees were gathered together, Jesus asked them, 42) Saying, What think ye of Christ? whose son is he? They say unto him, The Son of David.

You did not travel very far from yesterday as we are right back at the same verse. I wanted to share some additional thoughts about people in the Bible as far as the question of "What think ye of Christ"? We will start with the blind man that was healed and then consider some others mentioned. First off, the blind man was healed: *John 9:30 The man answered and said unto them, Why herein is a marvellous thing, that ye know not from whence he is, and yet he hath opened mine eyes.* We have a blind guy that is testifying about Jesus. He said, "This is a Marvelous thing"! Have you ever stopped and pondered your life before Jesus and declared, "This is a marvelous thing"? Is my life and your life a "Marvelous" thing? When we surrendered to Jesus Christ and accepted Him as our Savior, we can ask the same thing. Is my life MIRACULOUS and MARVELOUS or is it TRAGIC and RIDICULOUS? Only two people can answer that question and that would be You and God. The blind man is healed, but now what? *John 9:35-38 35) Jesus heard that they had cast him out; and when he had found him, he said unto him, Dost thou believe on the Son of God? 36) He answered and said, Who is he, Lord, that I might believe on him? 37) And Jesus said unto him, Thou hast both seen him, and it is he that talketh with thee. 38) And he said, Lord, I believe. And he worshipped him.* Do we think enough of Jesus Christ to worship Him freely and often? It will be reflected in our lifestyle by what we do according to the Word of God. When you got saved, your eyes are now opened to the truth. When the eyes are open, we become responsible to how we handle the "truth". Let me repeat the blind man, "Why herein is a "Marvelous" thing". It is only marvelous if our physical life matches up with our spiritual sight. It is marvelous when we know what Jesus wants us to do and we do it. Who was Jesus Christ to the blind guy, "Jesus was a Healer and the Son of God". When we continually see Jesus Christ as the Son of God, we reject the Sin of Satan. Christ is only a Deliverer to those who want delivered. *1 Peter 2:9 But ye are a chosen generation, a royal priesthood, an holy nation, a peculiar people; that ye should shew forth the praises of him who hath called you out of darkness into his marvellous light*: Our praise of Him should start with our life. No one should make a mockery of what Jesus did at the cross. Did He really die for all sins? Did He pay the ultimate sacrifice for all sins? Are you willing to leave any sin on the cross, or do you prefer to carry them everywhere you go? WHAT THINK YE OF CHRIST? It will be revealed by how we live not by what we say. What we think about Jesus to others is already known to everyone around. A Hypocrite will look like a Pharisee on Sunday and a heathen the other six days of the week.

November 29

Luke 6:46
And why call ye me, Lord,
Lord, and do not the things which I say?

To keep you on track with these questions, I want to recap with you the last few days for edification reasons. The questions that Jesus has asked so far are as follows. What about your own sin? Why are you so fearful? Do you believe I can do this? Who do you say that I am? What Think "YE" of Christ? The question today from Jesus is, "*Why call ye me, Lord, Lord, and do not the things which I say*"? Why do some call Him Lord, when it is just not so? The name Lord as applied to Jesus is not just a term of endearment. It is someone having power or influence over you. It is Lord as in He is our Master or our Ruler. It is used as Lord meaning someone superior to you and me. Is He really the Lord and how can I assess myself? Calling Him Lord to some just might not be who He really is spiritually and personally. What is our confirmation? Does our life stack up with His position of LORD in our life? *Matthew 7:21-23 21) Not everyone that saith unto me, Lord, Lord, shall enter into the kingdom of heaven; but he that doeth the will of my Father which is in heaven. 22) Many will say to me in that day, Lord, Lord, have we not prophesied in thy name? and in thy name have cast out devils? and in thy name done many wonderful works? 23) And then will I profess unto them, I never knew you: depart from me, ye that work iniquity.* Because someone calls HIM King or LORD does that mean they are saved? *Matthew 27:29 And when they had platted a crown of thorns, they put it upon his head, and a reed in his right hand: and they bowed the knee before him, and mocked him, saying, Hail, King of the Jews! Mark 15:18-19 18) And began to salute him, Hail, King of the Jews! 19) And they smote him on the head with a reed, and did spit upon him, and bowing their knees worshipped him. John 19:3 And said, Hail, King of the Jews! and they smote him with their hands.* **Many** called him LORD, but are those "**many**" really saved, and that answer would be no. The QUESTION: "*Why call me LORD and MASTER and then do your own thing*"? If you continued reading, it is about a house built on sinking sand. It is about not having a firm foundation for your life. We say Jesus is Lord, but we decide what is best for us and in reality, we are the lord. Some may say, "Jesus is the Real Thing", but in reality, will do their own thing. *John 5:14* {**Lame Man**}, *Afterward Jesus findeth him in the temple, and said unto him, Behold, thou art made whole: sin no more, lest a worse thing come unto thee.* When Jesus becomes someone's Savior the slate is wiped clean. I am not saying there are no consequences for sin. I am saying the slate is wiped clean and you can at least have a fresh start. If we can have a fresh start, then why would we want to take a marker and mark up the slate? *John 8:11* {**Woman at the Well**} *She said, No man, Lord. And Jesus said unto her, Neither do I condemn thee:* **go, and sin no more**. Jesus did not come to condemn the world. Jesus came to redeem the World. Jesus came to destroy sin, not support sin. Jesus came to offer repentance from sin, not acceptance of sin. Jesus came to die for our sin so we could live without sin. Some questions and words to consider from the Bible are: *Why do you not do the things I say* such as: Thou shalt have no other gods before me. We are to love the Lord with all thy heart, soul, and mind. We are to love our neighbor as ourselves. Is it easy to do what Jesus wants us to do? I really do not think that the LORD will give us any sin to hang on to. We are responsible for our own sin and what we hang on to. Is doing the right thing always easy? Maybe not, but it is always the right thing. Is

He really our Lord? Then we should do what He says to do. If He is Lord and we do our own thing, then He really is not the LORD. We need to be honest and acknowledge who He really is to us personally. When any of us do our own thing, we are simply telling God that I am smarter than you. We are saying that I know better than you what is best for me! We need to ask God what He thinks is best for us and then follow Him down that path.

November 30

Luke 8:30
And Jesus asked him, saying, What is thy name? And he said, Legion: because many devils were entered into him.

The thought for today is based on another question from Jesus when He asks, *"What is thy name"?* How many think that Jesus probably already knew who this was? Jesus did not ask because He did not know; He asked to get a response. Jesus asked, "What is your name" or "What are you called or recognized by"? We have a demon possessed man that knew his name based on what he contained internally. Devils or not, when Jesus asks a question there will be a response. The Response was. "My name is LEGION" because there were many devils in him. A Roman legion could be a few or quite possibly several thousand. If we give place to Satan in one area, we will give place to Satan in several areas. *Luke 16:15 {**Pharisees**}, And he said unto them, Ye are they which justify yourselves before men; but God knoweth your hearts: for that which is highly esteemed among men is abomination in the sight of God.* Do people justify their sin today? People can have their reason for doing so, but it is still sin. This verse says sin is highly esteemed among men, but is an abomination to God. There are things today that used to be forbidden and they should be. Now many satanic things that are contrary to the Word of God are widely practiced and accepted today. Many times, kids following a parent will be messed up because of an example. They may not know what the Bible taught, but by watching their parents, it is what they caught. *James 4:17 Therefore to him that knoweth to do good, and doeth it not, to him it is sin.* Jesus does not want us to justify sin. He wants us to do justly about sin. Jesus does not want us to conform to sin, He wants us to condemn sin. The question from Jesus was, *"what is thy name"*? Based on what our testimony is, "what is our name"? *Psalms 44:20-21 20) If we have forgotten the name of our God, or stretched out our hands to a strange god; 21) Shall not God search this out? for he knoweth the secrets of the heart.* We may have secrets from others, but God knows all. Some tragedy will be like David the King. He was told that what he did in Secret, (Bathsheba), or in darkness, would be revealed to everyone around him in the light of Day. It all ends up in nothing but shame and embarrassment. One question could be with what I have going on in my life right now, what is my name? Second question could be that if I completely turn my life over to Jesus Christ what would my name be to others? Based on my conduct, what have I been labeled by others. Like it or not people monitor if who we say we are, is really who we are. Jesus has a name above all names, but what is our name recognized as? Our name to God if you are saved is you are a child of the most HOLY KING. Have you ever heard this expression about someone, "they have made quite a name for themselves". That can mean prosperous or extremely poor. That can mean successful or not so much. That can mean spiritually rich or spiritually poor. You and I, based on what we do, really tells the story about who God is to us. If anyone hears our name, what is the first thing on their mind? People can and will linger on our past, but they cannot deny the present. When we do things for God in the present, we must make sure we keep on doing things for God in the future. Why? The world needs to see Christians that are rock-solid and committed to Jesus. The world needs to see that we will not compromise the Word of God. The world needs to see that when someone is called by the name of Christian, that we are living by the standard associated with it. We are Christians by choice, and we are followers by choice. Jesus is the name above all names and by Association let the world know we love Him! *Psalms 8:9 O LORD our Lord, how excellent is thy name in all the earth! Psalms 22:22 I will declare thy name unto my brethren: in the midst of the congregation will I praise thee.* (We declare it by how we live) *Psalms 23:3 He restoreth my soul: he leadeth me in the paths of righteousness for his name's sake.* (Are people seeing Jesus in us and through us)? *Psalms 74:18 Remember this, that the enemy hath reproached, O LORD, and that the foolish people have blasphemed thy name.* Our name to the world, and based on those that know us best, is _____? You fill in the blank? We can in fact turn over a brand-new leaf today. We can not only turn over a new leaf, but through Jesus we can flip over a whole new tree.

December 1

Luke 18:41
Saying, What wilt thou that I shall do unto thee?
And he said, Lord, that I may receive my sight.

Another question Jesus asks is in *Luke 18:41 Why call ye me, Lord, Lord, and do not the things which I say*? This is more or less a takeoff of Question three when Jesus says, *"Believe ye that I am able to do this"*? Do you believe I can, and it is either yes or no. The Lord already knows and still asks, *"What do you really need"*? If we do not know what we need then how can we really ask? *Luke 18:41 Saying, What wilt thou that I shall do unto thee? And he said, Lord, that I may receive my sight.* Do you believe that God already knows what you need? Let me give you a cross-reference for that answer in *Matthew 6:8 Be not ye therefore like unto them: for your Father knoweth what things ye have need of, before ye ask him.* Our prayers are to conform us to God's will not to conform God to our will. *James 5:16 Confess your faults one to another, and pray one for another, that ye may be healed. The effectual fervent prayer of a righteous man availeth much.* The first thing is to acknowledge is you have a need. If someone does not believe they are lost; they cannot be saved. You must recognize spiritual blindness before you can have spiritual insight. You must have a desire for spiritual sight before blinders are removed. For the blind man, *"Lord, I come to you with this request of sight"*. Spiritually for us we must ask the Lord, "Help me see the "ERRORS" of my ways". Did Jesus have the ability to restore this man's sight? Could Jesus have healed him without the request? Yes, but He waited for the request. Do you think Jesus was surprised at the request or did not see it coming? The tragedy for today is many see spiritual blindness but will not respond for healing. The tragedy is that Jesus will give spiritual sight, but you must look in the Bible. It is so easy to get distracted by many things. A distraction from Jesus comes in many sizes, shapes, and colors. With sight, what were this man's capabilities for serving Jesus? I did not say that those blind physically cannot serve. One of the best music leaders and singers I know is blind. It is the human side that causes limitations in how God will use us. The goal is to look beyond what we think we are capable of and look to what God is capable of accomplishing in and through us. Can we conquer spiritual blindness and overcome all things through Jesus Christ? *1 Corinthians 2:16 For who hath known the mind of the Lord, that he may instruct him? But we have the mind of Christ. 2 Timothy 2:7 Consider what I say; and the Lord give thee understanding in all things. 2 Timothy 2:15 Study to shew thyself approved unto God, a workman that needeth not to be ashamed, rightly dividing the word of truth. I John 4:4 Ye are of God, little children, and have overcome them: because greater is he that is in you, than he that is in the world. I John 5:4 For whatsoever is born of God overcometh the world: and this is the victory that overcometh the world, even our faith.* When you and I request having Jesus' sight we will see things differently. Maybe things you used to be in bondage to have now become disheartening. More often than not, we want others to be closer to Jesus than what they want to be. You want more for others spiritually than what they want for themselves. You hurt for people spiritually and emotionally, but you cannot really change anything. The closer you and I get to Jesus, the more His light will reveal our shortcomings. If shortcomings are not being revealed, then praise God for that. By completely surrendering to Jesus, you can conquer spiritual blindness.

December 2

Luke 18:41
Saying, What wilt thou that I shall do unto thee?
And he said, Lord, that I may receive my sight.

For me to not to sell you short on the devotional verse from yesterday I want to pick back up with you the same question from Jesus. *Luke 18:41 Saying, What wilt thou that I shall do unto thee? And he said, Lord, that I may receive my sight.*

I really want to dissect this verse with you for additional clarification. When Jesus poses any question, it demands an answer? The word **wilt** is used, and it can be translated as "what do you prefer, choose, or wish for"? The word "I" is used, and this man did not throw out a request to the world, he threw it out to Jesus. Jesus is addressing the blind man one on one, and He asks him specifically, "What do "YOU" want me to do"? Jesus is asking, "What are you commissioning me for, or what should I ordain, or perform for you"? In simpler terms Jesus is asking, "My child what can I do for you today"? In reality we ought to be asking, "Lord what can I do for you today". God is always waiting on His children to reach out to Him! That last sentence is really the definition of seeking God's will. The blind man addresses Jesus as Lord, which is who Jesus is. Jesus is acknowledged as the Supreme Authority or Master. In all honesty, Jesus cannot be your Lord if He is not your Master. Only an individual can determine who Jesus is to them. How do you decide that? How do our decisions for Jesus Christ look today? How do our decisions based on the Bible look? I care what it says, or I do not care what it says? In the midst of this question the blind man says, *"that I may receive my sight"*. Now the word "may" is an interesting word in a legal sense. It can imply that there is a possibility. It can also insinuate something is only an option. It can also imply something that is mandatory. You cannot force Jesus to heal, but He does heal. The blind man is saying, "According to your authority, power, and ability, "LORD", will you restore my sight"? **Request**: *Luke 18:41 Saying, What wilt thou that I shall do unto thee? And he said, Lord, that I may receive my sight.* **Answer:** *Luke 18:42 And Jesus said unto him, Receive thy sight: thy faith hath saved thee.* **Result**: *Luke 18:43 And immediately he received his sight, and followed him, glorifying God: and all the people, when they* *saw it, gave praise unto God.* What is the outcome? He followed Jesus and how can anyone not fully follow Jesus after salvation? I will share a couple of words from a hymn I trust you know. Amazing Grace how sweet the sound that saved a wretch like me. I once was lost, but now am found, was blind but now I see. How is your vision today and do you see God's will for your life clearly? We glorify God by what we do over what we say. This man was blind "physically", but it is worse to be blind "spiritually". Maybe you do not like your spiritual eyesight right now? Make an appointment with God today. He is the greatest optometrist ever known. The good news is that there is no appointment necessary. Just go on in and have a seat. By the way, you will not have to fill out any medical forms because God knows all about you.

December 3

John 18:7
Then asked he them again,
Whom seek ye? And they said, Jesus of Nazareth.

Before we go on to this question from Jesus, and how we can apply it, we really need to recap where we have been so far with Jesus' questions. I believe as you rehearse these questions over and over in your mind it will help you as you help others. And here are the questions: What about your own sin? Why are you so fearful? Do you believe I can do this? Who do you say that I am? What Think YE of Christ? Why call ye me, Lord, Lord, and do not the things which I say? What do you want me to do? And the question for today is in this *John 18:7 Then asked he them again,* **_Whom seek ye_**? *And they said, Jesus of Nazareth*. The context is a group of people finding Jesus in the garden. Some of them had indeed followed Jesus and they were His disciples. There also came some whose purpose was to arrest Jesus and turn Him over to the religious leaders. One group took Him into custody and another group ran as fast as they could to get away. I am thinking that this just might be how it may be today. Some will fully follow Jesus, and some will follow half-heartedly or not at all. We have a simple and honest question from Jesus about who or what were they seeking? The Bible is current today, and are you seeking Jesus of Nazareth? We answer that question every single day through various means. I love the word "seek" in this verse and it has two totally different meanings. One meaning is to seek as in worship, and another use of the word seek is to plot against or destroy. Eleven disciples sought to worship and learn from Him and one betrayed him with a kiss. If I am seeking Jesus, what do I do and what does it look like? What will be noticeable as I seek Jesus Christ? *Romans 12:1-2 And be not conformed to this world: but be ye transformed by the renewing of your mind, that ye may prove what is that good, and acceptable, and perfect, will of God.* There will be unity among the brethren. *Philippians 1:27 Only let your conversation be as it becometh the gospel of Christ: that whether I come and see you, or else be absent, I may hear of your affairs, that ye stand fast in one spirit, with one mind striving together for the faith of the gospel*; As we all seek God individually and corporately we will have unity of the Spirit. It would be hard to work together in unity or corporately without seeking Jesus as an individual first. Look at the wise men in *Matthew 2:1-2 1) Now when Jesus was born in Bethlehem of Judaea in the days of Herod -the king, behold, there came wise men from the east to Jerusalem, 2) Saying, Where is he that is born King of the Jews? For we have seen his star in the east, and are come to worship him.* The wise men had the Word of God and a "star" to follow to seek Jesus. You have the Word of God and the Holy Spirit to "guide" you to Jesus and truth. For Christians, look at *Colossians 3:1 If ye then be risen with Christ, seek those things which are above, where Christ sitteth on the right hand of God. Matthew 6:20 But lay up for yourselves treasures in heaven, where neither moth nor rust doth corrupt, and where thieves do not break through nor steal: Colossians 3:2 Set your affection on things above, not on things on the earth. Matthew 10:37 He that loveth father or mother more than me is not worthy of me: and he that loveth son or daughter more than me is not worthy of me.* Humanly speaking that sounds very mean to even ask us to not place family or anything before Jesus. Spiritually speaking we are to put nothing before Jesus. We must continually keep on seeking Jesus and it will bring with it spiritual blessings. If there are times we seek things more than Jesus, it will positively be reflected in how we are living for Jesus.

December 4

John 18:7
Then asked he them again,
Whom seek ye? And they said, Jesus of Nazareth.

Before you move on from this question from Jesus and how you can apply it, we need to consider some additional thoughts. Write these questions from Jesus down and rehearse them over and over in your mind. I promise it will help you as you help others. The questions you have considered so far are in order as far as what I have presented to you. What about your own sin? Why are you so fearful? Do you believe I can do this? Who do you say that I am? What think YE of Christ? Why call ye me, Lord, Lord, and do not the things which I say? What do you want me to do?

And the question for today is in this *John 18:7 Then asked he them again, **Whom seek ye**? And they said, Jesus of Nazareth.* The context is a group finding Jesus in the garden. You have the question from Jesus and here is the answer in *John 18:5 -6 5) They answered him, Jesus of Nazareth. Jesus saith unto them, I am he. And Judas also, which betrayed him, stood with them. 6) As soon then as he had said unto them, I am he, they went backward, and fell to the ground.* There was a group sent on a mission to find and arrest Jesus. The group finds Jesus and then go backward and fall to the ground, which to me is amazing in and of itself. The group falls down and yet they still arrest Jesus and turn Him in. The fact that they fell to the ground to Jesus was short-lived. This is exactly the kind of world we live in. Some will just sprinkle a little bit of Jesus on themselves and then rise up to do their own thing. Remember the old phrase; "If I were arrested for being a Christian, would there be enough evidence to convict me"? It is always a good time to fall on our face before God. There is no greater feeling than to bow the knee to the King as we seek Him. To the world Jesus is just an acquaintance that they do not seek after. To the body of Christ, Jesus is our Savior and who we are to follow. We must keep on seeking Jesus with a passion. I believe there is only one time in the King James Version where the word "Passion" is used. *Acts 1:3 To whom also he shewed himself alive after his passion by many infallible proofs, being seen of them forty days, and speaking of the things pertaining to the kingdom of God.* This passion is Jesus showing himself alive after the suffering/beating He took. If you and I seek Jesus with the same passion that He endured His sufferings "we" will never be the same. This verse portrays Jesus in *Proverbs 18:24 A man that hath friends must shew himself friendly: and there is a friend that sticketh closer than a brother.* {Jesus is this Friend}. As you seek Jesus personally, the friendship of Jesus will grow passionately. Never back down, reject, or sell-out any principle in the Bible. Seeking Jesus and the truth of the Bible is not to make your life difficult. It is to make your life richer and fuller.

December 5

2 Timothy 2:15
Study to shew thyself approved unto God, a workman that needeth not to be ashamed, rightly dividing the word of truth.

Do you believe that your testimony is one of the most important things you possess and is absolutely free? I believe that as well. Everyone has a testimony whether it is good or bad. Do people really remember the good or the bad? Someone's perception could be yours is bad and find out it was good. Why would they change their mind? Because of time and really figuring out who you are in Jesus Christ. Do others see Jesus in your life is the ultimate question. Take a spiritual walk today and be honest about what you think others may see in you. As a Christian what are we driven to do and this is not an exhausted list. Let the Bible define the process for everything we look at. We are to set the standard and are to be the example. Are you "Learning" the word, and if so, read again our text for today in *2 Timothy 2:15 Study to shew thyself approved unto God, a workman that needeth not to be ashamed, rightly dividing the word of truth. 1 Peter 2:2 As newborn babes, desire the sincere milk of the word, that ye may grow thereby: 2 Peter 1:20 Knowing this first that no prophecy of the scripture is of any private interpretation.* We have the Holy Spirit to teach us if we desire to be taught. If someone says they have a new and improved word from God you better run. If someone says

God gave them a new revelation of truth contrary to the Bible, you had best "RUN". *John 5:39 Search the scriptures; for in them ye think ye have eternal life: and they are they which testify of me. Psalms 86:11 Teach me thy way, O LORD; I will walk in thy truth: unite my heart to fear thy name. 2 Timothy 3:16 All scripture is given by inspiration of God, and is profitable for doctrine, for reproof, for correction, for instruction in righteousness*: You have read a lot of cross reference verses about studying. You can positively know what the Bible says through the teaching from the Holy Spirit. Never let anyone convince you as a believer that you are unteachable. You are a child of God, and the sky is the limit as to what God can convey through His word to you.

December 6

Deuteronomy 5:33
Ye shall walk in all the ways which the LORD
your God hath commanded you, that ye may live, and
that it may be well with you, and that ye may prolong
your days in the land which ye shall possess.

Yesterday you looked at learning the word of God and today we will look at living the Word. You will understand scripture better by cross-referencing verses from the Bible. *Psalms 101:6 Mine eyes shall be upon the faithful of the land, that they may dwell with me: he that walketh in a perfect way, he shall serve me. 1 Timothy 1:12 And I thank Christ Jesus our Lord, who hath enabled me, for that he counted me faithful, putting me into the ministry; Luke 4:4 And Jesus answered him, saying, It is written, That man shall not live by bread alone, but by every word of God. Ephesians 5:8 For ye were sometimes darkness, but now are ye light in the Lord: walk as children of light: 2 Thessalonians 3:14 And if any man obey not our word by this epistle, note that man, and have no company with him, that he may be ashamed. Colossians 1:10 That ye might walk worthy of the Lord unto all pleasing, being fruitful in every good work, and increasing in the knowledge of God; Psalms 119:133 Order my steps in thy word: and let not any iniquity have dominion over me.* You saw yesterday that learning the Word is paramount and key to everything. Living the Word must be based on what you learned under the influence of the Holy Spirit as you study your Bible. You positively cannot apply what you do not know. Ignorance of God's word is not an excuse for not living the Word. Be a living testimony of God's word and if necessary, use words. In *Deuteronomy 5:33 Ye shall walk in all the ways which the LORD your God hath commanded you, that ye may live, and that it may be well with you, and that ye may prolong your days in the land which ye shall possess.* Living the word is something that God commands us to do. That last verse you read says your days may be prolonged by walking with the Lord as His word commands you. God said live it and things will be well with you. I am not suggesting that you will live a perfect life. I am saying that you will cope better with whatever comes your way. I am not suggesting that you may live longer by obeying God's word. From Adam to today we have corrupted our bloodlines through sin, and death is the outcome for all of us. God's standards are healthy for our body, soul, and spirit. It is better to stay in communion with God as we read, study, meditate, and apply His truths.

December 7

John 14:23
Jesus answered and said unto him, If a man love me,
he will keep my words: and my Father will love him,
and we will come unto him, and make our abode with him.

In three days of devotions, you have gone from learning the word, to living the word, to today's topic of Loving the Word. Loving the Word is measured by how we live by what we know. Do you really Love the Word? *Psalms 119:140 Thy word is very pure: therefore thy servant loveth it.* What else can you read that is 100% reliable? God wants what is best for you and it is contained in one BOOK, and it is 100% pure. Pure, meaning there are no impurities such as a goldsmith or refiner would find when putting the fire to gold or silver. Pure as in God has preserved perfectly what He wanted preserved. You can love and rely on God's truth every second of your life because of its perfectness. I heated up some lead one time with an enormous amount of heat to see what would happen. After it started to breakdown and melt all this gross looking stuff that makes up lead came out. I poured only the remaining liquid into a ceramic mold and something beautiful came out. This is what loving the word of God does for you. It puts something beautiful inside of you, and you are transformed in front of the world as a thing of beauty. How do you gauge or evaluate your love for the word? None of us need anyone to give their opinion of how we love the word because we already know. For God's word, no one can love what they do not know. Have you ever not liked a food and you have never tried it? You just know you would hate it. Oysters: Even if I liked the taste, I cannot stand what they feel like in my mouth. When God's word rebukes us and we deny it, we do not like the feeling of conviction. When I was a lost guy I thought I was okay. When I became a saved man, I had a lot of rough edges that needed knocked off. I had a lot of God's truth to apply and still do. To Love the Word can only occur when we obey the Word. Ever had a baby you were feeding spit some food out? When we "READ" the Word and come across truth that corrects our living, we either apply what it says or we spit it out. We either eat the truth or we spit it out. *1 John 2:5 But whoso keepeth his word, in him verily is the love of God perfected: hereby know we that we are in him.* This word perfected means to be made complete. The word perfected is used so that we can accomplish something for the LORD. The word perfected is used meaning to complete and complement our character. You are to represent Jesus Christ to the best of His ability, not yours. *Psalms 119:162 I rejoice at thy word, as one that findeth great spoil.* The word spoil is when one army defeats another and takes everything valuable. When God shows us something we have never seen before it is "great spoil". As you search the truth, may God richly and abundantly bless your socks off.

December 8

John 14:23
Jesus answered and said unto him, If a man love me,
he will keep my words: and my Father will love him,
and we will come unto him, and make our abode with him.

This is the exact same verse you have been contemplating the last few days. You started out learning the word and progressed to living the word. You saw the positive results of living the words and now you love the word. Now that you love the word you will positively have a **Longing** for the word, which is our topic for today. Longing for the word is measured by how often we hold it in our hands. Consider that this longing for the word is also a longing for Jesus. Longing for the word is a natural craving, desire, or yearning to know more. If you were from one of the southern states you might have a "hankering" to know more. A longing is to be hungry for something and it is right at your fingertips. What a shame to starve to death when there is a refrigerator and cabinet full of food. We can also starve to death spiritually with the truth of the Bible right under our nose. A simple question to consider is do you long for the word? *1 Peter 2:2 As newborn babes, **desire** the sincere milk of the word, that ye may grow thereby*: Let me really define longing for the "Word" in two ways. The Word/Bible is the printed word and mind of God. The word is also Jesus, the only begotten Son of God, and Savior. Please check out *John 1:1* and *John 1:14* if you need a reminder of Jesus and who He is and how long he has been around. When I say we are to "LONG" for the word, it is the Bible, God, Jesus, and the Holy Spirit. Let God open your mind to something new and exciting "**according**" to His word. The Bible is not a serpent that will bite you, and it is never too late to start. *Isaiah 40:8 The grass withereth, the flower fadeth: but the word of our God shall stand for ever.* Do we agree that wo do in fact die a little every single day? *James 4:14 Whereas ye know not what shall be on the morrow. For what is your life? It is even a vapour, that appeareth for a little time, and then vanisheth away. Proverbs 8:17 I love them that love me; and those that seek me early shall find me.* Seek Jesus first as you start your day, and He will never play hide and seek with you. Through faith in Jesus we have been reconciled spiritually, but we need to stay reconciled to God relationally by longing for Jesus, who is the word. We get our thirsty soul quenched by Jesus as we long for the word. Our flesh can only be encouraged longing for Jesus. You will be fed spiritually by longing for the truth of God's word. May your faith in Jesus nurture your longing for the word. I promise that your love for Him will grow beyond your wildest imagination. You will become someone that people will be drawn to because of your demeanor. May you never come to the place where you think you have too much Jesus.

December 9

Luke 11:28
But he said, Yea rather, blessed are they
that hear the word of God, and keep it.

Today is a brand-new devotion verse, but here is where you have been the previous four days. You have looked at learning the word, which is the basis for everything. Living the word, which is how we measure what you have learned. Loving the word will indicate how much you apply what you have learned. Longing for the word is desiring to know more about the truth of God's word. Today you can address **listening** to the Word. To listen to the word is to sit still and wait expectantly for God to speak. Do you listen to the word? Let us define the "WORD" one more time before moving on. *John 1:1 In the beginning was the Word, and the Word was with God, and the Word was God. John 1:14 And the Word was made flesh, and dwelt among us, (and we beheld his glory, the glory as of the only begotten of the Father,) full of grace and truth.* All of us can become guilty of saying we are waiting on a Word from God the Holy Spirit. There are some things that do not require prayer or a prolonged listening session. Praying about whether you should pray for one another does not require listening for a word from God. *James 5:16 Confess your faults one to another, and pray one for another, that ye may be healed.*

The effectual fervent prayer of a righteous man availeth much. Do I serve God does not require prayer? *Psalms 100:2 Serve the LORD with gladness: come before his presence with singing.* Do we love one another does not require prayer. *1 John 4:7 Beloved, let us love one another: for love is of God; and every one that loveth is born of God, and knoweth God. 1 John 4:11 Beloved, if God so loved us, we ought also to love one another.* **Listen** to God the Holy Spirit, who is the teacher, and in Him is no error to the truth. Do not think for a second that you cannot hear a Word from God. *Luke 8:21 And he answered and said unto them, My mother and my brethren are these which hear the word of God, and do it.* Those that do not hear are either lost or in sin. How can it be fixed? Turn your life over to Jesus, repent, and sin no more. *Psalms 29:4 The voice of the LORD is powerful; the voice of the LORD is full of majesty.* As you listen to God's word it may not be loud like thunder or a trumpet. When God speaks to an individual it is very clear, concise, and completely consistent with the Word of God. God never speaks to anyone to stay in sin. God will never help us justify wrongdoing as that is Satan's work. *Psalms 46:10 Be still, and know that I am God: I will be exalted among the heathen, I will be exalted in the earth.* Finding a quiet time may require a sacrifice of getting up early or staying up late. What an honor a believer has in knowing that you can hear from God. God is never too busy, and He is always right on time. How do I know if I hear from God? Does it stack up with scripture? I do not concern myself with what others listen to, but I choose Christian music. Songs are powerful, and the truth of Jesus is contained in most of them. Listening to the Word may be a radio message or a conversation with another believer. God is not limited as to how you can hear from Him. Listen for a word from God and you will see that there is no sweeter sound.

December 10

Psalms 119:11
Thy word have I hid in mine heart,
that I might not sin against thee.

Here is a recap of where you have been over the previous five days. You have looked at learning the word, which is the basis for everything. Living the word, which is how we measure what you have learned. Loving the word indicates how much you apply what you have learned. Longing for the word is a desire to know more about the truth of God's word. Listening to the word is to be still and wait expectantly for God to speak. Today, look at "**SERVE**" the word or how you handle divine opportunities. You cannot serve what you do not possess. Compare the things a waiter or waitress does in a restaurant. There are some that amaze me as far as their ability to not write anything down and you get what you order. I remember once being in a restaurant and sixteen of us were eating together. The waiter never wrote down one thing and yet we all received exactly what we ordered. I am sure that gentleman had spent years cultivating the ability to retain information or it was simply a gift from God. Serve the Word will be seen by how we handle divine opportunities. We serve the Lord by how we obey the word and others see it. What is your service for the Lord and do others see it? As a verb or action word then what does **serving** the Word look like? It is the behavior or actions you exhibit. Like it or not, if we claim to be a Christian we are on display. Even the lost will measure if your actions and conduct comply with the Word of God. Back to the restaurant and what does a waiter or waitress do? They bring you your food. Do you ever notice when you order food and they do not write it down you get a little nervous? There may be a time you do not have your Menu/Bible, and can you share scripture? *Psalms 119:11 Thy word have I hid in mine heart, that I might not sin against thee.* You and I cannot serve what is not on our menu that we call our memory. If people can memorize a menu, I would think you can memorize scripture. When someone is having trouble can you serve them the Word of God on a platter? If your testimony is clean, you can, but people do not want food brought with soiled clothes. How would you feel about someone bringing you your food on a dirty plate? *Luke 11:39 And the Lord said unto him, Now do ye Pharisees make clean the outside of the cup and the platter; but your inward part is full of ravening and wickedness.* We can wear a shirt and tie, but that does not make us clean. Would you like a server who is wearing a tuxedo and has not showered for a month? We must know what we are serving. Some you may serve have bigger problems and need a bigger menu. Look at the menu at your fingertips every single day: 1 Bible, 66 Books, 1189 Chapters, KJV 1611 has over 788K words. We have plenty we can serve, but we may not always know what someone is ordering. Someone you know may be having a problem and they may ask, "What do you recommend"? We can use God's word when people are struggling, but many times you have to serve or order for them because they do not know what they need. Sometimes a person just needs a light meal to get back on track. For some that are really struggling they may need a seven-course meal. God's word is the solution to every problem, but we cannot serve what we do not know. When it is you struggling, you can go to the buffet line of God's word and get what you need. One thing about God's word as a buffet is that you will always leave full and satisfied. In serving others apply *Galatians 6:10 As we have therefore opportunity, let us do good unto all men, especially unto them who are of the household of faith.* Look for ways to serve others and pray for divine opportunity to **_serve_** them the "TRUTH" of the word of God! Stay on the footsteps of Jesus and charge the gates of Hell as you serve others.

December 11

Joshua 1:8
This book of the law shall not depart out of thy mouth; but thou shalt meditate therein day and night, that thou mayest observe to do according to all that is written therein: for then thou shalt make thy way prosperous, and then thou shalt have good success.

For the past six days you have looked at to learn the word, live the word, love the word, long for the word, listen to the word, serve the word, and now **"linger"** on the word. Linger really means staying longer than you need to because you are reluctant to leave. Maybe you can linger in the Bible because you know it is a safe place to be. When it comes to the Bible we do not always have to be in a hurry. There are times to slow down and smell the coffee! In a coffee shop or restaurant during a time of fellowship, do you gulp down your food and drink to hurry out? No, you take your time and maybe get a refill because the company is good. That is exactly how God wants you to be. As you linger in the word and feel God's presence you want to spiritually bathe in that experience. Many times, even in prayer, you can bounce in and out of prayer. You can be praying one second and then recalling something that happened years ago. Linger is to not be in any hurry to go anywhere and the Bible is the place to be. Have you ever had a verse jump out at you as you read? That is when God is speaking to you, and you should linger on what it is saying. Sometimes you linger for a Word until God gives you a Word. I was preparing a message one time and my wife said, "What are you doing"? I said I was waiting on God to reveal what I am supposed to preach about, and I am not moving until He does. I did not budge and three guesses as to what happened. You guessed it; I received a word from God. The more you linger on the word; the more GOD can communicate HIS word and His thoughts. Read again our text today from *Joshua 1:8 This book of the law shall not depart out of thy mouth; but thou shalt meditate therein day and night, that thou mayest observe to do according to all that is written therein: for then thou shalt make thy way prosperous, and then thou shalt have good success*. The book will not depart out of our mouth if we keep it fresh in our mind. Is there plenty of God's word to linger on? There are over seven hundred and eighty thousand words of scripture to pick from in order to fill your mind with the truth, so the mouth can support the thoughts. If you put junk in your mind, you have your very own landfill. *1 Thessalonians 4:11 And that ye study to be quiet, and to do your own business, and to work with your own hands, as we commanded you.* There will be times when you must Linger on the Word to Memorize the Word. Many kids at their church's kid's program try really hard to memorize scripture and some do not. God's word as you linger on it will never return void even in the mind of a four and five year-old. Linger can be to recite over and over again a verse to commit it to memory. *1 Timothy 4:13-16 13) Till I come, give attendance to reading, to exhortation, to doctrine. 14) Neglect not the gift that is in thee, which was given thee by prophecy, with the laying on of the hands of the presbytery. 15) Meditate upon these things; give thyself wholly to them; that thy profiting may appear to all. 16) Take heed unto thyself, and unto the doctrine; continue in them: for in doing this thou shalt both save thyself, and them that hear thee.* I am a strong advocate of writing notes in the margin of your Bible for future reference. When we hear something that is profitable, we really ought to log that down. The Bible says, *"Give attendance to it"*. God will never reveal what I am not ready to receive. God will never explain His word if we are too much into the worldly. Linger is to reluctantly leave what you want to stay with. The opposite of linger is to breeze through life with no regard for God's word. We must recognize that we need God all the time.

December 12

1 Kings 8:56
Blessed be the LORD, that hath given rest unto
his people Israel, according to all that he promised: there
hath not failed one word of all his good promise, which
he promised by the hand of Moses his servant.

Have you ever been just plain dog-tired and the only thing you wanted to do is find a good soft recliner? Every now and then we can get sick and tired of being sick and tired. Today we are going to talk about rest, resting, or to cease work from anything strenuous in order to be refreshed. We do sleep away at least one third of our life anyway, but we rest so we can regain our strength. There is no one that does not need their physical batteries recharged by way of a good night's rest. When we are completely beat, has anyone said, "You look wore out"? You need to be careful when you say that because that may be how they look all the time. Today we can grow weary of life, circumstances, sin, or whatever.

SPIRITUALLY: Let's take a look at **_resting in God's Word_**. Resting in the Word and your text again is *1 Kings 8:56 Blessed be the LORD, that hath given rest unto his people Israel, according to all that he promised: there hath not failed one word of all his good promise, which he promised by the hand of Moses his servant.* When God gives you His word, you can rest that it is going to happen. Have you ever wondered if Adam gave his word to God? Probably not because later on mankind was destroyed by a flood because Adam did his own thing. A failure on our part has a trickle-down effect to others close by. Failure keeps on getting bigger and bigger. Moses and Aaron died before the Promised Land because of disobeying. However, God **said**, "I am taking Israel into the Promised Land" and it happened. Are we any different than Adam as far as not conferring with God, doing our own thing, and not obeying God's word? We appear to rest in our own power and ability instead of obeying God. God has never, and will never, break one of His promises. There is only one time a verse like this appears: *Titus 1:2 In hope of eternal life,* **_which God, that cannot lie_**, *promised before the world began*; I am promised and can rest on eternal life because of Jesus. I am promised that my soul is preserved by God for eternity. Why do we rest on this? Because God CANNOT LIE. The worst thing anyone can do is take our life and yet we will still be okay. Born-again believers are promised that God will keep our soul for safe keeping. When we get saved, we can rest on that. *John 10:28 And I give unto them eternal life; and they shall never perish, neither shall any man pluck them out of my hand.* No one can steal you away and God cannot lie about that. Look at the promises in this verse alone: Eternal Life and can never perish. NO ONE can pluck you out of His hand. NO ONE can steal you away. Is this truth? It must be because God cannot lie! God promised eternal life to those who have trusted in Jesus. Can we rest on that promise? *John 3:16 For God so loved the world, that he gave his only begotten Son, that whosoever believeth in him should not perish, but have everlasting life.* Can everyone rest on these promises? *2 Peter 3:9 The Lord is not slack concerning his promise, as some men count slackness; but is longsuffering to us-ward, not willing that any should perish, but that all should come to repentance.* We can rest in the fact that God wants everyone to be saved and we all need to witness for Jesus. God cannot lie and He does not want any to perish and I believe it. I believe it and rest on the promise that soul winning is not a waste of time. Pray that God would continue to use you fervently and passionately. *2 Timothy 1:9 Who hath saved us, and called us with an holy calling, not according to our works, but according to his own purpose and grace, which was given us in Christ Jesus before the world began.* Can I rest on the promise that God will use the willing, bless the obedient, and enlarge their borders? Today are you Resting or Restless? *Psalms 23:4 Yea, though I walk through the valley of the shadow of death, I will fear no evil: for thou art with me; thy rod and thy staff they comfort me.* Situations or circumstances should not steal our comfort. What steals our resting on God's promises is disobedience/sin. *Romans 15:4 For whatsoever things were written aforetime were written for our learning, that we through patience and comfort of the scriptures might have hope/rest. Philippians 4:6-7 6) Be careful for nothing; but in everything by prayer and supplication with thanksgiving let your requests be made known unto God. 7) And the peace of God, which passeth all understanding, shall keep your hearts and minds through Christ Jesus.* Rest can also mean HOPE. Our HOPE and our REST is in Jesus. Tomorrow we will look some more at rest and hope. Until then, rest in the hope you have today in Jesus, and tomorrow will take care of itself.

December 13

1 Kings 8:56
Blessed be the LORD, that hath given **rest**
unto his people Israel, according to all that he promised: there hath not failed one word of all his good promise, which he promised by the hand of Moses his servant.

You left off yesterday looking at *resting in His word*. The last thought was based on rest as it is also seen as hope. Our hope is in Jesus who is the Word. We have a promise that we can rest comfortably in Him. I did not say a perfect life without tribulation. But we can rest in God and know He will take care of His children. By looking at rest or hope we can define hope. Hope is an expectation. I expect to be carried by Angels to heaven just like the beggar was in Luke 16:22. When I draw my last breath I rest in that truth. Hope is also a feeling of trust. I trust or rest in the fact that the Word of God is infallible and inerrant. Hope is believing something will happen even in the future. I believe my soul is kept by an Almighty God. I believe when I got saved, He died for my past, present, and future sin. I believe I will live and reign for eternity with Jesus on the throne and I rest in that promise. I believe those who have gone on before me will be reunited with me. I believe I will have a glorified body that can never perish. I rest on these promises because GOD cannot lie. You and I can rest from the weight of sin, and we have God's word on it. We can rest from care, worry, and anxiety. *Matthew 11:28 Come unto me, all ye that labour and are heavy laden, and I will give you rest.* When Jesus said on the cross, "IT IS FINISHED", it meant His redemptive work was complete. When we got saved our work began and we run our best race. I can rest on the fact that I have my race and you have yours. I can rest on the fact that God does not want any of us to just sit on the bench. We rest and rely on God's word three hundred and 365 days a year and know that it is profitable for us. *Joshua 1:13 Remember the word which Moses the servant of the LORD commanded you, saying, The LORD your God hath given you rest, and hath given you this land.* Moses reminded Israel of what God, (**who cannot lie**), had promised them. God could not lie to Moses and His word cannot lie to us. *1 Kings 8:56 Blessed be the LORD, that hath given rest unto his people Israel, according to all that he promised: there hath not failed one word of all his good promise, which he promised by the hand of Moses his servant.* When God gives a promise not one thing will fail to happen. The main problem people face today is not really trusting God or resting in God's word. We cannot rest with one eye on Jesus and the other on the world. I posted recently, "You cannot shack up with Satan and have God pay the rent". God will not give us rest, peace, or hope until we desire it. There is an old saying, "There is no rest for the wicked". There is no rest or peace for those living outside the confines of the Word of God.

December 14

Psalms 34:1-4
I will bless the LORD at all times:
his praise shall continually be in my mouth. (2) My soul shall make her boast in the LORD: the humble shall hear thereof, and be glad. (3) O magnify the LORD with me, and let us exalt his name together. (4) I sought the LORD, and he heard me, and delivered me from all my fears

Let us look starting today at exactly what Praise will produce? In *1 Samuel 21* David changed his behaviour before Abimelech. Here is the scenario as it played out. David had fled from Saul and was on the run. King David ended up receiving bread and the sword of Goliath from Ahimelech. And now he is afraid of Achish the King , plays a mad man, and the king sends him away. Saul chased and chased David, but to no avail and David is at his wits end. So what does David eventually do? He more than likely remembered this time in his life, and he penned *Psalm 34*. Have you ever noticed that sometimes we praise God after the fact when in reality we should be praising Him before the fact? We praise the Lord after good results but forget to praise him no matter what the results. Our praise is not to be reliant upon our circumstances or predicaments. Having a good day – we will praise the Lord! Having a bad day – we may not praise the Lord! If we break these verses down by verse and by day, as far as a devotional goes, we start out in verse 1 and it says, I will bless the Lord at all times. It means it is an individual decision. How can I bless the Lord? How I live my life. How I do my job. How I treat my spouse. How do I treat my kids and grandkids? How am I as a steward with what God has given me such as tithing or time? How do I serve the risen Lord Jesus Christ? It is hard to believe that we can bless the Lord, but the word says we can. What do I do when no one is watching? David says he is going to bless the Lord so let us define the **Lord**. The Lord is Jehovah, Supreme Master, King of Kings, Lord of Lords, and the creator of the universe. The Lord is He who knew us before we were formed in the womb, *Jeremiah 1:5 Before I formed thee in the belly I knew thee.* So how often are we to bless the Lord? The verse says it is to be at "all" times. Maybe that is easier said than done. When things are great it is easy. How about when things have gone terribly wrong? How do you think Job felt when God allowed Satan to buffet Him? Not sure I would have weathered that storm like Job did. Anyone got an answer as to how Job could bless the Lord? One thing he did not do was curse God as his wife suggested. He simply said, "O foolish woman". In *Job 2:10* foolish is also translated as wicked or stupid. You would have to be wicked or stupid to curse God. Amen? Other than some silly conversation with his friends Job was calm. I am certainly not saying that Job may have been more than a little confused or confounded over his circumstances. If Job could praise the Lord in his storm, certainly you and I can do the same in ours.

December 15

Psalms 34:1-4
I will bless the LORD at all times: his praise shall continually be in my mouth. (2) My soul shall make her boast in the LORD: the humble shall hear thereof, and be glad. (3) O magnify the LORD with me, and let us exalt his name together. (4) I sought the LORD, and he heard me, and delivered me from all my fears

Another day and another opportunity to gain experience about praising the LORD! I am to bless the Lord and what an opportunity we have before us. Praise is not always done collectively, but sometimes we need to individually set aside some time for Him. As Christians we have been called to be a blessing to the Lord and especially when no one is watching. If I am a blessing to the Lord, will I be a blessing to those around me? If I live my life as a blessing to the Lord what will others see in me? Will they see a person that will feed the hungry? Will they see a person that will not just offer prayer, but will lend a hand? Will they see a person that is a cheerful giver when the offering plate is passed? Will they see someone that clearly has the joy of the Lord all over them? Will others see someone that has a life on Sunday and a totally different life the rest of the time? Back in our text, and namely verse 1, it says His praise shall continually be in my mouth. Not praises about me or you, but "His" praise shall continually be in my mouth. Let's look at a couple of verses about what can be in this mouth of ours. *James 3:10 Out of the same mouth proceedeth blessing and cursing. My brethren, these things ought not to be. Ephesians 4:31 Let all bitterness, and wrath, and anger, and clamour, and evil speaking, be put away from you, with all malice.* Is it safe to say that if we are not careful, we can be pretty darn mean? We absolutely must guard our minds so we can hold our tongue. A friend and I have talked about what alcohol or drugs do to someone's mouth. If praise is going to roll off our tongue, then we cannot put junk in our brain, and alcohol or drugs in our body. What are some songs about that some listen to? What are some movies out there that some actually pay to rent or go to see? You know the saying; if we have to grab the remote control because Jesus just walked in the room, we probably should not be listening to or watching it. Amen? I watched a television documentary where the brain was highlighted. It showed just how much of a negative effect video games have on a person. Praise is not just singing a hymn; it is a lifestyle. Praising God is a life sold out and consecrated to the Lord Jesus Christ. Praising God is an example of what living like a Christian should be all about. It is living a life representative of a life that is changed through faith in Jesus Christ. It is not just looking holy on Sunday. It is living a lifestyle patterned after Jesus. We have a personal testimony, and it is seen everywhere we go by what we do. Sometimes we do not praise God because of the influence of who we continually run with. We must ask, "Are they dragging me down or am I lifting them up"? Our testimony of praise to the Holy One goes way beyond the walls of any church building. We are to praise God and walk like Jesus Christ would have us walk, whether we are in a church building or walking down the street. You can praise God today and never sing a note or utter a word.

December 16

Psalms 34:1-4
I will bless the LORD at all times: his praise shall continually be in my mouth. (2) My soul shall make her boast in the LORD: the humble shall hear thereof, and be glad. (3) O magnify the LORD with me, and let us exalt his name together. (4) I sought the LORD, and he heard me, and delivered me from all my fears.

Same Psalm from yesterday, just a different day to consider praise and stimulate your thinking. Today you can concentrate on verse 2 of our text. *Verse 2, My soul shall make her boast in the LORD: the humble shall hear thereof, and be glad.* Look at your Soul – the very inner being of how you are to boast of the Lord. The Soul – Your every emotion and everything you base your morals on will boast in the Lord. The Psalmist is going to boast in the Lord, but what can I boast of concerning the Lord? How about boasting about what you were like before you met Jesus? Do not linger long on where you have been. Lingering on where you have been can bring too much emphasis on Satan and that goof needs no emphasizing. Stick with how Jesus continues to mold you into his image. How about how the Lord can take the worst of the worst and change them for the good? How about boasting about how we are looking forward to eternity with Jesus? Every good thing can be used to boast in the Lord. Sometimes when God chastises us to shape or mold us into His image it is grounds for praise. The word boast is also translated as rave. Rave is to go on and on about how good the Lord is. The word boast can be translated as "to celebrate". Are we celebrating God's goodness? Who will hear you and be glad? The humble shall hear and be glad. Who are the humble? Those saved that are encouraged by your testimony. Those lost that have heard or have seen your testimony and want Jesus. Those who have possibly strayed and are rededicating their life to Jesus. The entire world needs to hear about Jesus through your praise and we have much to celebrate in HIM.

December 17

Psalms 34:1-4
I will bless the LORD at all times: his praise shall continually be in my mouth. (2) My soul shall make her boast in the LORD: the humble shall hear thereof, and be glad. (3) O magnify the LORD with me, and let us exalt his name together. (4) I sought the LORD, and he heard me, and delivered me from all my fears.

We have been a few days in Psalms 34:1-4 and addressing the issue of praise. For me, Psalms 34:1 has always been the heartbeat for praise in the Bible. Verse 1 is personal as it addresses the "I" for us. It points out how often praise is to be offered up and it is continually. Today we will concentrate on verse 3 and see what we can pull from that. Verse 3 says *O magnify the LORD with me, and let us exalt his name together.* O magnify means to lift up or to promote the Lord. In the course of a day what do we promote? We can promote a spouse, kids, grandkids, self, others, and on and on. We promote those things by what we do or by what we say. Do we consistently promote God the Father, God the Son, and God the Holy Spirit? What is louder or easier to understand? Will it be the words we use or the things we do? The Psalmist says to magnify the Lord with me such as to a group or a congregation in unity. Can we agree that it is great to praise the Lord individually? Praise can be the start of a revival if we come together in the same place, in one spirit, and all to magnify the name of the Lord. A revival is not an event, a place, or a speaker. It is a decision to do what is right and to be revived. Praise can be standing together shoulder to shoulder and proclaiming the goodness or good news of Jesus. No matter what is going on in this world we have cause to celebrate the greatness of God. The verse says to let us exalt His name together. The verse goes from "I" to "US". We are in this together because we are part of the body of Christ. Individual praise is our responsibility, but praise is to be done collectively as well. As the body of Christ should we be in harmony to exalt the name of the Lord? I have no doubt about the awesome unity in many churches. So then how can we exalt his name together? *Acts 4:12 Neither is there salvation in any other: for there is none other name under heaven given among men, whereby we must be saved.* Soul winning and living a life that points others to Jesus is a beautiful thing. Sharing how Jesus has changed your life may be the most powerful tool you have? Exalting the name of Jesus is not telling someone, *"Do as I say not as I do"* We are to exalt his name. If you or I were arrested for being a Christian would there be enough evidence to convict us? Do I look like this perfect little saint on Sunday and live like the dickens Monday thru Saturday? Exalting His name is when someone recognizes or asks are we a Christian. *Romans 12:1 I beseech ye therefore brethren, by the mercies of God, that ye present your bodies a living sacrifice. Holy, acceptable unto God, which is your reasonable service.* So what is reasonable as far as praising the name of the Lord and that is a great question. Reasonable means to serve as God calls. Reasonable is to repent when we know we need to repent. Reasonable is to live a life that points to Jesus. Reasonable is someone watching us and seeing us as Christ-like. Reasonable is to apply *Psalms 46:10 be still and know that I am God*. Reasonable is to make our own list of things we need to do in our life that will point to Jesus and exalt his name. There is not enough paper, ink, or time to fully describe all the ways we can praise the Lord. Our personal testimony, (if it points to Jesus), is all the paper and ink we need for the world to see.

December 18

Psalms 34:1-4
I will bless the LORD at all times: his praise shall continually be in my mouth. (2) My soul shall make her boast in the LORD: the humble shall hear thereof, and be glad. (3) O magnify the LORD with me, and let us exalt his name together. (4) I sought the LORD, and he heard me, and delivered me from all my fears.

You are probably becoming very familiar with this Psalm 34 as we have been there a few days. Today is no exception as we look specifically at verse 4. *Verse 4 says, I sought the LORD, and he heard me, and delivered me from all my fears.* Verse 1 pointed out the word I and it is a personal choice to seek the Lord. This verse 4 is definitely pointing out that when we seek the Lord, He will hear us. We also must address the question of when do we seek Him? We are to seek Him at all times. The word seek is not just a casual glance to the Lord, but a diligent search to know him. Seek such as in *Proverbs 8:17 I love them that love me; and those that seek me early shall find me.* I believe the Lord wants us first thing when we are fresh and after a good night's rest. I believe it is much better than at the end of the day when we may be worn out and tired. Verse 4 also says, *He heard me.* Have you ever been accused of ignoring your spouse? We have a risen Savior that will never ignore or forsake us. We are probably guilty at times of not having the greatest prayer life even though the Bible says to pray without ceasing. Prayer is our opportunity for Him to hear us and for us to "hear" Him. Verse 4 ends with the words, *And delivered me from all of my fears*. Can we agree that David probably had fears from being chased like a dog all over the countryside by Saul? After the whole movie played out for David he could look back and make this statement that God delivered me from all my fears. Was David perfect or did he ever make any mistakes? He did, but he would also turn back to the Lord when he knew he had sinned. Solomon started out strong and look what happened to a man with so much wisdom from God. *1 Kings 11:4 For it came to pass, when Solomon was old, that his wives turned away his heart after other gods: and his heart was not perfect with the LORD his God, as was the heart of David his father.* The opposite is found in *Job 1:1 There was a man in the land of Uz, whose name was Job; and that man was perfect and upright, and one that feared God, and eschewed evil.* Why are we like what we are? Hopefully, we can all answer that by saying, "I am what I am because of Jesus". I am born again, and I am a new creature in Christ and according to *2 Corinthians 5:17 Therefore if any man be in Christ, he is a new creature: old things are passed away; behold, all things are become new.* Are we allowing the Lord to mold us into His image a little bit every day? Jesus Christ released us from sin. The Word of God applied will keep us from sin. *John 8:36 If the Son therefore shall make you free, ye shall be free indeed.* Let us all praise God together collectively and as an individual because Jesus Christ has set us free. When Jesus says you are free, you are free. Free from sin and free to praise.

December 19

Deuteronomy 13:4
Ye shall walk after the LORD your God,
and fear him, and keep his commandments, and obey
his voice, and ye shall serve him, and cleave unto him.

The more I read and study God's word, the more I see natural progressions. In *Deuteronomy 13:4* we can follow a path that will lead us to service for Him. We will go from following Him, which is good, to hanging on tight to Him. Hanging on so tight that we would feel the very dust from Jesus' feet kicking up in our face as we are that close. When we partake of the Lord's Supper we have time to do a self-evaluation of where we are at with God relationally. No matter what may be going on, who is willing to stand for Christ and do whatever will please HIM? Look *at Joshua 24:15 And if it seem evil unto you to serve the LORD, choose you this day whom ye will serve; whether the gods which your fathers served that were on the other side of the flood, or the gods of the Amorites, in whose land ye dwell: but as for me and my house, we will serve the LORD.* As far as the flood of Noah's day, what exactly can that stand for in our life? Maybe the flood is the sin in your life before you were saved? The Flood – are you still there, wading in the water, (sin), or repentant and clean? The Flood – If God saved us then why would we stay in the water of sin? The Flood – If God saved us then why would we go back in the water of sin? The Flood – Get in the boat, THE ARK OF JESUS and live for Him! The verse starts out with the saying, Ye shall walk after the LORD your God. With that said, where did Jesus' path take him? Take a quick look at Jesus' path. *John 8:4 They say unto him, Master, this woman was taken in adultery, in the very act and Jesus delivered her. Luke 8:30 And Jesus asked him, saying, What is thy name? And he said, Legion: because many devils were entered into him and Jesus healed him. Matthew 14:21 And they that had eaten were about five thousand men, beside women and children and Jesus fed them all. John 19:17 And he bearing his cross went forth into a place called the place of a skull, which is called in the Hebrew Golgotha and Jesus sacrificed it all.* Jesus went down many paths and it was filled with serving people and looking for the lost who had no hope. Can we not do the same thing with our life? Who will stand with Christ no matter what? Jesus said it repeatedly, "Go and sin no more"! Every path Jesus went down was to fulfill the will of God. Every path Jesus took was to minister and serve people. *Mark 10:45 For even the Son of man came not to be ministered unto, but to minister, and to give his life a ransom for many*. Jesus came to serve, and if we are to be Christ like, what do we do? Is this life all about us? It is about God, Family, and then the Church. One thing will steal your joy and ruin your testimony and that is sin. The end of Jesus' path appeared to the world to be death, but *Luke 24:46 And said unto them, Thus it is written, and thus it behoved Christ to suffer, and to rise from the dead the third day.* Satan thought he had gotten the victory over Jesus. The only reason we can sing Victory in Jesus is because Jesus' path brought victory to those who will accept the victory. Jesus' path took Him to serve others and should ours be any different? We can serve others and we can serve self. If we serve others, we are in reality serving God himself. God wants one sacrifice on our path, and it is obedience. I just don't think that is too much to ask of us.

December 20

Deuteronomy 13:4
Ye shall walk after the LORD your God,
and fear him, and keep his commandments, and obey
his voice, and ye shall serve him, and cleave unto him.

Yesterday we looked at walking after the Lord and specifically the path Jesus took. As a comparison today let us both look at what our path is. We have two choices in life. We can walk a path of defeat and in bondage to sin, self, and Satan. We can walk a path of victory sold out to God who loves us. Anyone dwelling in sin will have to pay the piper eventually. If you pray about what God would have you do, then that is the path you should take if it is God's will for you. Do we want to hang on to sin and then partake of the Lord's Supper? How is my prayer life for others? If I have messed up, what is keeping me from repenting? We must ask God daily what would you have me to do? What is keeping me from serving? We may be on the same path in ministry for a brief time and it could change. We may stay on the same path for a long time. Someone's path may be to start up a Children's Church. If you do not have a particular ministry that you participate in, then start one, or get involved in a ministry already active. If you are unclear what path you should be on you should look where you see God active and go there. As we go down a path we want to know where we are going. If we do not have a goal, then where will your path take you? If the person we are following has no goal set towards following Jesus, then we really would not know where we are headed. Here is the key to the ultimate service in my opinion. *Isaiah 50:6-7 I gave my back to the smiters, and my cheeks to them that plucked off the hair: I hid not my face from shame and spitting.* Do you think Jesus put the cross to the back of His mind? Do not take your eyes off your goal. If you do, you will not see victory, you will see obstacles. Where will your path take you if you choose to follow Jesus Christ? *Psalms 16:11 Thou wilt shew me the path of life: in thy presence is fulness of joy; at thy right hand there are pleasures for evermore.* Sin may bring joy for a moment, but Christ's joy is eternal. Some paths may look good, but are they good for us? Christians hook up with the wrong person and the path is jagged at best. For couples dating, no matter how hard you try you will probably not change anyone after you are married. Marry a godly woman if you are a man, or marry a godly man if you are a woman. The rest will take care of itself. Following Jesus will bring peace and joy to your path. *Psalms 27:11 Teach me thy way, O LORD, and lead me in a plain path, because of mine enemies.* The word plain in this Psalm twenty-seven literally means a place of uprightness and righteousness. Can you have sin in your life and appear upright and righteous? We can think we are and justify it, but God knows. When we are in a place surrounded by evil and enemies, you want to be in a place of uprightness. Do not go down or stay on a path where you should not be. I truly believe it is just as easy to repent as it is to sin. It is obviously as easy to stay in sin as it is to get out of it. Some will say, "Well I just could not get out of there" but read *1 Corinthians 10:13 There hath no temptation taken you but such as is common to man: but God is faithful, who will not suffer you to be tempted above that ye are able; but will with the temptation also make a way to escape, that ye may be able to bear it.* Not only is being at the end of a bad path not good, but the journey along the way to the end might be the last place you would want to be. Remember, when you get to the end of a path filled with sin it can be too late to turn back. In life there are no do overs. Satan wants to destroy you and you do not want to allow that to happen. Serve Jesus and stay on His path. We only get one chance to do things right. Remember, when you draw your last breath, you cannot wish or pray that you would have done things differently.

December 21

Deuteronomy 13:4
Ye shall walk after the LORD your God,
and fear him, and keep his commandments, and obey
his voice, and ye shall serve him, and cleave unto him.

You have been reading and studying about what path to be on. It is so much better to stay on a path walking with Jesus. Do not let poor choices influence what path you are on because you just might hate what is waiting at the end for you. Do not let peer pressure drive your decisions. You will not give an account to your peers. You and I will be giving an account at the Judgment Seat of Christ. Your path is to be plain, upright, and righteous because of Him. Jesus did His part, and we must do ours. *Isaiah 64:6 But we are all as an unclean thing, and all our righteousnesses are as filthy rags; and we all do fade as a leaf; and our iniquities, like the wind, have taken us away.* Jesus' path is a good path so walk and talk with Him. If you are saved, then you must surrender and let him lead you on your path. If you are lost, you must surrender and get on His path. Most people are following someone or something. Please be sure that who or what you are following is who or what you should be following. There is an old saying that we can become guilty simply by association. Every one of us need one Master and Shepherd and that is JESUS! What do we have in common with Jesus Christ from just the last few days? Follow along as we contrast back and forth between Jesus and self. A Cross – Jesus carried His and died and we are to take up our cross daily and LIVE. *Mark 8:34 And when he had called the people unto him with his disciples also, he said unto them, Whosoever will come after me, let him deny himself, and take up his cross, and follow me.* A Will – Jesus and all of us are to do the Will of God. If we drive on then we need to read our text of *Deuteronomy 13:4 Ye shall walk after the LORD your God, and **fear him,** and keep his commandments, and obey his voice, and ye shall serve him, and cleave unto him.* What does to ***fear him*** mean in this verse and that is a great question. Fear is to stand in awe of God. Fear is to honor and respect God. Fear is to have reverence and a godly fear of God. Fear here is not like someone hiding in a corner, but rather reverently serving God openly. If we stay in sin, are we really reverencing God? I would have to say ABSOLUTELY NO! *Psalms 34:9 O fear the LORD, ye his saints: for there is no want to them that fear him.* God will take care of you. *Psalms 67:7 God shall bless us; and all the ends of the earth shall fear him.* Blessings will follow reverence and obedience to God. *Psalms 103:11 For as the heaven is high above the earth, so great is his mercy toward them that fear him.* Anyone ever needed a little mercy? The fear of God is not something I see a whole lot of in the news. The world does not appear to be too concerned about the final judgement of God coming. People do not fear God, and sin and rebellion is running rampant in every nation and corner of the world. People do not appear to worry about the consequences of sin. People do not worry about eternity, but rather the here and the now. People are not concerned about when they may draw their last breath. People do not consider where they will spend eternity. Most people will spend very little time pondering, "could this be my last day on earth and where will my soul spend eternity"? God is good all the time and all the time God is good. We must fear Him, trust Him, and serve Him. People need to hear the truth and God is depending on you and me to share the good news of Jesus Christ for salvation.

December 22

Deuteronomy 13:4
Ye shall walk after the LORD your God,
and fear him, and keep his commandments, and obey
his voice, and ye shall serve him, and cleave unto him.

Over the last few days we have learned that there is a path to follow and stay on. There is in fact what I would call having a desire to be godly as He is godly. We are to keep His commandments because He says so and that is sufficient. In this verse **we are to keep His commandments**. We are to do what his Word says. Why would we want to obey God's commandments anyway? *Psalms 33:4 For the word of the LORD is right. Psalms 119:11 Thy word have I hid in mine heart, that I might not sin against thee.* It creates healthy living. *Psalms 119:140 Thy word is very pure: therefore thy servant loveth it.* The word pure is used in the same sense as gold when it is put to the fire. When put to the fire gold loses all impurities and is priceless and perfect. Our life can head toward that process of being Christ-like. As a servant do you love God's word and are you daily in it? Not only do we trust God's Word, but we are to live by God's word. *Proverbs 13:13 Whoso despiseth the word shall be destroyed: but he that feareth the commandment shall be rewarded.* How do you know if you despise God's word or fear it? Simply do a self-evaluation of where you think you are spiritually. Does your life stack up with the Word of God? Is sin reigning in our life? When did you open your bible and read it last? Are you consistently in God's word or whenever you can fit it in? If you do not like where you are at spiritually then there are two choices. One is to fix it, or two, to live with the consequences. So according to this verse we should be walking on Jesus' path. We need reverence towards God, keep His commandments, live a life that points to the Bible, and obey his voice. If you were to obey His voice what would the Lord say to you? I think He would first say either slow down, stop, or listen. The Bible is literally the voice and mind of God. *John 10:27 My sheep hear my voice, and I know them, and they follow me.* Are you hearing from God, or can you not hear because your sin is too "loud"! *Jeremiah 7:23 But this thing commanded I them, saying, Obey my voice, and I will be your God, and ye shall be my people: and walk ye in all the ways that I have commanded you, that it may be well unto you.* Is God's word God's Voice? *I John 2:4 He that saith, I know him, and keepeth not his commandments, is a liar, and the truth is not in him.* There are only two people who can measure your love for God. One is you and the other is God. So the question becomes how are you measuring up? How obedient are you? What a sobering verse in *Matthew 7:22-23 22) Many will say to me in that day, Lord, Lord, have we not prophesied in thy name? and in thy name have cast out devils? and in thy name done many wonderful works? 23) And then will I profess unto them, I never knew you: depart from me, ye that work iniquity.* What a terrible thing to hear from Jesus, "**I NEVER KNEW YOU**"! Are you living by how the bible instructs? I can only answer for me, and you have to answer for you.

December 23

Deuteronomy 13:4
Ye shall walk after the LORD your God,
and fear him, and keep his commandments, and obey
his voice, and ye shall serve him, and cleave unto him.

A quick recap of where you have been the last few days and I pray the devotions have had influence in your life. We have a path or a journey for and with God. We have or should have a "godly reverence" towards God. We should be "obeying" God's word and not just when it is convenient. If we are saved, we "ought" to hear HIS voice. Lost people – Do you want to hear from Jesus, then turn to Jesus. Saved people – Not hearing from God? Is it because you do not want to hear or is there sin. The verse says, *and ye shall serve Him*. Why would we serve him, and the answer is because it is reasonable. Look at *Romans 1:1-2 1) I beseech you therefore, brethren, by the mercies of God, that ye present your bodies a living sacrifice, holy, acceptable unto God, which is your reasonable service. 2) And be not conformed to this world: but be you transformed by the renewing of your mind, that you may prove what is that good, and acceptable, and perfect, will of God.* Be not conformed or buy into what the world says is okay. Just because liberal news says it is okay does not make it okay. No news channel is superior to the word of God. Do we accept abortion, drugs, alcohol, filthy language, abuse, on and on and on? What does conform really mean? It means to comply with rules, standards, or laws. Conform can be to either accept or reject what is socially acceptable. Sometimes peer pressure is used to conform someone and sometimes it is not. Who are we supposed to conform to? Jesus is our example of who to mimic. So if Jesus wanted to spend a day with us, what would we do? Technically, if the Holy Spirit is living within believers, are we not in fact really hanging out with God? Does the world at times laugh at or make fun of "Christianity"? Why is that? Because at times "Christians" look like the lost. Do you know the biggest difference between someone lost or saved? The lost may not justify anything they do, but simply sin. The saved will sin, but will justify or explain the sin in their mind. Can anyone really explain to the Holy Spirit that is residing within us that the sin we may hang on to is acceptable? Jump back to serving God and know that He will not ask us to do anything that is beyond **His** capabilities. You may think that you cannot do anything beyond your capabilities. God will never ask you to do something that He is not able to equip you for. God will perfectly equip you for the ministry He has called you to. There is a spiritual battle waging in your life every day between God and Satan and God will never lose. The more you stay on track with God, fear God, listen intently to God, and serve God, the greater your blessings will be.

December 24

Deuteronomy 13:4
Ye shall walk after the LORD your God,
and fear him, and keep his commandments, and obey
his voice, and ye shall serve him, and cleave unto him.

We are moving on to another key phrase in this verse, *"And cleave unto him"*. The more we serve, the more we will hang on to Him, and the sweeter our relationship. A good cross-reference would be *Deuteronomy 30:20 That thou mayest love the LORD thy God, and that thou mayest obey his voice, and that thou mayest cleave unto him: for he is thy life, and the length of thy days: that thou mayest dwell in the land which the LORD sware unto thy fathers, to Abraham, to Isaac, and to Jacob, to give them.* Obedience will bring spiritual prosperity. The more we love and obey the Lord, the more we will cleave to the Lord. Why? Because it is good for the soul. The more we cleave or hang on to the Lord, the more our lifestyle will reflect it. We are going to reflect something, and the question becomes what are we reflecting? When it comes to being in right standing with God, how are we doing relationally? Right standing for salvation is only by accepting Jesus to be your personal Lord and Savior. Stop and praise God right now if you have already done that. When we are not cleaving to the Lord relationally, immoral behavior will raise its ugly head. Wrong behavior is staying in sin and nothing more than a classic case of being selfish. Selfish is when someone does something or commits an act for personal profit or pleasure. Selfish is having no regard for others including God Himself. Selfish is having zero regard for the welfare of others. We should all want to tell others about how Jesus changed our life. We must make sure it has changed before you can tell them. The result of cleaving to the Lord will be an honest, happy, and fulfilled life. I did not say you will not have any problems, but I did say you will feel fulfilled. God has a desire for the world to be saved and we can contrast what God desires versus the reality of many. God asks that we accept Him, and yet some will reject Him. God asks us to love Him, and yet some will despise Him by what they do. God asks for obedience, and some will only render disobedience. God longs for loyalty and He receives betrayal. God deserves reverence, and He received spit in the face. God longs for our embrace, and He received a crown of thorns. God enjoys spending time with us, but we cannot fit Him into our planners. God wants what is best for us and we give Him our worst. God wants all to avoid Hell and some will say I can party in Hell. Some will sing "I Love You Lord" on Sunday and never give Him another thought all week. Some will sing "O Victory in Jesus" and live a defeated life and in complete bondage to Satan and sin. Some will sing "Have thine own way Lord", but do not bother me with it. When we cleave to the LORD people will see a changed life. They will at least listen to what they have seen in and through you. Our actions are a whole lot louder than our words. Our words are what can lead people to Jesus Christ. Stay steadfast in your walk, cleave to the LORD, and you will bear fruit. If Christ is not as important today as he was in times past, are you ready to fix it? If you have never sold out to Jesus, will you do so? Is there anything keeping you from being sold out to Jesus and on a path with Jesus? Does God have to use us? No, but He desires that we would partner with Him. Give Jesus your best and live for Him. Jesus loved us so much that he was willing to die for us and that is exactly what He did!

December 25

MERRY CHRISTMAS

You will recognize right off that for one day we have left *2 Timothy*, but we will go back there tomorrow. Since today is the day we recognize the birth of Jesus, I will talk about this special day with you. This will be a long devotional that you can put into personal practice in your home should you choose to. Maybe you can set up some different colored candles in a row at this time of year, and if asked, have an explanation for each one. These specific candle colors are what I use and may they spark conversation in your house as well. Have a "GOLD" candle and it can represent the deity of God. God the Father, God the Son, and God the Holy Spirit. The deity is found in various verses, but we can go to *John 10:30 I and my Father are one. 1 John 5:7 For there are three that bear record in heaven, the Father, the Word, and the Holy Ghost: and these three are one.* God who is the giver of gifts. Jesus who is the Savior of the World. The Holy Spirit who is the Comforter, Guide, and Teacher. December 25th was actually a pagan day and chosen later that the birth of Jesus would also be December 25th. Do not get hung up on the date, but rather celebrate the event. Now set you up a "SILVER" candle to represent the Redemption of Jesus Christ to us. Look at the days preceding and following that "blessed" Christmas Day. *Matthew 1:18 Now the birth of Jesus Christ was on this wise: When as his mother Mary was espoused to Joseph, before they came together, she was found with child of the Holy Ghost.* First, we have a virgin birth of Jesus. God was the Father and it had never happened before, and it will never happen again. Men, women, boys, and girls will respond to Jesus in one of two ways. One, I accept him by faith to save my soul. Two, I reject Jesus as my Savior and my soul will end up in hell. I use silver as redemption, as it was silver that was paid out, and would ultimately lead to Jesus' arrest, beating, and death. Judas, who betrayed Jesus said in *Matthew 26:15 And said unto them, What will ye give me, and I will deliver him unto you? And they covenanted with him for thirty pieces of silver.* It would be thirty pieces of Silver for our redemption by man, but Jesus' life completed it. Now find you a "PURPLE" candle to represent or point to the King of Kings. Purple was often worn by royalty such as Kings and Nobles. Purple was very expensive to have and to make. You did not run down to the corner store and get some dye. Thousands of snails were gathered and boiled in lead vats to produce it. It was a very tedious process, and the poor could not afford it.

Mark 15:17-19 17) And they clothed him with purple, and platted a crown of thorns, and put it about his head, 18) And began to salute him, Hail, King of the Jews! 19) And they smote him on the head with a reed, and did spit upon him, and bowing their knees worshipped him. As far as the purple goes, the soldiers mocked Jesus as the King of Kings. The soldiers mocked his royalty. This purple candle for believers today signifies who Jesus said He was and who He is. *Matthew 22:32 I am the God of Abraham, and the God of Isaac, and the God of Jacob? God is not the God of the dead, but of the living.* The King said in *John 11:25 Jesus said unto her, I am the resurrection, and the life: he that believeth in me, though he were dead, yet shall he live*: The Master said in *John 13:13 Ye call me Master and Lord: and ye say well; for so I am.* Now find you a "BLUE" and a "PINK" candle and let that represent that Jesus died for all men and women. Let the blue be for men and the pink for women. *1 John 2:2 And he is the propitiation for our sins: and not for ours only, but also for the sins of the whole world. John 3:16 For God so loved the world, that he gave his only begotten Son, that whosoever believeth in him should not perish, but have everlasting life.* May all men and women be as the wise men of *Matthew 2:1-2 1) Now when Jesus was born in Bethlehem of Judaea in the days of Herod the king, behold, there came wise men from the east to Jerusalem, 2) Saying, Where is he that is born King of the Jews? for we have seen his star in the east, and are come to worship him.* Today, wise men will still seek Him. *Matthew 2:11 And when they were come into the house, they saw the young child with Mary his mother, and fell down, and worshipped him: and when they had opened their treasures, they presented unto him gifts; gold, and frankincense, and myrrh* Today, wise men will still offer up their best to Jesus. You and I are the best possible gift that we could offer to Jesus Christ! If someone does not know God personally, they will not find nor seek Jesus. Men and Women around the world will find Jesus when they recognize they are lost without Him. Now set you up a "RED" Candle to represent Jesus' Blood, which was the ultimate sacrifice for sin. Not everyone "loved" the King and not everyone "loves" the King. For Herod the King we have *Matthew 2:16: Then Herod, when he saw that he was mocked of the wise men, was exceeding wroth, and sent forth, and slew all the children that were in Bethlehem, and in all the coasts thereof, from two years old and under, according to the time which he had diligently enquired of the wise men.* The King wanted no ruler, but himself. Is that how many people are today? Jesus started in a cradle, headed to a cross, stopped at an empty tomb, and He will end up on a throne. God the Father gave us the "GIFT" of His Son. The blood of Jesus would be the ultimate sacrifice for mankind and the account of it is found in *John 19:30 When Jesus therefore had received the vinegar, he said, It is finished: and he bowed his head, and gave up the ghost.* On this Christmas day we can give a hundred gifts, but do not forget about "THE" gift. The gift of Jesus Christ who came in humble means, died a humiliating death, but will return triumphantly. The next time Jesus returns it will not be in a manger, it will be in the clouds. Because of the shed blood of Jesus represented by this "RED" candle we can now be reconciled to God. Jesus paid the price and fulfilled the plan that God had for lost man. Now set up a "GREEN" candle and let it represent a new life. Just like springtime when everything is coming back to life, our faith in Jesus offers us new life because the old man is dead. *2 Corinthians 5:17 Therefore if any man be in Christ, he is a new creature: old things are passed away; behold, all things are become new. 1 Corinthians 15:22 For as in Adam all die, even so in Christ shall all be made alive. Romans 8:37 Nay, in all these things we are more than conquerors through him that loved us. Colossians 2:10 And ye are complete in him, which is the head of all principality and power.* Finally, light a "WHITE" candle and place it right in the center of all of them. White will represent God's purity, holiness, and righteousness. We all know the children's story of the night before Christmas, but today we are celebrating the birth of Jesus, not the coming of Santa Claus. Light the bigger "WHITE" Candle representing Purity, Holiness & Righteousness. We are here to rejoice that God sent His Son Jesus and the Savior was born. Without God, Jesus, and the Holy Spirit a man or woman cannot be complete. There can be no purity, holiness, and righteousness away from God. The deity of God has different functions, but one goal in mind. That goal is that none would perish, but all would come to repentance. Let everything we do point to the risen Lord Jesus Christ. I think that is enough candles for today, but if you want to feel complete after setting up all the candles and what they represent, then read *Luke 2:1-20*, which is an account of the Christmas story. Merry Christmas!

December 26

2 Timothy 1:4
Greatly desiring to see thee, being mindful
of thy tears, that I may be filled with joy;

Our example today is answering the question of do we desire to be in the presence of other saints. Paul cherished his time with Timothy. Are we like that with the saints or do we just stay sitting on the porch or in the house? Be active and look for someone who is on the porch of isolation. Everyone wants to feel loved and needed. Bible study, reading God's word, and prayer is important. However, if that is all we do then how could we witness? Every now and then you must venture out of the house or make a phone call to someone God lays on your mind. Do not wait for others to make a move, but look for ways to reach out and stay in fellowship with other believers. Remember that Paul and Timothy had cried together and Paul remembered that as well. Other believers will always remember when you cried and when you laughed with them. We will never weep, laugh, mourn, or dance with someone that we do not know personally and intimately. There is a lot more to life than 4 walls and a big screen TV. Here is the deal with fellowship; you can hang out occasionally and call it fellowship, but without spending time with one another regularly you can never have a relationship. Are we seeking fellowship with others within or outside of our circle? There are a couple of different uses of the word fellowship. When fellowshipping with unbelievers, Satan, or devils the word fellowship is used in a sense of being a comrade or having something in common with them or to do what is evil. If we are not careful, we can even be an accuser of the brethren. When fellowship is used in the context of time spent with other believers or with Jesus and His word it takes on a different meaning: The word fellowship means having extreme intimacy. You or I will never experience intimacy without time spent with one another, and Jesus must be included in the mix. If we do not seek time with Him, we will not love Him right either. What a shame that would be for sure.

December 27

2 Timothy 1:5
When I call to remembrance the unfeigned faith that is in thee, which dwelt first in thy grandmother Lois, and thy mother Eunice; and I am persuaded that in thee also.

Look today at the heritage Timothy had been brought up with and how that is so very important. I was not brought up in a Christian home, but I broke that chain or cycle when I accepted Jesus to be my Savior in the spring of 1989. There can be no doubt that Timothy was grateful for a godly mom and grandma. That is what we know about his mom and grandma, but what about his dad? What do we really know about his father? *Acts 16:1 Then came he to Derbe and Lystra: and, behold, a certain disciple was there, named Timotheus, the son of a certain woman, which was a Jewess, and believed; <u>but his father was a Greek</u>.* The best we can come up with is that Timothy had two godly women in his life, but his dad was a Greek. Listen up dad, is that really the best we want our kids and acquaintances to know about us? I am not knocking anyone who is of a Greek descendant, but that is not much of a legacy to leave behind to your son or your daughter. That is the equivalent of saying we had a godly mom and grandma, but my dad was from **??????** county and big stinking deal. When it comes to salvation and passing on a legacy it will not matter what our nationality is or where we live. It will be based on what did we tell our children about Jesus. Our testimony is so important to not only our family, but our friends as well. Someone told you about Jesus so you could continue the chain of salvation to your family. If you found Jesus like I did, you broke the chain of lostness, but please pass it on. My prayer for both of us is that we will be instrumental in someone turning to

Jesus. We must make sure that people really see that we care about them. May we have an unfeigned faith like Timothy's mom and grandma and not live a backslidden life. I believe these two women were a witness to their son and grandchild of a life without hypocrisy. Invite others to your church and there will be times you can expect to hear that they will not go because the church is full of hypocrites. Remind them that the store they shop at may be full of hypocrites as well, but they shop there.

December 28

2 Timothy 1:7
For God hath not given us the spirit of fear;
but of power, and of love, and of a sound mind.

You and I can serve God without any reservation or with regard for ourselves. God does not use us because of us, but rather He uses us despite us. God can take the ordinary and turn them into something extraordinary. God has given us all things but look what he has not given us. This verse says God has not given us the Spirit of Fear, which is what we would call timid or lacking in self-confidence. Our confidence should be in the Lord Jesus Christ, and what He can do in our life. There are times when we must simply step out by faith and serve the Lord. As far as fear goes, God will not send us anywhere that He has not already been. Fear can also be a lack of courage because we forget that God equips His children to do anything. Log down any fears you may have on a piece of paper. I am not sure if you have a paper shredder or not, but log down those fears and let God be your paper shredder. Do we believe if God is leading that we can have confidence in Him? *1 John 4:4 Ye are of God, little children, and have overcome them: because greater is he that is in you, than he that is in the world. Psalm 31:24 Be of good courage, and he, (THE LORD), shall strengthen your heart, all ye that hope in the LORD.* If we believe God is leading, we must take the first step towards obedience and serve Him. May your first step be right behind God's step so you can walk in cadence with Him. The opposite is to not go forward as God directs, and we will head backward and that is exactly where Satan wants us to go. Direct your eyes back to our verse for the day and rest on the word "POWER". Low and behold, look what God has given us to combat any fear or trepidation. The word for Power is Dunamis where we get the word "dynamite". *Matthew 22:29 Jesus answered and said unto them, Ye do err, not knowing the scriptures, nor the **power** of God. Matthew 24:30 And then shall appear the sign of the Son of man in heaven: and then shall all the tribes of the earth mourn, and they shall see the Son of man coming in the clouds of heaven with **power** and great glory. Luke 4:36 And they were all amazed, and spake among themselves, saying, What a word is this! for with authority and **power** he commandeth the unclean spirits, and they come out. Ephesians 3:20 Now unto him that is able to do exceeding abundantly above all that we ask or think, according to the **power** that worketh in us*. We received the **power** of God within us when we received Jesus as our Savior. That thought ought to give you goosebumps everywhere. With God's **power** we must ask are we using it? God's **power** is given so we can glorify the KING and what He can do in and through all of His children!

December 29

2 Timothy 1:13-14
13) Hold fast the form of sound words, which thou hast heard of me, in faith and love which is in Christ Jesus. 14) That good thing which was committed unto thee keep by the Holy Ghost which dwelleth in us.

I figured out a long time ago that Paul was filled with a whole lot of joy because of what he had been appointed to do. Paul knew his calling and we must know ours. Paul knew what the cause was and who he believed and trusted. We can know the same thing, but it is what we do with what we know! Be a part of helping someone find their cause or their purpose. Play a role in someone believing and trusting in the Lord Jesus Christ. Look at what Paul wrote to Timothy to help him grow spiritually. If we apply the same things, we will be the better for it as well. Before we look at the word for **hold fast,** we need to understand that it is in the present tense. We need to do it now and forever more. It is used in an active voice, so it requires action on our part. The mood of the word is imperative meaning it is for our own good that we do it. Echo (ekh'-o) is the word used for **hold fast**. Do we echo God's word through our life, our words, and our ministry? If God gives us a divine encounter, do we take advantage of it? Someone asks us a Bible question; can we find a Bible answer? **Hold fast** is to know that we can literally or physically hold the Word of God in our hand. So what if we do not have our Bible in hand? Are we still holding fast to what we know is truth by our memory? When opportunity crops up do we share the truth? Do we memorize scripture so we can at least quote the truth? Do we hold it as a precious thing or as a whatever thing? To hold means are we wearing the truth and are we clothed in Jesus' word? You can hold a tool and when you are done with it you put it away. The word of God is not to be put away or left on a shelf. When your world gets shook up is when you need it the most. If you have God's word hid in your heart it will help you from getting tripped up and falling into sin. *Romans 13:14 But put ye on the Lord Jesus Christ and make no provision for the flesh.* We are to hold fast and "cling" to the sound words of our Holy Bible as the Holy Spirit instructs. Look at some other passages about why we should cling to the truth of God's word. *2 Timothy 4:3 For the time will come when they will not endure sound doctrine; but after their own lusts shall they heap to themselves teachers, having itching ears. Titus 1:9 Holding fast the faithful word as he hath been taught, that he may be able by sound doctrine both to exhort and to convince the gainsayers.* How exactly do you really change anyone's thinking? You use sound doctrine, the word of God. You use God's word to exhort or lift someone up. You use it to convince someone of truth. This verse for today does not say we will necessarily convince anyone of truth by our efforts, but by the Word of God. God's word does not need to be defended; It needs to be presented. Our life will be so good when we stay hooked up and cling to the Word of God and sound Biblical truth. People around the world have opinions. The Bible has been proved countless times, but there will be scoffers who will discount it. You will become sound in your faith when you become sound in your doctrine.

December 30

2 Timothy 4:6
For I am now ready to be offered,
and the time of my departure is at hand.

Paul is in Rome and locked up in prison and I doubt there were many comforts there. Based on the verse for today there should be no fear in dying if you know you are going home to be with Jesus. Despite any shortcomings any of us have, this earth is not our home. You and I have God's WORD on it. When we fail, (and we do), that one moment does not define us. We can fail a thousand times and that does not define our eternal standing in Heaven. What defines us is this: Was Jesus Christ our personal Lord and Savior. We will all draw our last breath eventually and that will be our defining moment. Was Jesus Christ our personal Lord and Savior or was He not? In *2 Timothy* Paul shares in just four chapters his calling, his heart, his trials, and his commitment to Jesus Christ. We get all that from him and end up at *verse 6* where he believes his time to die physically is near. Can we say beyond a shadow of a doubt that, *"I am now ready to be offered"*? Do we pray Lord you're coming back, but hold off until I'm done doing _____? Do we believe that we are accomplishing what God wants us to accomplish? Are we in the game serving God or going through the motions on "Rare Occasions"? There are three types of Christians. Those who are Actively serving = You are ready to be offered. Those who are Passively Serving = Claim to be a Christian, but only when it is convenient. Those who are Not serving at All; I don't have a comment for that. You see Jesus died for ALL, but ALL will not LIVE for Him. Are you really ready to be offered and draw your last breath and meet God? When you die there will be a very brief moment of time when it is just you and God. Your fate is already sealed for heaven or for hell. Paul's time was at hand, and he had a prison to prove it. None of us know for certain when our time is at hand. How many people leave home knowing they will be a fatality? None of us have a crystal ball so I am suggesting we live this life right. We cannot be a phony, but are to live in sincerity and in truth serving Jesus. *Joshua 24:14 Now therefore fear the LORD, and serve him in sincerity and in truth: and put away the gods which your fathers served on the other side of the flood, and in Egypt; and serve ye the LORD.* Are the gods we serve toys? Are the gods we serve friends? Are the gods we serve fishing, hunting, sports, or etcetera? Is the god we are serving the "god" of sleeping? Is the god we are serving the god of "food and TV"? A god is anything that interferes with your relationship with God, Jesus, and the Holy Spirit. Paul had fought a good fight, was imprisoned, and beaten. You and I will more than likely never experience what Paul did. Jesus fought a good fight all the way to the cross. Paul fought a good fight all the way to prison and then would be martyred. No matter whether we live to be two hundred years old, are we ready to be offered because we have lived a life for Jesus. No matter what comes our way in serving Jesus, and no matter the consequences, we must serve the resurrected king. May we all hear *Matthew 25:23 His lord said unto him, Well done, good and faithful servant; thou hast been faithful over a few things, I will make thee ruler over many things: enter thou into the joy of thy lord.*

December 31

2 Timothy 4:7
I have fought a good fight,
I have finished my course, I have kept the faith:

What kind of a fight is before us, and we must cross-reference a verse for comparison. *Ephesians 6:12 For we wrestle not against flesh and blood, but against principalities, against powers, against the rulers of the darkness of this world, against spiritual wickedness in high places.* Just how in the world are we doing? Is Satan winning or is God getting the victory in our life? This battle has been going on since Adam fell and humanity has never been the same. Look at what was going on in Noah's day in *Genesis 6:5 And GOD saw that the wickedness of man was great in the earth, and that every imagination of the thoughts of his heart was only evil continually.* Does that sound any different than the world we live in today? *Psalms 7:11 God judgeth the righteous, and God is angry with the wicked every day.* Angry in this Psalm 7 is to be literally enraged. Angry as in a dog that is so mad it looks like a rabid dog foaming at the mouth. The wicked will be dealt with by the wrath of God, (seven years of tribulation) and ultimately a Lake of Fire. We must look and respond like *1 Timothy 6:12 Fight the good fight of faith, lay hold on eternal life, whereunto thou art also called, and hast professed a good profession before many witnesses.* Maintain a good fight of faith to Jesus. We have been called to eternal life to do something with our new life. *2 Corinthians 5:17 Therefore if any man be in Christ, he is a new creature: old things are passed away; behold, all things are become new.* We can stay fresh spiritually and serve Jesus well. We received a new chance to start over with a brand-new life with forgiveness from Jesus. Finish your course as only you can do under the influence of the Holy Spirit. God does not want us to live a defeated life, but a victorious life. There is nothing that can stop you from running your race and finishing the course set before you. *1 John 4:4 Ye are of God, little children, and have overcome them: because greater is he that is in you, than he that is in the world.* Who do others see winning in your life spiritually? *1 Corinthians 15:57 But thanks be to God, which giveth us the victory through our Lord Jesus Christ. 1 John 5:4 For whatsoever is born of God overcometh the world: and this is the victory that overcometh the world, even our faith.* How is your faith, and we will end our last devotion for the year with that question. Is your faith unwavering in any circumstance? Do you have the courage to share your faith without fear? Do you have the stamina to run your race? We would call that race God's will for you. Is there anything you would like to lay aside in order to serve Jesus better? Tomorrow is a brand-new day so plan accordingly to spend time with the LORD. You are ending today, but tomorrow is a brand new one. Make a commitment to Jesus for the coming New Year.

CLOSING

The sole purpose of this devotional book was to give me and whoever may read it a greater appreciation and mutual understanding of the need to praise, serve, and worship the Father, Son, and Holy Spirit. All through the word of God He is there in some way or another to guard, protect, and to save those who will come to Him. When there was a time of captivity, God brought deliverance and the people praised Him. When someone was feeling distraught God brought them comfort. If someone was a little too prideful God brought humbleness. If there was a little bit of sadness God brought forth joy. When someone was imprisoned, God gave freedom. If someone needed to be saved God offered up His Son Jesus Christ. There are several examples of when the only hope available was through God. God has been our deliverer, comforter, rescuer, protector, sacrifice, and our Saviour. It is a good thing to trust in people, but a man or a woman can and will let you down. The reason for this emphasis on praise, service, and worship is because we have a living God that we can know personally and intimately. By reading through all 66 books it only stands to reason that we could and would praise, serve, and worship Him. *Ephesians 4:6 One God and Father of all, who is above all, and through all, and in you all.* I will leave you with the two verses to consider together. *Revelation 22:21 The grace of our Lord Jesus Christ be with you all. Amen. Psalms 34:1 I will bless the LORD at all times: his praise shall continually be in my mouth.* The first verse in Revelation 22 shows His love for us, and the second verse of Psalm 34 shows our love for Him. Until we personally meet, wave at those who are motorcycle riders because one of those just might be me!

Sinner's Prayer If You Are Not Saved

Lord Jesus, I come to you right now confessing that I am a sinner and that I want to turn my life completely over to you. I pray that you would come into my heart right now and save my soul for all of eternity. By faith I accept your sacrificial death on the cross. I believe that according to scripture Jesus died, was buried, and after 3 days He arose triumphantly from the grave. In the name of Jesus I pray and receive your grace. Amen!!!

If this book has helped you in your walk with Jesus Christ, please send me a note. If you just prayed the prayer above and made Jesus your personal Savior, please drop me a note for that as well. I will do my best to get back with you as quick as possible.

Here is the E-Mail address:
thewordonwheels@earthlink.net

The Author's Personal Testimony

My upbringing consisted of how I was taught good work ethic, but nothing about Jesus. I heard the name of Jesus and God, but as profanity. I was not taught that drinking alcohol was okay, but my dad chugged it down daily. I had zero recollection from parents or grandparents that any one of them knew Jesus as their Savior. At the age of thirty-two and a half years old, two different people verbally told me about Jesus. I discounted the first one's words for personal reasons and I will not share that on these pages. I really could not discount the second person's testimony as it was believable. I told him I would check it out and as an unbeliever I read the New Testament in two weeks. I got absolutely nothing out of it, "EXCEPT", for one verse that haunted me every day. The verse in *Matthew 1:21 And she shall bring forth a son, and thou shalt call his name JESUS: for **he shall save his people from their sins***. I understood sin. The third person that witnessed to me did not use words. It was how Beverly, (and we were married a couple of years later), lived her life for Jesus. In short order, I gave my life to Jesus Christ and broke the chain of lostness. I went through Discipleship one and two classes, and four years of Shepherd School of ministry. Fast-forwarding a few years later we were driving to Kansas City and I heard a booming voice from God that said you will be a Pastor. I will not bore you with the details, but I woke my wife up and told her of that calling. Three days later a Pastor was stepping down from his position and asked if I would take over for him. It has been a blessed road serving God and writing this book. I pray it is a blessing for you and others. In the meantime, kickstand is up, and off I go!!!

Made in the USA
Columbia, SC
26 July 2024

e83cc10f-1f58-4cb1-802c-9cca6bff1b55R01